INVITATION TO THE
NEW TESTAMENT

W. D. DAVIES was born in Wales and received his M.A. degree from the University of Cambridge and his D.D. degree from the University of Wales. He is the author of *Paul and Rabbinic Judaism, Torah in the Messianic Age and/or the Age to Come, Christian Origins and Judaism,* and *The Setting of the Sermon on the Mount,* acclaimed by critics as the definitive volume on its subject. One of the foremost biblical scholars in the world, Dr. Davies received the Burkitt Medal of the British Academy for distinguished contributions to biblical studies. He is currently a professor at Duke University.

Invitation to the
New Testament

A GUIDE TO ITS MAIN WITNESSES

by W. D. Davis

ANCHOR BOOKS

DOUBLEDAY & COMPANY, INC.

Garden City, New York

Invitation to the New Testament was originally published by Double-day & Company, Inc., in 1965. The Anchor Books edition is published by arrangement with Doubleday & Company, Inc.

Anchor Books edition: 1969

All Bible quotations, unless otherwise noted, are from *The New English Bible: New Testament.* © The Delegates of the Oxford University Press and the Syndics of the Cambridge University Press 1961. Reprinted by permission.

Grateful acknowledgment is made to the following for their permission to use copyrighted material: Burns & Oates, Ltd., London, and Sir Francis Meynell for "Christ in the Universe" by Alice Meynell. The Christian Century Foundation for "The Third Day" by Amos N. Wilder, copyright 1965, Christian Century Foundation. Reprinted by permission from the April 14, 1965, issue of *The Christian Century.* Clarendon Press, Oxford, for material from *The Hermetica,* edited by W. Scott, and from *Milton's Poetical Works.* Used by permission. Farrar, Straus & Giroux, Inc., Thomas Y. Crowell Company, and Leslie A. White for material from *The Science of Culture* by Leslie A. White. Harper & Row, Publishers, for the chart from *The Epistle to the Romans* by C. H. Dodd, found on p. 303. Alfred A. Knopf Incorporated for material from the Preface by John Galsworthy to *Green Mansions* by W. H. Hudson. Raphael Loewe for material from *A Rabbinic Anthology,* edited by C. G. Montefiore and H. Loewe. Macmillan & Co. Ltd. for the chart from *The Four Gospels* by B. H. Streeter, Eleventh impression, 1964, found on p. 93. Noble and Noble Publishers, Inc., for lines from *Idylls of the King and The King's Henchman.* Oxford University Press for lines from "Jacob" by T. Sturge Moore in *Longer Modern Verses,* edited by E. A. Parker. Penguin Books Ltd. for material from *The Four Gospels,* translated by E. V. Rieu. Sidgwick & Jackson Ltd. for lines from "A Prayer" from *The Collected Poems of John Drinkwater.* Used by permission of the publisher. The Society for Promoting Christian Knowledge, London, for material from *Paul and Rabbinic Judaism* by W. D. Davies. The University of Chicago Press for material from "The New Approach to the Synoptic Problem" by Rudolf Bultmann, which appeared in the *Journal of Religion,* Vol. VI, 1926. A. P. Watt & Son and Professor G. P. Wells, F.R.S., for material from *The Outline of History* by H. G. Wells. Copyright © 1949, 1956, 1961 by Doubleday & Company, Inc. Copyright 1920, 1931, 1940 by H. G. Wells. The Westminster Press and Darton, Longman & Todd Limited for material from *Christian Origins of Judaism* by W. D. Davies. © 1962, W. D. Davies. The Westminster Press. Used by permission.

5644

To
Rachel

PREFACE

The publication of this work fulfills a long-cherished desire to present, as clearly as possible, the essence of the faith of the New Testament. The work is not written for scholars, and not primarily for students of the Bible. It is written for those, in schools, colleges, churches, adult classes, and every walk of life, who have neither the time nor the guidance for detailed study of the New Testament, but who yet desire to grasp the central thrust of the foundation document of Christianity. In short, the aim is to take inquirers behind the dust of scholarship to the faith that pulsates in the New Testament. There is no attempt at persuasion, but only at description and explanation. That the faith revealed here has relevance for the mid-twentieth century is for the reader to decide. It has not been possible to cover the whole of the New Testament, but it is hoped that its major documents are sufficiently treated so as to set forth the New Testament alternative for this generation, which, more perhaps than most of its predecessors, is adrift on change and harassed by the irrepressible new.

The volume grew out of lectures delivered on television, in the "Summer Semester" series for 1963, under the sponsorship of the Columbia Broadcasting System, the Protestant Council of the City of New York, and the New Jersey Council of Churches. The lectures were entitled "As It Is Written: The New Testament in the Light of the Old." To the Columbia Broadcasting System and to the two Councils, I tender my most grateful acknowledgment. I am particularly thankful to the staff and crews who worked on the lectures, and for the help of Dr. John Bachman, now President of Wartburg College, Waverly, Iowa; Professor Roy Dwight Wilhelm and Miss Constance Clarke of Union Seminary; and Dr. Charles Urquhart of the Department of Radio and Television of the New Jersey Council of Churches, all of whom spared no pains to make the series effective.

In such a work as this, it has not been desirable to refer to the scholars from whom I have profited, but the reader will be aware that such a work of clarification is only possible because of what Professor Paul Tillich has called "the tremendous scientific toil" dedicated to the illumination of the Bible by many generations. It is a pleasure to record my debt to Miss Mary Norman Whiteside, of The Chapin School, New York City. She read the typescript with meticulous care, saved me from many infelicities of style, kept me aware of the pitfalls of theological jargon, and, what is more, shared with me her conviction in the necessity of my task. My assistant at Union Seminary, Mr. Robert Hamerton-Kelly, now Assistant Professor at Scripps College, Claremont, California, aided by his wife, gave ungrudgingly of his time and energy to make it possible for the book to appear at this time. He read the typescript, prepared the index, took the responsibility for the final proofreading, and made many valuable suggestions. I must also mention the ready help given me throughout by Mrs. Lawrence Apgar in preparing the manuscript for the press. Her long-suffering was only equalled by her efficiency. Mr. Alexander Liepa and Miss Maud Savage of Doubleday & Company took an interest in the volume that went far beyond the call of duty.

But I owe most to my daughter, to whom I have dedicated the work. It is her criticisms and questions that have made me most realize how remote Biblical scholarship can become from the world that now is. This book is an attempt to eliminate something of that remoteness.

W. D. Davies

Knox Hall
Union Theological Seminary
New York City
July 18, 1965

CONTENTS

PART IV: THE FOURTH GOSPEL

PART I

Introduction

... and the glory of the Lord
shone round about them ...

(Luke 2:9, KJV)

CHAPTER I

THE ONE BIBLE

An old Rabbi was once walking down the village street. He met a member of his congregation who began to boast that he had read through all the volumes of the Talmud three times. Instead of praising him, the Rabbi replied: "The important thing is not how many times *you* have been *through* the Talmud, but whether the Talmud has been *through you!*" The aim of this work is not to take us through the Bible but to let the Bible get through to us.

You will notice that I refer to the Bible as if it were one book. In fact, it is many volumes and, in particular, is made up of two parts, the Old Testament and the New. These are very often kept apart, as if the Old Testament belonged mainly to Judaism and the New Testament to Christianity. The assumption is made that the New Testament has replaced or superseded the Old. Sometimes they are still contrasted: the old clichés are repeated—that in the Old Testament we find the God of Law, in the New, the God of Grace; in the Old, the God of Wrath, in the New, the God of Mercy. But such contrasts are alien to the New Testament, and I begin by emphasizing as strongly as I can that the Old Testament and the New are two parts of a single whole: they constitute one volume, the Bible.

The difference between the two Testaments

But we have to recognize that these two parts are different and alike at the same time. Their differences we can gather under three heads.

1. *Language.* Apart from very brief sections at Ezra 4:8–6: 18, 7:12–26 and Daniel 2:46–7:28 and a verse at Jeremiah 10:11 and two words at Genesis 31:47, which are written in Aramaic, the Old Testament is written in Hebrew. This Hebrew language, although of mixed origin, became the language of a small nation; it was confined to a country which was smaller than New Jersey, and which would go into New York State several times. And it was not well fitted for use outside that small nation of Israel and outside that small land of Palestine. It was simple; a superb instrument for vivid poetry and prophecy, but ill suited for the rough and tumble of abstract thought and ill prepared to adapt itself to new peoples and lands. Hebrew remained the beautiful language of the few.

But the language of the New Testament was different. The New Testament was written in Greek, but Greek of a peculiar kind. At first Greek, too, had been the language of a small nation. However, owing mainly to the work of Alexander the Great, it had spread to other people and countries and had become almost a new language, a universal language to which the name *Koinê* or common Greek has been given. While this can be overemphasized, it is true that the language of the New Testament consists mainly of this unliterary Greek, which was above all a cosmopolitan language, a language born of the need for adaptability. It was a language confined to no one people or country, as was Hebrew, but understood in varying degrees throughout the known world of the first century from India to Spain. The language of the Old Testament was the language of a nation and a land; the language of the New Testament was that of all peoples and all countries; it was a world language.

2. *Geography*. It is true that the documents of the Old Testament move from place to place and country to country. They take us down to Egypt, to the land of Mesopotamia, to Assyria and Babylon, and they cast their eyes far away to the isles of the seas. In this way they confront us with many cultures. But, on the whole, the center of interest in the Old Testament is in the land of Israel; it is through the eyes of Israel that the other nations and countries are seen. The Old Testament is concerned with the Holy People, the Holy Land, the Holy City (Jerusalem)—these are the centers of the universe from which it looks out on all around. Its geographic awareness is in tune with its linguistic character.

In the New Testament things are different. The land of Israel, as such, plays little part in it. The epistles bear titles which immediately transport us away from the confines of Palestine to Corinth, Ephesus, Galatia, Thessalonica, Philippi, Rome, and, ultimately, to Spain. Jerusalem, the city of David, has become for many writers the apostate city which rejected the Lord. The poignant words of Jesus over it are significant; it has become an object of sorrow. "O Jerusalem, Jerusalem, killing the prophets and stoning those who are sent to you! How often would I have gathered your children together as a hen gathers her brood under her wings, and you would not!" Paul as early as Galatians has already ceased to center his emotions on the earthly Jerusalem. "Now Hagar is Mount Sinai in Arabia"; he writes in an allegory, "she corresponds to the present Jerusalem, for she is in slavery with her children. But the Jerusalem above is free, and she is our mother" (Gal. 4:25–27). Similarly, he consciously asserts that geographic and other divisions do not count. "There is neither Jew nor Greek, there is neither slave nor free, there is neither male nor female; for you are all one in Christ Jesus" (Gal. 3:28).

In a similar fashion, Luke sets the birth of Jesus on a world stage. This is why he begins his birth narrative with the wide-sweeping words: "In those days a decree went out from Caesar Augustus that all the world should be enrolled." The birth of Jesus is part of that wide world, placed against a universal canvas. And the last book of the New Testament proclaims that the "Kingdoms of this world" had become "the Kingdom of our Lord and his Christ" (Rev. 11:15). Universalism is known in the Old Testament (Is. 2:1 ff.); it breaks through at several points in it. But universalism is the very breath of the New Testament.

3. *Time*. The Old Testament spans at least ten centuries. It recalls the Exodus of Israel from Egypt at least thirteen centuries before Christ, but it advances from there right down to the time of Antiochus Epiphanes, a few centuries B.C., into the book of Daniel. The tradition that it contains spans the centuries. Contrast with this the New Testament, all of which came into being within a comparatively brief period. If we date the death of Jesus near to A.D. 30, then we may claim with certainty that within one hundred years of that date, all the books of the New Testament had come into being. The time span of the Old Testament is, therefore, at least ten times longer than that of the New. This fact alone should warn us against always applying the same methods to the interpretation of the Old as to that of the New Testament.

The unity of the two Testaments

In these three ways—language, geographic orientation, temporal span—the Old Testament and the New differ. But they constitute one book. How can this be claimed? Let me divide the reasons for the sake of clarity as follows.

1. *Both Testaments are concerned with the same God.* The God who speaks in Jesus Christ in the New Testament is the God of Abraham and Isaac and Jacob. The God who works

redemption in Christ in the New is the God who brought Israel out of the land of Egypt, who led her through the wilderness, spoke to her at Sinai, gave her the prophets, and brought her safely out of Babylon. The New Testament never doubts that the God of which it speaks is also the God of the Old Testament. The God who acted in creation in Genesis has acted also in Jesus Christ. As Paul puts it, "For it is the God who said, 'Let light shine out of darkness,' who has shone in our hearts to give the light of the knowledge of the glory of God in the face of Christ" (II Cor. 4:6). The God who spoke to Israel in diverse ways and manners also spoke in his son Jesus Christ (Heb. 1:1 f.).

There have often been those in the church who have sought to deny this truth. In the second century, for example, there were Marcion and his followers, who drew a rigid distinction between the inferior God of the Old Testament and the God of the New. In more recent years, there have been those who have found the value of the Old Testament only in its excellence as literature; religiously it can be ignored, they have implied. But such people, ancient and modern, ignore the evidence of the New Testament itself that the God of the Old Covenant is also the God of the New Covenant, that the voice heard on Sinai and on Calvary is the voice of the same God.

2. *Both Testaments are concerned with the same people.* By this I do not mean simply that the names of the same persons appear in both testaments, although this is true. Moses, Abraham, Elijah, Isaiah, Jeremiah—these and many other Old Testament figures re-emerge on the New Testament stage. But this is not as important as another fact. The Old Testament is concerned from first to last with Israel, the People of God —its origin, history, failures, triumphs, and destiny. Under several figures—the vine, the vineyard, the remnant, the peculiar people—the Israel of God is described; it is the traffic between God and Israel that constitutes the dominant note of

the Old Testament. Because Israel is designed to be God's agent in the world, to this end was a *people* chosen at the Exodus; and in a real sense the whole of the Old Testament is the record of God's attempt to prepare for himself a peculiar people that should make known his ways.

But what is true of the Old is also true of the New Testament. In the New, as in the Old, God's purposes are to be achieved through a community, the Church. The Church is now the Israel of God; it is the Israel of God continuous with that of the Old Testament but entered upon a new stage of its development. The new people centered in Christ has become "Israel" and is destined in the New Testament to carry on the function of the Old Israel. There is newness in the "People of God" in the New Testament but no radical break with the "People of God" of the Old Testament. Therefore, in their communal aspect (that is, in their concentration on God's people in the world), both Testaments are alike.

3. *The events of the Old Testament are types of events in the New Testament.* Since the Church, which created the New Testament, is Israel in a new phase of its development, it is not surprising that the history of the Old Israel supplies parallels to that of the New Israel. Thus individual figures in the Old Testament become examples of behavior in the New Testament. One need only refer at this point to Hebrews where in Chapter XI we have what has been called a portrait gallery of the Old Testament designed to provide inspiration and examples for Christians. But more important is the use of whole situations or events in the Old Testament to illumine the situation of Christians. An explicit example of this occurs in I Corinthians 10:1–13:

> You should understand, my brothers, that our ancestors were all under the pillar of cloud, and all of them passed through the Red Sea; and so they all received baptism into the fellowship of Moses in cloud and sea. They all ate the same supernatural

food, and all drank the same supernatural drink; I mean, they all drank from the supernatural rock that accompanied their travels—and that rock was Christ. And yet, most of them were not accepted by God, for the desert was strewn with their corpses.

These events happened as symbols to warn us not to set our desires on evil things, as they did. Do not be idolaters, like some of them; as Scripture has it, "the people sat down to feast and stood up to play." Let us not commit fornication, as some of them did—and twenty-three thousand died in one day. Let us not put the power of the Lord to the test, as some of them did—and were destroyed by serpents. Do not grumble against God, as some of them did—and were destroyed by the Destroyer.

All these things that happened to them were symbolic, and were recorded for our benefit as a warning. For upon us the fulfilment of the ages has come. If you feel sure that you are standing firm, beware! You may fall. So far you have faced no trial beyond what man can bear. God keeps faith, and he will not allow you to be tested above your powers, but when the test comes he will at the same time provide a way out, by enabling you to sustain it.

Here the events of the Exodus, the birth of the Old Israel, become prototypes of the birth and life of the Church. And the Exodus, in particular, played a considerable part in the thought of those who wrote the New Testament. They saw a parallel, or a common pattern, between that event and their own age. The coming of Jesus they interpreted as constituting a New Exodus leading to a New Sinai under a New Moses. This comparison must not be exaggerated, but it is real, as are other parallels, for example, between Elijah and John the Baptist, between the situation of Noah and that of Christians (Matt. 24:38 ff.; I Peter 3:18–22). The precise nature of the parallelism to which we refer is hard to define; and there are varieties in its use. We may claim that the New Testament presents not only parallels to the Old Testament events but also fulfillments of them; that is, the New Testament event is not only the antitype of the type presented by the Old Testament but its completion.

4. *The New Testament is the fulfillment of the Old.* This last point is most important. Constantly the writers of the New Testament draw upon the Old in order to show that it is now fulfilled. This happens in two ways. Sometimes there are echoes of the Old Testament in the New Testament passages which are so woven into the text that their presence is not always at first realized. For example, passages in Mark recall the Psalms. Take, for example, Mark 15:21–39. In these few verses, the following references to the Psalms are woven into the text:

> Then they fastened him to the cross. They divided his clothes among them, casting lots to decide what each should have. (15:24)
> (Compare Psalm 22:18—They divide my garments among them, and for my raiment they cast lots.)

> So too the chief priests and the doctors of the law jested with one another: "He saved others," they said, "but he cannot save himself." (15:31)
> (Compare Psalm 22:7–8—All who see me mock at me, they make mouths at me, they wag their heads; "He committed his cause to the Lord; let him deliver him, let him rescue him, for he delights in him!")

> . . . and at three Jesus cried aloud, *"Eli, Eli, lema sabachthani?"* which means, "My God, my God, why hast thou forsaken me?" (15:34)
> (Compare Psalm 22:1—My God, my God, why hast thou forsaken me?)

> A man came running with a sponge, soaked in sour wine, on the end of a cane, and held it to his lips. (15:36)
> (Compare Psalm 69:21—They gave me poison for food, and for my thirst they gave me vinegar to drink.)

More obvious are those passages where, not only are there words and phrases which evoke passages from the Old Testament, but there is direct citation of it. These quotations are most obvious in Matthew in verses where a special formula is employed, as in 1:22 (following the story of the birth of Jesus):

> All this happened in order to fulfil what the Lord declared through the prophet: "The virgin will conceive and bear a son, and he shall be called Emmanuel."
>
> (Compare Isaiah 7:14—Therefore the Lord himself will give you a sign. Behold, a young woman shall conceive and bear a son, and shall call his name Immanuel.)

But Matthew is not peculiar in this. Mark begins his gospel with a combination of words from Malachi 3:1 and Isaiah 40:3.

> Here begins the Gospel of Jesus Christ the Son of God.
>
> In the prophet Isaiah it stands written: "Here is my herald whom I send on ahead of you, and he will prepare your way. A voice crying aloud in the wilderness, 'Prepare a way for the Lord; clear a straight path for him.'"

These words are taken up, with slight variation, in Luke 3:4 f. and John 1:23. Paul again uses certain formulae when he quotes from the Old Testament. He uses the phrase: "as it is written," or something similar, followed by a quotation, short or long, about thirty times. Read, for example, Romans 4:16–25, which in three places contains references to the Old Testament. Throughout the New Testament, appeal is made to the Old. The life, death, and resurrection of Jesus of Nazareth and the emergence of the Church are understood in terms of the Old Testament as its fulfillment. At this point, however, two factors are to be recognized as of extreme importance.

First, although the New Testament writers draw upon the Old Testament to illumine what had happened in the Gospel, they do not draw upon all the Old Testament indiscriminately. There were some prophecies which they ignored and others which they modified. Not all Old Testament expectations were suitable for the events which they were interpreting. There is an example of this in the quotation made by Matthew in 11:4–6 which draws upon Isaiah 35:5–6.

> Jesus answered, "Go and tell John what you hear and see: *the blind recover their sight, the lame walk, the lepers are clean, the deaf hear, the dead are raised to life, the poor are hearing the good news*—and happy is the man who does not find me a stumbling-block."
>
> (The italicized words are from Isaiah 35:5–6.)

But in the same context in Isaiah 35:4, there is a prediction of vengeance which Matthew deliberately omits. Isaiah has the verse:

> Behold, your God
>   will come with vengeance,
> with the recompense of God.
>   He will come and save you.

This verse Matthew ignores. This means that the New Testament is not dominated by the Old. It is the Gospel itself that provides the pattern for the understanding of the Old, as of all things: the New Testament interprets the Old in the light of Christ; it does not merely interpret Christ in the light of the Old. To put the matter in another way, the New Testament did not paint a picture of its Lord out of all the colors found in the Old Testament. It used the Old Testament selectively, in a creative way; it rejected some colors and used others in the light of Jesus, the Christ.

But the second point to be emphasized is that the quotations from the Old Testament are of profound significance. The writers of the New Testament were not playing an interesting game with texts in a mechanical way; they were not adults playing at a Biblical jigsaw puzzle. In quoting the Old Testament, they were asserting their conviction that Christianity was not a mushroom growth, no sudden bolt from the blue, a new movement unrelated to the past, for which there was no preparation. On the contrary, it was the culmination of a long historic process revealed in the Old Testament. The coming of Christ and all that ensued thereon was the fruition of an age-long purpose which the God of Israel had cherished and had now fulfilled. It was no accident that Jesus was a Jew. Only within Judaism could He have appeared, because only there was the soil ready for him to appear and grow. He is the flowering of the hope of the Old Testament. In the quotations to which we referred, the New Testament expresses the conviction that Christianity is as old as Israel; it began when Israel was called out of Egypt, or when Abraham left Ur of the Chaldees, or, even earlier, at the very creation of the universe by the God of Israel.

In this sense the Old Testament is the substructure of the New and indispensable for its true understanding. It is mainly from this point of view that we shall approach the New Testament here.

CHAPTER 2

THE BACKGROUND
IN THE GRAECO-ROMAN WORLD

The roots of the New Testament, then, are in the Old Testament. But those roots had to grow in a particular soil—the world of the first century, not only in Palestine, but also in the Roman Empire. What were the main features of the world within which the New Testament emerged? We shall indicate five of these.

A world at peace

The dominant factor politically, when the New Testament documents were written, was the extent and power of the Roman Empire. For two hundred years, wars and rumors of wars had troubled Roman soil. By 275 B.C. Rome had spread its power from the city itself through Italy. Then, as a result of the Punic Wars, it had gradually gained control of the western Mediterranean. Julius Caesar (100–44 B.C.), a military genius, had furthered its conquests. On his death, Rome was to enter a period, not of further expansion, but of peace. In 27 B.C., Octavian, who became Augustus Caesar (63 B.C.–A.D. 14), entered upon his rule as virtually the first Roman Emperor. Both he and the emperors who followed him devoted their energies to the consolidation of the territories gained by conquest, and, as a result, the Empire became more and more a stable unit. Several factors contributed to the increasing power and stability of Rome.

First, Augustus Caesar saw the importance of a definite imperial policy. Before his time the provinces of Rome had been administered by proconsuls, who had used them for their own enrichment. Discontent had been rife. Augustus determined to change this state of affairs. He set up a system under which the rulers of the provinces were to be held responsible for their conduct. He divided the provinces into two groups, the Senatorial and the Imperial. In the Senatorial provinces the Senate appointed officers who were responsible to itself. Most of these Senatorial provinces were situated on the peaceful coasts of the Mediterranean so that they needed no garrisons: each was governed by a *proconsul*, who usually held office for a year. In such provinces the Emperor also kept a control over things through a *procurator* of his own appointment. Normally in charge of finances, the procurator also served as the Emperor's "eye."

More in number, and of greater importance, were the Imperial provinces. These were administered by a governor, called the *propraetor*, appointed by the Emperor. The propraetors exercised military and civil authority. Since the Imperial provinces were situated on the frontiers of the Empire, they had standing armies. By the creation of such provinces, and by keeping a secondary control on the Senatorial provinces, the Emperors established a political system that was highly effective.

Secondly, the unification of the Empire was helped by what is known as the Roman Peace, Pax Romana. The only province that broke the peace, which began with the accession of Augustus and continued to the death of Marcus Aurelius (A.D. 180), was Judaea. The Emperors brought deliverance from continual war, quelled internal factions, did away with fears of invasion. This absence of war came like a benediction; it furthered the unification of the world. But this was further helped by other factors.

Thirdly, then, three more factors made for unity. They may

be classified as physical, legal, and linguistic. The physical factors which helped toward unity were the presence of both sea and land routes which made intercommunication far easier than ever before. Diverging from Rome as their center, roads were built to connect the most remote countries. A courier could travel on these roads at the rate of fifty miles a day, carriages could go twenty-five miles, pedestrians fifteen; the roads were paved; they were guarded; they provided means of shelter and entertainment. Similarly, navigation was greatly extended; the seas were rid of pirates. Land and sea routes made a constant interchange of commodities, ideas, and peoples possible as never before. Travel was quicker, easier, and safer; and all roads tended to a unity centering in Rome itself.

Equally important was it that, on the legal side, the Roman Empire was consolidated by a magnificent system of law. The Empire respected local and national customs, but it was also concerned to establish a common justice for all its peoples. Gradually, local, tribal, provincial, and national ideas—for example, about the rights of fathers over sons, husbands over wives, etc.—gave place to principles of a more universal kind. The unifying force of the law was further increased by the extension of the privileges of Roman citizenship. Ultimately, by a decree of the Emperor Caracalla, A.D. 212, the distinction between Roman and non-Roman was abolished. More and more individuals, and even communities, were granted citizenship—a citizenship that granted the boon of legal protection everywhere and opened the door to the highest offices in the State. In this way national distinctions were obliterated; men of all nations and languages competed freely under the same political system for the highest honors, political and other.

This was still further made possible by the linguistic factor to which we referred. The most excellent means of physical transportation would be of little use without language as a medium through which to enter into familiar, easy intercourse. The chief medium of this is language. Here the Roman Empire was well served. To the East of Rome, one language dominated, but to the West, another. Spain, France, Italy, Britain, and, in a lesser degree, Germany, traded, were ruled, and intensified their culture by means of Latin. Asia Minor, Greece, Syria, Phoenicia, Egypt found in Greek a common speech. Rome became bilingual, and gradually Greek spread westward beyond Rome. By the first century, Greek, in its *Koinê* or common, diluted form was understood and spoken almost everywhere by educated classes, and there was some acquaintance with it everywhere, even among the less educated. *Koinê* Greek became the lingua franca of the Empire.

In all these ways—the Roman Peace, a common system of government, improved means of communication, and a common language—the Empire became unified in law, order, and sentiment.

A world of plenty

Let us next look at the economic conditions of the Empire at the time of the New Testament. It was fashionable in the early years of this century to interpret the rise of Christianity, partly at least, in terms of economics. The conditions of life for the underprivileged masses of the Graeco-Roman world were so desperate that they turned very readily to the Carpenter-Saviour, Jesus of Nazareth. Jesus was a workingman, and, as such, he made a special appeal to the poor of his day. Primitive Christianity was a movement of the proletariat, explicable because of its appeal to the underprivileged.

It is true that the Gospel always was, and always must be, good news to the poor. But does our knowledge of economic conditions in the first century support the view that it was the desperation of the working classes with their lot that made them turn especially to Christianity? There are certain factors that are pertinent.

First, what was the economic status of the leaders of primitive Christianity? They were certainly not of noble birth, not what we should call aristocratic. Not many wise, not many noble had been called (I Cor. 1:26 f.). But among them were people of some means—Paul himself, Barnabas, Erastus, Gaius (Acts 18:8, 19:3; Rom. 16:23; I Cor. 1:14)—so that the wholly proletarian origins of the early Church must not be over-emphasized.

Secondly, there is considerable evidence that during the period of Augustus (27 B.C.–A.D. 14) there was prosperity. True, he was followed by spendthrift Emperors; for example, Caligula (A.D. 37–41), who indulged in costly games and lavish entertainments, and Nero (A.D. 54–68), whose extravagances led him to seize half of the province of North Africa. But the Emperor Vespasian (A.D. 69–79) brought back something of the old Augustan prosperity. Vespasian was frugal and determined to find work for the poor. He authorized public works for this purpose. The Colosseum, for example, was an ancient Works Progress Administration project. During Vespasian's reign, the income of the Empire was three times what it had been under Augustus. And despite extravagant Emperors, there was much prosperity before Vespasian's time. There was, then, in the first century a genuine well-being. This manifested itself superficially in Rome itself; in the provinces, it was marked by a sense of security. The one exception was Palestine where there was dire poverty. But the over-all picture does not suggest a peculiarly strong economic reason for the success of Christianity in the first century. Although the Christian Gospel did appeal to the poor, its appeal was not merely in terms of compensation for injustice but of a challenge to love even in the midst of injustice.

A *world of many religions*

We have seen that, politically, the first century was characterized by unity; economically, by a degree of prosperity. Religiously, the scene was the exact opposite of what it was politically; it was marked by diversity. The first century was a period of intense spiritual yearning, combined with widespread popular superstition.

We have to distinguish between the religions of the ignorant masses and those of the more enlightened. The popular deities that Rome had inherited from Greece and elsewhere still retained the allegiance of the many; but their hold on the intelligentsia, even on the priests themselves, was waning. They could no longer satisfy. But where were the enlightened to turn? Just as the traditional Gods of Greece and Rome were failing, so was the confident humanism of ancient Greece. It was a mark of the Greek genius in classical times that it had sought to see life steadily and see it whole. Man was confident in his own power to think clearly and to solve rationally the perplexing problems that confronted him. But, by the first century, the old securities were gone—the old city-states with their comforting amenities were in decay; there had been foreign conquest, wars, pestilence, famine. The great changes and chances of existence in the period following Alexander the Great made men insecure, apparently helpless victims of forces beyond their control. Men ceased to feel at home in the universe. The old confident humanism of classical Hellas, the rationalism that had looked out on the world with fearless directness—these waned. A mood of pessimism developed, a suspicion of the power of philosophy to attain truth. The old spirit of inquiry gave place to a sense of the enigma of the unknown and of the need for a sure word of revelation.

And this mood was met by certain religious developments. First, *the development of Emperor Worship*. The Roman

Emperors had brought peace to the world. To a war-weary world it seemed as if they had brought in a "millennium." It was natural that many thought that the potentates responsible for "peace" were divine. Politicians encouraged the belief for the sake of imperial unity. The divinity of rulers had long been known among the Greeks. The Ptolemies at Alexandria and the Seleucids at Antioch had received divine honors and had been called gods. And in 29 B.C., the Romans followed the same path. In that year, Augustus, the first Roman Emperor, allowed a temple to be built in his honour. Doubtless he was worshipped, not simply for political reasons, but because, in the popular mind, he was seriously regarded as a divine being, a God upon earth. But equally clear is it that the worship of Emperors could not have profound religious significance; it could hardly meet the spiritual needs of men.

Secondly, the *Mystery Religions*. One outcome of the insecurity of the Hellenistic Age was the growth of individualism. Men no longer felt that they were bound up with their State, but stood in stark loneliness. To meet this individual loneliness, Mystery Religions arose. In speaking of these, great caution is necessary. The Mysteries observed secrecy, and our sources for them are late. We do know, however, that by the first century voluntary religious associations centering in a Mystery which had grown up all over the Eastern part of the Empire, spread through the Western part also. Some of them were dignified; for example, the Mysteries of Attis in Phrygia, Osiris in Egypt, Adonis in Syria. But the fundamental conceptions underlying them were essentially the same. After a period of ritual purification and preparation, the initiate took part in a sacred drama in which the adventures of the God were re-enacted by the worshippers. He, thereby, himself entered into the experience of the God and became conscious of intimate spiritual fellowship with him, which was understood as *deification*. Doubtless, some Mysteries had an elevating moral effect, but some were marked by disgusting ceremonial orgies; they produced "thrilling" individual experiences but, as far as we are aware, offered no "community" to the initiate. Thus they spread, not because they satisfied the need to conquer loneliness, but by creating a sense of mastery over *fate* and *death* (the twin enemies of man in the Hellenistic Age) through a spurious deification.

Closely related to the Mysteries was the gnostic movement (although the earliest date for this is uncertain), which offered salvation by knowledge—not rational or scientific knowledge, but a knowledge gained through secret lore, leading to mystic contemplation or vision. With this movement, however, we shall deal later. We merely note here that along with Stoicism, Epicureanism, Emperor Worship, and the Mysteries, a kind of Proto-gnosticism offered salvation to men—a salvation by way of an esoteric illumination, although full-blooded Gnosticism was later than the first century.

A world of many philosophies

Apart from the religions which offered salvation, philosophy played a considerable role in satisfying the aspirations of men. The higher intellects and more austere minds of antiquity, though often sympathetic to them, were not attracted by the Mysteries; they turned instead to philosophy for light on life and conduct. Can we describe this philosophy?

Behind all the philosophic tendencies of the first century, there towers, in the distance, the figure of Plato (428–347 B.C.). The *Platonic philosophy* to which he gave birth is perhaps best understood as the union of two previous forces, Socraticism and Heracliteanism. Plato agreed with Heraclitus (flourished 513 B.C.) that all things seen are ceaselessly flowing. As a result, they cannot be known, for the object of knowledge must be constant. At the same time, he believed that Socrates was right in the view that definition is concerned with universals. But what is universal? It cannot be something perceivable because perceivables are never constant. So what is permanent and universal must be other than what is perceptible and sensible. It was in this way that Plato arrived at his general notion that everything sensible is separate from its idea while at the same time participating in it. The idea itself is one and not many; it is changeless and eternal; it is perfect. Plato's "Ideas" constitute:

> A world above man's head, to let him see
> How boundless might his soul's horizon be,
> How vast, yet of what clear transparency.

They constitute a world of transcendental models or archetypes, the truly existent reality corresponding to all our dreams of perfection. Platonism, then, maintained the supremacy of eternal ideas over temporary phenomena. It was theistic—the Supreme Good is the end of all things; it was ethical—looking toward present and future rewards and punishments; it was religious—its ethics, politics, and physics are grounded in the Ruler of the Universe.

This Platonism, however diluted, lies behind the philosophies of the first century and is part of the air that intellectuals and others of that time breathed. Two other major philosophies alone can be mentioned.

Stoicism, founded about 310 B.C. by Zeno, a native of Cition in Cyprus, established itself first in Athens but spread widely among cultured people. It was born out of the failure of nerve which we noted above, in a time when life seemed aimless and the world incomprehensible. To the question: What is the good life?, Zeno gave the answer: it is the life which is in accordance with nature (*physis*). The whole universe is of one substance (*physis*) in various states, and this one substance is Reason, God. It is true that two principles of being were differentiated: the material (the passive) and the divine (the active); but there is nothing which is not in its ultimate origin God. In Him man lives and moves and has his being. The *physis,* which is God, aims at producing the highest possible; its purpose is to care for the world, to bring it to perfection. Hence, the wise part for man is to find out what the purpose of Nature (*physis*) is and to live accordingly. To serve and help that purpose is the good life; to thwart it is evil.

There was much in Stoicism that makes it similar to Judaism. Its monotheism, however different from that of Judaism, was real; it shared the moral seriousness of Judaism. But its total concentration on fulfilling the purpose of Nature, the immanent Reason, led to an emphasis on self-sufficiency. Since nothing is good but virtue, that is, conformity to Nature, everything else becomes a matter of indifference. The good man is, therefore, indifferent to poverty and riches, suffering and joy. Conformity of the will to the immanent Reason of the Universe alone is important.

Such a doctrine could appear inhuman. But this apparent inhumanity was softened by another aspect of Stoicism, the emphasis on the "sympathy of the Universe." Since the providence of God runs through all the created Universe, then all the universe is one. When a man fails to feel for others, he is manifestly isolating himself and rejecting the purpose of Nature for him, that is, the acceptance of his part in the whole.

But this doctrine did not succeed in delivering Stoicism from a kind of chronic depression; its relentless concentration on duty alone could not but, in the end, strike cold. A. E. Taylor writing of the fears of the Emperor Marcus Aurelius, asserts: "If Stoicism as a system is responsible for these fears, it is, I think, because the doctrine offers only a 'God within' and 'no God without' to whom one can call for grace against temptation."[1]

Next we mention *Epicureanism,* which has been much more misunderstood than Stoicism. Its founder was Epicurus, a man born in Samos in 342 B.C., but who by descent was Athenian and, with his disciples, resided in Athens where he lived a life of contemplation and abstemiousness. He was innocent, kind, and simple. His thought is generally considered under two heads: first, his view of the world. He considered the universe to be the outcome of a clash of atoms. These, in falling downward through space, swerved slightly and collided. Out of this collision, caused by an accidental swerve, emerged the physical universe and the whole existence of man. In this way, following Democritus, Epicurus was able to explain the physical world apart from the Gods.

Secondly, the ethics of Epicurus were influential. The aim of life should be to follow the natural impulses and instincts as they arise in us. Pleasure is to be cherished; pain avoided. But what gives real pleasure? It is the practice of virtue and avoidance of the pangs of conscience.

But not all could see that virtue was pleasant. In less innocent lives than his own, the materialism and hedonism of Epicurus could and did lead to license. If Stoicism, in concentrating too much on virtue for its own sake, led to depression, Epicureanism, in making virtue dependent upon happiness, often ended in sensuality.

A world of many crosscurrents

Our summary of the philosophic schools must end by pointing out that, by the first century, these various schools had intermingled a great deal. The time immediately preceding the Christian era was an "age of syncretism." There had emerged a philosophical and religious amalgamation. Edwyn Bevan writes as follows: "At a time when many men, not philosophers in any sense, wanted some guide for life which was raised above the old mythologies and which yet met their sense of some greater spiritual reality encompassing the life of men, it was natural that a kind of body of popular philosophic doctrines should come into vogue, made of the commonplaces of the different schools, with a blurring of their distinctive peculiarities."[2]

Through Posidonius (born 135 B.C.), a Stoic, and many other figures, there filtered through into the popular mind the concepts and terms of Stoicism and other philosophies. The first century was, therefore, a sophisticated world, long familiar with the language and ideas of philosophers. But this should not be exaggerated. The gifts of philosophy have always been for the few; she has often been unable or unwilling to walk in the streets; the masses she could despise. "The father of the world," Plato has said, "it is difficult to discover and it is impossible to make him known to all." Despite the influence of philosophy and the higher religious thought in the Graeco-Roman world, the populace was taught by swarms of teachers, more unscrupulous and adventurous than serious and informed. Because philosophy soared too high, astrologers and all sorts of "odd" teachers often reached the people and were their real teachers.

The first century, then, was a century in search of a spiritual and philosophic foundation for its political unity. The Christian faith when it appeared had to compete with other movements offering salvation by "knowledge" (the Mysteries, Proto-Gnosticism), by "ethics" (Stoicism and Epicureanism), and by Emperor worship. But it had also to meet the challenge of another "movement"—the very religion which gave it birth, Judaism.

CHAPTER 3

THE BACKGROUND
IN FIRST-CENTURY JUDAISM

The background of the New Testament in the Graeco-Roman world we dealt with above. Even more important is its background in Judaism. Jesus was a Jew; his disciples were Jews; for some time the Christian movement continued within Judaism. What was this Judaism within which Christianity was born? "Like mother, like child": to understand first-century Judaism is to go a long way toward understanding the New Testament, which was born out of it.

But to begin with, we must note two developments in recent scholarship. First, in the past, it was customary to draw a sharp distinction between the Judaism of Palestine and the Judaism outside Palestine in the time of the New Testament. Hellenistic Judaism was regarded as very different from Palestinian Judaism. But now, it is increasingly recognized that this difference has been grossly exaggerated. For a long time before the first century, Palestine had been open to Greek influences. Archaeologists have found Hellenistic figures in Palestinian synagogues; Rabbis were familiar with the Greek language and culture; there was constant interchange of ideas between the Jews of Palestine and those outside, in what was called the Dispersion; the annual temple tax paid by all Jews kept the synagogues of the Dispersion aware of Jersualem and its life, while pilgrims to Palestine from the Hellenistic world were constant. For these and many other reasons, the customary rigid division between the Palestinian and non-Palestinian or Hellenistic Judaism has broken down.

And, in the second place, recent discoveries have influenced our approach to Judaism in the first century. While the Dead Sea Scrolls have not revolutionized our understanding of the latter, they have made even more clear to us how varied and fluid was Judaism in the time of Jesus; it was a coat of far more mixed colors than was ever realized. Can we describe such a variegated complexity?

The Beliefs

Let us first look at the basic beliefs of a religious Jew in the first century.

(a) *The One God:* He would begin by assuming that there was *One, Living, Personal God,* burning in his purpose, who gave meaning to life from outside life and demanded love of and obedience to himself. In other words, monotheism for first-century Judaism was an assumption. Since the exile, idolatry had ceased in Israel, and it goes without saying that that monotheism was the ethical monotheism of the prophets: that is, the One God was Holy in his will, and asked of man to love mercy and to do justly.

This One Holy God was the constant theme of the thinking of the Jew. Sometimes he conceived of him almost familiarly, anthropologically; but the majesty, spirituality, and otherness of God, and the mystery of his holiness were also preserved. For example, texts in the Old Testament which referred crudely in an anthropomorphic manner to God were changed in the Greek Old Testament; phrases unworthy of God were avoided. From the third century B.C. onward, in order to preserve God's transcendence, the name *"Yahweh"* (for God) used in the Old Testament was not pronounced.

But did not the insistence on the "otherness" of God banish him from his world? Was the warm nearness of God lost in the experience of the first-century Jews? Was their God aloof and their religion dominated by fear and not by love? Many Christian scholars have often in the past urged that this was so. But the otherness of God in Judaism did not mean remoteness; it did not even mean transcendence in the philosophic sense. God was in heaven and man on earth, but through his Shekinah (Presence) and his Glory, the Jew could experience God's presence on earth. Or again, God could and did come to many of his own through his Holy Spirit. Nor should we forget the significance of the belief in angels in Judaism. It can be argued that they were merely a bridge between a remote God and his distant creatures. But it is far more likely that they were a sign of God's concern for men in the smallest details of their lives. The loving God provides guardian angels. On the other hand, there were very numerous evil angels whose origin and purpose is obscure. These demons did not serve to bring the distant God near. The same ambiguity arises when we consider the figure of wisdom, the mediator between God and the world, which we find in Proverbs—it can be interpreted as indicating both God's interest in and remoteness from the world. But one thing we can certainly say, that Judaism did know the love of God for his own and emphasized this as much as it did the fear of the Lord.

(b) *The One People:* Tied up with the assumption of the reality of the One loving good God, there was another—the assumption that there was a special relation between the One God and One People—Israel. This relation was, in a sense, a necessary one. Belief in God in Judaism was not the outcome of human or intellectual reflection, but of revelation. This revelation was given in and through a particular event, the Exodus of Israel from Egypt. The very act in which the Creator of the whole universe was revealed was also the act which gave birth to the people of Israel as a nation. There was, therefore, a peculiarly close relation between Israel and God. Israel is the people of God; the bride of God; his first-born son. In the affliction of

Israel, God was afflicted; he is her guardian and friend. It was a little step from this to the view that a special character was ascribed to the land of Israel. There it was that the Shekinah loved to dwell because God had sanctified it. There was the Holy Spirit to be experienced within the holy community in a holy land. And at the center of the Holy Land stood Jerusalem, the Holy City—and this was the center of the world.

Did this concentration on God's love for Israel affect the attitude of Israel to other nations? Often Israel had occasion, and just occasion, to think of the ruling Gentile nations as beasts out to devour her. But she also preserved a kindlier attitude toward the nations. Some Rabbis were careful to explain that God had offered the Law to the Gentiles; they attempted to understand and account for the moral weaknesses of the Gentiles; they were ready to recognize their virtues. In the Messianic Age, many expected the Gentiles to join in the common worship of the God of Israel; they emphasized the essential unity of all mankind. There was both a particularism and a noble universalism in Judaism then as always. The explanation of this juxtaposition is in the third assumption to which we now turn.

(c) *The One Law*: The Jew assumed the reality of the Living God and the eternal relation between him and Israel. The link between them was the Law, or, better, the *Torah*. Judaism assumed that the God of Israel had revealed his will to her in the Law. He had so loved her at Sinai that he had given her detailed instructions how to walk in his ways.

At this point it must be emphasized that the translation of the Hebrew word *Torah* by the English word *Law* has been doubly unfortunate. "Torah" is a far wider term than the English "Law"; it stands for direction, teaching, instruction of a religious and moral kind. Indeed, it stands for what we call "revelation"— the totality of God's will as revealed. It always retains a reference to law or commandment, but it is never exhausted in these terms. We shall, therefore, enlarge on its significance.

The Law was thought to have existed before the world came
into being; it was, in fact, the agent or instrument by means of
which God created the world. Before God did so, he consulted
the Law, as an architect looks at his plans before beginning to
build. The ground plan of the universe was the Law; or, as we
should put it, the world was founded on Law.

But the Law, which pre-existed creation and according to
which the universe was built, was revealed to Israel on Mt. Sinai.
What precisely was meant by the Law that had been given to
Moses and handed on from generation to generation? We may
distinguish four aspects of it.

1. The Ten Commandments, which were the essential parts
of the Law.

2. The first five books of the Old Testament, the Pentateuch.
It was to these that the term "Law" was most often applied.

3. The whole of the Old Testament was regarded as composed under the influence of the Holy Spirit. Primacy was accorded to the Pentateuch, however, according to some. While
the rest of the Old Testament might eventually disappear, the
Pentateuch would persist into the Age to Come.

4. The Oral Law, or the traditions of the Fathers. Judaism
had long recognized the necessity for adapting the Law to
changing conditions. This led to the growth of laws which were
not written in the Old Testament but formed a protective
"hedge" around the laws found there. For example, the Written
Law forbade work on the Sabbath. But what constitutes work?
In their anxiety to avoid any infringement of the Written Law,
the Rabbis eventually formed thirty-nine definitions of work to
be avoided on the Sabbath. In this way, by constant adaptation
and interpretation, the Written Law was made relevant to life;
it was made practicable. There were many different, and even
conflicting, interpretations of the Law and different schools of
interpretation developed. At one point it was feared that the One
Law might be so differently interpreted as to become two Laws.

Nevertheless, it was only by interpretation and adaptation that the One Law could live.

What was the relative importance of the Oral Law? In principle, it enjoyed the same authority as the Written Law, and some Rabbis in time came to regard it as even more important than the Written Law. They claimed that the Oral Law also went back to Sinai. This was not a historical judgment but a recognition of the value of the Oral Law. But whatever the relative importance of the Written and Oral Law, it is essential to grasp that Judaism regarded the Law, in all its forms, as a gift of God's grace. The miracle of grace, which was the giving of the Law, not by mediation but directly by God, not secretly but to all the people of Israel, and indeed to all nations—this was a constant theme of Jewish discussion. It was this experience that Judaism was concerned to re-enact in every generation at Passover.

The Practices

So far we have recognized certain basic beliefs of Judaism. Judaism assumed a God who had called Israel to be his peculiar people and supplied a Law to guide her. This meant that Judaism was a religion of gratitude for what God had done for and given to his people. But gratitude is perhaps the most ethical of all the emotions. It prompts the question: "What shall I render unto the Lord for all His benefits?" How shall God be recognized for what he has done? Here again the Law showed the way; certain activities emerged in Judaism to express gratitude to God. Here we can only mention the chief of these.

We note the significance of the worship at the Temple in Jerusalem. The centrality of the Temple goes back at least to the time of Ezra and Nehemiah. The moving descriptions of its ritual, which are so often found, point to its vitality. The very structure of the Temple was impressive. In the time of Jesus, it had been restored by Herod and stood out strikingly in gold and white, so that its glory was praised afar. The stream of sacrifices offered there could not but have made a deep impression.

What was the religious significance of the Temple? It was the place where the Shekinah loved to dwell; it signified the perpetual presence of God among his people. Its holiness and purity as the abode of the Lord was indicated by its very structure; the impure were progressively excluded from the innermost shrine. The Gentiles were only allowed into the Court of the Gentiles. Into the Holy of Holies, only the High Priest himself could enter, and that only once a year and after the most elaborate purifications. The Temple was, therefore, the abode of God, the Holy One himself. But it was not only this. It was the place where the Holy One offered forgiveness of sin. Here had he ordained a sacrificial system administered by authorized priests to reconcile his people unto himself. No wonder that, despite its many abuses, Judaism honored the Temple and its worship.

The Temple, then, signified the *perpetual* presence of the Lord among his people. But Judaism recognized that there were certain events in history when God had been especially near and had intervened on behalf of his people. They remembered these events by holding certain festivals. Thus Passover re-enacted the deliverance of Israel from Egypt; Pentecost recalled the giving of the Law at Sinai; the Feast of Tabernacles, Succoth, re-created the sojourn of the people in the wilderness. These and other festivals were intended to make live again events in Israel's history in which God had signally revealed himself. They aimed at re-creating in the experience of the Jew the experience of his people, and thus incorporating him "in Israel." This is as true of Hanukkah and Purim as of the festivals already mentioned. It is not quite so true of the Day of Atonement—the day of fasting, confession, and sacrifice, and of the New Year Festival, which recalled the creation of the world.

But apart from the Temple Services and the Festivals, how did the Law affect the lives of Jews? It created above all an institution, the Synagogue, where the centrality of the Law and of its study was recognized. The significance of the Synagogue for first-century Judaism, as for all Judaism always, cannot be over-emphasized. It made of the religious life a means of study and of prayer; it was the source of that knowledge of the Law which was to govern life in all its details. It is indeed probable that, even before A.D. 70, when the Temple in Jerusalem was destroyed, the Synagogue had already become the effective center of Jewish life. And with the Synagogue went the School.

The Pharisees, the Sadducees, and the Essenes

The Law, the Temple, the Festivals, the Synagogue—around these did the life of Jewry turn. And it was their attitude toward these centralities that determined how Jews were divided. They can especially be divided in terms of their attitude to the Law. Although the majority of the people of Israel were *am haaretz*, people of the land, who were not interested in religion, the other Jews understood the Law in many different ways. The main groups alone can be mentioned here: the Pharisees, the Sadducees, and the Essenes.

The Pharisees have been variously understood—as the intelligent artisan element in first-century Judaism, as Persianizers, and even as Hellenizers. But whatever their origin, their position can be summarized as follows. They accepted as axiomatic that the divine will was revealed in the Law and that every aspect of human life is to be governed by the Law. But the Pharisees also recognized that no written document can cover every detail of life. Changing conditions demand not an immutable code but a living, adaptable one. The Pharisees, therefore, claimed that, in addition to the Written Law, the Oral Law had authority. Moreover, they were in favor of adapting the Law more and more to make it relevant to their times. Their other beliefs are easily summarized—the resurrection of the dead, the existence of angels and spirits, a certain measure of free will. Within Judaism, the Pharisees were what we should today call "liberals"—men anxious to make religion living, vital, and contemporary.

Over against them stood the Sadducees. These, as compared with the Pharisees, were literalists; what we might loosely call "fundamentalists." They accepted the Written Law but refused to accept the authority of the Oral Law. The reason for this seems clear. They were comfortably situated, economically and socially; they were few in number but distinguished men of wealth and position. They had every reason to be satisfied. A Law written centuries before, which was not too awkward and relevant to their condition, they could tolerate. But a living, changing Law they resented. Thus it was that they insisted that only the Written Law was binding. The Oral Law was not to be taken seriously. In short, they made of the Law an antiquated "dogma," a museum piece that meant little for the present. It agrees with all this that they saw no need for a resurrection of the dead; their lives had been pleasant enough here. They saw no need for guardian or any other angels—for what? And they insisted that every man has free will—he can decide his fate. They were lusty individualists who had little time or need for the consolations of religion.

Recently, a third group—the Essenes—has come into prominence owing to the discovery of more of their literature. In all probability the Dead Sea Scrolls are Essene, and they enable us to read at first hand about the organization by a priest known as the Teacher of Righteousness of the sect of the New Covenant. After his martyrdom at the hand of a wicked priest, the Sect fled to Damascus, apparently under another leader known as the Star, but they later returned to Judaea and Qumran. They were known previously to us in the works of Philo and Josephus so that we can now draw a fairly detailed picture of their way of life. It was a way of life governed by a particular interpretation of the Law. They were even more rigid in their interpretation than the Pharisees, and it is this radicalism that led them to a more and more rigorous obedience, which led them to a highly organized withdrawn and abstemious existence in which they tried to obey all the Laws. That they constituted a very important element in the background of the New Testament is now clear.

The Hopes of Judaism

So far we have dealt with the assumptions and activities of first-century Jews. Their assumptions gave to their lives a backward look; they looked back to the Exodus when God had revealed himself and given to them his Law. They were, thus, governed by a memory. But this memory also gave them hope for the future. Gratitude for the past became in Judaism a lively expectation of favors to come. And there were many who were intensely concerned with the future. These are usually referred to as Apocalyptists or Eschatologists; they were people absorbed in their anticipations. Some have argued that Apocalypticism belongs only to the fringes of first-century Judaism, but this is not the case. The Pharisees themselves often shared in their apocalyptic hopes.

And with the eschatological or apocalytic elements we connect especially the messianic hope of Judaism. This hope was governed by the past; the end would be like the beginning. Sometimes the Messiah was conceived in terms of a new Moses, comparable to, though greater than, the first, or of a Son of David, the ideal King of the past. The ideal figure of the future would be like him. At other times, when there was despair of all human aid, the hope was expressed for a supernatural figure who would introduce a new heaven and a new earth, a Son of Man such as the one depicted in Daniel 7. And by the first century, the hope had arisen of a World or Age to Come. This was sharply contrasted with this age and would be marked by life rather than death, virtue rather than sin. There was no single dominant doctrine of the future, but a multiplicity of expectations. There is evidence that these anticipations were particularly active in Judaism in the first century.

Our survey is over. First-century Judaism lived on the memory of what God had done in the past at the Exodus and at other times, on the guidance that God gave in the present through his Law, and on an anticipation that as he had acted in the past so he would act in the future—only more gloriously.

The mingling of Judaism and Hellenism

But before leaving the Jewish and Hellenistic background of the New Testament, we have to note an important fact. By the first century, the two worlds of Judaism and Hellenism had intermingled in many parts of the known world. Especially since their return from the Exile in Babylon (586 B.C.), the Jews had increasingly spread very widely. Every considerable city in the Graeco-Roman world had its Jewish inhabitants, who usually retained their own religion and national identity wherever they settled. The numbers of Jews in the Roman Empire in the first century have been given as 6–7,000,000. Egypt is claimed to have had 1,000,000; and Rome, in the time of the Emperor Tiberius (A.D. 14–37), 50–60,000. These figures are exaggerated, but the strength of the Jews throughout the Empire was great. To the Jews scattered outside Palestine the name "The Dispersion" has been given.

The Roman authorities had to come to terms with this powerful, widespread, and united group which appeared to penetrate everywhere. To suppress such a group was impossible. The alternative was to seek to maintain its good will. Accordingly the Empire allowed to the Jews real privileges. In religion, they were allowed freedom of worship in their own synagogues. Certain aspects of the imperial cult were modified to suit Jewish monotheism, and the synagogues were allowed to be free from all imperial and other images. Other religious privileges cannot be described here. In law, the Jews were also highly privileged. For example, Jews—resident aliens and citizens—were allowed to marry according to Jewish (not Roman) law. To avoid offense, taxes on Jews were not collected on the Sabbath or Jewish Festival Days, and no Jews could be summoned to law on the Sabbath.

Such privileges and many other social, political, economic, and even philosophic factors made the Jews unpopular. As in many modern societies, anti-Judaism was real and the Jews insecure. But the Jews reacted strongly to the pressures of the Graeco-Roman world. One of the most important events in the history of western religion was the translation of the Old Testament into Greek (somewhere between 250 B.C. and the first century B.C.). The spread of Christianity and its interpretation to the Hellenistic world was immensely helped by this translation, in which Hebraic words and ideas had already been rendered into Greek before Christianity, which had to undertake the same task, had emerged.

In addition to the Septuagint, certain other writings arose. These may be divided into two groups: first, those which are historical such as 2 and 3 Maccabees and the works of Josephus (born A.D. 37–8), a Jew, who came under the protection of the Romans and who wrote: (1) *The Jewish War* (A.D. 70), which surveys Jewish history in the Hellenistic-Roman period; (2) *The Jewish Antiquities,* written between A.D. 81–96, covers from the patriarchs to the outbreak of the war against Rome in A.D. 66; (3) *Against Apion,* which was designed to refute calumnies against the Jews. These histories not only satisfy historical curiosity but offer apologies for Judaism. This leads us to the second group of writings by Jews of the Dispersion, literature designed to defend and propagate Judaism and especially presentations of Judaism to the Hellenistic world in a philosophical manner. In this group the works of Philo (born 20 B.C. in

Alexandria) are especially important. His writings are volumi-
nous. They can be classified as follows:

1. Writings of purely philosophical content.
2. Interpretations of the first five books of the Old Testament.
3. Historical-apologetic writings.

Philo is generally understood as a Jew concerned to show that
life according to the Jewish Law was compatible with Greek culture and philosophy. Moses contained all that Greek philosophy
had to teach. Throughout his life Philo aimed at showing that
the latter was the handmaiden of Judaism.

It is not surprising that very frequently Judaism in the Dispersion attracted many Gentiles. Two groups of such Gentiles
are to be distinguished. On the one hand, there were proselytes
—Gentiles who were so drawn to the Jewish faith that they undertook all the steps necessary to become Jews in the full sense,
that is, circumcision, baptism, and the presentation of an offering in the Temple. On the other hand, there were Gentiles who
were drawn to Judaism—its worship, tradition, and ethics—who
did not actually become proselytes. They were called "God-
fearers" or "devout." Both proselytes and God-fearers were numerous. Throughout the Empire there were Synagogues where
not only Jews by birth but proselytes and God-fearers gathered
regularly. There is evidence that in the time of Jesus, Judaism
was moved by a missionary urge which it had not known before
that time and has not known since.

It was this world in which Hellenism and Judaism were intermingled that forms the background of many of the writers of
the New Testament. The significance of Hellenistic-Judaism,
which was the result of this intermingling, can hardly be exaggerated for the early Christian movement, as will become clear
in the following pages.[3]

CHAPTER 4

THE GOSPEL AS THE GLORY OF GOD

So far we have pointed out that the New Testament belongs to the Old and that to understand it we have to read it in relation to the Old. It is also a document which emerged in the Graeco-Roman world and within the world of the Judaism of Palestine in the first century, so that these two worlds have also to be used in the interpretation of it. Like people, the New Testament is a part of its world and its world is part of it.

But the immediate *foreground* of the New Testament is still narrower—it is the life of the Christian Church. The documents of the New Testament were all written by Christians. This means that they are essentially products of the Christian communities of the first century. The New Testament was written by the Church, for the Church, and from the Church. In this sense, it is an ecclesiastical document. It bears the mark of the needs and concerns of the Church on every page. The liturgy of the Church—its cultic activity, prayers, hymns, catechism—have influenced what we find in the New Testament; the apologetics of the Church are there and its conflicts, and above all its preaching.

And, because it is the product of the Church, the New Testament reflects all the variety of the life of the Church. It is a coat of many colors; it is as mixed as the life of the Church itself. And twenty years or so ago, it was the variety of the New Testament that was emphasized. The New Testament was understood, not as one book, but as a variety of books. Each book was studied separately, and its distinctive message examined. The approach to the New Testament was analytic.

But, in recent years, there has been a change. The analytic approach of earlier times has given place to a synthetic one; the emphasis is now placed on the oneness of the New Testament. It has been seen that it not only reflects the variety of the Church but its essential *unity*. Just as the primitive Church, however diverse, had behind it a single thrust or energizing conviction; so the New Testament. Despite its variety, it witnesses to an essential impulse which lies behind the Early Church. Can we discover this? What is it that gives its unity to the Church, as to the New Testament, despite their diversity?

The answer that the New Testament writers would doubtless give would be that they shared a common Gospel or Good News. Can we recover the essence of this Gospel which they believed in and preached?

Fortunately the New Testament itself has defined this Gospel for us in a very succinct phrase. In I Timothy 1:11, it is defined as follows:

It is the Gospel of the glory of the Blessed God.

Both the King James Version and the Revised Standard Version translate the term "glory" here as if it were an adjective and render: "the glorious Gospel of the Blessed God." But that is misleading; "glory" here is not merely an adjective. It defines the content of the Gospel. The Gospel is concerned with the glory of God. So too, according to the Epistle to the Hebrews (1:3), the Jesus to whom witness is borne "reflects the glory of God"; and in the Epistle of James, "He is the Lord of Glory" (2:1); "I endure everything," says the author of II Timothy, "for the sake of the elect, that they also may obtain the salvation which in Christ Jesus goes with eternal glory." The conception comes out with special force in II Corinthians 4:3-6, where Paul deals with the ministry and the Gospel which is committed to him. It reads:

> And if indeed our gospel be found veiled, the only people who find it so are those on the way to perdition. Their unbelieving minds are so blinded by the god of this passing age, that the gospel of the glory of Christ, who is the very image of God, cannot dawn upon them and bring them light. It is not ourselves that we proclaim; we proclaim Christ Jesus as Lord, and ourselves as your servants, for Jesus' sake. For the same God who said, "Out of darkness let light shine," has caused his light to shine within us, to give the light of revelation—the revelation of the glory of God in the face of Jesus Christ.

Here the purpose of the Gospel is defined as the giving of the glory of Christ. But he is the image of God, and his glory, therefore, is the glory of God; the mystery of creation itself is illuminated in his face.

When we turn to the Gospels the same conception meets us. Mark begins his Gospel with a quotation from Malachi 3:1 and Isaiah 40:3: John the Baptist is

> A voice crying aloud in the wilderness, "Prepare a way for the Lord; clear a straight path for him."

But it is well to recall the following words in Isaiah 40:4 and 5:

> Every valley shall be lifted up,
> And every mountain and hill be made low;
> The uneven ground shall become level,
> And the rough places a plain:
> And the glory of the Lord shall be revealed,
> And all flesh shall see it together;
> For the mouth of the Lord has spoken.

John the Baptist is the prelude to the revelation of the glory of the Lord in Jesus of Nazareth. Even more clear is the association of the glory of God with Jesus in the Gospel of Luke. Luke interprets the birth of Jesus in these terms:

All at once there was with the angel a great company of the heavenly host, singing the praises of God: "Glory to God in highest heaven, And on earth his peace for men on whom his favour rests. (2:14)

In the Fourth Gospel the concept of glory becomes a major one.

So the Word became flesh; he came to dwell among us, and we saw his glory, such glory as befits the Father's only Son, full of grace and truth. (1:14)

No one has ever seen God (Jn. 1:18), but his glory is revealed in Jesus. One great German scholar has divided the whole of the Fourth Gospel in terms of this concept. He regards chapters 2–12 as concerned with the revelation of the glory of God before the world; 13–20 with the revelation of the glory before the Church. We may safely claim then that the Gospel is concerned with the glory of God.

The Meaning of "Glory"

But to say in modern English that the Gospel deals with the glory of God does not take us very far. Language such as this has for us a strange unreality. Can we pierce the centuries to grasp what the early Christians meant by the glory of God?

In the Oxford Dictionary, the term "glory" is defined as "resplendent majesty, beauty or magnificence, the effulgence of heavenly light, imagined unearthly beauty, the bliss and splendour of heaven." In short, "glory" in modern English suggests the unknowable perfection of God's being. This is different from the usage of the New Testament, where God's glory is revealed and known. Again, it is unlikely that classical Greek literature can help us to understand the use of the term "glory" in the New Testament. In classical Greek, "glory" denotes simply "opinion" and "view"; that is, what a man thinks.

From this it also comes to signify reputation; that is, what one thinks of a man.

Where, then, can we find help in understanding the meaning of the Gospel as the "glory of God." We must look in the Old Testament and the New Testament itself. In the Old Testament the following meanings are associated with the term "glory."

1. *It has a secular meaning.* Glory is sometimes synonymous with riches, property, wealth. This seems to be its connotation in Genesis 31:1:

> Now Jacob heard that the sons of Laban were saying, "Jacob has taken all that was our father's; and from what was our father's he has gained all this wealth."

Here the word translated "wealth" is, literally, "glory." Such is the case in Genesis 13:2:

> Now Abraham was very rich in cattle, in silver and in gold.

Here where the English has "very rich," the Hebrew is "glory." Compare also Genesis 45:13 and I Kings 3:13 where "glory" denotes success and power.

2. *More important is the religious connotation of the term.* In many places "glory" is that which in some way or other makes the invisible God visible; the glory of God is the revelation of God, that which reveals or makes him known. In some passages the glory of the Lord is associated with natural phenomena—storms, tempests, lightnings, thunder. Psalm 29 in its entirety is instructive:

> Ascribe to the Lord, O heavenly beings,
>   ascribe to the Lord glory and strength.
> Ascribe to the Lord the glory of his name;
>   worship the Lord in holy array.
> The voice of the Lord is upon the waters;
>   the God of glory thunders,
>   the Lord, upon many waters. (Ps. 29:1–3)

So also in Psalm 97, the glory of God is associated with clouds and thick darkness, fire, and lightning.

> The Lord reigns; let the earth rejoice;
>   let the many coastlands be glad!
> Clouds and thick darkness are round
>   about him;
>   righteousness and justice are the
>   foundation of his throne.
> Fire goes before him,
>   and burns up his adversaries
>   round about.
> His lightnings lighten the world;
>   the earth sees and trembles.
> The mountains melt like wax before
>   the Lord,
>   before the Lord of all the earth.
>
> The heavens proclaim his righteousness;
>   and all the peoples behold his glory. (Ps. 97:1-6)

Especially impressive is the way in which God's "glory" appears on Mount Sinai, as in Exodus 24:15-18:

> Then Moses went up on the mountain, and the cloud covered the mountain. The glory of the Lord settled on Mount Sinai, and the cloud covered it six days; and on the seventh day he called to Moses out of the midst of the cloud. Now the appearance of the glory of the Lord was like a devouring fire on the top of the mountain in the sight of the people of Israel. And Moses entered the cloud, and went up on the mountain. And Moses was on the mountain forty days and forty nights.

3. Related to the second usage is the third, where the term "glory" *is used of a kind of element which belongs to the upper regions,* as in Psalm 19:1:

> The heavens are telling the glory of God.

In all the above passages, the glory of God is radiant and usually terrible. It is mysterious even as it reveals God; it is like lightning, terrifying and illuminating at the same time. The term "glory" in the Old Testament never loses the connotation of majesty and magnificence. But this "majesty" is not inaccessible, necessarily transcendent; in two ways particularly God's "glory" approaches men.

(a) It comes to dwell among men in certain objects or places, as in the *Tent of Meeting* in the wilderness. Exodus 40:34 reads:

> Then the cloud covered the tent of meeting and the glory of the Lord filled the tabernacle.

In I Samuel 4:21 f., the glory is almost identified with the *ark*. "And she named the child Ichabod, saying, 'The glory has departed from Israel! because the ark of God had been captured.'"

In Psalm 24:7–10, the King of glory enters into the *Temple* at Jerusalem.

> Lift up your heads, O gates!
>> and be lifted up, O ancient doors!
>> that the King of glory may come in.
> Who is the King of glory?
>> The Lord, strong and mighty,
>> the Lord, mighty in battle!
> Lift up your heads, O gates!
>> and be lifted up, O ancient doors!
>> that the King of glory may come in!
> Who is this King of glory?
>> The Lord of hosts,
>> he is the King of glory!

The Temple is the special dwelling place of God's glory. In I Kings 8:10 f. we read:

> And when the priests came out of the holy place, a cloud filled the house of the Lord, so that the priests could not stand to minister because of the cloud; for the glory of the Lord filled the house of the Lord.

And in Psalm 26:8 we have:

> O Lord, I love the habitation of thy house
> And the place where thy glory dwells.

But when crime and sacrilege desecrate the Temple, "the glory" can depart from it and appear elsewhere, as in Ezekiel (1:4 ff.).

(b) Not only does the glory appear in certain places, it is associated with particular times and events. Thus glory of the Lord was especially connected with the Exodus from Egypt. But even there, it was so dazzling that even the great Moses was allowed to see it only by reflection from the rear.

> And the Lord said to Moses, "This very thing that you have spoken I will do; for you have found favor in my sight, and I know you by name." Moses said, "I pray thee, show me thy glory." And he said, "I will make all my goodness pass before you, and will proclaim before you my name 'The Lord'; and I will be gracious to whom I will be gracious, and will show mercy on whom I will show mercy. But," he said, "you cannot see my face; for man shall not see me and live." And the Lord said, "Behold, there is a place by me where you shall stand upon the rock; and while my glory passes by I will put you in a cleft of the rock, and I will cover you with my hand until I have passed by; then I will take away my hand, and you shall see my back; but my face shall not be seen." (Exod. 33:17–23)

Again, for Second-Isaiah the deliverance of Israel from captivity in Babylon would be a revelation of the glory of the Lord (Is. 40:5).

In the Old Testament, therefore, the idea of the glory of God is many-sided, and no simple formula can cover all its nuances. In its developed form it stands for the revelation of God, his manifestation of himself through his control of the lives of nations and men. Thus the glory of God is not a static but a dynamic concept; God's glory is revealed not so much as knowledge of what he is in his essence, as in what he does; it is his active revelation of himself, particularly in certain events.

One thing remains to be said about the Old Testament conception of "the glory of God." In Ezekiel, the expectation is expressed that the glory would return in the future to a purified Jerusalem.

> Afterward he brought me to the gate, the gate facing east. And behold, the glory of the God of Israel came from the east; and the sound of his coming was like the sound of many waters; and the earth shone with his glory. And the vision I saw was like the vision which I had seen when he came to destroy the city, and like the vision which I had seen by the river Chebar; and I fell upon my face. As the glory of the Lord entered the temple by the gate facing east, the Spirit lifted me up, and brought me into the inner court; and behold, the glory of the Lord filled the temple. (Ezek. 43:1-5)

> Then he brought me back to the outer gate of the sanctuary, which faces east; and it was shut. And he said to me, "This gate shall remain shut; it shall not be opened, and no one shall enter by it; for the Lord, the God of Israel, has entered by it; therefore it shall remain shut. Only the prince may sit in it to eat bread before the Lord; he shall enter by way of the vestibule of the gate, and shall go out by the same way." (Ezek. 44:1-4)

In Isaiah 59:19, God's glory will in the future be revealed from East to West:

> So they shall fear the name of the Lord
> From the west
> And his glory from the rising of the sun.

Compare also Isaiah 60:1-5:

> Arise, shine; for your light has come,
>   and the glory of the Lord has risen upon you.
> For behold, darkness shall cover the earth,
>   and thick darkness the peoples;
> but the Lord will arise upon you, and his glory
>   will be seen upon you.
> And nations shall come to your light,
>   and kings to the brightness of your rising.

Lift up your eyes round about, and see;
 they all gather together, they come to you;
your sons shall come from far, and your
  daughters shall be carried in the arms.
Then you shall see and be radiant,
 your heart shall thrill and rejoice;
because the abundance of the sea shall
  be turned to you,
  the wealth of the nations shall come to you.

And in Daniel 7:13 f.:

I saw in the night visions, and behold, with the
 clouds of heaven
 there came one like a son of man,
and he came to the Ancient of Days
 and was presented before him.
And to him was given dominion and glory and kingdom,
 that all peoples, nations, and languages
  should serve him;
his dominion is an everlasting dominion,
 which shall not pass away,
and his kingdom one that shall not be destroyed.

Thus it is fair to say that however much realized by his presence in the Temple, and however much revealed in past events, the glory of God in its fullness is an object of hope in the Old Testament: it belongs to the future.

The Gospel of the Glory of God

Let us now return to the New Testament. It defines the Gospel as "the gospel of the glory of God." To say this is to claim that it is concerned with that activity or presence in which God reveals himself. And, in the context in which the phrase occurs in the New Testament, it must refer to certain events in which God acts in history. Just as Second-Isaiah saw the glory of God revealed in the return of Israel from exile in Babylon, so the New Testament sees the glory of God revealed in another event—the life, death, and resurrection of Jesus and the life of the Church that issued thereupon. In this sense the Gospel of the New Testament, which gives unity to all its diversity, claims that, in a particular set of events centering around Jesus of Nazareth, the glory of God is present. The assumption behind the New Testament is that at a particular time, in a particular life, God was decisively at work; its concern throughout is to witness to these events. By this is meant not that it merely pointed to a person, Jesus of Nazareth; this alone would not have availed. Rather, it witnessed to him by appropriating his life and living in him so that his life was its life. The New Testament is concerned with events as they are appropriated and become alive in the lives of Christians:

> Tho' Christ in Bethlehem a thousand times was born
> Unless He was born in thee, thy soul's forlorn.

The Gospel points to events which happened in the past but are made present in the response of faith and life. It is these events, in this sense, that give unity to the New Testament (see chapter 7).

CHAPTER 5

THE PRIMITIVE CHRISTIAN PREACHING

In the previous pages it was asserted that the New Testament is the creation of the Christian Church. It reveals both the variety of the life and faith of early Christians and the original, living thrust which lies behind them; that is, the conviction that in Jesus of Nazareth the glory of God was revealed. Christians lived out of this conviction in the world and often evoked its admiration for the reflection of Jesus in their lives. But they also proclaimed this conviction to the world. The form in which they presented their gospel is fortunately traceable, to a considerable extent, in the New Testament. What was that form? It was clarified by C. H. Dodd.

The earliest evidence is found in Paul. That apostle distinguished sharply between the foundation of Christian truth, which he had received, and the building which he himself had based upon this. The foundation was common to him and to other Christians. Occasionally Paul refers to his own gospel —"my gospel" (Rom. 2:16; 16:25; II Tim. 2:8) and to "our gospel" (II Cor. 4:3; I Thess. 1:5; II Thess. 2:14). But this does not mean that he claimed to have his own private kind of Christianity. For example, the phrase "my gospel" in Romans 2:16 merely refers to a future judgment which cannot be regarded as a peculiarly Pauline teaching. Paul recognized a foundation which he shared in common with other Christians. He seems to mean by this a "factual core," "given data" without which there could be no gospel. In I Corinthians 3:10 f., he writes:

> I am like a skilled master-builder who by God's grace laid the foundation, and someone else is putting up the building. Let each take care how he builds. There can be no other foundation beyond that which is already laid; I mean Jesus Christ himself.

Not even Paul can ignore the fundamental foundation which is common to all Christians.

The same comes out in Romans 15:20. It had been his ambition "to preach the gospel, not where Christ has already been named, lest I build on another man's foundation." Here the "foundation" is simply defined as "Christ."

But in other passages Paul enlarges upon this foundation. Note the following:

> You stupid Galatians! You must have been bewitched—you before whose eyes Jesus Christ was openly displayed upon his cross! (Gal. 3:1)

> Jews call for miracles, Greeks look for wisdom; but we proclaim Christ—yes, Christ nailed to the cross; and though this is a stumbling-block to Jews and folly to Greeks, yet to those who have heard his call, Jews and Greeks alike, he is the power of God and the wisdom of God. (I Cor. 1:22–24)

The crucified Christ preached is equated with "the power and the wisdom of God." Compare with this the next passage.

> As for me, brothers, when I came to you, I declared the attested truth of God without display of fine words or wisdom. I resolved that while I was with you I would think of nothing but Jesus Christ—Christ nailed to the cross. I came before you weak, as I was then, nervous and shaking with fear. The word I spoke, the gospel I proclaimed, did not sway you with subtle arguments; it carried conviction by spiritual power, so that your faith might be built not upon human wisdom but upon the power of God.

> And yet I do speak words of wisdom to those who are ripe

for it, not a wisdom belonging to this passing age, nor to any of its governing powers, which are declining to their end. (I Cor. 2:1–6)

Most important is I Corinthians 15:1–11:

> And now, my brothers, I must remind you of the gospel that I preached to you; the gospel which you received, on which you have taken your stand, and which is now bringing you salvation. Do you still hold fast the Gospel as I preached it to you? If not, your conversion was in vain.
>
> First and foremost, I handed on to you the facts which had been imparted to me: that Christ died for our sins, in accordance with the scriptures; that he was buried; that he was raised to life on the third day, according to the scriptures; and that he appeared to Cephas, and afterwards to the Twelve. Then he appeared to over five hundred of our brothers at once, most of whom are still alive, though some have died. Then he appeared to James, and afterwards to all the apostles.
>
> In the end he appeared even to me; though this birth of mine was monstrous, for I had persecuted the church of God and am therefore inferior to all other apostles—indeed not fit to be called an apostle. However, by God's grace I am what I am, nor has his grace been given to me in vain; on the contrary, in my labours I have outdone them all—not I, indeed, but the grace of God working with me. But what matter, I or they? This is what we all proclaim, and this is what you believed.

Here Paul uses terms of a technical nature to describe the acceptance and transmission of tradition ("handed on"; "were imparted to"): the things of first importance are shared with others as a common faith.

In addition to the above explicit references, in other places in the Pauline epistles there are outcrops of the essential content of the gospel. Romans 1:1–5 has been claimed to contain an incipient creed or confession of faith which Paul shared with other Christians. He seems to quote it effortlessly; his manner of writing suggests an almost unconscious recital of a formula for the faith. It reads:

From Paul, servant of Christ Jesus, apostle by God's call, set apart for the service of the Gospel.

This gospel God announced beforehand in sacred scriptures through his prophets. It is about his Son: on the human level he was born of David's stock, but on the level of the spirit—the Holy Spirit—he was declared Son of God by a mighty act in that he rose from the dead: it is about Jesus Christ our Lord. Through him I received the privilege of a commission in his name to lead to faith and obedience men in all nations.

Similarly, in Romans 10:9, there emerges a kind of catechetical recital; that is, there breaks through into Paul's writing the sound of a confession of faith.

If on your lips is the confession, "Jesus is Lord," and in your heart the faith that God raised him from the dead, then you will find salvation.

What appears in Paul also emerges in Acts, where the preaching of earliest Christians is purported to be preserved. In Acts 2:14–36 we read:

But Peter stood up with the Eleven, raised his voice, and addressed them: "Fellow Jews, and all you who live in Jerusalem, mark this and give me a hearing. These men are not drunk, as you imagine; for it is only nine in the morning. No, this is what the prophet spoke of: 'God says, "This will happen in the last days: I will pour out upon everyone a portion of my spirit; and your sons and daughters shall prophesy; your young men shall see visions, and your old men shall dream dreams. Yes, I will endue even my slaves, both men and women, with a portion of my spirit, and they shall prophesy. And I will show portents in the sky above, and signs on the earth below—blood and fire and drifting smoke. The sun shall be turned to darkness, and the moon to blood, before that great, resplendent day, the day of the Lord, shall come. And then, everyone who invokes the name of the Lord shall be saved."'

"Men of Israel, listen to me: I speak of Jesus of Nazareth, a man singled out by God and made known to you through miracles, portents, and signs, which God worked among you

through him, as you well know. When he had been given up
to you, by the deliberate will and plan of God, you used heathen
men to crucify and kill him. But God raised him to life again,
setting him free from the pangs of death, because it could not
be that death should keep him in its grip.

"For David says of him:

'I foresaw that the presence of the Lord would
   be with me always,
For he is at my right hand so that I may not be
   shaken;
Therefore my heart was glad and my tongue spoke
   my joy;
Moreover, my flesh shall dwell in hope,
For thou wilt not abandon my soul to Hades,
Nor let thy loyal servant suffer corruption.
Thou hast shown me the ways of life,
Thou wilt fill me with gladness by thy presence.'

"Let me tell you plainly, my friends, that the patriarch David
died and was buried, and his tomb is here to this very day. It
is clear therefore that he spoke as a prophet who knew that
God had sworn to him that one of his own direct descendants
should sit on his throne; and when he said he was not abandoned to Hades, and his flesh never suffered corruption, he
spoke with foreknowledge of the resurrection of the Messiah.
The Jesus we speak of has been raised by God, as we can all
bear witness. Exalted thus with God's right hand, he received
the Holy Spirit from the Father, as was promised, and all that
you now see and hear flows from him. For it was not David
who went up to heaven; his own words are: 'The Lord said to
my Lord, "Sit at my right hand until I make your enemies your
footstool."' Let all Israel then accept as certain that God has
made this Jesus, whom you crucified, both Lord and Messiah."

The recital of the preaching given in the above follows upon a
declaration that in the coming of the Spirit the prophecy of
Joel 2:28–32 had been fulfilled, and the items of the preaching are clear—the attestation of Jesus by works, wonders, and
signs during his ministry, his death, his resurrection. The con-

nection of the preaching with the Holy Spirit is also made in Acts 2:38; and again in Acts 3:12–26, 4:8–12, and especially 10:34–43, the notes struck in 2:14–36 recur.

And the same notes, with variations, recur in I Peter. I Peter 1:10–12 reads:

> This salvation was the theme which the prophets pondered and explored, those who prophesied about the grace of God awaiting you. They tried to find out what was the time, and what the circumstances, to which the spirit of Christ in them pointed, foretelling the sufferings in store for Christ and the splendours to follow; and it was disclosed to them that the matter they treated of was not for their time but for yours. And now it has been openly announced to you through preachers who brought you the Gospel in the power of the Holy Spirit sent from heaven. These are things that angels long to see into.

Here the connection between the preaching of Christians with the activity of Old Testament prophets is asserted. The latter had testified beforehand to the sufferings of Christ. This they could do because the Spirit that was active among Christians had also been active in them. Compare I Peter 1:3.

In another passage, II Peter 1:18–21, a creedal formulation of the Christian conviction again breaks forth, and the elements of the preaching elsewhere indicated shine clear again. It reads:

> This voice from heaven we ourselves heard; when it came, we were with him on the sacred mountain.
>
> All this only confirms for us the message of the prophets, to which you will do well to attend, because it is like a lamp shining in a murky place, until the day breaks and the morning star rises to illuminate your minds.
>
> But first note this: no one can interpret any prophecy of Scripture by himself. For it was not through any human whim that men prophesied of old; men they were, but, impelled by the Holy Spirit, they spoke the words of God.

Further passages of significance in the same epistle are I Peter 2:21–24; 3:22. In both of these it is difficult not to trace creedal elements; these are not so much quoted as incorporated naturally and freely.

Taken together the above passages present the chief emphases in the preaching of early Christians. These may be summed up as follows:

1. The coming of Jesus Christ into history is the fulfillment of prophecy. It is the end to which the purpose of God revealed to us in the Old Testament points. In Jesus Christ that purpose has reached its preordained conclusion. But at the same time Jesus is the beginning of a new epoch. He carries further the purpose of God and inaugurates a new creation. In him the Age to Come of Jewish expectation has begun on earth.

2. In this coming of a new order, as the fulfillment of God's revealed purpose, Jesus has a unique role. He is the Messiah, the Son of David, the Son, the Son of Man. The fulfillment and new beginning is indissolubly related to him; it is in him that they emerge.

3. In referring to Jesus Christ, the Church recalled his actual ministry on earth—his going about doing good, the authority of his teaching, his acts of healing. He was a man approved of God by "signs and wonders."

4. Emphasis was placed on the passion of Jesus. The cross was by the foreknowledge of God; not an accident, it was essential to the divine purpose. Suffering is a mark of Jesus as the Messiah.

5. Similarly emphasized was the resurrection of Jesus. All the strata of the New Testament assume it: witnesses of the resurrection are cited; its actuality is firmly established.

6. Through his passion and resurrection, Jesus is raised to the right hand of God. By this is meant that he is Lord over the new people created by him and invested with authority.

7. On this new humanity, God has poured forth his spirit. It is a common conviction that this new humanity is God's own people; it is the Israel of God, marked by the gift of the Spirit.

8. There was offered within this Israel of God the forgiveness of sin.

9. The Christ who sits at the right hand of God was expected to come again to judge the world and to bring to its full flowering the New Age inaugurated by Jesus. At his return his work will be completed.

It is, then, in the convictions expressed in the above preaching that the early Church found its focus. But how real is the above catalogue? Some have criticized it; for example, the last item noted (9) has been denied a place in the earliest preaching. More important, the whole of this approach to the early Christian movement has been questioned. The isolation of the preaching as outlined above has been criticized on three main grounds.

First, in isolating the primitive preaching, appeal is made to the early chapters of Acts and I Peter as preserving it. But is this position really tenable? Many now urge that those chapters do not present us with the earliest preaching but with what the author of Acts considered ought to be preached in his own day, that is, in the second century. Secondly, it is purely accidental that the items listed above occur fairly frequently in the New Testament. It is possible and probable that convictions about which we hear little or even nothing in the New Testament played an important role in the early Christian communities. The suggested preaching, as enumerated above, may merely be due to statistical accidents. Thirdly, the discovery of a unity in the New Testament centering in this preaching is due to the influence of recent theological and ecclesiological movements. The last half-century has witnessed a growing desire among churches to unite. Theologians have accordingly sought for a ground of unity behind the conflicting theologies of Christendom within the New Testament. This quest led to the discovery of the preaching outlined above as a focal point of unity within the New Testament around which churches, otherwise divided, could be united. That is, the centrality of the preaching is not so much the result of objective, scientific study of the New Testament as of easily definable theological and ecclesiastical concerns. Emphasis on this preaching was fathered by ecumenical enthusiasm rather than by exegetical exactitude; it is a superb example of wishful thinking.

On these grounds many have not been moved by the Kerygmatic approach to the New Testament, which we welcomed so enthusiastically. To counter these criticisms, however, is not difficult. Let us take each in turn. First, the date and character of the preaching reported in the early chapters of Acts must always be open to dispute. While many scholars take the view that the speeches in Acts 1–5 are late, and designed to instruct the Church at the close of the first century, if not in the second, others have discovered behind them Aramaic sources containing very early tradition. But the reality of the Kerygma does not stand or fall with the data of Acts. The evidence culled from the Pauline epistles and elsewhere, not to mention the Kerygmatic interest traceable in the Gospels themselves, is very cogent. To question the existence of a common core of early Christian preaching is to ignore much evidence outside Acts altogether. We need not spend long over the second objection. It is doubtful procedure to claim for what does not appear in the New Testament a significance equal to that of the elements of the Kerygma, which appear very frequently in it. What is often mentioned is likely to have been central. An illustration may help. I have been associated in America with two universities, which I name with honor. During five years spent at the one the word "alumni" scarcely ever came to my ears; during four years at the other, I was seldom free from its sound. Was this statistical difference in the incidence of the term "alumni" significant in the life of the two universities? It most certainly was. It would be no great exaggeration perhaps to say that while the one university produced alumni, the other university was maintained by alumni. Statistics are not always misleading. The items which recur in the New Testament in its various strata can rightly be taken to indicate what was of real significance in the life of the communities which produced it. As for the third criticism, it is to be readily admitted that the New Testament student is necessarily the child of his time, and, if he be at all alive, he brings to his task of interpretation the influences and concerns of his age. There can be little doubt that theological and ecclesiological interests which have moved our time have not left the student of the New Testament untouched. But this cuts both ways. The times which may condition our exegesis may also illuminate it. Is it not true, in more spheres than one, that these times of "the breaking of the nations" have opened our eyes to things which in more velvety days were hidden from us? Not far from my home in Wales there is an old Norman Castle, Castell Dinefwr. In summer when the trees which surround it are in full leaf the castle is hidden; it can be seen only in glimpses. But when winter comes, and the trees have lost their foliage, the castle walls stand forth in the stark clarity of their ancient splendor. The living of our days has been wintry, but may it not have helped us to see with a new awareness the constitutive structures of the New Testament documents? Even if it were admitted that the emphasis on the Kerygma in recent

scholarship was the result of conscious or unconscious pressures
to discover a New Testament ground for the unity of the
Church (a view to which I could not subscribe), this would
not necessarily belittle the validity of the Kerygmatic emphasis.[4]

None of the criticisms mentioned, therefore, have been
found convincing. But the emphasis on the word "preaching"
in the above pages can be misleading. The presentation of the
preaching as a scheme might suggest that early Christians had
a fixed formula by which they neatly interpreted and summarized their faith. But this was not so. The list of items cited
above is no more the reality of the Gospel than is his skeleton
the reality of a man. Bare bones alone do not constitute a man;
they have to be clothed with flesh and blood. And the items
of the preaching are, by themselves, abstractions. To supply
them with reality, they have to be clothed with the life and informed by the Spirit of the Christian communities. They are
not to be separated from that life and spirit; that is, from the
total ministry of the Church in healing, teaching, forgiveness.
Treated in isolation, these items are like the empty scaffolding
of a building; to be significant, they must be seen as the rein-
forcement of the living building of the Church. Another way
of stating the same point is to recognize that the items of the
preaching refer not merely to external events—the life, death,
and resurrection of Jesus—but to those events as appropriated
by the Christian. It is in the living response to Jesus, in his life,
death, and resurrection, that the significance of these becomes
real.

In the above list of items from the primitive preaching,
there are both such as can be described simply as events
(No. 3), and those which imply that they are already interpreted (Nos. 1, 2, 4, 5, 6, 7, 8, 9, where there are events and
meaning). The preaching contained both the proclamation of
what had happened and the meaning ascribed to this. Without

the "facts," there could be no interpretation; without the interpretation, the "facts" would be dead data. What gives to the events, to which the preaching points, their importance is that they are seen in the setting of God's purpose and in the light of the experience of the community to which they gave birth and continued, pulsating life. The events and the significance given to them become inseparable in the preaching. An illustration may clarify this. I lived for some years within sight of the Palmer Stadium of Princeton University. Frequently, during the football season, I saw the athletes practicing; and during practice they often kicked a ball across the goal post. But there was no resulting thunderous roar or moan. The ball crossed the bar in an innocuous setting; the kick, excellent as it might be, had no significance. But when a match was on, let us say between Princeton and Harvard, when Palmer Stadium would be crowded with interested spectators, then things turned out differently. Let a ball be kicked by Harvard over the Princeton post and the crowds either exulted or despaired. A single such kick of a ball over a post might win or lose a match—*in that setting, given those spectators.* So is it with the life, death, and resurrection of Jesus. It is their occurrence in the setting of the early Christian life that lends them significance. Without the life, death, and resurrection of Jesus as "data," there could be no Church; but it was people, expectant and tense, that saw in these events the glory of God and thus their significance. In the totality of the life, death, and resurrection of Jesus, the coming of the Spirit, the emergence of the Church, the forgiveness and newness of life, and the hope of his coming again—in all these, in which fact and interpretation are so closely intermingled, the early Church saw the manifestation of the glory of God or saw in Jesus of Nazareth a window through the surface of things into the very ground of our being. The Church understood the ultimate in terms of Jesus Christ and sought, by its life, to point to him. This life was its sermon, and indeed it is doubtful whether there were "sermons" in our modern sense in the early Church, but only proclamations for witness. By the whole of their life in word and deed, the Christian communities referred men to the Person in whom the glory dwelt, to the fact on which their life depended.

CHAPTER 6

THE HISTORICITY OF JESUS

If it was the faith evoked among Christians that gave significance to the life, death, and resurrection of Jesus, as was asserted in the last chapter, what importance has the figure of Jesus himself for the Christian movement? Some have claimed not only that Jesus is secondary in the rise of Christianity, but that he is not necessary at all to explain that phenomenon. The Christian movement emerged, so it has been urged, in response to the widespread religious yearnings of the Graeco-Roman world. These were so complex, varied, and unsatisfied that they thrust to the forefront a new faith to meet a spiritual vacuum. Christianity can be understood as having arisen, not from any impulse supplied by a historical figure, Jesus of Nazareth, but as the crystallization of religious yearnings around a "fictional" peg to which the name Jesus was given.

Such ideas began to appear in the eighteenth century in France, where some claimed that Jesus was neither man nor God, but a solar deity among many such as have always been worshipped. But even the archcritic Voltaire rejected this position. Later, in the nineteenth century, in a book entitled *Christ and the Caesars*,[5] a German scholar, Bruno Bauer, argued that Christianity was born at the beginning of the second century. It grew out of the meeting of different currents of thought, issuing from three centers—Judaea, Greece, and Rome. A Dutch school, at the beginning of the nineteenth century, which dated all the Pauline epistles in the second century, denied the historicity of Jesus because of the unreliability of the Gospels as historical sources and the lack of any non-Christian evidence for this. And in the twentieth century in a number of works, particularly those of Arthur Drews in Germany,[6] Jesus has been explained as a purely mythological figure.

The existence of Jesus as a historical figure is not now seriously questioned. But the works of writers such as those mentioned still exercise popular influence among the uninformed. I recall a village schoolmaster who, whenever we met, always furiously engaged me in the struggle to prove that Jesus ever existed. In view of this historical scepticism outside Christian circles and of tendencies within Christian circles to minimize the role of Jesus of Nazareth, as such, in the emergence of Christianity, it is necessary to pin down, objectively, the evidence for his actual existence. This evidence can be treated under two headings.

Evidence from Jewish sources

First, there is the Jewish historian, Josephus. To assess properly the evidence he supplies, it is profitable to glance at his career. He was born in Jerusalem around A.D. 37 or 38. When war broke out between the Jewish people and the Roman Empire in A.D. 66, he at first opposed it, but later held an important command on the Jewish side in Galilee. He was taken prisoner in A.D. 67, but he was freed when a prophecy of his that Vespasian should be made Emperor was fulfilled. He then assumed the name of Flavius, and during the last campaign against Jerusalem remained on the Roman side. The rest of his days he spent at Rome, enjoying the protection of the Emperors and devoting himself to historical and literary work. He died, probably about A.D. 110. Among his writings are the *Jewish Antiquities,* in twenty books. This gives an account of Jewish history from the creation of the world to A.D. 66.

In the *Antiquities* there are two passages where Josephus refers to Jesus. These are:

(1) *XVIII iii. 3*. Now, there was about this time Jesus, a wise man, *if it be lawful to call him a man,* for he was a doer of wonderful works, a teacher of such men as receive the truth with pleasure. He drew over to him both many of the Jews, and many of the Gentiles. *He was (the) Christ.* And when Pilate, at the suggestion of the principal men amongst us, had condemned him to the cross, those that loved him at the first did not forsake him; *for he appeared to them alive again at the third day; as the divine prophets had foretold these and ten thousand other wonderful things concerning him.* And the tribe of Christians, so named from him, are not extinct at this day.

Most if not all scholars agree that the words *italicized* in the above passage must be regarded as Christian interpolations. But there is difference of opinion as to whether the whole passage is a later addition to the text that Josephus wrote. Of those who have dealt with it, the majority take the passage as authentic and attesting the historicity of Jesus.

(2) *XX ix. 1*. Festus was now dead, and Albinus (the newly appointed procurator) was but upon the road; so he assembled the sanhedrin of judges, and brought before them the brother of Jesus, who was called *Christ*, whose name was *James*, and some others. And when he had formed an accusation against them as breakers of the law, he delivered them to be stoned;

There is the same difference of opinion about this passage, but, again, most scholars accept its authenticity. There is no textual evidence against either passage.

Josephus attests the historicity of Jesus, then, as a wise man and miracle worker. But his comparative silence is striking. Can this be explained? Many suggestions have been made. Josephus may have been ignorant of all but the barest existence of Christianity. That movement in his day was insignificant. Despite its Messianic character it had produced no fiery political revolution, and Josephus might well have ignored it. It is always possible for historians to ignore major events and record trivia. (For example, it is still possible to find histories of the Victorian era which do not mention the publication of Darwin's *The Origin of Species* in 1859). This is more likely than that he was friendly to Christianity, and for this reason, deliberately avoided drawing hostile attention to it, as some have held. But it is still more likely that the silence of Josephus is due to the character of his work: his career suggests what his aim was in his writings. He desired to remain in the good graces of the Roman Emperor: to do so he avoided in his history all that might offend Roman susceptibilities. To mention Christianity, a Messianic movement that proclaimed another King than Caesar (Acts 17:7), would be to expose Judaism, which in Rome might not be distinguished from Christianity, to "guilt by association." Perhaps Josephus would not cavil at discussing a dead Messianic movement, which no longer offered any threat to Rome, but Christianity was alive and militant. The part of prudence was to ignore it. He could not ignore it altogether, but he could and did assign it little space.

Other evidence for the existence of Jesus occurs in the Talmud. There are two forms of the Talmud. Rabbinic schools in Palestine developed their own interpretation of the Mishnah, the collection of Jewish law formulated by Rabbi Judah the Prince about A.D. 200, and produced the Palestinian Talmud, consisting of the Mishnah and Gemara ("commentary") upon it, about A.D. 400. Similarly, Rabbinic schools in Babylon produced their Talmud, the Babylonian Talmud, around A.D. 500.

There are passages which preserve comparatively late references to Jesus and others which are Tannaitic, that is, earlier than the Mishnah. Among the latter passages the chief are the following:

(1) TRACTATE SANHEDRIN OF THE BABYLONIAN TALMUD 107b.
Our Rabbis taught: Let the left hand repulse but the right hand

always invite back: not as Elisha, who thrust Gehazi away with both hands, *and not like* R. *Joshua b*. Perahjah, who repulsed Jesus [the Nazarene] with both hands. (The italicized words occur only in uncensored editions.)

(2) TRACTATE SANHEDRIN OF THE BABYLONIAN TALMUD 43a. AND A HERALD PRECEDES HIM (i.e., the condemned criminal) etc. This implies, only immediately before (the execution), but not previous thereto. (In contradiction to this) it was taught: On the eve of the Passover Yeshu was hanged. For forty days before the execution took place, a herald went forth and cried, "He is going forth to be stoned because he has practised sorcery and enticed Israel to apostasy. Any one who can say anything in his favour, let him come forward and plead on his behalf." But since nothing was brought forward in his favour he was hanged on the eve of the Passover! . . . Ulla retorted: Do you suppose that he was one for whom a defence could be made? Was he not a Mesith (enticer), concerning whom Scripture says, *Neither shalt thou spare, neither shalt thou conceal him?* With Yeshu however it was different, for he was connected with the government (or royalty, i.e., influential).

Our Rabbis taught: Yeshu had five disciples, Matthai, Nakai, Nezer, Buni and Todah.

The Rabbi referred to above, R. Ulla, belongs to the third century. Rabbinic authorities at that time, we may gather, did not deny that Jesus worked signs and wonders, but they interpreted them as acts of sorcery which exposed Israel to danger (compare Mark 3:22; Matt. 9:34; 12:24). It is also clear that the death of Jesus was being discussed and efforts made to claim that he was given a fair trial, properly publicized, not a hasty one such as is recorded in the Gospels. But the Jewish scholar Klausner recognizes that this passage is unhistorical and polemical. Its aim was not to record history, but to gain a point in debate.

In the above, no attempt has been made to present an exhaustive list of references to Jesus. But enough material could be gathered to justify certain conclusions. First, there are statements arising from hostility to Christianity which can be discounted. References to the illegitimacy of Jesus and to the manner of his trial are recognized by Jewish scholars to be untrustworthy. But, secondly, Jesus is known by the name Yeshua or Yeshu of Nazareth; his miracles, his teachings, his disciples, his crucifixion—these are all referred to. The picture that emerges from the Talmudic sources is of a Jesus who was a "crucified false teacher." No attempt is made to deny that the death of Jesus was, in part, due to Jewish authorities or to claim, as in some modern liberal circles, that he was condemned unjustly. It is implied that he had a considerable following and that he did lead Israel astray. But he is always recognized as a Jew, and among the Tannaim there is no bitter hatred against him. Bitterness creeps into the sources only later when Christian-Jewish relationships had become very hostile: Jewish-Christian bitterness is the sad fruit of a sad history.

The essential significance of the above Jewish evidence, however, is clear. Had there been any justification for denying the existence of Jesus, the Jewish authorities would surely have insisted upon it. Meager as it is, the above material is conclusive that such a figure as Jesus of Nazareth did exist.

Evidence from other sources

The following sources are to be considered:

The Church Father, Bishop Eusebius of Caesarea (around A.D. 260–340), wrote a chronicle in two books, giving a summary of universal history with a table of dates. In this he preserves fragments of the work of a Christian writer called Julius Africanus Sextus (about A.D. 160–240) on the history of the world; it covers down to A.D. 217. This same Julius Africanus, in turn, refers to a writer called Thallus, the Samaritan (about A.D. 50). He writes: "Thallus in the third book of his history, calls this darkness an eclipse of the sun, but in my opinion he is wrong." The reference is to the darkness which, according to the Gospels (Mark 15:33 and parallels), accompanied the death of Jesus. This event Thallus explained as a natural one. Thallus probably wrote about A.D. 55 and dealt with the period down to A.D. 52. His words thus attest two things: (1) that the Gospel tradition, at least the Passion, was known in Rome in non-Christian circles toward the middle of the first century, and (2) that attempts were made to interpret this tradition naturally.

Pliny the Younger was Governor of Bithynia (A.D. 111–113) during the reign of the Emperor Trajan (A.D. 98–117). He regarded Christianity as a crude superstition, and wrote a letter to the Emperor asking how he was to deal with Christians in his province. This letter tells us much about Christians but little about Jesus. He informs us that Christians assembled regularly on a certain day and sang "a hymn to Christ as to a god." The existence of Jesus may be implied indirectly from this, since they sing to Christ "quasi Deo," "as if to a god," the assumption being, perhaps, that he was really only a man. But Pliny's evidence cannot be regarded as impressive. We may merely assume that Christians in Bithynia, around A.D. 87, believed that Christ had existed, because Pliny asserts that some had professed the faith for twenty years.

Tacitus, a Roman historian, born after A.D. 61 and surviving after A.D. 117, wrote, among other things, his *Annals*, covering the years A.D. 14–68, that is, from the death of Augustus to the death of Nero. In the *Annals* XV:44, the fire at Rome, in A.D. 64, in the reign of the Emperor Nero (A.D. 54–68), is dealt with, as far as it is pertinent here, as follows:

> But neither human help, nor imperial munificence, nor all the modes of placating Heaven, could stifle scandal or dispel the belief that the fire had taken the place of order. Therefore, to scotch the rumors, Nero substituted as culprits, and punished with the utmost of cruelty, a class of men, loathed for their vices, whom the crowd styled Christians (*Christianos*). Christus, the founder of the name, had undergone the death penalty in

the reign of Tiberius, by sentence of the procurator Pontius Pilatus, and the pernicious superstition was checked for a moment, only to break out once more, not merely in Judaea, the home of the disease, but in the capital itself, where all things horrible or shameful in the world collect and find a vogue.

The reference to Christ in the above passage is regarded by all philologists as authentic. It has been suggested that Tacitus was here drawing upon official Imperial archives dealing with the trial of Jesus, but this cannot be proved and is, perhaps, unlikely since such archives were secret. But Tacitus, without depending on Jewish or Christian sources, shows his acquaintance with the crucifixion of Jesus under Pontius Pilate.

Suetonius, the Roman historian, who flourished at the end of the first and the beginning of the second century, wrote, as his chief work, *The Lives of the Caesars*. In his *Life of Claudius* (Divus Claudius, Emperor A.D. 41–54), in a section dealing with Claudius' treatment of "men of foreign birth," occurs the following:

Since the Jews constantly made disturbances at the instigation of Chrestus, he expelled them from Rome.

This agrees with Acts 18:2. But is the reference to Jesus Christ or to someone of the name Chrestus or Chrestos? Almost certainly it is to Christ, because the confusion of Chrestos and Christos was a natural one. The Church Father, Tertullian (A.D. 160–220), refers to the wrong pronunciation of Christianus as Chrestianus by rulers of the Roman Empire. He explains in his *Apologeticus,* 3:

But Christian, so far as the meaning of the word is concerned, is derived from anointing. Yes, and even when it is wrongly pronounced by you "Chrestianus" (for you do not even know accurately the name you hate), it comes from sweetness and benignity. . . .

Note further that only one manuscript (Codex Mediceus) has the form Chrestianos in Tacitus, *Annals,* XV:44, which was noted above. There is no reason for seriously doubting that Suetonius, therefore, refers to Christ. On the other hand, if, as is implied, Suetonius believed that Christ had been to Rome, his information must have been very vague. Nor can he have bothered to deal seriously with it. He knows of Christ, but his statement tells us more about the Christian community in Rome in the fifties of the first century than about its Lord.

The passages referred to above, both Jewish and Gentile, sufficiently attest the historicity of Jesus. That Jesus was a crucified teacher who caused embarrassment to Judaism and to Rome is clear. For our present purposes this evidence is adequate; it does pin down the existence of Jesus of Nazareth beyond doubt. And it is easy to understand why Jewish and Gentile sources do not reveal more. Today Christianity is a worldwide religion, and Jesus has become the object of reverence for millions. In the first century, the Christian movement and its Lord were insignificant and, for Roman writers especially, objects of suspicion and contempt. The silence of non-Christian sources, except for the details given above, is understandable. Beyond the bare fact of Jesus as a crucified teacher, it is from the specifically Christian sources that knowledge about him and his church must be learned. This is another way of claiming what was asserted at the end of the last chapter, that Jesus, as a figure in history, gains significance only through those who responded to him. What are the sources which derive from them, that is, from the Church?

PART II

The First Three Gospels

(The Synoptics)

... they are the Magna Charta of the human spirit.

(E. V. Rieu)[7]

CHAPTER 7

THE GOSPELS

So far we have examined the background of the New Testament in the Graeco-Roman world and in Judaism. We have seen that behind all the documents of the New Testament giving them an essential unity, is the conviction that in certain events—the life, death, and resurrection of Jesus—the glory of God has been revealed, the hope of Judaism has been fulfilled. We also saw that there is no reason to doubt that, in fact, there was a historical figure such as the New Testament points to; his existence is alluded to outside all Christian sources.

We have now to ask: what are the Christian sources which deal with this figure in any way, and how are they to be approached? We may roughly classify these Christian sources as follows.

The Non-Canonical Gospels

There were Gospels other than the four found in the New Testament. Some of them which have long been known in fragments, like the Nazarene Gospel, the Ebionite Gospel, and the Gospel according to the Hebrews were of Jewish-Christian origin; others are of Gnostic origin, like the recently discovered Gospel according to St. Thomas, The Gospel of Truth (which, however, is not and does not claim to be a Gospel), and the Gospel according to Philip. The Jewish-Christian Gospels generally concentrate chiefly on the birth and death of Jesus. In this they are not unlike the Gospels found in the New Testa-

ment, some of which also pay increasing attention to the birth
and death of Jesus. For example, much of the material peculiar
to Matthew and Luke deals with the birth of Jesus. In some of
the non-canonical Gospels there is much material that is
grotesque and much that merely serves to entertain. The Gospels of Gnostic origin purport to convey teaching of a secret
character which goes back to Jesus. It is unlikely that any of
the non-canonical Gospels embody much, if any, trustworthy
tradition. Both the Gospels that have long been known to us
and those recently discovered illumine not so much the life
and teaching of Jesus as the various ways in which these were
dealt with in the early Church.

The Agrapha[8]

By "agrapha" we mean sayings attributed to Jesus preserved
outside the accepted text of the canonical Gospels. These vary
in attestation and credibility. As examples of these we note:

(a) A verse in Acts 20:35:

> . . . remembering the words of the Lord Jesus, how he said,
> "It is more blessed to give than to receive."

(b) Codex Bezae at Luke 6:4 has a famous addition; here
Jesus addresses a man who is working on the Sabbath and tells
him:

> Man if indeed thou knowest what thou doest, thou art blessed:
> but if thou knowest not, thou art cursed and a transgressor of
> the Law.

(c) Again there is a saying quoted by Origen in a Homily on
Jeremiah:

> The Saviour himself says: "He that is near me is near the fire:
> He that is far from me is far from the Kingdom."[9]

It is difficult to decide as to the authenticity of the *Agrapha*.
Some commend themselves; others are obviously spurious. It is

reasonable to think that many sayings of Jesus have survived outside the canonical Gospels. But those known to us, except for very few, are not significant.

The New Testament and, especially, the Gospels

But, first, what is a Gospel as a literary form? It is doubtful whether the term "gospel," *euangelion*, is used of a document in the New Testament itself. Paul seems to use the term *euangelion* of historical "events" upon which his preaching was based.

> And now, my brothers, I must remind you of the gospel that I preached to you; the gospel which you received, on which you have taken your stand, and which is now bringing you salvation. Do you still hold fast the Gospel as I preached it to you? If not, your conversion was in vain.
>
> First and foremost, I handed on to you the facts which had been imparted to me: that Christ died for our sins, in accordance with the scriptures; that he was buried; that he was raised to life on the third day, according to the scriptures; and that he appeared to Cephas, and afterwards to the Twelve. Then he appeared to over five hundred of our brothers at once, most of whom are still alive, though some have died. Then he appeared to James, and afterwards to all the apostles. (I Cor. 15: 1–7)

In Mark 1:1, it may mean the theme of Christian preaching or a book. But probably the term "gospel" was first applied to a book, as its title, in the Epistles of Ignatius written when he was on his way to Rome to meet martyrdom. We certainly have it in the writings of Justin Martyr (1:66). He refers to to the reminiscences of the apostles "which are called gospels."

But to what literary genre do these memoirs that are called "gospels" belong?

1. *Simple Memories?* Justin Martyr seems to compare them with the *Memorabilia* of the Greek historian Xenophon (444–354 B.C.). In the *Memorabilia*, Xenophon wrote four books to

defend the memory of Socrates, his master, against the charge
of irreligion and of corrupting the Athenian youth. They constitute the best picture we have of Socrates as a man. And in
many ways the Gospels are like the *Memorabilia;* they both
give room for much dialogue and are not too much concerned
with setting. But the Gospels are not anecdotal in the way in
which the *Memorabilia* are; while they concentrate on the death
of Jesus in many ways, the *Memorabilia* do not emphasize the
death of Socrates.[10]

2. *Myths?* If the Gospels were to be judged by their form and
by the distribution of their contents, they most probably would
remind us of some pagan myths; like the myths, for example,
of Persephone, who was carried off to Hades and returned—
that is, who died and rose again. But, at the same time, there
is a historical factual dimension to the Gospels which sets them
apart from the myths. None would be tempted to take Demeter
and Persephone as historical figures, whereas the Gospels deal
with such—Jesus, who suffered under Pontius Pilate, Peter and
James and John—all are tangible historical personages. Whatever formal similarities there are to the Greek myths, the historical reference of the Gospels sets them in a class apart.

3. *Biographies?* But does this historical reference make them
histories or biographies of Jesus? There were precedents for
writing histories in the first century; but in the Gospels, the
historical interest which is present coexists with some other
concern. The Gospels do not tell us much that, from a purely
historical point of view, we should like to know. Their primary
purpose is not to tell us all that happened in the life of Jesus.
We may contrast them with biographies written in the first century and with the kind of biographies which are being written
today, about Churchill or, let us say, Mahatma Gandhi. Biographers of Churchill tell us how many cigars he smoked a day
and other minute trivia; biographers of Gandhi report on his
frugal meals and minor matters in a most detailed manner. Such

attention to purely personal details about Jesus are almost entirely absent from the Gospels. We are not told what Jesus looked like, and geographic and chronological data about his activities, except those of the vaguest kind, are not given. In Mark, especially, we are plunged, without any preamble, into the ministry of John the Baptist and then presented with what seems, at first sight at least, a haphazard conglomerate of sayings and events culminating in his Passion. The end of Mark is notoriously brief—if it ended at 16:8. It is clear that the Gospels are not biographies in the modern sense of the term.

4. *History Interpreted?* Here caution is necessary. To claim that the Gospels are not modern biographies might create the impression that they are not concerned with what happened or with the reliability of what was asserted to have happened. To do justice to them, it is necessary to ask how and when the Gospels emerged and what they purported to achieve in the light of this.

First, how did they emerge? Assuming without discussion that Mark is the earliest of the Gospels, it is clear that there were traditions about the works and words of Jesus, possibly collections in Aramaic, Hebrew, and Greek, which Mark received. It is also evident that these traditions, for various reasons, were handed on in "sermons" to the outside world and cherished in the services of the Church before Mark came to be written. They were traditions in which Christians preserved and recalled what they had seen and heard and which had caused them to become a living community. We saw before that Judaism was governed by a memory—the memory of that event, the Exodus, which had called Israel into being. Every year, especially at Passover, that event was recalled as the necessary ground of Judaism. So it was with Christians; they, too, looked back and remembered him who had called them into being as the Church, and at the same time they recognized his presence with them—in the Eucharist and the services of worship. Behind the church was a common conviction about the essential event that had created it—the life, death, and resurrection of Jesus of Nazareth. To this event Christians bore witness. They witnessed to the whole life of Jesus: his activity in healing and exorcism, his words that were with authority, his death at the hands of Gentiles and Jews, his coming back to them after death so that he was with them.

At first this witness was preserved orally. There were many factors which account for this. The earliest Christians were by and large non-literary people; they were mostly simple folk, many of whom were no doubt illiterate. Education in the first century was largely confined to the aristocracy and the well-to-do; literature could not easily emerge among Christians, who were largely uneducated. It has been held that the production of literature in any form was costly, and that this was an added reason why the tradition was not at once put into writing. In fact, papyrus was exceedingly cheap and was used with great freedom by the poorest. Even more important was the fact that probably in many Christian circles greater credence was given to the word preserved orally than to that written down. The oral transmission of tradition was the vogue in first-century Judaism, and early Christians would share very naturally in such transmission. The amazing capacity to remember, which is often a mark of the Semite, would at first render it unnecessary to write things down. Coupled with this is the fact that early Christians had a vivid expectation that the end was at hand. They expected that soon the whole of history would come to an end. In such a situation there was no motive for the writing of books of any kind, and doubtless many Christians were convinced that the time was so short before the end that it was not necessary to write down what was remembered.

For these reasons, and others, there was no attempt made for some time to put on record what the Church remembered. We know that behind our Gospels there are collections of materials —of narrative and teaching material. These were made for the convenience of preachers and catechists. But apparently Mark was the first to write a full Gospel. He did this by combining and arranging traditional materials which had already taken shape. The other Gospels, like Mark, emerged very slowly out of the combination of pre-existing traditional materials. All these materials had as their aim to witness, in some way or other, to Jesus of Nazareth, and in this manner to serve the needs of the Christian communities.

Can we point to those things which were not merely of temporary significance for the production of Gospels? What made it necessary for the Church to have something like Gospels? Three things were probably crucial.

Passing of Eyewitnesses. First, there was the gradual passing away of those who had been eyewitnesses of the ministry of Jesus. The Church lived on a memory; its present life depended on the continual recalling of an event in the past. The validity of this past event rested upon the witness of those who had first experienced it. Without such witness the foundation of the Church would itself become shaken; indeed, the first apostles, who had accompanied Jesus, were the foundation of the Church. But when these witnesses began to pass away, their testimony had to be preserved. This is one of the fundamental reasons for the emergence of the Gospels—in part, at least, they were designed to supply the witness of those witnesses who were no longer alive. The memory of the Church had now to be concentrated in documents which would preserve and give it in its authentic forms. In this sense, the Gospels were a necessity for a Church whose pillars were passing away.

The World Still Survives. Secondly, while the pillars of the Church were passing away, the world was *not* passing away. It has to be recognized again that one reason why the tradition

had not come to be written down at an earlier date was that
the earliest Christians anticipated a speedy end to the world.
The evidence is overwhelming that the early Church, if not
Jesus himself, was dominated by the conviction that the end
was at hand; they expected history to be wound up, and that
soon, on the return of Jesus as judge of the quick and the dead.
As long as this expectation was alive, the production of Gospels
might be regarded as unnecessary: the end was at hand; records
were redundant. The end of history would make history—even
the history of Jesus—unnecessary. But the end did not come,
and the need for history—the history of the beginnings and
their meaning—asserted itself. As delay succeeded delay, it became necessary to make sure that the works and words of
Jesus were recorded. The delay of the Parousia removed the
prohibition of writing; it made reflection upon the life and meaning of Jesus a necessity, and it demanded a new assessment of
the meaning of what had happened in him. The expectation of
the return of Jesus had not only been living, it had been intense, and it had been an expectation of his immediate return.
As long as it was widely believed that he was right at hand,
there was no urge to speculation and reflection. The Lord was at
hand; that sufficed. But when the Lord did not return, the
situation changed. The Church was compelled to re-examine
what had happened. To do this it had to consolidate and preserve what had happened, and partly out of this need arose
the Gospels. The Gospels from this point of view are part of a
crisis in primitive Christian eschatology, that is, in the early
Christian's understanding of and expectations for the end of history.

  The Spreading of the Church. Again as the Church spread
further and further into the Graeco-Roman world, it became
more and more necessary for it to secure its base, as it were.
Just as an army can go too far away from its base, so as to
jeopardize its reinforcements, so the primitive Church could

have jeopardized its very existence by removing itself too far from that event which was its foundation. In the Graeco-Roman world, the Palestinian Gospel came into contact with all sorts of religious and philosophic movements. Men challenged it and could have perverted it by turning it into a metaphysical system or a mystery or a Gnostic cult, without connection with that historic figure who gave it birth; that is, they could have cut it from its root. To prevent this, the Gospels came into being; they kept the Church attached to its base—in the actualities of the ministry of Jesus; they preserved Christianity from degenerating into a theology of the Word or of an idea, and preserved the community rooted in the Word made flesh, that is, in the historically real Jesus.

The purpose of the Gospels, then, is to witness to Jesus of Nazareth, and to him as the Lord of the Church. How far in presenting their witness were they interested in giving the story of his life? It has often been asserted that early Christians were little interested in knowing about Jesus of Nazareth as such, but only as he was their Lord. They were concerned with him, not historically, but religiously, as their present living Lord. But this is a false antithesis. We should not rule out a biographical interest among Christians; they were not uncurious about him in whom they believed. But more important than this was their conviction that it was precisely in Jesus of Nazareth that the glory of the Lord had appeared to them. The event—the life of Jesus—has primacy as the touchstone of any theology or interpretation which the Church might develop. It is no accident that the Church presented its witness in the form of Gospels, because the Gospel story was essential to its life.

CHAPTER 8

THE SOURCES OF THE GOSPELS

So far we have pointed to the Gospels as witnessing to Jesus of Nazareth as the Lord of the Church. When we ask more closely who that figure is to which the Gospels witness, we are in difficulty, because this witness is not the same in all the Gospels, and the materials in the Gospels, even apart from their variety, are so difficult to understand that any simple approach to them is ruled out. Probably no documents in the history of the world have been subjected to such a rigorous scrutiny.

But are they not simple witnesses? They are, and they are not. What they point to—the centrality of the mystery and glory of Jesus of Nazareth—is clear; but they themselves are complex. In their witness to the one many splendored thing, they differ from each other. They draw upon different traditions and use them differently. To reach the figure to whom the many Gospels point, although he shines through them, requires a sifting of their witness. This it is that has led to the modern study of the Gospels, to the work of the so-called Biblical Critics. "Criticism" and "critic" are not happy expressions, because they have so often suggested hostile, destructive intentions. But both terms come from a Greek verb, *Krinô*, meaning to judge, to discriminate, to investigate. And Biblical Criticism—in its "Higher" form—connotes the scholarly investigation of the date, authorship, sources, destination, plan, and purpose of a Biblical document. After more than a century of scholarship, certain probabilities have emerged.

The two groups of Gospels

The first step which critics of the Gospels came to recognize was the necessity to distinguish between two groups of the Gospels. The differences between the three first Gospels—Matthew, Mark, Luke—and John are so marked that the latter must be treated separately. These differences, as will appear later, are not as rigid as was once claimed, but they are still real enough to demand that Matthew, Mark, and Luke should be "isolated" from John for critical purposes. There are differences in the chronology and geography of the ministry of Jesus, in the nature of his teaching and its form, and in the general approach to the person of Jesus as found in John which set it in a category of its own. On the other hand, Matthew, Mark, and Luke are so much like one another as to form a group which should be studied together. For this reason they have been called the "Synoptic Gospels"—Gospels to be examined one alongside the other—and present us with the "Synoptic Problem."

The Synoptic Problem

The Synoptic Problem is the problem of the interrelation of the Gospels of Matthew, Mark, and Luke, which are accordingly called "The Synoptic Gospels." It asks the questions, "How do they come to be so closely related?" and "How, if they have so much in common, do they have so many differences?"

FACTS GIVING RISE TO THE PROBLEM

The first fact that created the Synoptic Problem is that there are agreements between them; and agreements of different kinds which have to be explained. These are:

a. *Agreements in substance or contents.* Mark consists of 103 narratives, of which all but five are included in Matthew, while Matthew has parallels to two or three of the five. The second Gospel, Mark, is thus fully embedded in Matthew. Equally certain is the incorporation of Mark in Luke, though the coincidence of material is not so complete. This agreement of substance is all the more striking when we remember that behind the Gospels is a process of selection from a large body of material. They do not contain one-half of what Jesus said and did during his ministry (John 21:25), and so we may well ask whether the incorporation of Mark in the other two is the work of chance or due to the fact that Mark was copied and used by Matthew and Luke.

b. Again, there are *agreements in the order of the narratives*. Omitting the first paragraphs in Matthew and Luke as introductory, we find that the three Synoptics, in presenting the ministry of Jesus, largely follow the same plan, namely, a brief period in the Jordan Valley and the Wilderness, before the active ministry begins. Then follows a period of teaching and working in cities around the Sea of Galilee with Capernaum as the center, and ending with the journey to Jerusalem, the trial, and the crucifixion. We find the baptism, temptation, and the order of events in the last days, recorded by the Synoptics with extraordinary similarity, and sometimes we find the same order followed even when there is no reason to suppose that the events happened in the way indicated; e.g., in Mark 2:3–22, Matthew 9:2–17, Luke 5:18–38, we find that the three evangelists relate the following: the healing of the sick of palsy, the call of publicans, and the discussion on fasting. The three relate these items in the same order though it is not obvious that the narratives are connected with each other. Sometimes we find the same order followed when clearly it is not the right one. An excellent example is found in Mark 6:14 and Matthew 14:1, where the two evangelists go out of their way to interrupt the narrative in order to relate the story of the death of John the Baptist. Luke does not follow Mark on this occasion, having already made a brief reference to the death of the Baptist in Luke 3:19 and 20.

c. Next, in Matthew, Mark, and Luke we find much *agree-*

ment in language and style. In order to appreciate this fully, the Gospels must be studied in Greek, but the agreements to which we refer are so striking that we are bound to conclude that there is mutual dependence between them. For example, in Mark 2:10, Matthew 9:6, and Luke 5:24, we have the same kind of sentence in all three Gospels—a repetition of the words of Christ with a parenthetical sentence in the middle. This parenthesis affords a striking agreement in style. The passage reads:

". . . But to convince you that the Son of Man has the right on earth to forgive sins"—he turned to the paralysed man— "I say to you, stand up, take your bed and go home." (Mk. 2:10)

It is almost exactly the same in the three Gospels.

Another example of such stylistic agreement occurs in Mark 1:16 and Matthew 4:18. The verse in Mark reads:

Jesus was walking by the shore of the Sea of Galilee when he saw Simon and his brother Andrew on the lake at work with a casting net; for they were fishermen.

Matthew has:

Jesus was walking by the Sea of Galilee when he saw two brothers, Simon called Peter and his brother Andrew, casting a net into the lake; for they were fishermen.

The phrase "for they were fishermen" is a redundant expression. Such redundancies are a feature of Mark's style, and it is difficult to suppose that Matthew is not here deliberately following Mark.

In addition, particular expressions, which occur nowhere else in the New Testament, occur in parallel passages in the three Gospels—Matthew, Mark, and Luke. Consider the following passages:

Mark 2:21, with parallels in Matthew 9:15; Luke 5:35:

But the time will come when the bridegroom *will be taken away* from them, and on that day they will fast.

The verb "to be taken away" is only found in the New Testament in these passages. Does not this suggest that the three Gospels are related?

These agreements in points of Greek are all the more significant in view of the fact that the language of Christ and his apostles was Aramaic, which belongs to the same group as Hebrew and is one of the Semitic languages. This is of special importance in the case of the agreements in the records of the teaching of Jesus. The words of Christ are mainly recorded by Matthew and Luke, rather than Mark. Mark's gospel is chiefly narrative. We find that Matthew and Luke not only agree with Mark in the narratives of the events in the life of Jesus, but also agree with one another in reporting the words or discourses of Jesus. See the Sermon on the Mount and other passages. This means that, while Mark was used by Matthew and Luke in writing the story of the events of the life of Jesus, for their report of his words both of them must have had access to another document which they used in common.

The second major fact which created the Synoptic Problem is the differences between the Gospels.

As we know, the gospels differ as well as agree. Ancient people worried over the differences, while moderns wonder why they agree so much. There certainly are differences which must be taken account of. We have different accounts of the same event—Baptism, Temptation, Resurrection, Transfiguration. Then the order differs. Matthew and Luke do not give the second and third Temptation in the same order. Each of the gospels has peculiar sections; i.e., a section found only in one or the other of them. Luke, in particular, has eight or nine paragraphs from 9:51–18:14 which contain almost entirely narratives and sayings, most of which find no parallel in the others. We have many smaller differences. In Mark 6:3, Christ is called *The Carpenter*; in Matthew 13:55, *The Carpenter's Son*; and the

Synoptic Problem must have regard to these differences as well as to the agreements.

We have, thus, three things to account for: (1) agreements and disagreements between the three Gospels; (2) agreements and disagreements between two of them, particularly as regards the teaching in Matthew and Luke; (3) sections peculiar to one or the other of the three. This last problem perhaps is most conspicuous in the case of Luke, but we have it also in Matthew and in less degree in Mark.

A number of theories for the solution of the Synoptic Problem have been proposed.

The Oral Theory

This is an old theory, the simplest and most obvious. It is the theory of the existence of an original oral gospel, which was definite in general outline and even in language. It was later committed to writing, when it assumed various special shapes determined by the typical forms which it assumed in the preaching of different apostles. Whether it was first committed to writing in Aramaic and later in Greek, or in both Aramaic and Greek from the first, cannot be determined. But upon this common gospel, each evangelist drew independently; each knew nothing of the work of the other. This approach to the Gospels is especially associated with the great Bishop Westcott of Durham, England.

Much in this theory is reasonable. The Church did exist for some time before it possessed written Gospels: the differences in the Gospels are explicable in terms of it. For example, the difference in the order of the Temptations in Matthew and Luke may be due to one or the other leaving a written source which he possessed in deference to another order familiar in oral form to his church. But the theory cannot account for the uniformity of substance, order, style, and language among the Gospels noted above. If only an *oral* tradition was common to the evangelists, would they have such uniformities?

The Fragment or Pamphlet Theory

According to this theory the earliest stage of the history of the written gospels consisted of narratives or sayings collected in fragments or pamphlets. Some Christians collected parables, others miracles, others a brief account of the last journey of Jesus to Jerusalem, others a description of Jesus' activity in Galilee. Various evangelists drew upon these fragmentary collections. Clearly this theory might explain special sources used by evangelists which seem still to be detectable. For example, the section from 9:51–18:14 in Luke might come from a "pamphlet" or "fragment" of the kind suggested.

A recent scholar, the late W. L. Knox, has revived this theory by insisting that the Church quickly formulated various tracts on different themes upon which the Gospel writers drew. Behind Mark, for example, he discovers pamphlets or tracts dealing with the end of the world, Mark 13; Conflict, 2:1–3:6; Parables 4:1 ff.; a source dealing with the Twelve (this occurs in "fragments" throughout the Gospel) and the Passion.

But again, while this approach helps to illumine the concentration of certain blocks of material in the Gospels, it offers no explanation for the kinds of agreement to which we referred above, unless different evangelists used the same pamphlets.

The Two-Document Theory of Borrowing

The next attempt to explain the data giving rise to the Synoptic Problem concentrated on the similarities between Matthew, Mark, and Luke. The claim was made that Matthew and Luke had borrowed from Mark. This accounts for the almost complete embodiment of Mark in Matthew and Luke and for the large amount of narrative material which is common to all three. Mark was a primary source for Matthew and Luke; this has been a fundamental assumption of most synoptic criticism.

On the other hand, there is very little discourse material of any length in Mark, whereas there is much in Matthew and Luke. And much of this lengthy discourse material is very similar, if not always quite identical, in both Gospels. The conclusion is clear that Matthew and Luke, in addition to borrowing from Mark, also borrowed from a common sayings-source. To this source the title Q was given (from the German word "Quelle," source). A possible reference to this source may be present in a passage from Eusebius (about A.D. 260–340), Bishop of Caesarea, the Father of Church History. It reads:

> Matthew compiled *the logia* in the Hebrew [that is, the Aramaic] language and each person interpreted them as he was able.[11]

This statement is ascribed by Eusebius to Papias (A.D. 60–130), Bishop of Hierapolis in Asia Minor. Many interpretations of the term "the logia" have been given, but it seems most likely that it refers to a collection of sayings, the very collection to which our Matthew and Luke are indebted. In any case, whether Q be thought of as a written source or not, it designates material common to Matthew and Luke which they had drawn from the same source, oral or written.

Further refinements of the Theory of Borrowing

The Two-Document Theory did not, however, deal with all the data to be explained. What of the material which is only found in Matthew and Luke? Clearly there were special sources on which they drew. At this point, Canon Streeter of Oxford applied himself to the problem. He was disturbed by the tendency of many to regard materials that were not in Mark or Q as inferior in value or authenticity to those that were. This meant, for example, that the parable of the Good Samaritan, because it occurred only in Luke, could become suspect. Could it be established that materials peculiar to Matthew and Luke had originated in centers as reliable as that from which Mark had emerged? Streeter emphasized how early Christianity spread from city to city. He surmised that each of the big centers of the early Christian movement might have produced a significant document. Tradition connected Mark with Rome. Did churches at other big centers produce gospels? For various reasons Streeter connected Q with Antioch, and M (because of its Judaic character) with Jerusalem. Applying the same method to Luke, he traced L to the Church at Caesarea. Under Streeter, the sources behind the Gospels thus assumed definiteness of form and of geographic origin. It was generally felt that his theory dealt with all the data that had to be explained in the Synoptics—the differences and the similarities. The theory was still further elaborated. Before being finally used by Luke, L and Q had already been combined in a document to which the name Proto-Luke was given. The picture of the sources that emerged then was understandable and for a long time convincing.

Once the sources of the Gospels had been so neatly assorted, the examination of their characteristics followed. These may be summarized simply.

The Q source

This was regarded with the greatest possible interest because it preserved the moral teaching of Jesus, much that could be gleaned about his ministry, and the work of John the Baptist. It was dated generally around A.D. 50 and traced, as we saw, to Antioch, chiefly because of its favorable attitude toward the Gentiles (Lk. 7:2 ff.=Matt. 8:5 ff.; Lk. 10:13=Matt. 11:21; Lk. 11:31 f.=Matt. 12:41 f.). One scholar, however, traced Q to the country because of its rural flavor; see Luke 12:22–31= Matthew 6:25–34. Its origin was understood as catechetical, that is, it was a collection of materials from the teaching of Jesus

The Probable Sources of the Synoptics

Box/Node	Location	Date
Source of Luke I & II		
L	Caesarea	A.D. 60
Q	Antioch	A.D. 50
MARK	Rome	A.D. 60
M	Jerusalem	A.D. 65
PROTO-LUKE		
LUKE	(?) Corinth	A.D. 80
MATTHEW	Antioch	A.D. 85
Antiochene Tradition		

gathered to supply moral guidance to converts. Some scholars were so convinced that Q existed as a document that they thought it possible to detect two sources—in Aramaic and Greek —behind Q itself. Moreover, the disappearance of Q could easily be accounted for, because it had been absorbed by Matthew and Luke and so had become superfluous and perished.

The M source

The characteristics of M are clear. First, it contains an abundance of parables, many of which are introduced by a formula familiar in Rabbinic sources. The following are noteworthy parables: The Tares (13:24–30); The Hidden Treasure (13:44); The Pearl of Great Price (13:45–46); The Drag Net (13:47–50); The Unmerciful Servant (18:23–35); The Laborers in the Vineyard (20:1–16); The Two Sons (21:28–32); The Marriage Feast (22:1–14); The Virgins (25:1–13); The Talents (25:14–30); The Judgment (25:31–46). The introductory formulae in most of these parables vary only slightly: "The kingdom of heaven may be compared to . . ." (13:24; 18:23; 22:2; 25:1); "The kingdom of heaven is like . . ." (13:44, 45, 47; 20:1).

Secondly, the community reflected in it is turned toward Judaism; it reveals anti-Pharisaic tendencies (5:20; 23), and yet a concentration in its mission on Israel (10:6). For M, Christianity is a life under a new law, the Church is a kind of school, whose activity is like that of a Jewish community—it binds and looses (5:17 ff.; 11:27 ff.; 13:52; 18:18; 23:8; 28:20). For M, the Gospel is not a revolution but a reformation or fulfillment of Judaism, a fact made clear in the Old Testament quotations in 1:23; 2:6, 15, 18, 23; 4:15 f.; 8:17; 12:18–21, where the formula of fulfillment is important. All these characteristics point to Judaea as the place of origin for M and probably to Jerusalem itself. As to its date, 5:23–24a may mean that it regards the Temple as still standing and so points to a period before A.D. 65.

The L source

This source contains, in addition to some detached sayings, fourteen parables and thirty narratives. A list of the parables at once indicates the richness of L in these: The Good Samaritan (10:29–37); The Importunate Householder (11:5–8); The Rich Fool (12:13–21); The Barren Fig Tree (13:6–9); The Great Feast (14:15–24); Building a Tower (14:28–30); Embassy before Battle (14:31–33); The Lost Sheep (15:3–7); The Lost Coin (15:8–10); The Prodigal Son (15:11–32); The Dishonest Steward (16:1–13); Dives and Lazarus (16:19–31); The Unjust Judge and the Importunate Widow (18:1–8); The Pharisee and the Publican (18:9–14). Whereas Q, and to a lesser degree M, concentrated on the sayings of Jesus, L is most noticeable for parables and stories of a memorable kind. M attacked the casuistry and frequent hypocrisy of Pharisees directly; L, indirectly by emphasizing the need for humility and the loss of self-righteousness through stories and parables (see, e.g., Lk. 18:9). L is the comfort of the common man, remembering the friend of publicans and sinners. Jesus here emerges as a first-century prophet, surrounded by a band of simple disciples. He stays at the homes of rich friends; his message calls for faith in an uncomplicated manner; his tones are gentle; his raucous notes are few. No eschatological dogma or dream disturbs a Jesus who is sweet reasonableness itself and, above all else, sympathetic.

It should be recognized that L has been variously delineated. Some have included in it the accounts of the birth and passion of Jesus and regarded it as a complete gospel; others have deemed it simply an oral tradition or a mere collection of notes. Its place of origin has generally been taken to be Caesarea and its date about A.D. 60.

Proto-Luke

Three main facts led to the assumption that Q and L had been united to form one document, to which the name Proto-Luke has been given, before they were combined with Mark to form the Gospel of Luke.

1. The amount of Markan material in Luke is comparatively small in extent.

2. The non-Markan material in Luke seems to control the distribution of the Markan.

3. Material from Q is only combined with L material. This suggests that they were combined before the editor of Luke used them.

It is claimed that at Caesarea or in Rome just after he had left Caesarea, the author of Luke had combined Q and L and later added Mark, which he found in Rome.

The existence of Proto-Luke, however, has not been generally accepted. If it did exist, its importance is evident, but we cannot enlarge on this question here.

Above we have presented briefly the picture generally held of the sources behind the Synoptic Gospels (Proto-Luke has at no time won general acceptance and has increasingly encountered rejection). This picture was so neat that it immediately appealed to scholars and still governs the work of, perhaps, most New Testament scholars. But its validity has lately been questioned. It is premature to sign the death warrant of the four-document hypothesis, as Streeter's theory was called, and it is difficult to think that it will ever be wholly discarded. Nevertheless, in recent scholarship, the neat lines of Streeter's source analysis are being rubbed faint, if not entirely rubbed out. Attention has shifted more and more away from the fixity of sources to the living oral tradition behind the Gospels, which does not allow of the clean rigidity of the Streeterian lines. This last stage we shall deal with in chapter 11, but first it is necessary to turn to the work of those scholars who have concentrated on the oral tradition and thus brought about the change which we have indicated —the Form Critics.

CHAPTER 9

FORM CRITICISM

So far we have emphasized that behind the Gospels as we now have them there were probably written sources. But, when we have isolated such sources, can we go behind them still further to an earlier form or stage of the tradition? If these sources and, finally, the Gospels are the outcome or culmination of a process of oral tradition which had gone on from the time of the resurrection, how is this process to be understood? Can we trace the manner in which the tradition of the works and words of Jesus was handed down before it crystallized into written sources? It is this question that has occupied a great deal of New Testament scholarship since the end of the first world war. This kind of preoccupation with oral tradition has marked other fields of study; for example, students of early English and Celtic literature have been concerned with pre-literary developments, and classical scholars have sought to delve into the twilight before Homer from this point of view. But in the field of New Testament studies, this concern has been particularly evident. It has given rise to what is known as Form Criticism. As its name implies, Form Criticism is that discipline which examines the oral tradition lying behind the Gospels on the basis of the forms which it has assumed. The most significant Form Critics have been K. L. Schmidt, Martin Dibelius, Rudolf Bultmann, and Vincent Taylor. But it should be recognized that all serious students of the New Testament today are to some extent Form Critics.

Assumptions of Form Criticism

Let us first examine the main assumptions of this school.

I

They assume that the tradition, that is, the words of and stories about Jesus which we now have in the Gospels, serves the needs and purposes of the Church. The background of the New Testament, as we have seen before, was in the Graeco-Roman world and in first-century Palestine, but its immediate foreground was the life of the Christian Church itself. This has to be strongly re-emphasized. It is the first assumption of Form Critics that the Gospels are from the Church, by the Church, for the Church. The tradition about the works and words of Jesus was transmitted by the churches scattered around the Mediterranean; their evangelists, preachers, teachers, and exorcists used it and molded it, and even created parts of it. It was the needs of the churches in worship, in catechism, in apologetic, in exhortation, and in other ways that determined what tradition was transmitted and how it was used. And it is easy to see these needs at work in the Gospels.

With this first assumption of Form Criticism, it is impossible not to agree. It is possible, roughly at least, to fit the whole of the documents of the New Testament into the history of the Church; each stage in the Church's life seems to have produced literature appropriate to it. Thus we may broadly trace the history of the Church as follows.

1. *A period of expansion:* A.D. 30–65. To this belong the Pauline Epistles, which reveal the problems of an expanding Church at such places as Corinth, Thessalonica, Rome, and elsewhere, and the interaction of a Palestinian Gospel with the Graeco-Roman world, as well as with Judaism.

2. *A period of conflict:* A.D. 65–90. This period may be said to have openly begun with the persecutions of Nero. Christians

became aware of, and sometimes preoccupied with, the problem of their relation to the secular government; they had to be ready to give a reason for the faith that was in them. To this period belong I Peter, Hebrews, and Revelation.

In this period, also, the need arose for consolidation. The Church had expanded with astounding rapidity; it was in danger of overlooking its base or being cut loose from its moorings. Hence, the need arose to conserve the tradition on which it was built. This was one reason, as we saw previously, why the Gospels arose. Mark and the other Gospels show the need both to face persecution and to preserve the connection between Christianity and its roots.

3. *Consolidation and apologetic: from* A.D. *90 onward.* This coincides largely with the period of toleration under the Emperors Nerva (A.D. 96–98), Trajan (A.D. 98–117), and Hadrian (A.D. 117–138). To it we owe the literature of ecclesiastical concern in the strict sense (that is, literature dealing with such matters as church discipline, belief, and conduct in the Church)— the Pastorals, the Epistles of John and Jude, II Peter, and James. But it also produced great apologetic literature—Acts and the Gospel of John, which were designed to present the claims of Christianity to the world.

If the documents of the New Testament are placed thus over against the growing life of the Church, it is clear that their setting in life is that of the Church itself. It is the condition of the contemporary Church that supplies the clue to the form and contents of these documents. Form Criticism assumes this in its treatment of the Gospels especially, and urges that what confronts us primarily in these are not the actualities of the ministry of Jesus, or Jesus in his own setting, but Jesus in the setting of the early Church—seen through its eyes and ministering primarily, not to his own contemporaries, but to the contemporary Church.

II

But with this assumption goes another. Before our written sources for the tradition emerged, during the earliest years of the Church, there was an intense activity in the transmitting of tradition. So much was this the case that the tradition had assumed a certain "form" or "structure" before it came to be written down. And Form Criticism assumes that this "form" can be recognized.

If we look at the Gospel of Mark we find that a great deal of it consists of brief sayings and incidents, which cannot be grouped together, but seem to be self-contained entities. See, for example, the following passages from Mark:

1:40 ff.	The healing of the leper
6:1–6	The visit to Nazareth
6:7–13	The mission of the Twelve
6:14 ff.	The death of John the Baptist
7:25–30	The Syro-Phoenician woman
8:11–13	The demand for a sign
8:23–26	The blind man
10:13–16	Christ and the children
12:13 ff.	The question about tribute money

It may be well to have a typical unit of the tradition written in full. Mark 10:13–16 is a suitable passage. It reads:

And they were bringing children to him, that he might touch them; and the disciples rebuked them. But when Jesus saw it he was indignant, and said to them, "Let the children come to me, do not hinder them; for to such belongs the kingdom of God. Truly, I say to you, whoever does not receive the kingdom of God like a child shall not enter it." And he took them in his arms and blessed them, laying his hands upon them.

Clearly this story and many others like it are complete in themselves. They do not depend on accompanying passages in their context to give them meaning. They are isolated units of tradition. And they bear certain easily detectable formal characteristics.

1. *They begin with a stereotyped formula.* Consider at random, for example, the following passages from Mark:

> Once he was approached by a leper, who knelt before him begging. (1:40)

> Once more he went away to the lake-side. (2:13)

> One Sabbath he was going through the cornfields. (2:23)

> On another occasion when he went to synagogue. (3:1)

It is very few passages that do not begin in some such vague way: "And he entered" . . . "And they came to" . . .

2. *The form of the close of the episodes is more varied.* (a) Sometimes the close is very abrupt, as in the case of the story of the daughter of Jairus. After the little girl has been cured and the amazement of the crowd has been recorded, Mark adds in 5:43: "And he strictly charged them that no one should know this, and told them to give her something to eat." This is a sensible, down-to-earth piece of advice but hardly what would be expected at the close of such a tense story.

(b) Sometimes the crowd makes a comment. The comment is brief, but its effect, oddly enough, is reminiscent of the comments of a Greek chorus. Thus at the end of the story of the healing of a paralytic borne by four, in Mark 2:12, we read: "And he [the paralytic] rose, and immediately took up the pallet and went out before them all; so that they were all amazed and glorified God, saying, 'We never saw anything like that.'" Again after the healing of a man who was deaf and had an impediment of speech, the multitude near Decapolis exclaims: "He has done all things well; he even makes the deaf hear and the dumb speak." (Mk. 7:37—compare Gen. 1:31.)

(c) Very often the separate episodes end in a word proclaimed by Jesus, as a climax. See, for example, Mark

2:15–17; 23–28; 3:20–27; 3:31–35. For clarity, Mark 2:23–28 is given in full:

> One Sabbath he was going through the cornfields; and his disciples, as they went, began to pluck ears of corn. The Pharisees said to him, "Look, why are they doing what is forbidden on the Sabbath?" He answered, "Have you never read what David did when he and his men were hungry and had nothing to eat? He went into the House of God, in the time of Abiathar the High Priest, and ate the consecrated loaves, though no one but a priest is allowed to eat them, and even gave them to his men."
>
> He also said to them, "The Sabbath was made for the sake of man and not man for the Sabbath: therefore the Son of Man is sovereign even over the Sabbath."

(d) Sometimes the importance of a saying or incident is emphasized by an appended explanation, as in the following:

> Mark 7:18–19 is explained in 7:20–23.
> Mark 8:15 is explained in 8:17–21.
> Mark 9:14–28 is explained in 9:28–29.

In the last example cited, there is given an explanation not of a saying of Jesus but of his healing power. The disciples ask why they could not cast out a demon. The explanation is given by Jesus: "This kind cannot be driven out by anything but prayer."

(e) Again, the natural conclusion to an episode is followed by a generalizing summary not closely connected with the episode itself but linked in a general way with it. Examples of this are found in:

Mark 1:34. This follows on the healing of Peter's mother-in-law in Mark 1:29–31 and on an evening of healing activity. It reads: "And he healed many who were sick with various diseases, and cast out many demons; and he would not permit the demons to speak, because they knew him."

Compare Mark 4:33–34, a general statement on the parabolic teaching of Jesus, and 6:12–13, on the preaching activity of the twelve disciples. In these verses the tenses of the verb are in the imperfect tense in Greek to denote continuous action.

Although the examples cited above are from Mark, the same form emerges not only in the parallel passages in Matthew and Luke but also in episodes peculiar to them. See, for example, Matthew 17:24–27 on the temple tax; Luke 7:11–17, the story of the widow of Nain, and 17:11–17, the story of the ten lepers. The forms we have indicated seem to be characteristic of the tradition which lies behind all the Synoptics (and also John). These forms had already taken shape before the material came to be written down. These stories and sayings about Jesus had been retold many times in preaching, in catechetical activity, in liturgical settings, and elsewhere. Although sometimes additions would accrue to stories and sayings in the course of their transmission, they would also become rounded off, polished, vivid, direct, and concise. As pebbles in a river are carried on and gradually smoothed, so that they lose their awkward corners, so the stories about and sayings of Jesus were refined as they were conveyed down the stream of tradition.

III

A third assumption of Form Criticism has followed from this. The episodes giving the works and words of Jesus pursued their way like pebbles in a stream. This means that they were not only smoothed, but that they were isolated. The tradition was orally transmitted in self-contained units. This is a very important fact. It implies that any framework in which these episodes are now embedded is secondary. The basic unit of the tradition is not any structure, conglomerate or framework, but the separate, isolated items or stories. A Swiss scholar, Professor Karl Ludwig Schmidt, insisted that, apart from the story of the Passion, all the material in Mark is in the form of isolated units. The structure of Mark is secondary: the outline of events is imposed upon the tradition, not derived from it; no outline could be derived from the tradition, because it was a moving pebbly stream. The episodes in Mark have no essential chronological or geographical sequence, and cannot be regarded as preserving a "life" of Jesus. On this view, Mark turns out to be a series of episodes, arranged as if they were on a string but, in fact, having no inner connection. Mark is, to use a metaphor, a string of beads without "a string," or a row of pebbles.

It is with these three main assumptions that Form Critics have often approached the form of the tradition contained in the Gospels. The *contents* of this tradition they divide into two main groups which may roughly be designated as Teaching and Narrative. Various scholars have used different terms for these groups. Dibelius refers to Paradigms and Tales respectively; Bultmann to Apophthegmata and Miracles; the English scholar, Vincent Taylor, prefers to use the terms Pronouncement Stories and Stories, which are most illuminating.

First, then, there are *Pronouncement Stories*. The interest in these does not lie in the setting or action described but in a significant saying for which the setting and action only serve as a foil or occasion. The pronouncement character of a passage may not always be perfectly clear. For example, in the healing of the paralytic in Mark 2:1–12, there is a pronouncement given in verse 10; that is, Jesus announces "that the Son of Man has authority on earth to forgive sins." But this is followed by a further climax in 2:12. The complexity is probably due to the combination of two stories in 2:1–12. Notice that here, as in Mark 2:15–17, Jesus eating with publicans and sinners, there are geographical notes given although they are vague. The healing of the paralytic in 2:1–12 occurs at Capernaum, and in 2:15–17 Jesus is at the house of Levi, the publican.

But in other episodes there are no indications of time or place. Consider, for example, Mark 10:2–9, dealing with divorce. The introduction is vague; it has no obvious connection with 10:1. Consider also Mark 10:13–16, the blessing of the children; 12:13–17, the discussion on the payment of taxes; and 12:18–27 on the resurrected life. In all these we are not told when or where the episodes happened. These passages are all marked by extreme brevity; they all emphasize, as their climax, a particular saying which can have wide application. In such passages Form Critics assert that the story or framework merely exists for the sake of the saying; they are presumably imaginatively conceived to provide settings for pronouncements.

Why was it necessary to provide such anecdotal settings for sayings? The answer is natural that the episodes were designed to illustrate and illumine actual problems that were faced by Christians in their individual and corporate life. There were unavoidable questions. Should Christians pay taxes? A story leading on to an authoritative pronouncement would be valuable, such a story as emerges in Mark 12:13–17, for example. What is the true way in dealing with marriage? Should divorce be allowed to Christians? Are children desirable? What is the correct attitude toward wealth? A glance at Mark 10:2–9, 10–13, 13–16, 17–22, shows how such questions were met in story-pronouncement forms. In pronouncement stories, seldom does anything appear which cannot be deduced from the pronouncement itself. Details of time, place, and personnel are usually or often lacking; all such data are reduced to a minimum.

In the second place, there are the pure stories, the narrative material. Among these, for example, are the following, all from the first nine chapters of Mark:

The storm on the lake, 4:35–41.
The demoniac and the swine, 5:1–20.
The healing of the daughter of Jairus, 5:21–43.
The woman with the issue of blood, 5:25–34.
The feeding of the five thousand, 6:30–44.
The walking on the sea, 6:45–52.
The blind man at Bethsaida, 8:22–26.

These and similar stories are marked by the following characteristics:

1. Apparently there is no edificatory motive in many of them. They are designed to interest or to entertain, not necessarily to teach.

2. They contain details sometimes of a very trivial kind. Consider the detail in Mark 7:32–37. The actual healing of the man who was deaf and had an impediment in his speech is described thus in 7:33–34:

> He took the man aside, away from the crowd, put his fingers into his ears, spat, and touched his tongue. Then, looking up to heaven, he sighed, and said to him, "Ephphatha". . . .

Compare with this Mark 8:23. The stories as they passed along the stream of tradition sometimes lost many such superfluous details. The story of the Gerasene demoniac is different in Mark and Matthew and Luke; the Markan version is far more elaborate than those in the other two Gospels.

Matthew 8:28–29	*Mark* 5:1–9	*Luke* 8:26–30
When he reached the other side, in the country of the Gadarenes, he was met by two men who came out from the tombs; they were possessed by devils, and so	So they came to the other side of the lake, into the country of the Gerasenes. As he stepped ashore, a man possessed by an unclean spirit came up to him from	So they landed in the country of the Gergesenes, which is opposite Galilee. As he stepped ashore he was met by a man from the town who was possessed by devils.

Matthew 8:28–29	Mark 5:1–9	Luke 8:26–30
violent that no one dared pass that way. "You son of God," they shouted, "what do you want with us? Have you come to torment us before our time?"	among the tombs where he had his dwelling. He could no longer be controlled; even chains were useless; he had often been fettered and chained up, but he had snapped his chains and broken the fetters. No one was strong enough to master him. And so, unceasingly, night and day, he would cry aloud among the tombs and on the hillsides and cut himself with stones. When he saw Jesus in the distance, he ran and flung himself down before him, shouting loudly, "What do you want with me, Jesus, son of the Most High God? In God's name do not torment me." (For Jesus was already saying to him, "Out, unclean spirit, come out of this man!") Jesus asked him, "What is your name?" "My name is Legion," he said, "there are so many of us."	For a long time he had neither worn clothes nor lived in a house, but stayed among the tombs. When he saw Jesus he cried out, and fell at his feet shouting, "What do you want with me, Jesus, son of the Most High God? I implore you, do not torment me." For Jesus was already ordering the unclean spirit to come out of the man. Many a time it had seized him, and then, for safety's sake, they would secure him with chains and fetters; but each time he broke loose, and with the devil in charge made off to the solitary places. Jesus asked him, "What is your name?" "Legion," he replied. This was because so many devils had taken possession of him.

A glance at these columns shows how the Markan account has shed its "superfluities" in Matthew and, less so, in Luke.

3. They concentrate on the miraculous. Jesus emerges as a wonder-worker.

4. In the case of the healing stories, a simple pattern is followed—symptoms described, healing achieved, proof thereof supplied.

The above are the main emphases in the work of Form Critics. Other aspects of their contribution must be examined in the next chapter.

CHAPTER 10

THE STRENGTH AND WEAKNESS OF FORM CRITICISM

> Yet, as a preliminary to the story of the Gospels, too large a
> dose of Form Criticism might well reduce one to the condition
> of a man who stands before a Raphael and keeps on asking
> where the artist got his paints. . . .   (E. V. Rieu)[12]

In the light of what was written in the last chapter, Form
Criticism has very greatly enriched our understanding of the
forms which the oral tradition behind the Gospels assumed.
It is when we ask not *what* forms that oral tradition took, but
how it did so that questions arise. How did the pronouncement stories and tales originate and evolve? At this point, a
glance at the work of two Form-Critical scholars who give
different answers to this question is necessary.

According to Martin Dibelius, supreme importance should
be given in the preservation and transmission of the works
and words of Jesus to the activity of preachers. In the beginning was the sermon. "The mission," writes Dibelius, "offered the cause and the sermon the means for the spreading of
what the followers of Jesus spread as a memory." It was the
stories about Jesus and his words which were useful in preaching which were preserved and passed on, that is, stories that
could often be used as illustrations by preachers. But the
preachers did not spin these out of their own minds; they
derived them from teachers in the Church who had previously
collected them and given them to missionaries when they set

out on their campaigns. But what is important is that Dibelius recognized a real transmission of tradition *from Jesus downward,* a tradition having its point of departure in the ministry of Jesus himself. He regarded Jesus as the source of a deposit of works and words which was used, modified, and handed down by the Church. Dibelius went too far in claiming that there was a special group of teachers in the early Church whose specific task was to hand on the tradition, but, in understanding Jesus himself as the originator or beginning point of a tradition, he is on more certain ground.

It is at this point that Bultmann's work has been more radical than that of Dibelius. Bultmann has examined both the Pronouncement Stories (*Apophthegmata*) and the Tales (*Miracles*) with minute thoroughness. The former he divides into the following five main categories:

1. *Logia* or *Wisdom Sayings* like those of the Old Testament. Many of these were originally Jewish proverbial sayings which have been attributed to Jesus by the Church.

For example, Matthew 6:34b: Each day has troubles enough of its own.

2. *Prophetic and Apocalyptic Sayings* in which the arrival of the Kingdom of God is declared and a call to repentance issued. Since Jesus clearly appeared as a prophet and announced the Kingdom, genuine sayings of his are preserved among these.

For example, Mark 8:35: Whoever cares for his own safety is lost; but if a man will let himself be lost for my sake and the Gospel, that man is safe;

Mark 8:38: If anyone is ashamed of me and mine in this wicked and godless age, the Son of Man will be ashamed of him when he comes in the glory of his Father and of the holy angels.

3. *Laws or rules for the community,* some of which may go

back to Jesus, but many of them can only be the creation of the community itself.

For example, Mark 7:15: . . . nothing that goes into a man from outside can defile him; no, it is the things that come out of him that defile a man.

4. *Sayings in the first person singular:* these are not likely to be from Jesus. They reflect the world of Hellenistic religion.

For example, Luke 19:10: . . . the Son of Man [=I] has come to seek and save what is lost.

5. *Parables and parabolic sayings* of which some can be regarded as deriving from Jesus himself, especially those of an ethical and eschatological nature.

For example, Mark 2:17: It is not the healthy that need the doctor.

Bultmann's treatment of the stories in the Gospels is that many of them were suggested by a pronouncement or a pronouncement story which was reshaped. The miracle stories, especially, reveal the same style and structure as stories of miracles in Hellenistic sources. He writes:

> Since we know a great many miracle-stories, we can make a careful comparative study of the miracle-stories found in the Gospels. We then discover that the Gospel stories have exactly the same style as the Hellenistic miracle-stories. Accounts of miraculous healing run as follows: first, the condition of the sick person is depicted in such a fashion as to enhance the magnitude of the miracle. In this connection it is frequently said that the sickness has lasted a long time. Occasionally it is stated that many physicians had attempted in vain to cure the sick person. Sometimes the terrible and dangerous character of the sickness is emphasised. All these traits are found in the Synoptic narratives just as they also appear in the stories which are told concerning the pagan miracle-worker Apollonius of Tyana. After the introductory description of the illness comes the account of the healing itself. The Hellenistic miracle-stories often tell of unusual manipulations by the miracle-worker; the Gospel accounts, however, seldom mention this trait (Mk. vii.

33, viii. 23). The Gospels, however, do retain other typical items. They narrate that the Saviour came near to the sick person—perhaps close to his bed—that he laid his hands upon the patient and took him by the hand and then uttered a wonder-working word. Following a custom also characteristic of pagan miracle-stories, the narratives of healing in the Gospels occasionally reproduce this wonder-working word in a foreign tongue, as for example "Talitha cumi" (Mk. v. 41) and "Ephphatha" (Mk. vii. 34). Another typical trait appears when it is sometimes said that no one was permitted to see the actual working of the miracle (Mk. vii. 33 and viii. 23). The close of the miracle-story depicts the consequence of the miracle, frequently describing the astonishment or the terror or the approval of those who witnessed the miraculous event. In other cases the close of the narrative shows the one who is healed demonstrating by some appropriate action that he is entirely cured.[13]

It follows from the above that for Bultmann a great deal of the material—sayings and stories—in the Gospels is the creation of the Christian communities as they wrestled with the problems that confronted them. Any biographical treatment of the life of Jesus is, at least, exceedingly problematic because the structural elements in the Gospels are secondary. This scepticism must not be exaggerated, and Bultmann himself was able to write a brilliant book on the teaching of Jesus. But two things can safely be asserted: (1) that he ascribes a highly creative role in the formation of the tradition to the Christian community, which felt free to ascribe its own insights to Jesus; and (2) that much of the tradition, in his judgment, only emerged on Hellenistic soil and, therefore, cannot but be secondary. To these two factors is due the extreme scepticism which has marked much New Testament scholarship about the figure of Jesus of Nazareth and the reliability of the witness of the Gospels to him. On this view, the Gospels become primarily, though not wholly, evidence for the life and faith of early Christians, not for the life of Jesus. The words of an

Oxford Form Critic (the bluntness of which he later softened) have become famous: "The form of the earthly no less than of the heavenly Christ is for the most part hidden from us. For all the inestimable value of the Gospels, they yield us little more than a whisper of his voice; we trace in them but the outskirts of his ways."

For this reason Form Criticism has been regarded by many as a kind of "nightmare" in which the solid, historical foundations of Christianity seemed to dissolve. Accustomed to a vivid picture of a real Jesus and often conceiving Christianity as, above all, demanding a personal, living relationship with this tangible Man who walked the Galilean hills, many have been surprised and, then, appalled at his disappearance behind the dust of scholarship. They have felt in encountering Form Criticism as the Devil in Milton's *Paradise Lost* felt when journeying to the earth. Suddenly he

> . . . meets
> A vast vacuitie: all unawares,
> Fluttering his pennons vain, plumb down he drops
> Ten thousand fadom deep . . . .
> Quencht in a Boggie *Syrtis*, neither Sea
> Nor good dry Land: nigh founderd on he fares,
> Treading the crude consistence, half on foot,
> Half flying . . . .
> O'er bog or steep, through strait, rough, dense or rare,
> With head, hands, wings, or feet pursues his way
> And swims or sinks, or wades, or creeps, or flyes. . . .[14]

The scholars seem to have taken away their Lord in taking away Jesus. Under the impact of Form Criticism Jesus seems to be reduced to an unsubstantial ghost.

It is not surprising that many recoiled from studies that produced such a result. But such a reaction cannot be justified. Form-critical scholars have followed the truth where it led them, and it seems often to have led them to scepticism about the historical reliability of much in the Gospels. But whether such scepticism be necessary or not, through their scholarly pilgrimage these scholars have made an immeasurable contribution to our understanding of the Gospels. They have illumined the form which the tradition of the works and words of Jesus assumed; they have made it forever impossible to ignore how the preaching, exhortation, apologetic, polemic, and discipline of the primitive Churches have influenced the stories and sayings recorded in the Gospels. Moreover, it should not be overlooked that there is no such thing as Form Criticism in the abstract but only a number of scholars applying this method and arriving at different results. Each scholar has had his own preconceived ideas or presuppositions as to what was likely or unlikely in the transmission and formation of tradition. All sorts of qualifications are necessary in any assessment of the over-all impact of Form Criticism. Nevertheless, it cannot be gainsaid that that discipline did encourage a sceptical attitude toward the historicity of the Gospels. Is this scepticism justified? There are certain overemphases in Form Criticism in its total impact which have to be recognized.

First, many Form Critics asserted or implied that the earliest Christians were not concerned to remember what Jesus did and said. It is certainly true that the Jews in the time of Jesus were not interested in biographies of their great leaders. We have no contemporary biographies of such great figures as Hillel, Rabbi Johannan ben Zakkai, or Akiba. Not the life of a Rabbi was important but what he said. So, it was claimed, among Christians there was little concern to preserve the biography of Jesus. But can we rule out a distinctly biographical or historical interest in Jesus among early Christians? This is unlikely. Like other Christians of a later age in India and elsewhere, who, having heard the preaching of the Gospel, demand to know more and more about the Jesus proclaimed, so too, we cannot doubt, the first Christians became curious about

Jesus and the first disciples anxious to preserve what they remembered him to have uttered and done.

Consider the alternatives placed before a student of the tradition about Jesus. The first alternative is to believe that for some time after his death and resurrection what Jesus did and said was neglected and so forgotten. But, as the Church developed, it became necessary for her to find rules for conduct, teaching for catechumens, material for "sermons." To meet this need, the Christian communities created their own sayings or borrowed materials from Jewish and Hellenistic sources and ascribed them to Jesus. The other alternative is to recognize that what Jesus actually taught was remembered by his followers and adapted by the Churches as the need arose.

On grounds of historical probability, the second alternative is the more likely by far. Much Form Criticism has been unnecessarily sceptical about the amount of teaching which can be traced back to Jesus himself. If the coming of the Christ in the flesh interested Christians, they must have been concerned with the details of his life in the flesh. Another way of asserting the same thing is to recognize that Form Criticism has ascribed to the Christian communities a role, in the creation of the tradition preserved in the Gospels, which is exaggerated. The New Testament witnesses to virile, expanding Christian communities, it is true, but also to confused and immature ones. It is more likely that the thrust, the creativity, the originality which lies behind the Gospel tradition of the works and words of Jesus should be credited to him rather than to the body of Christians. The kind of penetrating insight preserved in the Gospels points not to communities—mixed and often muddled in their thinking—but to a supreme source in a single person, Jesus, Rabbi and prophet.

It also seems that Form Criticism of the Gospels has been unduly influenced by the history of tradition in the Old Testament and in other folk literature. But any comparison between such literatures and the New Testament must be dubious. The Old Testament covers at least ten centuries; folk literature usually stretches over long periods of time. The New Testament, on the other hand, probably was all composed within a century. Only one generation probably separates Jesus from the last New Testament document. And the tradition in the Gospels is not strictly a folk tradition, derived from long stretches of time, but a tradition preserved by believing communities who were guided by responsible leaders, many of whom were eyewitnesses of the ministry of Jesus. The Gospels contain materials remembered recently, at least as compared with other traditional literatures, so that the rules which governed the transmission of folk tradition do not always apply to the tradition found in the Gospels.

Furthermore, Form Criticism has often assumed that it is possible to pass from a judgment about the literary form of certain sayings and stories to their authenticity or historicity. But such a direct transition from judgments of form to judgments of historicity is not legitimate. Just as the form of an advertisement on the radio or television (and such advertisements often assume a similar "form," dictated by the effectiveness of certain structures, rhythms, and mnemonic devices) is, in itself, no indication of the validity of its claims, so the forms of sayings and stories in the Gospels do not decide their authenticity or historicity. Frequently the form of the tradition has wrongly been taken to indicate that it was unhistorical. The literary activity of Form Criticism should not automatically become historical criticism.

Again, the Hellenistic characteristics of much in the tradition have been emphasized. These characteristics, it has been claimed, imply that the traditions concerned arose, not during the ministry of Jesus, but later, after the Christian movement had left Palestine behind and entered the Hellenistic world. The interest in the miraculous found in the Gospels has often been held to point to a Hellenistic background. But traces of Hellenistic influences on the tradition have to be very carefully assessed. As long as it was possible to draw a sharp line between Palestinian and Hellenistic Judaism, there was some justification for making confident assertions that certain stories and sayings had to be derived from the Hellenistic world and were, therefore, not to be traced back to Jesus. But since this sharp line can no longer be drawn (see pp. 26–27), it is more difficult to distinguish what is early and Palestinian from what is late and Hellenistic.

Finally, it is difficult to understand—if the early churches were uninterested in the life of Jesus to any considerable degree—why Gospels should have emerged at all. On the other hand, if the early Churches were concerned to witness to the "story" of Jesus, the emergence of the Gospel form becomes easily intelligible, and the preservation of geographic and chronological data in the Gospels natural.

Form Criticism, then, both deserves our praise and demands our caution. We must be grateful for the light it has thrown upon the Gospels. It has forced us to ask of each item of the tradition what it meant to the Church within which it arose. But we cannot follow Form Criticism all the way. It is necessary to ask also what each item, modified as it may be, meant in the ministry of Jesus. Form Criticism has spurred our scepticism about the possibility of knowing Jesus as he lived; but by doing so, as we shall see later, it has also, by its very negations, compelled us to renew the quest for Jesus.

CHAPTER 11

RECENT EMPHASES IN GOSPEL CRITICISM

In the village where I grew up it was a custom among the boys when they met, even after the briefest separation, to greet each other with the question, "What's the latest?" So far in the previous chapters we have touched only upon old news. "Source Criticism," "Form Criticism"—these have long been discussed. But what are the recent emphases in the criticism of the Gospels?

A new understanding of first-century Judaism

First, there has been considerable discussion about the nature of Judaism in the first century in Palestine. Until recently a rigid distinction was drawn between the Judaism of Palestine and the Judaism of those Jews who lived in the Hellenistic world, the Diaspora Jews. In Palestine was the authentic Judaism. The religious Jews living there believed in an intensely personal God, great and awful, but also merciful and loving. The Law was not a burden to the Jews of Palestine but a source of joy on earth and in the world to come; it was a source of spiritual blessedness and intellectual activity. The Judaism of Palestine was marked by optimism and a glad acceptance of life. It was a joyous, simple religion and yet intellectual and rational.

Over against this happy, sunny, Palestinian Judaism, scholars of the past often placed Diaspora Judaism. In the Hellenistic world, Jews came into contact with pagan life, philosophy, and religion. Their God became, under the influence of philosophy, less intimate and affectionate than the God of Palestinian Judaism. God became distant and less approachable. Pessimism marked the Jewish religion in the Diaspora; despair was familiar to it. The Law was a source of tension; it had ceased to be a source of joy. Diaspora Judaism was colder and more somber than Palestinian Judaism. It emphasized sin and human failure.

This traditional distinction between Judaism inside Palestine and Judiasm outside Palestine has within recent years been questioned. Two reasons can be given for this questioning.

First, there has been the increasing recognition that Judaism changed from one period to another. Behind the view mentioned above, is the assumption that the Judaism of Palestine in the time of Jesus was like later Rabbinic Judaism, and that there was little change in Judaism from the first century A.D. to the fourth. But this view has been challenged. It is now recognized that the Judaism of Palestine in the time of Jesus was far more variegated and complex and far less monolithic than older scholars recognized, and that after A.D. 70, when Pharisaic Judaism triumphed, many currents within Judaism were either suppressed or died a natural death. This means that we cannot describe first-century Palestinian Judaism as if it were simply the happy Rabbinic Judaism of later times. It was much more complex and difficult to describe. Older scholars drew a sentimentalized version of first-century Palestinian Judaism which enabled them to contrast it sharply with Hellenistic Judaism.

Secondly, recent scholarship has shown that Palestine in the first century was very largely Hellenized. Palestine was dominated since 333 B.C. by the Greeks and from 63 B.C. by the Romans. From the time of Alexander the Great, it was always open to strong Hellenizing influences. The Greek domination was not merely political. Palestine, during the period of the Seleucids 198–168 B.C., was subjected to a definite propaganda for its Hellenization. Thus although Aramaic was the language of the common people of Palestine in the first century, Greek was also known, at least to the learned. Palestine was bilingual. Greek terms were used to designate such essentially Jewish institutions as the Sanhedrin; there are very many Greek terms in the Talmud itself. Moreover, the many wars which Jews had suffered had decreased their numbers in Palestine. By the first century, Jews had become a tiny political unit around the city of Jerusalem. In the rest of Palestine they were surrounded by Hellenistic influences, and there were Hellenistic influences in Jerusalem itself. According to one source, R. Simeon b. Gamaliel II had 500 lads learning Greek wisdom in his house. Thus in Palestine itself Judaism was being Hellenized.

And, in addition, there were constant contacts between the Judaism of Palestine and of the Dispersion. Every Jew, wherever he lived, paid an annual ½ shekel tax to maintain the Temple. Pilgrims from the Diaspora constantly visited the city in large numbers. The Synagogue gave to Judaism everywhere a marked unity, and there were constant journeys made by Jewish religious leaders from Synagogues in one country to those of another.

In all these ways the Judaism of Palestine was open to influences from outside Palestine. Within and without, Hellenism pressed upon it. This is abundantly attested by archaeological remains. Hellenistic motifs had invaded the synagogal and other Jewish architecture of the first century in Palestine and elsewhere. Moreover, the variety and syncretistic character of first-century Palestinian Judaism has been further reinforced for us by the Dead Sea Scrolls.

The upshot of all this is that the traditional division between Palestinian and Hellenistic Judaism is false. There was far greater fluidity and complexity in the Palestinian Judaism of the time of Jesus than we had previously supposed. The results of this new awareness of first-century Judaism have not yet been apparent. But they will be important. Let me give one example. We saw that many of the traditions found in the Synoptic Gospels were thought to be the products of Hellenistic Christianity and, therefore, late. But much in the Synoptics which it has been customary to label Hellenistic may turn out to be Palestinian. The lines between Judaism and Hellenism had become, in the time of Jesus, often blurred.

Confirmation of Form Criticism

I now turn to the second area where a comparatively new emphasis has appeared, although in fact it is a return to an old emphasis. You will recall that we spent some time on the sources behind our Gospels—behind Mark we mentioned a disciples' source, between Matthew and Luke we discovered Q and M and L, and Proto-Luke. Most New Testament students have taken these written sources with seriousness and have applied them in their researches.

But, for some time, there has emerged a tendency to question whether we should speak of written sources in this way. The existence even of Q has recently been questioned, and to M and L and other sources usually recognized, the epithet "shadowy anonymities" has been applied. These so-called sources never existed. Instead of such sources, we should think of a living oral tradition upon which the various evangelists drew and which each arranged in his own way—sometimes this way was immensely complicated. Some recent scholars also emphasize that this oral tradition was largely uncontrolled and that we should not emphasize the role of the leaders of the Church in its preservation.

Thus we are faced with a curious phenomenon: at the time when the existence of written sources behind the Gospels is becoming more credible historically, they are being denied in

New Testament studies. The reason why they are more reasonably credible is that the Dead Sea Scrolls have been discovered. We now know, in the light of the Scrolls, that there was perhaps a stronger popular literary tradition in first-century Judaism than had previously been recognized. Nevertheless, recent students of the Gospels have paid less and less attention to source criticism as such, and in many recent commentaries on the Synoptics there is very little space given to source criticism at all. Rather, emphasis is placed upon the fluid oral tradition which lies behind the Gospels—a tradition that had not become formulated or fixed in documents but existed in an undifferentiated form. Perhaps this change is not a very significant one. But a few comments must be made. First, it is unlikely that we should dismiss, as cavalierly as is now done, the accumulated results of the source criticism of the Synoptic Gospels. Thus, it is hardly likely that we should dispense with Q and M, although in the case of L and Proto-Luke there may be doubt. It is exceedingly dangerous to ignore the problem of sources, and despite recent tendencies in this direction, source analysis is still being forced upon us by the Gospels themselves; thus behind Mark, we are constantly compelled to recognize sources. But, secondly, it does seem clear that the discussion of tradition—whether oral or written—is likely to occupy New Testament scholars more and more in the near future. Attention to tradition in the New Testament, its form and transmission in all its forms is already prominent among N.T. scholars. This means that the concerns of Form Criticism are still very much alive.

One problem of the tradition which has occupied scholars is its relation to the cultic life of the early Church. The view has grown that the actual worship of the Church has influenced the tradition. This emerges very clearly in several ways.

To begin with, let us compare the versions of the Lord's Prayer which are found in Matthew and Luke respectively.

Let us look first at the Lord's Prayer as it is in Matthew, the form with which we are all most familiar because we use it regularly in our Churches. It reads:

> Our Father in heaven,
> Thy name be hallowed;
> Thy kingdom come,
> Thy will be done,
> On earth as in heaven.
> Give us today our daily bread.
> Forgive us the wrong we have done,
> As we have forgiven those who have wronged us.
> And do not bring us to the test,
> But save us from the evil one. (6:9–13)

Compare with this the form in Luke 11:2–5 which reads:

> Father, thy name be hallowed;
> Thy kingdom come.
> Give us each day our daily bread.
> And forgive us our sins,
> For we too forgive all who have done us wrong.
> And do not bring us to the test.

Notice that "Father" in Luke has become in Matthew, "Our Father in heaven."

"Thy kingdom come" in Luke has become in Matthew, "Thy Kingdom come, Thy will be done."

"And do not bring us to the test" in Luke has become in Matthew, "And do not bring us to the test, but save us from the evil one."

The Doxology "For thine is the kingdom, the Power, the Glory," which occurs in some manuscripts for Matthew, does not occur at all in Luke.

What accounts for the differences which I have pointed out? The answer is simple. The Matthaean form has been adapted to liturgical use in the services of the Church.

This liturgical character of Matthew has been noticed by

many scholars, particularly by Professor Kilpatrick of Oxford, who emphasizes that the author of Matthew has changed his sources at points in the interests of liturgical propriety. We can give only a few examples. In Matthew 6:26, we read: "Look at the birds of the air: they do not sow and reap." In the parallel passage in Luke 12:24, we have: "Think of the ravens."

Why has the Lukan "ravens," which in Greek is an ugly word (*Korakas*) which strikes harsh on the ear, become "the birds of the air" of Matthew? Again, the answer is clear. For reading in the Church, "the birds of the air" is much more suitable than the ugly sounding "ravens" of Luke. But not only so. Matthew has clarified his material in many ways so as to fit it for liturgical purposes.

But one scholar has gone much further than Kilpatrick. The former Archbishop of Quebec, Dr. Philip Carrington, wrote a volume on the Gospel of Mark which he called *The Primitive Christian Calendar*. This is a brilliant work. Its thesis roughly is as follows. How did the tradition about the works and words of Jesus, asks Carrington, come to be gathered together? The answer he gives is simple.

In Judaism there are certain central festivals—*Passover, Pentecost, the Day of Atonement, The New Year,* etc. These central days of the Jewish year were familiar to early Christians, many of whom were Jews. On these days they would gather together for worship and recount the story of Jesus. Within fifteen years after his death, the tradition about Jesus came to be fixed in its main outlines around certain central festival days, such as Passover, Pentecost, Tabernacles, The New Year, the Day of Atonement.

Carrington starts by pointing out that the Feeding of the Five Thousand was related to the Passover Festival in the light of John 6:4 ("The Passover was near, the festival of the Jews"). The Passion narrative of Mark beginning at 13:1, he thinks, was read as a lection in the annual Christian Pass-over. The whole of Mark, in his view, not only reveals the influence of liturgical practices but is a lectionary, i.e., it was specifically prepared to provide the Church with a series of readings which could be used in the public services of the Church.

Carrington finds support for this view in certain manuscript evidence. The lectionary units into which Mark can be divided are reflected in the lectionary and script divisions of some of the oldest manuscripts of the New Testament. On these manu-scripts Carrington notes the presence of the sign √, and this sign, he thinks, indicates how much of the Gospel was to be read on a particular Sunday. In all there are sixty-two divisions in Mark: if we allow that ten additional divisions were read at Easter time, this would allow us to think of each division in Mark as designed for one of the fifty-two Sundays of the year. On this view, Mark is a primitive Christian lectionary, and the same is also true according to Carrington of Matthew. It is unlikely that we should accept Carrington's view, but his work is an example of the emphasis on liturgical factors in recent treatment of the Gospels.

It is not only the services of the Church which can be traced behind the tradition. The baptismal activity and the catechetical work of the Church breaks through in the Gospels. For example, in Mark 10:1–27, we have sections dealing first with marriage and divorce (1–12), then with children (13–16), then with the dangers of wealth (16 ff.). These sections are probably placed in this order because they had been used to teach Christians in these matters—the idea of marriage leading on to children and to the anxiety and worldliness which the care of families often entails. Or, again, to use an even clearer example of early Christian practice revealing itself in the Gospel tradi-tion, we may turn to Matthew 18 where there is a lengthy section on Church members, and on the way in which discipline is to be maintained in the Church. The following passage, 18:15 ff., for example, might well have been the rules of order or *Church Discipline* of a primitive community.

> If your brother commits a sin, go and take the matter up with him, strictly between yourselves, and if he listens to you, you have won your brother over. If he will not listen, take one or two others with you, so that all facts may be duly established on the evidence of two or three witnesses. If he refuses to listen to them, report the matter to the congregation; and if he will not listen even to the congregation, you must then treat him as you would a pagan or a tax-gatherer.
>
> I tell you this: whatever you forbid on earth shall be forbidden in heaven, and whatever you allow on earth shall be allowed in heaven.
>
> Again I tell you this: if two of you agree on earth about any request you have to make, that request will be granted by my heavenly Father. For where two or three have met together in my name, I am there among them.

Again, it is possible that we can trace in the Gospels the hymns of the primitive Church. What, for example, shall we make of the well-known passage in Matthew 11:25–30:

> At that time Jesus spoke these words: "I thank thee, Father, Lord of heaven and earth, for hiding these things from the learned and wise, and revealing them to the simple. Yes, Father, such was thy choice. Everything is entrusted to me by my Father; and no one knows the Son but the Father, and no one knows the Father but the Son and those to whom the Son may choose to reveal him.
>
> "Come to me, all whose work is hard, whose load is heavy; and I will give you relief. Bend your necks to my yoke, and learn from me, for I am gentle and humble-hearted; and your souls will find relief. For my yoke is good to bear, my load is light."

This is arranged in strophes and may be a highly finished hymn used at baptism.

Whether all the suggestions made above are to be accepted

or not, they show how the emphasis has been in recent study of the Gospels. They are seen as documents preserving a tradition molded and fashioned by the Church and reflecting at various points the lectionary activity, the prayers, the catechism, and the baptismal practice of the communities. That is, much in the Form-Critical approach is being confirmed in recent studies.

But there are other currents at work in recent scholarship which have a bearing on Form Criticism. We may group them in three ways: first, those that go against Form Criticism; secondly, those that come after Form Criticism without questioning the validity and importance of the Form Critical method; and, thirdly, those that go beyond Form Criticism:

Critics of Form Criticism

A recent trend is associated especially with the two Scandinavian scholars, Professor Harald Riesenfeld and his pupil, Dr. B. Gerhardsson. Their point of departure is certainly in opposition to the Form-Critical school. The Scandinavians question the view of the early Church and of Jesus held by Dibelius and Bultmann, the major Form-Critical scholars. In particular, they react violently against the dominantly creative role which the Form Critics have ascribed to the community. Over against the understanding of the Form Critics of a tradition developing mainly to meet the needs of the primitive community and, indeed, largely created by those needs, the Scandinavians present another. They make the following assumptions:

1. The early Church lived in a milieu in which the concept of tradition played an important role. This was true in the Hellenistic and Judaistic world. As early as Paul, we find in the Church an established conception of tradition which was regarded as authoritative.

2. The early Church recognized that the transmission of this tradition was so important and distinct that it used a technical

vocabulary to define it: the tradition was "received" and "delivered."

3. These terms suggest that there was a deliberate didactic activity on the part of definite doctrinal authorities—the formulation of definite sayings, the methodical delivery and reception of such sayings.

Riesenfeld and Gerhardsson, therefore, claim that the emphasis on preaching by Dibelius and on teaching, catechism, apologetics, polemics, discipline, organization, and study of the Scriptures by the Church by Bultmann do not adequately account either for the origin or the transmission of the Gospel tradition. This is because these scholars refuse to recognize those assumptions to which we referred above. As Riesenfeld and Gerhardsson interpret the case, behind the tradition preserved in the New Testament stands a "Holy Word." This was accorded a status similar in sanctity to that of the Old Testament. This "Holy Word" was probably solemnly recited in the early Christian assemblies for worship. Jesus himself, as Messiah, had taught the "Holy Word" to his disciples, who learned it by heart at his feet. It is this that explains why so much material in the Gospels can be easily memorized. There is, then, behind the Gospels a fixed, distinct tradition—partly memorized and partly written down in notebooks or private scrolls but invariably isolated from the teaching of other doctrinal authorities.

In support of this position the Scandinavians appeal to the Early Church Fathers; Gerhardsson offers also an understanding of primitive Christianity which supports his position. Thus he claims that Jerusalem was of great importance in the life of primitive Christianity; in Jerusalem, the Twelve were authoritative teachers, and from them there went forth to the world an authoritative tradition from the Messiah.

To examine this position is not possible here. The reader is asked to read a critique of this position offered elsewhere. One can only state that, in their reaction against Form Criticism, the Scandinavians have gone too far. Was there a "Holy Word," more or less fixed, handed on by authoritative teachers after a Rabbinic manner in the early Church? The tradition we now have in the Synoptics received its initial impulse in Jesus. This we can accept. But that it was a fixed deposit, strictly guarded, goes beyond the evidence. As a critique of the extreme scepticism of much Form Criticism, the Scandinavian protest is to be welcomed; but it is not to be accepted by itself as a fully valid approach to Christian Origins. The evidence of the Fathers, of textual criticism, and of the Gospels themselves demand this caution. It should be noted that the Scandinavian scholars have not been generally accepted.

After Form Criticism

So far we have dealt with critics of Form Criticism. We now turn to those scholars who accept that discipline but have gone beyond it. You will recall that by Form Criticism we mean that discipline which is concerned to examine the oral tradition which lies behind our Gospels. It made certain assumptions: first, that the Church transmitted, molded, and even created much of the tradition; secondly, that, before it came to be written down, the tradition had assumed certain forms which we can recover; but thirdly, it went a step further than this— it often asserted that any framework that the Gospels may have is purely secondary. Form Critics tended to report the Gospel tradition as made up of isolated units of tradition. Thus, Professor K. L. Schmidt reduced Mark to a series of independent "beads." There is no inner connection between its various stories, no unifying structure which controls the separate parts. Mark is simply a collection of unrelated stories—at least outside the Passion narrative. By and large, Form Critics atomized the Gospels, that is, reduced them to their component units and left them dismembered.

The result of such a view of the Gospels—as conglomerates—was to render any attempt at understanding them as wholes very difficult. Students became content very often with examining individual stories or sayings but gave up any effort to understand the Gospels as wholes. The Gospel writers were compilers, often, apparently, very dull ones. They received various traditions about Jesus, used them, but did not impose any scheme or interpretation upon them. They were, in short, somewhat trivial. The material they dealt with could not but, in consequence, be unimportant and unimpressive, as were the compilers themselves.

Recently, there has been a change from such an approach to the Gospel writers. To put it roughly, Form Criticism has led on to Redaction Criticism or Editorial Criticism. Many scholars have come to the conclusion that while the discovery of the sources behind the Gospels may be a first step, and the discovery of the oral forms and content of the tradition behind the written sources the second, it is necessary to go a third step. We must ask: What does the final editor of a Gospel intend to do with his material? Mark, Matthew, and Luke—to use these convenient terms for the moment for the authors of the Gospels —were not mere transmitters of what they had received. They were not mere copyists, content to record mechanically what they had mechanically received. No! They were more than copyists—they were editors, and editors with a difference. By what they retained from the tradition, by the way they introduced changes into it, minor as these appear at first, and above all, by the way they arranged the material at their disposal, the writers of the Gospels show that they were not mere collectors of a limited intelligence but, in a sense, authors. They imposed their particular concern or interest, even their point of view, on the Gospel material. In short, they present their Gospels with a particular slant.

Scholars are increasingly paying attention to the mind of the "authors" of the Synoptic Gospels themselves. Those who wrote the Gospels had a specific point of view which they had to express in their presentation of the Gospel materials.

I myself have sought to argue that Matthew, for example, has a specific purpose in compiling the Sermon on the Mount; that is, he was not merely concerned to put together the tradition about the teaching of Jesus, but to put it together in such a way as to serve his own purposes in confronting Judaism. Thus, in certain sections of the Gospels, we can see the purpose of the author or editor breaking through. Or, take another example. All the Synoptic Gospels have largely the same materials with which to present John the Baptist, but, in very subtle changes in this material, each Gospel presents him in its own way.

But it is not only in such details that the purpose of the writers of the Gospels breaks through. Three scholars in particular have dealt with three of the Gospels from this point of view. First, Professor Bornkamm of Heidelberg examined the Gospel of Matthew. By detailed examination of the various sections in Matthew, he has shown how Matthew has imposed his own purpose on his material, to present the higher righteousness, his own understanding of the Church, and the Christology that he himself espoused. In the same way, Professor Willi Marxsen has dealt with Mark and urged us to look at the Evangelist as imposing his point of view on the material. The most accessible work in English, however, from this point of view, is that of Dr. Hans Conzelmann under the title *The Theology of St. Luke* (London, 1960). Conzelmann shows that Luke has reflected upon the tradition about Jesus that he has received, and has interpreted it. He concludes that Luke presents the story of salvation in three stages:

(1) The Period of Israel: Luke 16:16.

(2) The Period of Jesus' Ministry (not his life), characterized in passages such as Luke 4:16 ff., Acts 10:38.

(3) The Period since the Ascension: the period of the Church.

The Second Coming is the end of saving history, not part of it. In the work of Bornkamm, Marxsen, Conzelmann and, as we shall see, Dodd, and others, the evangelists appear as "authors" concerned to bring out their own specific understanding of the Gospel tradition.

Beyond Form Criticism to Jesus himself

Recently, then, students of the New Testament have emphasized that the writers of the Gospels were not merely compilers and editors but authors, who interpreted the works and words of Jesus in their own way. Once more the Gospels can be read, not as collections of unrelated items, but as wholes presenting a unified view of their central character. It might be expected, that this new emphasis would establish more firmly than ever the view that that figure in whom the early Christians saw the glory of God is still further removed from us. Must we not recognize that Jesus is not only screened from us by the beliefs of early Christians, which have colored the oral tradition and written sources about Jesus, upon which the Gospel writers drew, but also by the minds of the Gospel writers themselves? Do not Matthew, Mark, and Luke, as interpreters, cast their own mantles around Jesus so that he himself is hidden more and more from our eyes? Oddly enough, this does not seem to have been the case. The rediscovery of the Gospel writers as authors has coincided with a movement which is called "the new quest for the historical Jesus."

In the last decades of the nineteenth century and in the early decades of the twentieth, New Testament scholarship was largely dominated by "the quest of the historical Jesus," that is, the quest to discover what really happened in the life of Jesus of Nazareth. It was in pursuit of this quest that scholars examined the world into which Jesus was born and sought for the sources upon which the Gospel writers had drawn.

But, as we indicated above, with the coming of Form Criticism it became clear that the sources at our disposal for understanding Jesus of Nazareth had been so colored by the interests of the early Churches, whose needs they reflected at every point, that any attempt to present a life of Jesus of Nazareth came to be deemed almost futile. Under the impact of Form Criticism, the tradition about Jesus preserved in the Gospels was broken up into small units of narratives or sayings, which could not be connected to give a clear story of his life. Details about places and times which occur in the Gospels were claimed to be historically unreliable. Any hope that the Gospels might provide a coherent account of the life of Jesus was abandoned. By and large, it was the faith of Christians not facts about Jesus which confronts us in the Gospels; the quest of the historical Jesus was considered impossible.

The results of Form Criticism were reinforced by the views of many leading theologians in the period when Form Criticism arose and flourished. In different ways they urged that knowledge of Jesus, as he lived, is not essential to Christian faith. "To believe" it is not necessary to know about Jesus but only to meet him in our experience as he comes to us as a living, present challenge in the preaching of the Church where he is set forth as God's final word to men. It is impossible and unnecessary to go behind this preaching. Professor Rudolf Bultmann, one of the greatest of the Form Critics and New Testament scholars of this century, wrote as far back as 1929 the following words:

It is not permitted to go beyond the 'proclamation' (*Kerygma*), using it as a 'source' in order to reconstruct the 'historic Jesus' with 'his messianic consciousness,' his 'inwardness' or his 'heroic character.' This would be precisely the . . . (Christ according to the flesh) who belongs to the past. It is not the historic Christ who is the Lord, but Jesus Christ as he is encountered in the proclamation.[15]

All that is necessary is response to the message preached by the believing community. Even if we could discover Jesus as he actually lived, this would not help, because he would embarrass us. Jesus as a figure in history, even if discoverable, must appear a stranger, an awkward stranger, to people living in the twentieth century. We are fortunate not to know too much about him as a historical figure, and need only know him as that person through whom is mediated to us the decisive call or challenge to place our trust not in ourselves but in God.

Form Criticism and theology, then, seemed to conspire to push Jesus of Nazareth into the twilight of the past.

But recently there has been a change; an attempt is afoot to bring him back into the full light again. The reasons for this are numerous. To begin with, although Form Critics and theologians claimed that Jesus could not be known and need not be known, interest in him, as he actually lived, did not entirely die. Professor Bultmann himself wrote a brilliant study called, *Jesus and the Word,* in which he presented the radical teaching of Jesus, and he always insisted that the fact of Jesus, that is, his reality as a historical figure, was essential to Christianity. But it is in the work of Bultmann's followers that the new quest has arisen, and it arose because they increasingly, although hesitatingly, came to realize that the preaching of the Church always points to Jesus; the Gospel calls to an encounter with God through him. In the end, it becomes impossible to ignore the questions that arise about him, and the preaching of Jesus as the Messiah or as the call to decision compels the question: "But who is this Jesus: whom do we encounter in the preaching?" To ask this is to set going again the quest for him. And recent Form Critics have been less sure than their predecessors that we do not have the sources for this quest—however much those sources are products of the Church. At this point, care is necessary to avoid exaggeration. British scholars, generally, have never been as sceptical as the German Form Critics, and there are even in Germany scholars, such as Professor Jeremias of Göttingen, who are convinced that after much sifting we may even recover the very words that Jesus uttered. The Form Critics who belong to the post-Bultmannian period, as it is called, are not so confident. They do not consider that the new quest is the same as the quest of an earlier period; they do not consider that a full life of Jesus is possible. But they do recognize that the Jesus of history is essential to the preaching of the New Testament, and that it is possible through his words or his deeds to grasp how Jesus understood himself and thus to find through his self-understanding a way to our self-understanding. Thus it is that, at a time when it seemed as if the figure of Jesus was being still further hidden from us behind the interpretation, this time, of the Gospel writers themselves, he has almost suddenly emerged from the dust of scholarship and again occupied the foreground of the New Testament. What, then, do the Gospels tell us about him?

CHAPTER 12

TOWARD UNDERSTANDING THE SYNOPTICS: THE NEW ORDER

The New Order

Many of you, who may have read thus far, may well be asking impatiently by now, "But when are we going to look at what the Gospels themselves contain?" We have so far discussed the background of the New Testament, its unity, the sources and oral traditions behind the Gospels, and the views of scholars about them. But what of the actual contents of Matthew, Mark, and Luke? Is it not time to look directly at them? With this kind of impatience it is easy to sympathize. And yet, as we now turn to the Synoptic Gospels themselves, it is necessary to realize that the Gospels, although they can be understood on one level by the wayfaring man, do not yield their secrets easily. Before we can enter into their world, we have to take at least three major leaps in imagination.

Three leaps in imagination

First, there is a leap in time. The Gospels belong to the early days of the Church; probably all date from before A.D. 100. They are ancient documents, and so they demand of us a leap backward in time. "Time flies," but it does not fly without changing us. To enter into the mind of another generation—even the generation preceding or following our own—is difficult. How often do we hear a father say of a son or daughter that he cannot understand him or her, that his children live in a different world from his own. This is probably true, although the father usually forgets that his own father had said precisely the same of him! Even in one generation we become strangers. I recently tried to reread a work by John Galsworthy, which had enthralled me in my teens. To my amazement, I found the novel already so dated that I could hardly read it. Most of the books that were popular in 1925 are now hopelessly outlived and gather dust on unused shelves. Consider how strange documents written almost twenty centuries ago must be. The gulf of twenty centuries has to be crossed if we would understand the Gospels. Books, like people, become strangers through time, and the chronological leap demanded of us by the Gospels is a tremendous one. The temptation is to avoid this leap, to modernize the Gospels or to archaize ourselves. But these shortcuts we must avoid.

Next, there is a leap of geography to be considered. Books, like people, are part of the soil and climate on and in which they are born. I shall never forget the first impression of strangeness made upon me by North Carolina (which, after all, is not very Southern!) when I first came to this country. I had left England in the grey, chilling mists of September to arrive in North Carolina in a blaze of sunshine and a temperature of over ninety degrees. The sounds, the colors, the odors of Durham, North Carolina, were so different from those that I had left behind in England that we seemed to be in a new world. So is it—and infinitely more so—when we westerners and northerners enter the lands of the Bible. It is a new and foreign land, which is likely to disconcert by its very strangeness. To understand the allusions of the Gospels, it is necessary to leap geographically across the seas and across the years to first-century Palestine.

And, finally, there is the leap demanded by language. Is it possible to understand another language fully? Do the words of one nation yield their innermost secrets to other nations? Words are living things; they have their own history. They are like trees that have many branches. Even the words of our own language are often difficult to comprehend fully. You may recall the story told about Sir Winston Churchill. In his early years he served at the British Embassy at Paris. He could speak little French and someone inconsiderately asked him why he had not learned that language. His reply was, "I am too busy learning English."

The New Testament is written in a language that is highly deceptive. It is in *Koinê* Greek, influenced by Aramaic and Hebrew. This language, despite its apparent simplicity, has meanings within meanings. The Gospels are, therefore, foreign in a profound linguistic sense. True, there are excellent translations of them available. But in the Preface to *The New English Bible* there is a revealing statement: the translators of this masterly rendering assert that translation is an impossible art. To approach the Gospels is like approaching an intricate jewel of the first century—who can do justice to their complexity?

The terms and motifs of the Gospels

I have emphasized these three leaps before we enter the Gospels because, however familiar, the Gospels are still strange. They demand a readiness to overcome a spurious familiarity and to confront the unfamiliar with sympathy. This is why, before we can deal effectively with the individual Gospels, we must first seek to grasp the meaning of certain terms and motifs which occur in all the Synoptics as their common coin. Later, having learned the coinage, we can examine the Gospels one by one.

And the first motif to be recognized is the awareness that in the life of Jesus of Nazareth a "new order" has appeared. This awareness is not only found in the Synoptics; it breaks through in all the New Testament. The following passages attest this. In Paul we read:

> For upon us the fulfillment of the ages has come. (I Cor. 10:11)

> Therefore, if any one is in Christ, he is a new creation; the old has passed away, behold, the new has come. (II Cor. 5:17)

> And although you were dead because of your sins and because you were morally uncircumcised, he has made you alive with Christ. For he has forgiven us all our sins; he has cancelled the bond which pledged us to the decrees of the law. It stood against us, but he has set it aside, nailing it to the cross. (Col. 2:13–14)

In Hebrews 1:1 we read:

> When in former times God spoke to our forefathers, he spoke in fragmentary and varied fashion through the prophets. But in this the final age he has spoken to us in the Son.

And in I Peter 1:18–20:

> Well you know that it was no perishable stuff, like gold or silver, that bought your freedom from the empty folly of your traditional ways. The price was paid in precious blood, as it were of a lamb without mark or blemish—the blood of Christ. He was predestined before the foundation of the world, and in this last period of time he was made manifest for your sake.

This sense of a new order as having arrived is everywhere in the Synoptics. Let us look at the following passages:

> John, who was in prison, heard what Christ was doing, and sent his own disciples to him with this message: "Are you the one who is to come, or are we to expect some other?" Jesus answered, "Go and tell John what you hear and see: the blind recover their sight, the lame walk, the lepers are clean, the deaf hear, the dead are raised to life, the poor are hearing the good news—and happy is the man who does not find me a stumbling-block."

When the messengers were on their way back, Jesus began to speak to the people about John: "What was the spectacle that drew you to the wilderness? A reed-bed swept by the wind? No? Then what did you go out to see? A man dressed in silks and satins? Surely you must look in palaces for that. But why did you go out? To see a prophet? Yes indeed, and far more than a prophet. He is the man of whom Scripture says,

'Here is my herald, whom I send on ahead of you,
And he will prepare your way before you.'

"I tell you this: never has there appeared on earth a mother's son greater than John the Baptist, and yet the least in the kingdom of Heaven is greater than he." (Matt. 11:2–11)

Here we are taken back to Isaiah 35:5–6 to a picture of a future Messianic Order or Age. Matthew declares that in the ministry of Jesus this new order has begun.

Once about that time Jesus took a walk on the Sabbath through the cornfields; and his disciples, feeling hungry, began to pluck some ears of corn and eat them. The Pharisees noticed this, and said to him, "Look, your disciples are doing something which is forbidden on the Sabbath." He answered, "Have you not read what David did when he and his men were hungry? He went into the House of God and ate the consecrated loaves, though neither he nor his men had a right to eat them, but only the priests. Or have you not read in the Law that on the Sabbath the priests in the temple break the Sabbath and it is not held against them? I tell you, there is something greater than the temple here. If you had known what that text means, 'I require mercy, not sacrifice,' you would not have condemned the innocent. For the Son of Man is sovereign over the Sabbath." (Matt. 12:1–8)

"I tell you, there is something greater than the temple here. The Son of Man is sovereign over the Sabbath." To feel the full force of this passage we have to recall what the Temple and the Sabbath meant in first-century Judaism.

Both the Temple and the Sabbath were regarded as so

important that they were declared to have pre-existed creation. The Temple was the place where God loved to dwell through his Shekinah. Its holiness and purity, as the abode of the Lord, was indicated by its very structure. The impure were progressively excluded from its innermost shrine. Thus the Gentiles were only allowed into the section called the Court of the Gentiles; and into the Holy of Holies only the High Priest himself could enter once a year, and that after the most elaborate purifications. But the Temple was not only the place where God chose to dwell, it was also the place chosen by him for making reconciliation with his people. Thus the Temple signified both the *perpetual* presence of God and also the means of forgiveness. And the Gospels declare that something greater than the Temple was in the midst—greater than the place of the presence of the Lord, greater than the whole sacrificial system. A new thing has appeared.

> At the Judgement, when this generation is on trial, the men of Nineveh will appear against it and ensure its condemnation, for they repented at the preaching of Jonah; and what is here is greater than Jonah. The Queen of the South will appear at the Judgement when this generation is on trial, and ensure its condemnation, for she came from the ends of the earth to hear the wisdom of Solomon; and what is here is greater than Solomon. (Matt. 12:41–42)

Here again, by referring to Jonah and the city of Nineveh and Solomon and the Queen of Sheba, the Gospel points to the amazing thing that has happened. The generations of Jonah had less reason to repent at the presence of Jonah than Israel at the presence of Jesus; so, too, a greater than Solomon is present in him.

> The disciples went up to him and asked, "Why do you speak to them in parables?" He replied, "It has been granted to you to know the secrets of the kingdom of Heaven; but to those others it has not been granted. For the man who has will be

given more, till he has enough and to spare; and the man who has not will forfeit even what he has. That is why I speak to them in parables; for they look without seeing, and listen without hearing or understanding. There is a prophecy of Isaiah which is being fulfilled for them: 'You will hear and hear, but never understand; you will look and look, but never see. For this people has grown gross at heart; their ears are dull, and their eyes are closed. Otherwise, their eyes might see, their ears hear, and their heart understand, and then they might turn again, and I would heal them.'

"But happy are your eyes because they see, and your ears because they hear! Many prophets and saints, I tell you, desired to see what you now see, yet never saw it; to hear what you hear, yet never heard it." (Matt. 13:10–17)

This passage makes clear especially two things:

(a) To the disciples, or to those who receive the presence of Jesus for what it is, is given to know the secrets of the Kingdom of heaven. What this phrase means we need not for the moment enquire. But it surely signifies at least some momentous truth.

(b) In the ministry of Jesus, men are confronted with something unprecedented. What the prophets had desired to see but had not—they can now see. Note especially Matthew 13:16–17: "But happy are your eyes because they see, and your ears because they hear! Many prophets and saints, I tell you, desired to see what you now see, yet never saw it; to hear what you hear, yet never heard it."

I tell you this: never has there appeared on earth a mother's son greater than John the Baptist, and yet the least in the kingdom of Heaven is greater than he.
Ever since the coming of John the Baptist the kingdom of Heaven has been subjected to violence and violent men are seizing it. For all the prophets and the Law foretold things to come until John appeared, and John is the destined Elijah, if you will but accept it. If you have ears that can hear, then hear. (Matt. 11:11–15)

It agrees with all the above that here in 11:11 ff. (compare Luke 16:16 f.) there is offered to us a division of history into two orders. A line is drawn between the order of the prophets, an order of expectation only, and the order of Jesus, an order of realization.

What was meant by the "New Order"

How is this "new order" to be understood? Paul speaks of a "new creation." He compares the coming of the "new order" in Christ with that of the first creation. But although this interpretation of it does emerge in parts of the Gospels, it is not a central one. We here encounter the necessity for the leap of language which we mentioned previously. What precisely do the above passages imply? Although we cannot exactly define the words employed, we can see the accompaniments of this "new order." We note four things:

(1) *It brings judgment.*

On the Temple, Mark 11:11, 15–18:

> He entered Jerusalem and went into the temple, where he looked at the whole scene; but, as it was now late, he went out to Bethany with the Twelve.
>
> So they came to Jerusalem, and he went into the temple and began driving out those who bought and sold in the temple. He upset the tables of the money-changers and the seats of the dealers in pigeons; and he would not allow anyone to use the temple court as a thoroughfare for carrying goods. Then he began to teach them, and said, "Does not Scripture say, 'My house shall be called a house of prayer for all the nations'? But you have made it a robbers' cave." The chief priests and the doctors of the law heard of this and sought some means of making away with him; for they were afraid of him, because the whole crowd was spellbound by his teaching.

On the Fig Tree, Mark 11:12–14 (The Fig Tree probably stands for Israel):

> On the following day, after they had left Bethany, he felt hungry, and, noticing in the distance a fig tree in leaf, he went to see if he could find anything on it. But when he came

there he found nothing but leaves; for it was not the season for figs. He said to the tree, "May no one ever again eat fruit from you!" And his disciples were listening.

On Israel, Mark 12:1–12:

He went on to speak to them in parables: "A man planted a vineyard and put a wall round it, hewed out a winepress, and built a watch-tower; then he let it out to vine-growers and went abroad. When the vintage season came, he sent a servant to the tenants to collect from them his share of the produce. But they took him, thrashed him, and sent him away empty-handed. Again, he sent them another servant, whom they beat about the head and treated outrageously. So he sent another, and that one they killed; and many more besides, of whom they beat some, and killed others. He had now only one left to send, his own dear son. In the end he sent him. 'They will respect my son,' he said. But the tenants said to one another, 'This is the heir; come, let us kill him, and the property will be ours.' So they seized him and killed him, and flung his body out of the vineyard. What will the owner of the vineyard do? He will come and put the tenants to death and give the vineyard to others.

"Can it be that you have never read this text: 'The stone which the builders rejected has become the main cornerstone. This is the Lord's doing, and it is wonderful in our eyes'?"

Then they began to look for a way to arrest him, for they saw that the parable was aimed at them; but they were afraid of popular feeling, so they left him alone and went away.

(2) *It brings to birth a New Israel.*
See Mark 12:1–12, cited above, and the following:

Then Jesus spoke to them again in parables: "The kingdom of Heaven is like this. There was a king who prepared a feast for his son's wedding; but when he sent his servants to summon the guests he had invited, they would not come. He sent others again, telling them to say to the guests, 'See now! I have prepared this feast for you. I have had my bullocks and fatted beasts slaughtered; everything is ready; come to the wedding at once.' But they took no notice; one went off to his farm, another to his business, and the others seized the servants, attacked them brutally, and killed them. The king was furious; he sent troops to kill those murderers and set their town on fire. Then he said to his servants, 'The wedding-feast is ready; but the guests I invited did not deserve the honour. Go out to the main thoroughfares, and invite everyone you can find to the wedding.' The servants went out into the streets, and collected all they could find, good and bad alike. So the hall was packed with guests." (Matt. 22:1–10)

(3) *It is a time of harvest, of cutting and reaping.*

So Jesus went round all the towns and villages teaching in their synagogues, announcing the good news of the Kingdom, and curing every kind of ailment and disease. The sight of the people moved him to pity: they were like sheep without a shepherd, harassed and helpless; and he said to his disciples, "The crop is heavy, but labourers are scarce; you must therefore beg the owner to send labourers to harvest his crop" (Matt. 9:35–38).

(4) *It brings victory over evil.*

He entered a house; and once more such a crowd collected round them that they had no chance to eat. When his family heard of this, they set out to take charge of him; for people were saying that he was out of his mind.

The doctors of the law, too, who had come down from Jerusalem, said, "He is possessed by Beelzebub," and, "He drives out devils by the prince of devils." So he called them to come forward, and spoke to them in parables: "How can Satan drive out Satan? If a kingdom is divided against itself, that kingdom cannot stand; if a household is divided against itself, that house will never stand; and if Satan is in rebellion against himself, he is divided and cannot stand; and that is the end of him.

"On the other hand, no one can break into a strong man's house and make off with his goods unless he has first tied the strong man up; then he can ransack the house." (Mk. 3:20–27)

But if it is by the Spirit of God that I drive out the devils, then be sure the kingdom of God has already come upon you. (Matt. 12:28)

All the Gospels point to the same fact: the coming of Jesus was a crisis, *the* crisis, in world history; he brings judgment, new birth, victory over evil.

CHAPTER 13

THE GOSPEL OF THE KINGDOM OF GOD

The Synoptic Gospels, then, like the rest of the New Testament, set forth the coming of Jesus of Nazareth as the beginning of a new order and the culmination of an old order. Do they use any terms to express this in shorthand, as it were? They do. They use the two familiar terms "The Gospel," that is, The Good News, and "The Kingdom of God." The coming of Jesus constitutes "The Good News" and can be understood in terms of the coming of God's Kingdom, or, to be more accurate, God's Rule.

The meaning of the term "Gospel"

Such a term as "The Gospel" seems self-explanatory; does it not simply mean that Jesus is "The Good News" for men? But, as we have so often seen previously, many of the words used in the New Testament have undertones of meaning which we can only painfully discover. "The Gospel" is one of these terms. Its meaning is as difficult to pin down exactly as such phrases as "The New Deal" or "The New Frontier"—phrases that are familiar enough and yet imprecise. What did the term "The Gospel" convey to Christians who read the Synoptic Gospels?

It is clear that the term is a Greek one, and some have urged strongly that it must be understood in the light of its meaning for Greeks and Romans in the first century. For these the word "gospel" had one particularly interesting connotation. In the sources we have, the term was used, in the plural number, in connection with the worship of the Emperors. The birthday of a Roman Emperor, who had come to be regarded as a divine being, was claimed to bring with it "gospels," "good news" or benefits. Similarly, the whole course of the Emperor's life might be called "gospels," that is, a series of benefits or blessings constituting "good news," and especially the gift of peace. The suggestion has been made that, when early Christians made use of the *singular* term "The Gospel" (notice the article "The") to describe the coming of Jesus, they deliberately set their good news—the *one* good news (this is the force of the article)—over against the many benefits of a lesser kind, claimed to be brought by the Roman Emperors who (as Christians thought) were foolishly worshipped. Jesus brought the one essential "good news," "The Gospel": Emperors brought only "gospels"—benefits, following one after the other to no avail. The great poet of the Roman Empire, Virgil (70–19 B.C.), had celebrated the birth of a child when

the great line of the centuries begins anew.[16]

This could only be true of the birth of Jesus! So *might* an early Christian, who *might* have known of Virgil's expectation, have exclaimed! We know that Luke was aware that Jesus could be set over against the Emperor, because he himself set the birth of Jesus deliberately in the reign of Caesar Augustus (2:1) and refers to Christians as those who said that there was another king than Caesar (Acts 17:7). The term "The Gospel," then, could evoke a contrast between the King of Kings and the Caesars.

But this was at a time when the Church had become suspicious of the State and the State hostile to her. It is unlikely that, at the beginning, Christians consciously used the term in opposition to Emperor worship. Paul at least was probably even anxious not to do so; he avoided the term "Kingdom" in setting forth "The Gospel" for this reason and was not anti-imperial. In Romans 13:1–7, Paul sets forth his attitude to the State.

Every person must submit to the supreme authorities. There is no authority but by act of God, and the existing authorities are instituted by him; consequently anyone who rebels against authority is resisting a divine institution, and those who so resist have themselves to thank for the punishment they will receive. For government, a terror to crime, has no terrors for good behaviour. You wish to have no fear of the authorities? Then continue to do right and you will have their approval, for they are God's agents working for your good. But if you are doing wrong, then you will have cause to fear them; it is not for nothing that they hold the power of the sword, for they are God's agents of punishment, for retribution on the offender. That is why you are obliged to submit. It is an obligation imposed not merely by fear of retribution but by conscience. That is also why you pay taxes. The authorities are in God's service and to these duties they devote their energies.

Discharge your obligations to all men; pay tax and toll, reverence and respect, to those to whom they are due.

For a man who wrote the above, it is unlikely that the term "The Gospel" had a polemic intent against the Emperor.

To understand the term, therefore, it is more likely that we should follow those who have explained it in the light of the Old Testament and Judaism. The noun "The Gospel," in the singular number, does not occur in the Old Testament, but the verb meaning "to bring good news" occurs in several passages. In I Kings 1:42, it is used of bringing the good news that David had made Solomon king. In Jeremiah 20:15, it describes the good news of the birth of a son. It is used especially of bringing good news of a victory in battle, as in I Samuel 31:8–10:

On the morrow, when the Philistines came to strip the slain, they found Saul and his three sons fallen on Mount Gilboa. And they cut off his head, and stripped off his armor, and sent messengers throughout the land of the Philistines, to carry the good news to their idols and to the people. They put his armor in the temple of Ashtaroth; and they fastened his body to the wall of Bethshan.

Compare with this passage I Chronicles 10:8–10, which is parallel. Three things, therefore, are clear about the verb "to bring good news," from which the term "The Gospel" comes:

1. It contains the idea of joyous, good news.
2. It is associated with the idea of victory in battle.
3. It is used of a celebration in, or in connection with, a sanctuary; that is, it has a religious nuance at times.

But most scholars have turned to one portion of the Old Testament in particular for the understanding of the term "The Gospel"—to what is referred to usually as the Second-Isaiah, who wrote Isaiah 40 and many chapters that followed. Second-Isaiah (so-called merely to distinguish him from the author of Isaiah 1–39) wrote at a time when the people of Israel were in exile in the Babylonian Empire; they were in a strange land, weeping for their homeland and longing for Jerusalem. To such a people the prophet brought a message of hope. He looked forward to a time when the exile would come to an end and "Israel" would be returned to her own land. Then a new age or a new world would dawn. God's victory over the foes of Israel would be assured; his rule or reign would be established in the earth. God would act in such a way in delivering his people that the might of his arm would be revealed. But before all this would happen, the prophet claims that God would send a messenger, an evangelist, to foretell this event, that is, to proclaim the good news of God's imminent intervention or salvation. And so the prophet issues his word of comfort to his people as follows:

> Comfort, comfort my people,
>   says your God.
> Speak tenderly to Jerusalem,
>   and cry to her
> that her warfare is ended,
>   that her iniquity is pardoned,
> that she has received from the
>   Lord's hand
>   double for all her sins.

A voice cries:
"In the wilderness prepare the way
   of the Lord,
      make straight in the desert a
      highway for our God.
Every valley shall be lifted up,
   and every mountain and hill be
   made low;
the uneven ground shall become
   level,
      and the rough places a plain.
And the glory of the Lord shall be
   revealed,
      and all flesh shall see it together,
      for the mouth of the Lord has
spoken." (Is. 40:1–5)

And again, in Isaiah 52:7–10:

How beautiful upon the mountains
   are the feet of him who brings
      good tidings,
who publishes peace, who brings
   good tidings of good,
   who publishes salvation,
   who says to Zion, "Your God
   reigns."
Hark, your watchmen lift up their
   voice,
   together they sing for joy;
for eye to eye they see
   the return of the Lord to Zion.
Break forth together into singing,
   you waste places of Jerusalem;
for the Lord has comforted his people,
   he has redeemed Jerusalem.
The Lord has bared his holy arm
   before the eyes of all the nations;
and all the ends of the earth shall see
   the salvation of our God.

The frequency with which Second-Isaiah is quoted in the New Testament justifies us in setting the term "The Gospel," in view of what we have written above, in his light. To refer the term "The Gospel" to the coming of Jesus implies, therefore, that a decisive victory over God's enemies has been achieved; a battle has been fought and won against the foes of "Israel" and her God; the redeeming or liberating power of God has been revealed; freedom has been achieved. There is, in short, a new age or epoch; the hope of "Israel" has been fulfilled. What the prophet had longed for has been realized. This figure, Jesus of Nazareth, may have been set over against Caesar but more important is it to recognize that, when he was interpreted in terms of "The Gospel," he was acknowledged as the inaugurator of a new epoch. A new beginning had been made in him; God had visited the world to emancipate it from evil and to establish his rule.

The Kingdom or Rule of God

The last term mentioned—the Rule of God—is a convenient point of transition to the other term which the Synoptic Gospels use to set forth the significance of the coming of Jesus of Nazareth. The evangelists not only describe the new order as "The Gospel," they refer to it also in terms of what they call "The Kingdom or the Rule of God." This concept is central for the understanding of the Synoptic Gospels. In Mark 1:14 f., there appears a summary statement of the ministry of Jesus of Nazareth, a "formula" giving the Gospel in a nutshell. It reads:

> After John had been arrested, Jesus came into Galilee proclaiming the Gospel of God: "The time has come; the kingdom of God is upon you; repent, and believe the Gospel."

Here the Gospel consists of two pronouncements—the time is fulfilled and the Kingdom of God is at hand. What does this second phrase, with which The Gospel is, at least partially, identified, mean? Unlike the term "The Gospel" it does not turn our thoughts to the Graeco-Roman world. But like that term, it does direct us to Judaism. It has an unmistakably Jewish ring.

Oddly enough, however, the phrase "The Kingdom of God" occurs only seldom in the Old Testament. In the earlier books, in the few places where it does occur, it usually has a political meaning. The Kingdom of the historical "Israel" in its various forms is the Kingdom of God. Only later in the Book of Daniel, written between 168 and 165 B.C., is there a clear distinction between the kingdoms of this present world and a future Kingdom of God. In 2:44–45, after listing the passing kingdoms of history as he knew them, the author writes:

> And in the days of those kings the God of heaven will set up a kingdom which shall never be destroyed, nor shall its sovereignty be left to another people. It shall break in pieces all these kingdoms and bring them to an end, and it shall stand for ever; just as you saw that a stone was cut from a mountain by no human hand, and that it broke in pieces the iron, the bronze, the clay, the silver, and the gold. A great God has made known to the king what shall be hereafter. The dream is certain, and its interpretation sure.

And at the end of history, in 2:44, 7:27, God hands over his ever-lasting kingdom to the people of his choice: the kingdoms of history rise and fall; beyond them God's Kingdom will stand. But it cannot be claimed that the Kingdom of God, as an express phrase or concept, plays a marked role in the Old Testament.

On the other hand, the idea that God is King is found throughout the Old Testament. Here religion, as always, reflects the culture within which it arises. The concept of God as King is an Oriental one. As the Oriental monarch or chieftain, so the Oriental God. God commands; his subjects are meant to obey. In return, just as the Semite expected his king to secure his subjects justice and protection, so God helps his worshippers in judgment and salvation. He rules. The marks of his rule we may sum up as follows:

1. *It is timeless:* "The Lord will reign for ever and ever" (Exod. 15:18).

> All thy works shall give thanks to thee, O Lord,
>   and all thy saints shall bless thee!
> They shall speak of the glory of thy kingdom,
>   and tell of thy power,
> to make known to the sons of men thy mighty deeds,
>   and the glorious splendor of thy kingdom.
> Thy kingdom is an everlasting kingdom,
>   and thy dominion endures throughout all generations.
> The Lord is faithful in all his words,
>   and gracious in all his deeds. (Ps. 145:10–13)

> The Lord will reign for ever,
>   thy God, O Zion, to all generations.
> Praise the Lord! (Ps. 146:10)

2. *It is closely connected with the people "Israel."* In the pre-exilic period, the Kingship or Rule of God is asserted over Israel. God alone is the true King of Israel and, in the mind of many, it is against his wishes that a human king was elected (I Sam. 8; 12:12). Even in the period after the exile, God is the King of Jacob (Is. 41:21), the Creator of Israel in particular (Is. 43:15), the King of Israel (Is. 44:6).

3. *In many passages the Kingship or rule is a hope or an expectation.*

> On that day the Lord will punish
>   the host of heaven, in heaven,
>   and the kings of the earth, on the earth.
> They will be gathered together
>   as prisoners in a pit;
> they will be shut up in a prison,
>   and after many days they will be punished.
> Then the moon will be confounded,
>   and the sun ashamed;
> for the Lord of hosts will reign
>   on Mount Zion and in Jerusalem
> and before his elders he will manifest his glory. (Is. 24:21–23)

> For the Lord is our judge, the Lord
>   is our ruler,
>   the Lord is our king; he will save us. (Is. 33:22)

Sing aloud, O daughter of Zion;
   shout, O Israel!
Rejoice and exult with all your heart,
   O daughter of Jerusalem!
The Lord has taken away the judgments against you,
   he has cast out your enemies.
The King of Israel, the Lord, is in your midst;
   you shall fear evil no more.
On that day it shall be said to Jerusalem:
"Do not fear, O Zion;
   let not your hands grow weak.
The Lord, your God, is in your midst,
   a warrior who gives victory;
he will rejoice over you with gladness,
   he will renew you in his love;
he will exult over you with loud singing
   as on a day of festival.
I will remove disaster from you,
   so that you will not bear reproach for it." (Zeph. 3:14-18)

Then every one that survives of all the nations that have come against Jerusalem shall go up year after year to worship the King, the Lord of hosts, and to keep the feast of booths. (Zech. 14:16)

Increasingly, then, the Kingship of God was interpreted as belonging to the future. God was, indeed, King in the present. But his Kingship was not obvious. At present, the rule of evil was too real to allow God's rule to be apparent. God's rule was in hiding. But, at long last, it would manifest itself.

What men expected from the Kingdom

The expectation of a future when God would establish his rule, that is, act decisively in history, was very vivid in the time of Jesus. Among the prayers of the synagogue which Jesus attended at Nazareth, he would probably have found a version of the following, which is still used in synagogues:

Magnified and sanctified be His great Name in the world which He hath created according to His will. May He establish His Kingdom during your life and during your days, and during the life of all the house of Israel, even speedily and at a near time; and say ye, Amen.

But what would the coming of God's Rule or Kingdom mean? There were varieties of expectations. Just as the Utopias about which men have dreamed have ranged from that of Thomas More to that of H. G. Wells, so Jews have differed in their understanding of the "good time" to come when God would establish his rule. Many colored the future in the light of the present, and interpreted it as deliverance from the typical evils of their day—foreign domination, the scattering of the people, the oppression by the wealthy. The views of the humble poor, among whom Jesus was reared and whose expectations he is claimed to have fulfilled, can be gathered from words used by Mary in Luke 1:46–55:

Tell out, my soul, the greatness of the Lord,
rejoice, rejoice, my spirit, in God my saviour;
so tenderly has he looked upon his servant,
    humble as she is.
For, from this day forth,
all generations will count me blessed,
so wonderfully has he dealt with me,
    the Lord, the Mighty One.
    His name is Holy;
his mercy sure from generation to generation
    toward those who fear him;
the deeds his own right arm has done
    disclose his might:
the arrogant of heart and mind he has put to rout,
he has torn imperial powers from their thrones,
    but the humble have been lifted high.

The hungry he has satisfied with good things,
    the rich sent empty away.
He has ranged himself at the side of Israel his servant;
    firm in his promise to our forefathers,
he has not forgotten to show mercy to Abraham
    and his children's children, for ever.

Or, again, by Zechariah in Luke 1:68–79:

Praise to the God of Israel!
For he has turned to his people, saved them and set them free,
and has raised up a deliverer of victorious power
    from the house of his servant David.
So he promised: age after age he proclaimed
    by the lips of his holy prophets,
that he would deliver us from our enemies,
    out of the hands of all who hate us;
that he would deal mercifully with our fathers,
    calling to mind his solemn covenant.
Such was the oath he swore to our father Abraham,
    to rescue us from enemy hands,
and grant us, free from fear, to worship him
    with a holy worship, with uprightness of heart,
    in his presence, our whole life long.
And you, my child, you shall be called Prophet of the Highest,
for you will be the Lord's forerunner, to prepare his way
    and lead his people to salvation through knowledge of him,
    by the forgiveness of their sins:
for in the tender compassion of our God
    the morning sun from heaven will rise upon us,
to shine on those who live in darkness, under the cloud of death,
    and to guide our feet into the way of peace.

Even some of the Pharisees, refined as they were, had what we might call a "jingoistic" or nationalistic view of the future rule of God. In the *Psalms of Solomon*, XVII, which are probably Pharisaic in character, there are long passages depicting what God's future vicegerent, The Messiah, would do.

O Lord, Thou art our King for ever and ever,
   For in Thee, O God, doth our soul glory.
How long are the days of man's life upon the earth?
   As are his days, so is the hope (set) upon him.
But we hope in God, our deliverer;
For the might of our God is for ever with mercy,
   And the kingdom of our God is for ever over the nations in
      judgement.

. . . .

Behold, O Lord, and raise up unto them their king, the son of
   David,
   At the time in the which Thou seest, O God, that he may
      reign over Israel Thy servant.
And gird him with strength, that he may shatter unrighteous rulers.
   And that he may purge Jerusalem from nations that
      trample (her) down to destruction.
Wisely, righteously he shall thrust out sinners from (the)
      inheritance,
   He shall destroy the pride of the sinner as a potter's vessel.
With a rod of iron he shall break in pieces all their substance,
   He shall destroy the godless nations with the word of his mouth;
At his rebuke nations shall flee before him,
   And he shall reprove sinners for the thoughts of their heart.

And he shall gather together a holy people, whom he shall lead
   in righteousness,
   And he shall judge the tribes of the people that has been
      sanctified by the Lord his God.
And he shall not suffer unrighteousness to lodge any more in
   their midst,
   Nor shall there dwell with them any man that knoweth wicked-
      ness,
   For he shall know them, that they are all sons of their God.
And he shall divide them according to their tribes upon the land,
   And neither sojourner nor alien shall sojourn with them any more.
He shall judge peoples and nations in the wisdom of his righteous-
      ness.

                                                        Selah.

And he shall have the heathen nations to serve him under his yoke;
  And he shall glorify the Lord in a place to be seen of (?)
  all the earth;
  And he shall purge Jerusalem, making it holy as of old:
So that nations shall come from the ends of the earth to see his
  glory,
  Bringing as gifts her sons who had fainted,
  And to see the glory of the Lord, wherewith God hath glorified
  her.
And he (shall be) a righteous king, taught of God, over them,
And there shall be no unrighteousness in his days in their midst,
  For all shall be holy and their king the anointed of the Lord.
For he shall not put his trust in horse and rider and bow,
  Nor shall he multiply for himself gold and silver for war,
  Nor shall he gather confidence from (?) a multitude (?) for
  the day of battle.
The Lord Himself is his king, the hope of him that is mighty
  through (his) hope in God.

All nations (shall be) in fear before him,
  For he will smite the earth with the word of his mouth for ever.
He will bless the people of the Lord with wisdom and gladness,
  And he himself (will be) pure from sin, so that he may rule a
  great people.
He will rebuke rulers, and remove sinners by the might of his word;
  And (relying) upon his God, throughout his days he will not
  stumble;
For God will make him mighty by means of (His) holy spirit,
  And wise by means of the spirit of understanding, with strength
  and righteousness.
And the blessing of the Lord (will be) with him: he will be strong
  and stumble not;
  His hope (will be) in the Lord: who then can prevail against
  him?
(He will be) mighty in his works, and strong in the fear of God,
  (He will be) shepherding the flock of the Lord faithfully and
  righteously,
  And will suffer none among them to stumble in their pasture.

He will lead them all aright,
> And there will be no pride among them that any among them
> should be oppressed.

This (will be) the majesty of the king of Israel whom God knoweth;
> He will raise him up over the house of Israel to correct him.

His words (shall be) more refined than costly gold, the choicest;
> In the assemblies he will judge the peoples, the tribes of the
> sanctified.

His words (shall be) like the words of the holy ones in the midst
of sanctified peoples.

Blessed be they that shall be in those days,
> In that they shall see the good fortune of Israel which God
> shall bring to pass in the gathering together of the tribes.

May the Lord hasten His mercy upon Israel!
> May He deliver us from the uncleanness of unholy enemies!

The Lord Himself is our king for ever and ever.

The future anticipated here resounds not only with righteousness but with judgment, not only with the ingathering of the scattered and the exaltation of Israel but with the slaughter of the ungodly. And the same picture of the future meets us again in the Dead Sea Scrolls. In one passage we read:

On the day of judgment God will exterminate from the
earth all those who serve idols, together with the sinners. (1 Qp
> Hab. XIII. 2–4)

But, in another passage:

And then shall the truth go forward in the world for ever . . .
And then will God in His truth purify all the deeds of a man—
and He will sprinkle him with a spirit of truth. (1 QS IV. 19–21)

Not all, perhaps, expected blood and thunder to accompany the future Rule of God, but many did, and the writers of the Gospels were familiar with their expectations.

The scandal of the Good News

The astounding nature of what the Gospels assert about Jesus, then, can only be appreciated over against these expectations.

The Gospels assert that, with Jesus, the Reign of God had drawn near and, indeed, had already begun. Was this really credible— that God was establishing his Rule in the life of Jesus? To believe this was to go against the cherished hopes of most of Judaism. To use a colloquialism, this was asking too much. This is what the Gospel writers mean when they claim that Jesus was a "scandal" to Israel.

But even granting this, is it at all conceivable that the Rule of God should be interpreted in terms of Jesus' ministry only? Evil was still rampant after his coming (and as Jewish leaders remind us constantly—it still is!). How then could it be claimed that the Kingdom of God had come? The answer is that in the Synoptic Gospels the Rule of God is not depicted as having fully or finally asserted itself. The new order has come, but the old order has not yet fully passed away. And so in the Synoptic Gospels there is a twofold aspect to the Kingdom of God—it is present, exerting itself in the works and words of Jesus, but its full force is yet to be revealed. This is the meaning of those many passages in which the Synoptics describe a future coming of Jesus and refer the Kingdom of God to the future. This is why the Lord's Prayer prays for the coming of the Kingdom, even though it is already present in Jesus. A future note creeps in again and again in all the Gospels. We may quote only one passage from Mark 13:24–27:

> But in those days, after that distress, the sun will be darkened, the moon will not give her light; the stars will come falling from the sky, the celestial powers will be shaken. Then they will see the Son of Man coming in the clouds with great power and glory, and he will send out the angels and gather his chosen from the four winds, from the farthest bounds of earth to the farthest bounds of heaven.

But however much such notes of an impending doom break into the Synoptics, it is the other note that is most persistent: the coming of Jesus *now* is "The Gospel." He himself, as he walks through Galilee and goes up to Jerusalem, healing, forgiving, teaching, is *here* and *now* showing what God's Rule really is. In short, the Gospels assert that the figure of Jesus has become the revelation of God's Rule. To look at him with clear sight is to see what God's Rule is like and what it demands of men. The Rule of God—God's will—is active in him; this is the stupendous claim of the Synoptics. History has taken a decisive turn in him. An illustration may clarify this point. One Sunday, during World War II, I was walking home from Church when a friend accosted me and said, "Have you heard the news?" I said, "What news?" And he replied, "Hitler has invaded Russia." And at once I answered, "Then the Allies have won the war." This was in 1943, and the war went on till 1946. But I knew—as did all who knew the history of Napoleon—that, once Hitler had engaged in a war on two fronts, West and East, his defeat was certain, however long the war continued. The turning point of World War II was the invasion of Russia. So, too, when early Christians sought to assess the significance of Jesus. In him, God's will had broken into their ken with marvellous intensity; they knew that a decisive turn had taken place in man's age-long struggle with evil. That struggle might go on for some time, but the decisive battle in it had already been won—in the life and death and resurrection of Jesus. In him, a break had been made with all the past; the Kingdom of God had come; man's war was over, although man's battles continued. A new order—the order of God's rule, understood in the light of Jesus, had arrived—this was the Good News. And because his light was so different from the light expected—this Good News became a scandal.

CHAPTER 14

THE SCRIPTURES FULFILLED

The first motif we emphasized in the Synoptic Gospels is the sense that in the appearance of Jesus a new order has come into being. History has taken a decisive turn. In this sense, Christianity is new; it inaugurates a new era; it is "The Gospel," the advent of God's Rule.

But there are passages in the Gospels which seem to contradict this. They suggest that "The Gospel" is not only new but also old; that while it is a new beginning in history, it is also the culmination of a long process stretching into the past. What is this long process which finds its completion in the coming of Jesus? It is the process revealed in the Old Testament—the process through which God had been creating for himself a people obedient to himself and thus ready to serve him in history, an "Israel" of God. This process has now reached its end, so the Gospels claim, in Jesus of Nazareth, who was obedient. In him, the purpose of God is fulfilled and the people of God brought to a new birth.

This conviction that the ministry of Jesus is the culmination of a long process that had been going on for centuries is expressed in the Gospels in one exceptionally clear way. They all assert that in the ministry of Jesus the Scriptures have been fulfilled; the ministry of Jesus is "according to the Scriptures" or "as it is written." The Church, as its thought is revealed in the Gospels, declared not only that the ministry of Jesus was in accordance with God's will but in accordance with God's will as it was defined or revealed in the Old Testament. This is why the writers of the New Testament are constantly adducing passages from the Old in order to expound the meaning of the events of the Gospel story. They imply that it is only over against the setting of the Old Testament that the meaning of the coming of Jesus is to be understood. In this sense, the Gospels themselves are a continuation of the Old Testament; they are its outcome and fulfillment.

The Testimonies of the Early Church

In working out this conviction, that the ministry of Jesus is the fulfillment of God's purpose revealed in the Old Testament, the Church displayed remarkable insight and intellectual acumen. Christians probably used collections of Old Testament texts, to which the name *Testimonia* (testimonies) has been given; these contained passages which *testified* to Jesus as the Messiah. Fortunately, some of these *Testimonia* have survived; the earliest we have is that used by Cyprian (died A.D. 258); it is entitled *"Testimonia against the Jews. Three books of testimonies against the Jews."* Until recently there was some doubt whether we should assume the existence of specific collections of *testimonia* in the first century. But the discovery of the Dead Sea Scrolls, which include *testimonia* for the use of the Dead Sea Sect, makes it highly probable that the earliest Christians had such *testimonia* also. Even if there were no books of *testimonia,* it is certain that the early Church did make frequent use of certain well-defined blocks of Old Testament passages.

The early Church was in some respects like a Bible class or Bible school. We can see its scholastic activity from stray references in Acts, for example. Think of the following passages: Acts 17:2: "And Paul went in, as was his custom, and for three weeks he argued with them from the scriptures, . . ." This was at Thessalonica. Or again, Acts 18:28: ". . . . for he powerfully confuted the Jews in public, showing by the scriptures that the Christ was Jesus." This was at Corinth.

We need not doubt the truth of the picture of Paul that Acts gives here. Paul spent a great deal of his time as an exegete. And what was true of Paul was true of the writers of the Gospels. They used the Old Testament as a foil for the ministry of Jesus and drew upon it for their interpretation. This process can be illustrated abundantly.

The ministry of Jesus in the light of the Old Testament

Passages from the Old Testament are quoted to illustrate or expound the fact that a new order had arrived in Jesus. Let us look at Mark 1:1–3. It reads as follows:

> Here begins the Gospel of Jesus Christ the Son of God.
> In the prophet Isaiah it stands written: "Here is my herald whom I send on ahead of you, and he will prepare your way. A voice crying aloud in the wilderness, 'Prepare a way for the Lord; clear a straight path for him.'"

In this passage Mark applies to the figure of John the Baptist two passages; the first is from Malachi 3:1: "Behold, I send my messenger to prepare the way before me, and the Lord whom you seek will suddenly come to his temple; the messenger of the covenant in whom you delight, behold, he is coming, says the Lord of hosts." If we look at the context of this quotation in Malachi we find the following:

> Behold, I send my messenger to prepare the way before me, and the Lord whom you seek will suddenly come to his temple; the messenger of the covenant in whom you delight, behold, he is coming, says the Lord of hosts. But who can endure the day of his coming, and who can stand when he appears?
> For he is like a refiner's fire and like fullers' soap; he will sit as a refiner and purifier of silver, and he will purify the sons of Levi and refine them like gold and silver, till they present right offerings to the Lord. (3:1–3)

Malachi looks forward to a time when God would send a messenger to prepare for his advent. He would exercise judgment, like that of fire, and bring purification and redemption. Mark sees in the figure of John the Baptist this predicted messenger who precedes the Lord's coming.

Similarly, Mark applies to John the Baptist a quotation from Isaiah 40:3–5:

> A voice cries:
> "In the wilderness prepare the way of the Lord,
>   make straight in the desert a highway for our God.
> Every valley shall be lifted up,
>   and every mountain and hill be made low;
> the uneven ground shall become level,
>   and the rough places a plain.
> And the glory of the Lord shall be revealed,
>   and all flesh shall see it together,
>   for the mouth of the Lord has spoken."

John the Baptist is the "voice," and he again precedes the revelation of the glory of God in Jesus Christ. By applying to the Baptist these two passages, Mark sets him forth as the forerunner of the coming of God's glory, for which the prophets had hoped. In this way the very threshold of the ministry of Jesus is a fulfillment.

But the coming of Jesus itself also fulfills prophetic hopes. The coming of Jesus was a victory over evil. But notice how this victory over evil is understood. The victory is over the demons. This is how it is expressed in Mark when he describes controversy over the casting out of demons by Jesus:

> The doctors of the law, too, who had come down from Jerusalem, said, "He is possessed by Beelzebub," and, "He drives out devils by the prince of devils." So he called them to come forward, and spoke to them in parables: "How can Satan drive out Satan? If a kingdom is divided against itself, that kingdom cannot stand; if a household is divided against itself, that house will never stand; and if Satan is in rebellion against himself,

he is divided and cannot stand; and that is the end of him.

"On the other hand, no one can break into a strong man's house and make off with his goods unless he has first tied the strong man up; then he can ransack the house." (3:22–27)

At first there seems to be no reference to the Old Testament in this passage. But if you turn to Isaiah 49:24–25, you will find there a parallel to the Markan passage. In the passage in Isaiah, there is a description of what was to happen when God should save his people; he would deliver the captive prey of a tyrant.

> Can the prey be taken from the mighty,
>   or the captives of a tyrant be rescued?
> Surely, thus says the Lord:
> "Even the captives of the mighty shall be taken,
>   and the prey of the tyrant be rescued,
> for I will contend with those who contend with you,
>   and I will save your children . . ."

It is this passage which probably lies behind Mark 3:22–27. The conditions described in the prophecy of Second-Isaiah have been realized in the ministry of Jesus, who sets at liberty those who are bound to the demonic.

In the same way, whenever Mark wants to exemplify the judgment which the coming of Jesus brings, he expounds this judgment in the light of the Old Testament. Let us take only one illustration of this from Mark 12:1–12, which we quoted above. After tracing allegorically the history of Israel and its treatment of the son sent to them, Mark adds:

> What will the owner of the vineyard do? He will come and put the tenants to death and give the vineyard to others.
> Can it be that you have never read this text: "The stone which the builders rejected has become the main cornerstone. This is the Lord's doing, and it is wonderful in our eyes"?

The son rejected by the old Israel has become the head of a new Israel. The evangelist understands the rejection and exaltation of Christ here in terms of Psalm 118:22–23:

> The stone which the builders rejected
>   has become the chief cornerstone.
> This is the Lord's doing;
>   it is marvelous in our eyes.

In the Psalm it is *Israel*, rejected by the nations, pushed hard by them, surrounded by them like bees, that is the stone that has become the head of the corner. What the Psalmist applied to the old Israel is applied in Mark to Jesus, who becomes the new Israel.

Similarly, the judgment on the Temple is interpreted in terms of Jeremiah 7:11 in Mark 11:15–17:

> So they came to Jerusalem, and he went into the temple and began driving out those who bought and sold in the temple. He upset the tables of the money-changers and the seats of the dealers in pigeons; and he would not allow anyone to use the temple court as a thoroughfare for carrying goods. Then he began to teach them, and said, "Does not Scripture say, 'My house shall be called a house of prayer for all the nations'? But you have made it a robbers' cave."

When we turn to the positive aspect of the coming of Jesus, that is, his creation of a new people of God in history, we find the same reference to the Old Testament. In Mark 14:22–25, we read as follows:

> During supper he took bread, and having said the blessing he broke it and gave it to them, with the words: "Take this; this is my body." Then he took a cup, and having offered thanks to God he gave it to them; and they all drank from it. And he said, "This is my blood of the covenant, shed for many. I tell you this: never again shall I drink from the fruit of the vine until that day when I drink it new in the kingdom of God."

This reference to the blood of the covenant is inexplicable apart from Exodus 24:8; although there is no explicit reference to Jeremiah 31:31 f., we are also probably to read Jeremiah 31:31–34 into the passage:

Behold, the days are coming, says the Lord, when I will make a new covenant with the house of Israel and the house of Judah, not like the covenant which I made with their fathers when I took them by the hand to bring them out of the land of Egypt, my covenant which they broke, though I was their husband, says the Lord. But this is the covenant which I will make with the house of Israel after those days, says the Lord: I will put my law within them, and I will write it upon their hearts; and I will be their God, and they shall be my people. And no longer shall each man teach his neighbor and each his brother, saying, "Know the Lord," for they shall all know me, from the least of them to the greatest, says the Lord; for I will forgive their iniquity, and I will remember their sin no more.

At the Last Supper, Jesus fulfills the hope of Jeremiah for a new covenant. Especially noteworthy is the way in which the whole of the Passion narrative in Mark, as in the other Gospels, is riddled with references to the Old Testament.

Jesus himself in the light of the Old Testament

So far we have seen how the ministry of Jesus in his conquest over evil, its judgment, and its creation of a new Israel was understood over against the Old Testament in the Gospels. But Jesus himself—apart from the ministry which he exercised —was set in the light of the Old Testament. Thus, passages which in the Old Testament refer to Israel are applied in the New to Jesus himself. Look, for example, at the story of the Temptation given in Matthew and Luke:

Jesus was then led away by the Spirit into the wilderness, to be tempted by the devil.

For forty days and nights he fasted, and at the end of them he was famished. The tempter approached him and said, "If you are the Son of God, tell these stones to become bread." Jesus answered, "Scripture says, 'Man cannot live on bread alone; he lives on every word that God utters.'"

The devil then took him to the Holy City and set him on the parapet of the temple. "If you are the Son of God," he said, "throw yourself down; for Scripture says, 'He will put his angels in charge of you, and they will support you in their arms, for fear you should strike your foot against a stone.'" Jesus answered him, "Scripture says again, 'You are not to put the Lord your God to the test.'"

Once again, the devil took him to a very high mountain, and showed him all the kingdoms of the world in their glory. "All these," he said, "I will give you, if you will only fall down and do me homage." But Jesus said, "Begone, Satan; Scripture says, 'You shall do homage to the Lord your God and worship him alone.'"

Then the devil left him, and angels appeared and waited on him. (Matt. 4:1–11)

What the Old Testament applies to Israel in Deuteronomy 8 is applied there to Jesus: he relives in himself the trials and temptations of Israel. In Matthew 4:1–11 the phrase, "Scripture says" occurs four times, that is, it is emphatic. The section contains quotations from Deuteronomy 8:3, 8:16, and other Old Testament passages. Jesus is Israel—the true Israel. In an indirect way we also saw how, in Mark 1:1 f., John the Baptist is the forerunner of the Lord; but the Lord in Malachi 3:1, which Mark cites, is God himself, whereas in Mark 1:2, the term refers to Jesus. Passages dealing with the Lord God in the Old Testament are referred to Jesus in the New.

In addition to the kind of quotations to which we have already referred, there are other passages where the events and personages of the Old Testament become "types" of the events of the ministry of Jesus. This is particularly manifest in Matthew, but I have referred to this previously (see chapter 1).

We see, then, that the new order, which is Christianity, is inseparable from the Judaism from which it sprang. This means that the new order, although new, is continuous with the old. But, finally, one thing must be emphasized. Although continuous with the old, it is not determined by the old. It is important to recognize that not all the quotations from the Old Testament in the New are of equal importance. And, again (and this is of extreme importance), not all the Messianic prophecies of the Old Testament are used in the New. Certain prophecies were rejected by the Church. Why were they rejected? Because the Church was governed in its interpretation of the Old Testament by the history of Jesus himself. The evangelists were not engaged in formulating a picture of a Messianic figure, Jesus, on the basis of the Old Testament. Rather, they used the Old Testament to interpret certain events which they regarded as Messianic. It was the life of Jesus that determined their use of the Old Testament; it was not the Old Testament that determined their understanding of Jesus or formed their conception of the Messiah. Thus Jesus himself becomes for them the theme of prophecy but only of that prophecy which was congruous with him. The figure of Jesus in the Gospels is not an artificial construction woven out of Old Testament passages; it is not dictated by the expectations of Judaism. Rather, Jesus has become a means for the sifting and reinterpretation of those expectations. The Jesus whom the Church remembered controlled its use of the Old Testament. He was rooted in the Old Testament but also burst its bounds. The new order is new even when it is old; much as a daughter is both an expression of her mother and also a "new creature."

CHAPTER 15

THE AGENT OF THE KINGDOM

So far we have traced three motifs which run through the Synoptics: a new order has begun; the Kingdom of God has drawn near; the Scriptures have been fulfilled. These motifs imply two things: that the Gospel is both new and old. It introduces a radically new departure in history, and also brings to fulfillment the age-long purpose of God revealed in the Old Testament. In this chapter, a new question is asked. What is the role or significance of Jesus in this New Order in which the Old Testament is fulfilled? We shall find that Jesus himself, also, is understood as both rooted in the past and free from it.

We find certain terms applied to him in the Synoptics, and we can best understand his role by an examination of these terms. It is tempting to divide them into two groups: (1) those titles that connect Jesus with Judaism and the Old Testament and thus emphasize the continuity of the Gospel with the past; to these would belong the titles, Messiah, Son of Abraham, and, possibly, Son of God; (2) those titles which emphasize his discontinuity with the past; to these belongs particularly the title Son of Man. Such a division is too arbitrary to do full justice to the terms which, however distinct, nevertheless have certain features in common. I shall, therefore, deal with each title in turn without attempting to classify them.

The Messiah

The use of the title Messiah on the lips of Jesus is very sparse and suggests that, even if he used it at all, he was chary of using it too freely and unguardedly. But the Synoptic Gospels assume that Jesus is the Messiah. Note the following passages:

(1) Mark 1:11.
(2) The Temptation.
(3) Matthew 11:2–6: Reply to John the Baptist.
(4) The triumphal entry into Jerusalem (cf. Zech. 9:9).
(5) The trial before the High Priest.

Assuming, then, that for the Synoptic writers Jesus was the Messiah, not merely one like a king or a high priest who had been anointed, but *The* Messiah of Jewish expectation, what are we to understand by the term?

Recent discussion of it has been in the light of two major studies. The first is by a Jewish scholar, Joseph Klausner. His work published long ago has now been translated into English; it is called *The Messianic Idea in Israel*. According to Klausner, Judaism was governed by its past: its past had been inglorious. The Hebrews had been slaves in Egypt. But they had known a deliverer—Moses. He had rescued Israel from material, political, and spiritual bondage. Thus, the figure of Moses became a symbol of the Redeemer in general. And Judaism, therefore, came to picture its future—an ideal future—in terms of its past. There would be a new Exodus after the pattern of the first Exodus, and a new deliverer like the first deliverer. It was from this expectation of a new deliverer, like Moses, that there arose the expectation of the Messiah; the Exodus was the authentic embryo from which the Messianic idea of necessity developed. With the Exodus came to be associated also the figure of David. Thus, the Messiah who was to deliver Israel was both new Moses and Son of David. The expectation for a new Exodus through a new Moses and a Son of David was deepened and refined morally under the influence of the Prophets.

Over against the position taken by Klausner, stands that of the Norwegian scholar, Professor Mowinckel, in his work translated as *"He That Cometh."* He traces the development of the Messianic idea, not to the Exodus, but to the idea of kingship in Israel. The King in ancient Israel was called "The Anointed," "The Messiah." The King is marked by three things:

(1) A close relationship to Jahweh.
(2) A sacred character and office.
(3) An abnormal endowment with Holy Power.

At first, the King was the Priest of the people.

Mowinckel further connects the idea of the King in ancient Israel with the idea of the King in the ancient Near East. The enthronement of a king was, he thinks, an annual festival which re-enacted creation and thus gave new life to the world. A symbolic victory over the King's historical enemies was also enacted. Thus, the creation and the nation were sustained by the annual enthronement, and, in Israel, the moral renewal of the people was also effected.

But earthly kings always disappointed Israel. Anointed they were, but they remained unsatisfactory. They were moral failures; disasters occurred during their reigns. Thus the actual King was never really the Messiah, although designated as such. The ideal King, the Messiah, became an object of hope. One day the ideal King would appear to put things right— to renew creation and redeem the people both politically and morally.

All these ideas have to be borne in mind when we consider the significance of the title Messiah applied to Jesus in the

Synoptics. If we follow Klausner, the Messiah was understood as the final figure, comparable to, but greater than, the first Moses, inaugurating a new Exodus. If we follow Mowinckel, he is also the final figure with cosmic, political, and spiritual significance. As applied to Jesus, in the Synoptic Gospels it undergoes a certain modification. The Gospels reject the political connotation the term had; they refuse to think of Jesus as a political leader. But they retain its cosmic and moral or spiritual connotations. The Synoptics assert that Jesus is the final redeemer in two ways. He is the Lord of nature. This is part of the meaning of the nature miracles—walking on the sea and stilling the storm. Jesus has cosmic significance. But he also brings moral and spiritual and physical healing. His exorcisms and all his miracles of healing attest this.

To sum up. The Synoptics, in calling Jesus the Messiah, present him as the final figure of all history, the ultimate figure. But the term connects Jesus with the hopes of his people in the past; it emphasizes that Jesus is of the Jewish people; he does not depart from Israel. As Son of David, the Messiah, Jesus belongs to the royal house of Israel, a member of a hereditary family and community, part of the culture of Judaism. To call Jesus The Messiah was to preserve his Jewishness as well as his finality.

The Son of Abraham and Son of Adam

We suggested that the term "Messiah" connected Jesus with his roots in Judaism and in the Old Testament. Two other titles, at least, do the same. These are, first, the title "Son of Abraham," which is emphasized by Matthew (1:2–17) and used by Luke (3:23–33). Abraham is above all the father of all Jews, and the title "Son of Abraham" is designed to connect Jesus directly with the Jewish people. Secondly, he is the Son of Adam. This is made clear in the genealogy of Jesus given in

Luke 3. This means that he is flesh of our flesh and bone of our bone. Although there is no passage in the Synoptics where Jesus is called the Son of Adam, there is much in the Synoptics to suggest a connection between him and Adam. The temptation stories recall the temptation of Adam, at least in Mark; Jesus endures temptation as a man, like the first Adam. But these two titles—Son of Abraham and Son of Adam—are secondary; more important is the next term with which we shall deal.

The Son of God

The term "Son of God," as applied to Jesus, occurs about twenty-four times, either explicitly or implicitly, in the Synoptic Gospels. In certain passages it is used *absolutely*, that is, without qualification, as a title. Two passages are important:

> At that time Jesus spoke these words: "I thank thee, Father, Lord of heaven and earth, for hiding these things from the learned and wise, and revealing them to the simple. Yes, Father, such was thy choice. Everything is entrusted to me by my Father; and no one knows the Son but the Father, and no one knows the Father but the Son and those to whom the Son may choose to reveal him.
>
> "Come to me, all whose work is hard, whose load is heavy; and I will give you relief. Bend your necks to my yoke, and learn from me, for I am gentle and humble-hearted; and your souls will find relief. For my yoke is good to bear, my load is light." (Matt. 11:25–30)
>
> But about that day or that hour no one knows, not even the angels in heaven, not even the Son; only the Father. (Mk. 13:32)

It is further noteworthy that the term "Son of God" seems interchangeable with the terms "Messiah," and "Son of Man." This emerges clearly in Luke 22:66–70:

When day broke, the elders of the nation, chief priests, and doctors of the law assembled, and he was brought before their Council. "Tell us," they said, "are you the Messiah?" "If I tell you," he replied, "you will not believe me; and if I ask questions, you will not answer. But from now on, the Son of Man will be seated at the right hand of Almighty God." "You are the Son of God, then?" they all said, and he replied, "It is you who say I am."

In view of this passage are we to conclude that "Son of God" is a Messianic, Jewish title, and that we do not need to search further for its meaning; is it merely a synonym for the Messiah?

To answer this question we have to recall two possibilities:

(a) *The Hellenistic derivation of the term.* The term "Son of God" would convey a specific, easily-understood meaning to a Gentile in the first century. There was in Hellenistic religion in the first century an inability to appreciate the distance between the human and the divine. Gods and men were confused. In several ways, a man could be considered divine. First, especially in Egypt, kings were conceived as begotten of gods. This made it easy, as we saw, to regard the Roman emperors as divine. Secondly, religious teachers, such as Apollonius of Tyana (a neo-Pythagorean philosopher, born about 4 B.C., who pretended to miraculous powers), laid claim to divinity. Thirdly, any person who believed himself possessed of divine powers could claim to be a "divine man." Such men were twopence a dozen in the first century.

Clearly, if the use of the term "Son of God" is derived from Hellenistic circles, it cannot be regarded as having any profound significance. This fact indicates, perhaps, that the adjective "divine," in the Hellenistic sense, was not thought suitable for Jesus, and the absolute use of the term "The Son," points to a deeper meaning than was suggested by the Hellenistic usage.

(b) *The Jewish derivation of the term.* Can we discover what the title may have meant in a Jewish milieu? In Judaism, the title "The Son of God" is used in two ways:

(1) *Of the people of Israel.* The classic passage is Exodus 4:21–23:

> And the Lord said to Moses, "When you go back to Egypt, see that you do before Pharaoh all the miracles which I have put in your power; but I will harden his heart, so that he will not let the people go. And you shall say to Pharaoh, 'Thus says the Lord, Israel is my first-born son, and I say to you, "Let my son go that he may serve me"; if you refuse to let him go, behold, I will slay your first-born son.'"

Notice that it is God himself who calls the people his "son." This title continues throughout the Old Testament. Since the Exodus, Israel had been adopted by God as his "son." Hosea places on the lips of God loving words about Israel and an unforgettable description of his patience with his people:

> When Israel was a child, I loved him,
>   and out of Egypt I called my son.
>
> . . . .
>
> Yet it was I who taught Ephraim to walk,
>   I took them up in my arms;
>   but they did not know that I healed them.
> I led them with cords of compassion,
>   with the bands of love,
> and I became to them as one
>   who eases the yoke on their jaws,
>   and I bent down to them and fed them. (11:1, 3–4)

In both the Book of Exodus and Hosea, the people of Israel as a totality are thought of as "The Son of God." In addition, individual Israelites are also "sons." One example will suffice:

> Hear, O heavens, and give ear, O earth;
>   for the Lord has spoken:
> "Sons have I reared and brought up,
>   but they have rebelled against me." (Is. 1:2)

But a passage from Isaiah 63:15–16 deserves quotation because it shows so clearly how God is thought of as the father of Israel.

> Look down from heaven and see,
> from thy holy and glorious habitation.
> Where are thy zeal and thy might?
> The yearning of thy heart and thy compassion
> are withheld from me.
> For thou art our Father,
> though Abraham does not know us
> and Israel does not acknowledge us;
> thou, O Lord, art our Father,
> our Redeemer from of old is thy name.

By the time of Jesus, the idea that Israel was the Son of God had become generally accepted in Judaism. The people of Israel and Israelite individuals are the apple of God's eye; they are "sons."

We may rightly ask, therefore, whether, when Jesus is called "The Son of God," it is intended to suggest that he himself is "Israel." This seems to be the case, for example, in the stories of the birth of Jesus in the second chapter of Matthew. There Jesus as a child is carried down to Egypt. He is then taken back to Nazareth. Matthew sees in this a parallel to the calling of the people of Israel out of Egypt: "Out of Egypt have I called my son" (2:15; cf. Hos. 11:1). Jesus relives the experience of the people of Israel. So, too, as we saw previously, the temptations of Jesus recall the temptations endured by the people of Israel in the wilderness. There can be little doubt that the Synoptic Gospels find in Jesus the representative of the true Israel of God. This is part of the meaning of the title "The Son of God" which they attribute to him.

But this does not explain fully why Jesus is called "The Son" in an absolute sense, as if he were especially "The Son of God." This brings us to the second use of the title in Judaism.

(2) *Of the Israelite King.* In II Samuel 7:14, God gives a promise to David, the King, in the following terms:

> I will be his father, and he shall be my son. When he commits iniquity, I will chasten him with the rod of men, with the stripes of the sons of men; . . .

The King is peculiarly the Son of God. Note that God's relation to the King is conceived of as eternal: the King withstands the vicissitudes of history.

> I will tell of the decree of the Lord:
> He said to me, "You are my son,
>   today I have begotten you.
> Ask of me, and I will make the nations your heritage,
> And the ends of the earth your possession." (Ps. 2:7)

> He shall cry to me, "Thou art my Father,
>   my God, and the Rock of my salvation." (Ps. 89:26)

Since the Messianic King of the future was the ideal King, we might presume that the Messiah also was called "The Son of God." In fact, there is no evidence that this was so in Judaism. But whether in Judaism the titles Messiah and Son of God are interchangeable or not, they are so in the Synoptics. Jesus, who represents the people of Israel, is its King and The Son of God. He stands in a special relation to God.

The Fatherhood of God in Jesus

Can we penetrate further into this relationship as it applies to Jesus? Was there a personal significance to this title, as applied to Jesus, which the Synoptic Gospels intended to convey?

Can the term "Son of God" be understood to reveal the quality of the life of Jesus? Here we are on extremely difficult ground. But even at the risk of distortion, we must now ask whether, as revealed in the Synoptics, Jesus as the "Son of God" had a special relation to the Father. This question brings us to the meaning of the Fatherhood of God in the Synoptic Gospels.

The doctrine of the Fatherhood of God was a commonplace in first-century Judaism; it was a very familiar theme among Jewish teachers. But the New Testament presents us with a curious phenomenon. On the one hand, the New Testament, as a whole, places great emphasis on the Fatherhood of God. On the other hand, in the earliest strata of the Synoptic Gospels, references to this doctrine are rare. The following are the data:

(a) In the Synoptic Gospels, the name Father is used by Jesus the following number of times: Mark, 4; Q, 8 or 9; M, 23 (circa); L, 6.

(b) In the Fourth Gospel: 107.

(c) In the rest of the New Testament: Acts, 3; Paul, 39; I and II Timothy and Titus, 3; Hebrews, 2; James, 3; I Peter, 1; I, II John, 16; Jude, 1; Rev., 4.

On the basis of these figures, some scholars have claimed that, in the Synoptics, God is conceived as Father of Jesus, the Messiah, and of the disciples to whom Jesus, as Messianic Son, willed to reveal him; but there is no suggestion that God is the Father of all men. The distinctively Christian doctrine of the Divine Fatherhood, then, is that God is the Father of those, and those only, who acknowledge the Messianic Sonship of Jesus, who belong in his new Messianic community, and are thereby entitled to claim that they are Sons of God through him. But such a position is not tenable. Statistics have been given too much weight in it. The exclusiveness of the Fatherhood of God need not be pressed in this way, and we need not think that Jesus repudiated the Fatherhood of God for all men: God rains on the just and on the unjust.

But why, then, is there such extraordinary reserve on the part of Jesus in using this name "Father" for God? There is a reserve—a secret—about the whole ministry of Jesus, as we shall see in our treatment of Mark, but this is not enough to account for the reserve of Jesus in using the term "Father." The late Professor T. W. Manson suggested that there was one main reason for this reserve: it was the intensity with which Jesus understood his relation to God. The Fatherhood of God was no mere theological commonplace to Jesus, but a matter of profound experience and conviction, so that he could not easily speak of it, even to his disciples. We find the same kind of reserve among great poets; they do not like to speak about their art. Étienne Gilson has written as follows:

> No one is humbler than the artist before his art, even if he is vain before man. He is even humble about his life, which is, he is aware, different from other lives. He asks by what unmerited grace he should be called from so many. This feeling goes so deep that when he is among men engrossed by the needs of ordinary life modesty will not let him speak of his own way of living. He hides it as a saint hides his life of prayer which can be talked about only among saints.[17]

I felt the truth of these words very forcibly when I met the poet Dylan Thomas. The last thing he would speak about was his own work! He had the reticence about which Gilson speaks. Such words as those of Gilson might be applied also to the reserve of Jesus in speaking of the Fatherhood of God. The reason why the authors of the other New Testament documents emphasize the Fatherhood of God, while Jesus so seldom seems to have spoken of it, was that they knew of its extraordinary intensity in the experience of Jesus. In the Early Church it was recognized that "The Father" meant a great deal more in the life and teaching of Jesus than would appear from the limited use of the name "Father" in the Gospels. Professor Manson refers to the baptism of Jesus, which he takes to be a profound religious experience of the Father on the part of Jesus, who is then declared to be the Son. Manson further appeals to the scene in Gethsemane where Jesus was obedient to the Father's will. From this sense of trust in and obedience to God as Father, comes the note of authority in the activity and teaching of Jesus. The realization of the Fatherhood of God was for Jesus a personal, religious experience of unparalleled depth. This explains both the reticence of Jesus and those passages where he is regarded as "The Son" in an absolute sense.

In this discussion, Professor Manson assumes that the Synoptic Gospels lead us to the mind of Jesus himself. This is an assumption with which many Form Critics would not agree. But, even if the method employed by Professor Manson would now be considered dubious, his conclusions have been supported by the work of another scholar, Professor Joachim Jeremias. In a learned article, he examined the occurrence of the term "Father" in Judaism. He concluded that there is, in the whole of Jewish literature, no parallel to the use of "Father," without a suffix, as an address to God, such as we find on the lips of Jesus. This use of "Abba, Father," is unique, he thinks, to Jesus.[18]

Perhaps this claim goes too far. It is always difficult to prove that something is unique. We can, however, hardly doubt that Jesus as "The Messiah" and as "The Son of God" was understood by the Early Church to have been in a unique filial relation to God. The title "Son of God" is, therefore, ambiguous. It links Jesus with "Israel," with the King of Israel, with every Israelite—all of whom are "sons" of God. But it also points to an awareness of God as Father on the part of Jesus about which he himself seldom spoke, but which early Christians recognized full well. The title "Son of God," in this sense, sets Jesus alone or apart from men. The same ambiguity meets us in the next title with which we shall deal.

The Son of Man

The phrase by which Jesus most frequently refers to himself in the Synoptics is "The Son of Man." In Hebrew and

Aramaic, the phrase simply means "an individual man," "a man." Thus, it is possible that, in using the phrase "The Son of Man," Jesus simply meant to refer to himself as "a man." But the phrase has a meaning beyond this. It had a history. There are four passages in the Old Testament which may shed light on its use by Jesus:

(1) . . . . what is man that thou art mindful of him,
    and the son of man that thou dost care for him?
Yet thou hast made him little less than God,
    and dost crown him with glory and honor. (Ps. 8:4, 5)

Here the phrase "Son of Man" refers to man both in his weakness or creaturely insignificance before God and also in his divinely appointed dignity over against the rest of creation. Man is a creature of whom God takes note. It seems to be, in any case, a synonym for "man" in his misery and grandeur.

(2) In Ezekiel, the prophet is addressed as a mere man; or as "Son of Man." When he is thus addressed, he is opposed to the Divine Majesty, and yet, at the same time, recognized to be worthy of converse with the Divine. The phrase here again paradoxically suggests insignificance and dignity. Since it is used eighty-seven times in Ezekiel, it must be of marked importance to him. A typical usage occurs in 1:28–2:1:

Like the appearance of the bow that is in the cloud on the day of rain, so was the appearance of the brightness round about.
    Such was the appearance of the likeness of the glory of the Lord. And when I saw it, I fell upon my face, and I heard the voice of one speaking.
    And he said to me, "Son of man, stand upon your feet, and I will speak with you."

(3) In Psalm 80, the phrase "Son of Man" comes to mean something far more inclusive than an individual man. It is a collective term standing for the nation of "Israel" as God's "right-hand man." The Son of Man is Israel as it is used by God for his divine purposes in history.

Turn again, O God of hosts!
  Look down from heaven, and see;
have regard for this vine,
  the stock which thy right hand planted.
They have burned it with fire, they have cut it down;
  may they perish at the rebuke of thy countenance!
But let thy hand be upon the man of thy right hand,
  the son of man whom thou hast made strong for thyself!
Then we will never turn back from thee;
  give us life, and we will call on thy name!

Notice here that the "Son of Man" is also God's vine, that is, "Israel" itself.

(4) What we find in Psalm 80 is carried much further very strikingly in Daniel 7:13. The whole of the pertinent passage reads:

As I looked,
thrones were placed
  and one that was ancient of days took his seat;
his raiment was white as snow,
  and the hair of his head like pure wool;
his throne was fiery flames,
  its wheels were burning fire.
A stream of fire issued
  and came forth from before him;
a thousand thousands served him,
  and ten thousand times ten thousand stood before him;
the court sat in judgment,
  and the books were opened.
I looked then because of the sound of the great words which the horn was speaking. And as I looked, the beast was slain, and its body destroyed and given over to be burned with fire. As for the rest of the beasts, their dominion was taken away, but their lives were prolonged for a season and a time. I saw in the night visions, and behold, with the clouds of heaven
  there came one like a son of man,
and he came to the Ancient of Days
  and was presented before him.

And to him was given dominion
and glory and kingdom,
that all peoples, nations, and languages
should serve him;
his dominion is an everlasting dominion,
which shall not pass away,
and his kingdom one
that shall not be destroyed. (Dan. 7:9–14)

Here a figure coming with the clouds of heaven is "like a Son of Man." The explanation of the figure is made explicit in 7:18, 22, 27. In all these three places, "the Saints of the Most High" take the place of one "like the Son of Man," that is, the one like a Son of Man is understood as the glorified "Israel" in the coming kingdom, or as the ideal "Israel" of the future. Following upon the various beasts, representing different nations that have oppressed Israel, the true Saints of the Most High, the Israel of God, appear. The first beast was like a lion and had eagles' wings (a combination of the British lion and the American eagle!)—this is Babylon; the second beast was like a bear (like the rugged Russian bear)—this stands for the Medes; the third was like a leopard, with four wings of a bird on its back and four heads—this stands for Persia; the fourth beast, "terrible and dreadful and exceedingly strong" stands for Greece—the Greece of Antiochus Epiphanes. The little horn is Antiochus Epiphanes. The Son of Man appears as the representative of Israel, but here he is not merely a representative of Israel. The Son of Man seems to be a kind of holy, angelic figure, who belongs to the end; he is the final figure of history standing for the final people of history.

(5) There is one further document to which we have to refer, namely, the Similitudes of Enoch (37–71). The pertinent passages read as follows:

46:1 And there I saw One who had a head of days,
And His head was white like wool,

And with Him was another being whose countenance had the
    appearance of a man,
And his face was full of graciousness, like one of the holy
    angels.

2 And I asked the *angel* who went with me and showed me all
    the hidden things, concerning that

3 Son of Man, who he was, and whence he was, (and) why
    he went with the Head of Days? And he
answered and said unto me:
This is the Son of Man who hath righteousness,
With whom dwelleth righteousness,
And who revealeth all the treasures of that which is hidden,

Because the Lord of Spirits hath chosen him,
And whose lot hath the pre-eminence before the Lord of Spirits
    in uprightness for ever.

4 And this Son of Man whom thou hast seen
Shall raise up the kings and the mighty from their seats,
[And the strong from their thrones]
And shall loosen the reins of the strong,
And break the teeth of the sinners.

5 [And he shall put down the kings from their thrones and
    kingdoms]
Because they do not extol and praise Him,
Nor humbly acknowledge whence the kingdom was bestowed
    upon them. . . .

48:1 And in that place I saw the fountain of righteousness
Which was inexhaustible:
And around it were many fountains of wisdom:
And all the thirsty drank of them,
And were filled with wisdom,
And their dwellings were with the righteous and holy and
    elect.

2 And at that hour that Son of Man was named
In the presence of the Lord of Spirits,
And his name before the Head of Days.

3 Yea, before the sun and the signs were created,
Before the stars of the heaven were made,
His name was named before the Lord of Spirits.

4 He shall be a staff to the righteous whereon to stay themselves
   and not fall,
   And he shall be the light of the Gentiles,
   And the hope of those who are troubled of heart.

5 All who dwell on earth shall fall down and worship before
   him,
   And will praise and bless and celebrate with song the Lord
   of Spirits.

6 And for this reason hath he been chosen and hidden before
   Him,
   Before the creation of the world and for evermore.

7 And the wisdom of the Lord of Spirits hath revealed him to
   the holy and righteous;
   For he hath preserved the lot of the righteous,
   Because they have hated and despised this world of unrighteousness,
   And have hated all its works and ways in the name of the Lord
   of Spirits:

   For in his name they are saved,
   And according to his good pleasure hath it been in regard to
   their life. . . .

49:1 For wisdom is poured out like water,
   And glory faileth not before him for evermore.

2 For he is mighty in all the secrets of righteousness,
   And unrighteousness shall disappear as a shadow,
   And have no continuance;
   Because the Elect One standeth before the Lord of Spirits,
   And his glory is for ever and ever,
   And his might unto all generations.

3 And in him dwells the spirit of wisdom,
   And the spirit which gives insight,
   And the spirit of understanding and of might,
   And the spirit of those who have fallen asleep in righteousness.

4 And he shall judge the secret things,
   And none shall be able to utter a lying word before him;
   For he is the Elect One before the Lord of Spirits according
   to His good pleasure.

Until the discovery of the Dead Sea Scrolls, the date of Enoch was uncertain, and since the Similitudes, from which the above verses come, have not been found among the Scrolls, there is still doubt whether the references in it to the Son of Man are pre-Christian or not. But, since many scholars have taken the Similitudes to be pre-Christian, we must refer to them here. The figure which emerges in Enoch has the following characteristics:

a. Graciousness (46:1).

b. Righteousness (46:3).

c. He reveals all the treasures of that which is hidden (46:3).

d. He has pre-eminence before the Lord of Spirits forever (46:3).

e. His name was before the Lord of Spirits before the stars of heaven were made. He was chosen and hidden before creation.

f. The Son of Man recalls the features of the Suffering Servant (48:4).

g. He also slays sinners by the word of his mouth.

h. From the first he was hidden.

i. He is given the power of universal judgment.

On many points there has been disagreement about this figure. First, it is not certain that the Son of Man pre-exists the world. He is named before creation. Does this mean that he really pre-existed creation or merely that he was an idea conceived before creation, or that he was then intended to come to existence in the future? Secondly, the connection of the Son of Man in I Enoch and in Daniel is in dispute: are they intended to refer to the same figure or not? Thirdly, there are passages which point to the individual nature of the Son of Man, and others to his corporate character; in some passages, the Son of Man is an individual man, in others a group. Fourthly, some have found in him a suffering figure, while others have violently rejected this.

One thing alone is clear: the phrase "Son of Man" in the first century must have suggested something mysterious; it had many undertones of meaning. He represented the people of God, Israel in its ideal aspect; again, he stood for an individual destined to redeem Israel; again, he had angelic aspects which pointed to a supernatural being; and again, he was simply man himself in his weakness or creatureliness. But in most passages, he challenges to thought; he compels the question, What does "The Son of Man" mean? And in Daniel and I Enoch, he becomes the final figure of history.

In the light of all this, we can turn to the Synoptics. It is very probable that Jesus spoke of himself as "The Son of Man" because this title stimulated his hearers to reflect, to face the mystery of his ministry, the question as to who he really was. This Jesus—Son of Man—is an earthly figure, humiliated and suffering; he utters the call to repentance. Is this figure also the final figure? Does men's response to him constitute the "final" test of life? Jesus—Son of Man—is with men and for men, but also mysterious judge of men for God. The title "Son of Man" insinuates itself into the minds of men—to disturb; it raises the awkward, needling question: "Is Jesus the 'final' or 'ultimate' figure with whom men have to deal?"

By using all the terms we have mentioned above, the Synoptic Gospels set forth Jesus as—Messiah, Son of Abraham, Son of Adam, Son of God, Son of Man; they rooted him in the history of his people—a Semite among Semites, a man among men, and also elevated him to transcend all things past and present, as the final figure of history—the revelation of God's glory now and forever. And his marks are clear—forgiveness and healing, authority in word and deed. The rule of God which he inaugurates is a rule of grace and judgment. It comes as gift and demand. The rule of God as grace, we have already suggested; we shall next deal with its demand.

CHAPTER 16

THE DEMAND OF THE KINGDOM

The last words of the last chapter might convey the impression that the gift of God's rule in the coming of Jesus Christ is distinct or separated from the demand of that rule. But this impression is false. Gift and demand go together in the rule of God which Jesus reveals. In order to make this clear, let us glance briefly at what has already been written and relate this to the demand which Jesus brings. In the coming of Jesus of Nazareth into history, the Synoptics, and indeed all the New Testament writers, see the purpose of God revealed in the Old Testament brought to a fulfillment. In this way a new order has dawned; this new order constitutes the coming of the Kingdom of God into history. The marks of this new order are seen in the activity of Jesus himself; he casts out demons, he forgives sin, he breaks down barriers. He calls to himself all the weary and heavy laden. In short, the marks of the rule of God are, above all, grace and forgiveness. And this grace and forgiveness, which men encountered in Jesus Christ, are the result of no merit in men; they come to the unworthy. God has extended to men a merciful forgiveness beyond their conception. In the ministry of Jesus, writes Professor Jeremias, "the hour of fulfillment is come, that is the urgent note that sounds through them all. The strong man is disarmed, the forces of evil are in retreat, the physician has come to the sick, the lepers are cleansed, the heavy burden of guilt is removed, the lost sheep has been brought home, the door of the Father's House stands open, the poor and the beggars are summoned to the banquet, a master whose grace is undeserved pays his wages in full, a great joy fills all hearts. God's acceptable year has come . . ."

But with this undeserved grace comes a demand. Incredible as is the grace, so intolerable seems the demand that Jesus brings. Consider the following familiar verses from the Sermon on the Mount:

> You have learned that our forefathers were told, "Do not commit murder; anyone who commits murder must be brought to judgement." But what I tell you is this: "Anyone who nurses anger against his brother must be brought to judgement. If he abuses his brother he must answer for it to the court; if he sneers at him he will have to answer for it in the fires of hell." (Matt. 5:21–22)

> You have learned that they were told, "Do not commit adultery." But what I tell you is this: "If a man looks on a woman with a lustful eye, he has already committed adultery with her in his heart." (Matt. 5:27–28)

We may well ask on reading these words, "Are they not impossible?" And while there are many words of a prudential kind placed on the lips of Jesus in the Synoptics, there can be no question that what is characteristic of him is this absolute demand, and especially the demand to show love toward all, deserving and undeserving.

The ministry of Jesus is thus governed by two poles. It offers to men limitless forgiveness and mercy; it demands of men limitless love. At first sight, at least, it seems too fantastic and unrealistic that we should be asked to love those whom we naturally cannot love. What are we to make of this absolute demand of Jesus to love? Several answers have been given to this question.

1. We may take the naïve view that it is possible to gain the kingdom by keeping these absolutes. This conception does justice to the need for obedience and discipline in the Chris-

tian life. The kingdom is to be sought (Matt. 6:33); we are "to enter in by the narrow gate" (Matt. 7:13). There is to be striving, discipline, growth, in following Jesus.

But there are two things that such a view overlooks. First, that everywhere the Kingdom of God is grace and a gift, not to those who have achieved any growth but to the ungodly; and, secondly, that to fulfill these absolute demands is impossible. After we have done everything we can, we know that we are still unprofitable servants, that is, still aware that we have failed to do what is commanded.

2. Others have sought to deal with the terrible absoluteness of the demand of Jesus by claiming that his ethical teaching is intended, not for this world of time and space and sense, but for another world. The ethic of Jesus applies only to an ideal world to come.

This view is honest; it acknowledges how utterly impossible it is to live fully the demand of Jesus in this world. But it goes too far. In fact, the kinds of demands that Jesus did make are applicable only in this world where there is a possibility of false swearing, a possibility of adultery, of conscription, of hate. However removed from our possibilities, the demands of Jesus encounter us in this world; they challenge us to obedience here and now.

3. This last fact is recognized by the third approach to the teaching of Jesus in its absoluteness. It may broadly be called the Roman Catholic approach. According to this, there are two grades in the Christian ethic. There is the honors grade, as it were—the life of the ascetics or monastics, who accept the full demand of the absolute; they leave the world so as to be able to live by ideal standards. This is the special code which Jesus gave to his apostles. This code is more exacting than that which was given to "ordinary" men. Let us look, for example, at Matthew 19:10. After the prohibition of divorce by Jesus, we read as follows:

The disciples said to him, "If that is the position with husband and wife, it is better to refrain from marriage." To this he replied, "That is something which not everyone can accept, but only those for whom God has appointed it. For while some are incapable of marriage because they were born so, or were made so by men, there are others who have themselves renounced marriage for the sake of the kingdom of Heaven. Let those accept it who can."

On the obvious interpretation of the above words, there are some who should submit to celibacy, because they are capable of it, for the sake of the Kingdom. But it is equally recognized that others are not so capable and should not be asked to undertake what they are not fitted for.

There is a certain heroism in the position I have just outlined—the heroism of those who accept a total commitment. But there is a point at which it fails to satisfy. The teaching of Jesus is not only absolute in certain heroic aspects of life, for example, in its demand to give up marriage and wealth. It is absolute over all its range, over our covert thoughts as well as our overt acts. And it is, therefore, not justifiable to claim that by giving up certain aspects of life, heroic as this may be, its demand is met. Admirable as so much Catholic devotion is at this point, we may still ask whether even the ascetic life of the cloisters of history can claim to have met the challenge of that absolute demand which the words of Jesus set forth.

4. We next come to the interpretation of the demands of Jesus proposed by Albert Schweitzer. He held that Jesus thought that the end of the world was imminent; in a very short time all history would be wound up; a new order utterly inconceivable would emerge. What, then, are the ethical commandments of Jesus? They are intended for the few weeks which remain before the end of the universe comes. It expresses the total demand of Jesus before the final crisis of all history. The demands of Jesus are meant only for an interim. But is this a sufficient account of the teaching of Jesus?

Let us admit two things about this view. It does justice to the urgency of the moral teaching of the New Testament; it preserves us from watering down the Christian demand. And, further, it recognizes that much in the teaching of Jesus was directed toward a special crisis bound up with the call of Jesus to men. But it must be insisted that at no point does the moral teaching of Jesus rest upon the shortness of the time before the end; nowhere is appeal made to the imminent winding up of all things.

5. There is another more recent approach to the teaching of Jesus. This emphasizes the call that the command of Jesus made to decide for or against God. But the specific laws which we find in the Gospels are, by and large, later accretions—due to the need to legislate for the Church. The essence of the call of Jesus is to decision—all other things are secondary. But this is too drastic a solution. We must recognize that Jesus reckoned with life in this world in its complexity. A bare call to decision by itself was not enough.

But what, then, is the content of the demand of Jesus? First, the Gospels assume the ethical tradition of the Old Testament. There is a holy, righteous God who calls for justice and peace among men and nations. The demand for social righteousness, in this sense, is assumed. However, the Gospels also understand the demand of God in the light of the Rule of God revealed in the ministry of Jesus. A new order has come—an order when God's grace is revealed and freely given. This new order is, in one sense, a return to the primordial will of God in creation, to his pure will uncorrupted by the necessities of history, by the disobedience of man. And this will of grace imposes a demand of grace. To receive the kingdom is to know also the demand of the kingdom. To be forgiven is to know the demand to forgive. This is the real absolutism of the moral teaching of Jesus—it is a call to those who have received grace to show grace.

What, then, are the motives offered for living a life of grace? Why should one seek to live as Jesus commanded? Rewards and punishments are offered; but the real motive offered is that men might be the sons of God. Live the good life, so that you may enter as sons into the Kingdom of God. To enter into a filial relation with God—this is the life of the new order; this filial attitude toward God is the ground of all morality and its reward. The disciple is to live out in life the meaning of this sonship conferred upon him by the love of God. It follows that the nature of the demand placed upon the sons is absolute. Just as it is impossible to measure what we owe to our fathers and mothers, so it is impossible to measure what we owe to God and what, therefore, we should do. Jesus' demands cut at the very roots of our being; they search our hearts. His demands transcend all natural, prudential standards. Jesus asks for absolute mercifulness. This means that we can never fulfill his demands. But, though unfulfilled and unfulfillable, the demands are there. To accept the call of Jesus is to know that the absolute demands are there, to know that they cannot be achieved, and yet to strive to achieve them. And they are all summed up in the command to love.

The coming of the Kingdom is the coming of love. It is, therefore, necessarily in conflict with the evil of the world. The Kingdom comes—and there are temptations to overcome, exorcisms to be performed, sins to be forgiven, suffering to be borne. The gift of the Rule of God thus becomes a demand. And in fulfilling this demand, which arises out of God's gift, man finds himself. Thus, for those who take upon themselves the yoke of the Kingdom, grace demands grace. There is no room for "perfectionism"—that is, for any claim that we have already at any point fulfilled the demands of grace, and yet there is always the recognition of the claims of grace. Nowhere is the truth of the matter better expressed than in Tennyson's *Idylls of the King*: to encounter Jesus in whom God's rule is active is to encounter one of whom it may be said:

> . . . tho' some there be that hold
> That King a shadow . . .
> Yet take thou heed of him, for, so thou pass
> Beneath his archway, then wilt thou become
> A thrall to his enchantments, for the King
> Will bind thee by such vows as is a shame
> A man should not be bound by, yet the which
> No man can keep; but so thou dread to swear,
> Pass not beneath this gateway, but abide
> Without, among the cattle of the field.[19]

H. G. Wells expressed the impact of the demand of Jesus un-forgettably.

He was too great for his disciples. And in view of what he plainly said, is it any wonder that all who were rich and prosperous felt a horror of strange things, a swimming of their world at his teaching? Perhaps the priests and the rulers and the rich men understood him better than his followers. He was dragging out all the little private reservations they had made from social service into the light of a universal religious life. He was like some terrible moral huntsman digging mankind out of the snug burrows in which they had lived hitherto. In the white blaze of this kingdom of his there was to be no property, no privilege, no pride and precedence; no motive indeed and no re-ward but love. Is it any wonder that men were dazzled and blinded and cried out against him? Even his disciples cried out when he would not spare them the light. Is it any wonder that the priests realized that between this man and themselves there was no choice but that he or priestcraft should perish? Is it any wonder that the Roman soldiers, confronted and amazed by something soaring over their comprehension and threatening all their disciplines, should take refuge in wild laughter, and crown him with thorns and robe him in purple and make a mock Caesar of him? For to take him seriously was to enter upon a strange and alarming life, to abandon habits, to control instincts and impulses, to essay an incredible happiness. . . .

Is it any wonder that to this day this Galilean is too much for our small hearts?[20]

CHAPTER 17

THE GOSPEL OF MARK

We have been concerned in the last few chapters to set forth the concepts and motifs which all the Synoptic Gospels share. But although they have so much in common, the Synoptics are all different. Although they all deal with the same theme, they each expound it in a particular way. In the next chapters, we shall seek to set forth the peculiar emphases of each of the evangelists or the special imprint which each places on his materials.

Mark is generally regarded as the earliest of the Synoptic Gospels because it is almost entirely included in Matthew and Luke. This fact, together with the way in which the material from Mark is distributed in Matthew and Luke, has convinced most students that Mark was written before Matthew and Luke and was probably the first full gospel ever to be written. Although some place it as late as A.D. 80, most favor a date for the Gospel around A.D. 65, and trace it to Rome. Mark, in the judgment of most, is the basic Gospel, the stuff out of which Matthew and Luke were largely made. For this reason, its importance can hardly be exaggerated. But its interpretation has been confusing.

At the end of the nineteenth century and at the beginning of the twentieth, Mark was regarded as presenting a fairly straightforward life of Jesus. True, it did not contain the story of the birth of Jesus and did not provide many details which historians would like to know, but, by and large, it did give the main outline of the career of Jesus from the ministry in Galilee through a shorter ministry in Judaea, to his Passion and Resurrection. Mark was taken seriously as the statement of a life; it was historical in its intention.

But the advent of Form Criticism raised awkward questions. When Form Critics examined Mark, they came to the conclusion that it does not give a "life of Jesus." There is no attempt at presenting one incident after another in the order in which they happened historically. Apart from the account of the Passion, which is a continuous recital of what happened almost day by day, the Gospel is made up of a number of isolated stories which have no connection with each other. The details about the time and place, when and where events happened, are claimed by many recent scholars to be unimportant, so that Mark cannot be regarded as a reliable source for a historical biography of Jesus.

But this scepticism led to a reaction. Professor C. H. Dodd holds that Mark drew upon three kinds of materials:

1. Isolated stories handed down independently.
2. Collections of stories and parables and sayings.
3. An outline of the whole ministry of Jesus designed perhaps as an introduction to the story of the Passion. Into this outline Mark could fit his other materials.

This outline can be traced in certain summaries which Mark uses. These are:

> After John had been arrested, Jesus came into Galilee proclaiming the Gospel of God: "The time has come; the kingdom of God is upon you; repent, and believe the Gospel." (1:14–15)
> They came to Capernaum, and on the Sabbath he went to synagogue and began to teach. The people were astounded at his teaching, for, unlike the doctors of the law, he taught with a note of authority. (1:21–22)
> So all through Galilee he went, preaching in the synagogues and casting out the devils. (1:39)

Once more he went away to the lake-side. All the crowd came to him, and he taught them there. (2:13)

Jesus went away to the lake-side with his disciples. Great numbers from Galilee, Judaea and Jerusalem, Idumaea and Transjordan, and the neighbourhood of Tyre and Sidon, heard what he was doing and came to see him. So he told his disciples to have a boat ready for him, to save him from being crushed by the crowd. (3:7–9)

With many such parables he would give them his message, so far as they were able to receive it. He never spoke to them except in parables; but privately to his disciples he explained everything. (4:33–34)

On one of his teaching journeys round the villages he summoned the Twelve and sent them out in pairs on a mission. So they set out and called publicly for repentance. They drove out many devils, and many sick people they anointed with oil and cured. (6:7, 12–13)

The apostles now rejoined Jesus and reported to him all that they had done and taught. (6:30)

Read consecutively, these passages supply the framework of Jesus' ministry. This framework is derived from the preaching of the primitive communities. But notice. Even if the historical character of Mark is in this way preserved, it is not simply history that Mark gives but a preached history. Mark is concerned with presenting the story of a life in the conviction that this life is the life of the Son of God. This conviction governs his presentation of the life. His history is preaching.

What, then, does Mark emphasize as he gives the story of Jesus? We have seen that that life is for him, as for the other Synoptics, the fulfillment of prophecy; it is the life of the Messiah, the Son of Man, the Son of God. But what are his peculiar emphases? They may roughly be stated as follows.

The authority of Jesus, the Messiah

Jesus is the Messiah of Jewish expectation. This is established for Mark because, during his life, Jesus had exercised what Mark calls "authority." This concept of "authority" plays a central role in the evangelist's view of Jesus. He illustrates by showing how Jesus has authority:

1. *As a teacher:*

> They came to Capernaum, and on the Sabbath he went to synagogue and began to teach. The people were astounded at his teaching, for, unlike the doctors of the law, he taught with a note of authority. (1:21–22)

2. *Over the Law:* In chapter 7:1–13 he rejects much of the tradition of Judaism, and in 7:14–20 seems to contravene the written Law:

> On another occasion he called the people and said to them, "Listen to me, all of you, and understand this: nothing that goes into a man from outside can defile him; no, it is the things that come out of him that defile a man."
>
> When he had left the people and gone indoors, his disciples questioned him about the parable. He said to them, "Are you as dull as the rest? Do you not see that nothing that goes from outside into a man can defile him, because it does not enter into his heart but into his stomach, and so passes out into the drain?" Thus he declared all foods clean. He went on, "It is what comes out of a man that defiles him."

In chapter 10, he sets one part of the Law over against another in discussing divorce.

3. *Over the Sabbath:*

> He also said to them, "The Sabbath was made for the sake of man and not man for the Sabbath: therefore the Son of Man is sovereign even over the Sabbath." (2:27–28)

4. *Over the Temple:* In chapter 11, Jesus seems to take command of the Temple and asserts his authority over its customs.

> So they came to Jerusalem, and he went into the temple and began driving out those who bought and sold in the temple. He upset the tables of the money-changers and the seats of the

dealers in pigeons; and he would not allow anyone to use the temple court as a thoroughfare for carrying goods. Then he began to teach them, and said, "Does not Scripture say, 'My house shall be called a house of prayer for all the nations'? But you have made it a robbers' cave." The chief priests and the doctors of the law heard of this and sought some means of making away with him; for they were afraid of him, because the whole crowd was spellbound by his teaching. (11:15–18)

Notice that the Law—including the Sabbath and the Temple system—was the ultimate religious authority for Judaism. In setting himself above the Law, the Temple, and the Sabbath, Jesus was virtually claiming to be the ultimate authority. This is the significance of the conflict stories in Mark.

5. *Over the mystery of the Kingdom of God:*

When he was alone, the Twelve and others who were round him questioned him about the parables. He replied, "To you the secret of the kingdom of God has been given; but to those who are outside everything comes by way of parables." (4:10–11)

6. *Over the forgiveness of sin:*

When Jesus saw their faith, he said to the paralysed man, "My son, your sins are forgiven."

Now there were some lawyers sitting there and they thought to themselves, "Why does the fellow talk like that? This is blasphemy! Who but God alone can forgive sins?" Jesus knew in his own mind that this was what they were thinking, and said to them: "Why do you harbour thoughts like these? Is it easier to say to this paralysed man, 'Your sins are forgiven,' or to say, 'Stand up, take your bed, and walk'? But to convince you that the Son of Man has the right on earth to forgive sins"—he turned to the paralysed man—"I say to you, stand up, take your bed, and go home." And he got up, took his stretcher at once, and went out in full view of them all, so that they were astounded and praised God. "Never before," they said, "have we seen the like." (2:5–12)

7. *Over unclean spirits:*

He entered a house; and once more such a crowd collected round them that they had no chance to eat. When his family heard of this, they set out to take charge of him; for people were saying that he was out of his mind.

The doctors of the law, too, who had come down from Jerusalem, said, "He is possessed by Beelzebub," and, "He drives out devils by the prince of devils." So he called them to come forward and spoke to them in parables: "How can Satan drive out Satan? If a kingdom is divided against itself, that kingdom cannot stand; if a household is divided against itself, that house will never stand; and if Satan is in rebellion against himself, he is divided and cannot stand; and that is the end of him.

"On the other hand, no one can break into a strong man's house and make off with his goods unless he has first tied the strong man up; then he can ransack the house." (3:19–27)

8. *Over nature:* Here it is sufficient to refer to the walking on the sea and the stilling of the storm in 4:35–41 and 6:45–52. The question is inevitable: "Who then is this, that even wind and sea obey him?" In these "miracles" Jesus assumes the prerogatives reserved in the Old Testament for God himself.

The hidden Messiah

Mark, therefore, presents Jesus as one having moral authority and control over nature. But this poses a problem! If his authority was so clearly expressed, why was Jesus rejected by the leading Jewish leaders of his day? Was it not natural for them to see that here, indeed, was the Messiah? What caused not only the politically minded Herodians and Sadducees but also the Pharisees, the best people of his day, to reject Jesus? To this puzzling question Mark gives certain answers. He makes use of the idea that Israel's heart has become hardened. The phrase "the hardening of the heart" refers primarily to a condition of the mind. The heart stands for the intellectual faculty in man. The term "hardening" suggests the term "calcified"; the mind has become calcified, or, as we should now say, "petrified," incapable of responding to challenges set before it. This "hardening" has fallen upon the mind of the Jewish leaders and often on the minds of Jesus' own followers. They have become incapable of accepting the intellectual, moral, and spiritual challenge posed by the presence of Jesus.

Again, Mark, without explanation, uses another term, "scandal," to describe the impact of Jesus on his contemporaries: they are "scandalized" by him. This term "scandal" means, in this context, that there is something about Jesus which causes people to stumble; it is not that he wants to trip them or to cause difficulty to them, but that, since he is what he is, they cannot but be "scandalized" in him. Why this was so Mark explains, but, before we deal with his explanation, we must mention another reason that Mark suggests for the rejection of Jesus by his own people.

There is one phenomenon which is very prominent in Mark. That is the refusal of Jesus to declare openly who he was. We have previously referred to the reserve of Jesus. Certainly this is emphasized by Mark. Only in one place, Mark 14:62, does Jesus come near to admitting that he was the Messiah. At Caesarea Philippi (8:27–33) his response to Peter's assertion that he is the Messiah is ambiguous: he refuses to allow the demons to proclaim his identity; when he is asked by what authority he acts, he refuses to give a direct answer, just as he elsewhere refuses to give a "sign" that he is the Messiah. Throughout the Gospel, he seems to hide his real character. He is Messiah, but he never wants to admit it; he hesitates to confess that he is Messiah because there is some secret about his Messiahship which he wishes to safeguard. And it was this secret that was also a "scandal" to the Jewish leaders.

What was this secret? It is the secret that the Messiah must suffer; that the Messianic figure is not a triumphant but a humiliated figure. Consider the following passages from Mark:

> Jesus and his disciples set out for the villages of Caesarea Philippi. On the way he asked his disciples, "Who do men say I am?" They answered, "Some say John the Baptist, others Elijah, others one of the prophets." "And you," he asked, "who do you say I am?" Peter replied: "You are the Messiah." Then he gave them strict orders not to tell anyone about him; and he began to teach them that the Son of Man had to undergo great sufferings, and to be rejected by the elders, chief priests, and doctors of the law; to be put to death, and to rise again three days afterwards. He spoke about it plainly. At this Peter took him by the arm and began to rebuke him. But Jesus turned round, and, looking at his disciples, rebuked Peter. "Away with you, Satan," he said; "you think as men think, not as God thinks."
>
> Then he called the people to him, as well as his disciples, and said to them, "Anyone who wishes to be a follower of mine must leave self behind; he must take up his cross, and come with me." (8:27–34)

Here it cannot be claimed that Jesus declares that he is not the Messiah, but he does insist that the Son of Man must suffer. To deny this, as does Peter, is to think the things of Satan and not of God. Jesus here shifts from the title Messiah to the title Son of Man, as if he preferred to think in terms of the latter. The same transition marks 14:61–63:

> But he kept silence; he made no reply.
>
> Again the High Priest questioned him: "Are you the Messiah, the Son of the Blessed One?" Jesus said, "I am; and you will see the Son of Man seated on the right hand of God and coming with the clouds of heaven." Then the High Priest tore his robes and said, "Need we call further witnesses?"

The title Messiah is not explicitly rejected, but it is immediately passed over in favor of that of the Son of Man. In 14:61–63, in the trial before the High Priest, this Son of Man is to appear triumphant, but he is, at present, a suffering figure. And this suffering is declared in 9:12 to be in accordance with the Scriptures. The prediction of suffering is made again in 10:33.

Jesus is, therefore, for Mark, a Messiah who hides himself; who prefers, not indeed to deny his Messiahship, but to express it in terms of the Son of Man. The reason for this is clear. To affirm his Messiahship outright would have been to court misunderstanding. His contemporaries would immediately have foisted upon him their traditional conception of the Messiah as one designed to slay their foes and lift them high. But Jesus was not such a Messiah; he was Messiah, but so unlike the picture of the Messiah which his hearers had in their minds that he wanted to avoid the term. He was the Messiah but not their Messiah. He might have used to a contemporary the words of Blake:

> The Vision of Christ [Messiah] that thou dost see
> Is my vision's greatest enemy . . .

But why was the suffering of the Messiah such a scandal? The answer is clear. The main currents in Judaism expected a conquering Messiah. To suffer did not comport with the Messiah; a suffering Messiah was a contradiction in terms. It is this contradiction that Mark proclaims as the heart of the Gospel: that Jesus, the Messiah, had chosen to suffer.

The suffering Messiah

For Mark, then, the point of emphasis in the life of Jesus is naturally its end on the cross, which is the "culmination" of his suffering. This is why almost one-half of Mark, from 8:27 onward, is overshadowed by the Passion of Jesus. Mark sets forth that Passion at length: he shows the sovereignty of Jesus, the King of the Jews; but also his silence before his accusers, his solitariness as he is forsaken by the crowds, by Judas, by all the disciples. Even the three nearest to him could only sleep while he agonized; and throughout the Passion,

Mark makes clear that we are witnessing the suffering of one who was sinless and alone.

But the Gospel ends, not with the cross, glorious as that is, but in the resurrection. Throughout his Gospel, Mark has looked beyond the Passion both to a second coming of Jesus as Son of Man and to a resurrection after three days. In the last chapter, the ending of which is probably lost, there is the story of Mary Magdalene and Mary, the mother of James and Salome, going to anoint Jesus in the tomb and finding that he was not there. They are told to go to Galilee to see him. Does this refer to appearances of the Risen Christ which they were to see, such as are recorded in Matthew and Luke and John, or does it refer to something even more stupendous—the second coming of Jesus? The evidence does not allow us to decide. Suffice that Jesus was risen. Throughout the Gospel, Mark links the suffering with the resurrection; and the end of the Gospel is of a piece with all that went before. Through suffering, Jesus, the hidden Messiah, becomes the manifested Messiah in his risen life, that is, in the disciples' experience of him as living in their midst.

Mark has wrestled, above all, with the suffering of Jesus. It may be that this particular aspect of the ministry of Jesus is emphasized by him because suffering was so much part of the life of Christians when he wrote. In A.D. 64, Nero had accused Christians of setting fire to the city; Paul and Peter had been put to death. Christians knew the extreme of suffering; persecution might break out at any moment again. They needed to be encouraged; Mark undertakes to do so by urging them to take up the cross. A whole central section of the Gospel is given over to such exhortation. Mark breathes the tension of a persecuted Church. Conflict bursts around Jesus from the outset. Each expression of his authority calls forth criticism and, in the end, he is put out of the way. The mystery of his death dominates Mark; all else becomes, to some degree, secondary. His Jesus is the stark Son of Man, destined to set his face to Jerusalem to die. The teaching of Jesus is emphasized but not recorded; and it is significant that the teaching which is made explicit by Mark usually concerns his suffering. The Jesus of Mark is the Jesus of the Passion. He stands before us in the glare of the fires lit by Nero. Perhaps that glare blinded Mark so that he failed to see some aspects of Jesus. But it certainly did illumine for him the cross of Jesus; all the light of the sacred story gathers round that for Mark. The strong, authoritative, and yet suffering Messiah of Mark bursts forth upon his readers with the sharp clarity and force of a painting by Goya. Nothing is there that is not passionate. No understanding of Jesus which ignores Mark's starkness can be true; no understanding of Jesus which does not see his glory in his suffering, his crown in and through his cross, can be true to him. And yet it is certain that Mark has passed over much in Jesus that we need to know. That is why the instinct of the Church led to Matthew and Luke.

CHAPTER 18

THE GOSPEL OF MATTHEW

Mark, we saw, presented Jesus in storm and stress, a suffering figure to inspire the persecuted. But this understanding of Jesus, as essential as it is, was inadequate to present the wholeness of Jesus. It is partially corrected in the next Gospel with which we now deal, Matthew.

The *sources* behind Matthew can easily be disposed of. It includes almost the whole of Mark; it shares a great deal of material with Luke, which it derived from the source Q, and, in addition, it has drawn upon a source which was unknown or neglected by the other evangelists, usually referred to as M. Whether the birth narratives in chapters 1 and 2 should be included in M or regarded as a distinct tradition is a matter of debate.

When was it written?

The date is much disputed. Since Matthew has incorporated Mark, it is at least to be dated after A.D. 65. Many have argued for a date as late as A.D. 90–100; others place it between A.D. 80 and 90. The reasons suggested for regarding Matthew as late are many.

In addition to its incorporation of Mark, which implies a distance in time from it, there are other indications that much time has passed since the days of Jesus. See Matthew 11:12; 27:8; 28:15:

Ever since the coming of John the Baptist the kingdom of Heaven has been subjected to violence and violent men are seizing it. (11:12)

This explains the name 'Blood Acre,' by which that field has been known ever since. (27:8)

So they took the money and did as they were told. This story became widely known, and is current in Jewish circles to this day. (28:15)

Scholars have also pointed to the developed idea of the Church in Matthew, with which we shall deal below.

There is a marked concentration in Matthew on the coming end of all things. This is revealed in some of the parables peculiar to Matthew: the parable of *The Ten Virgins*, ending with the warning: "Watch, therefore, for you know not neither the day nor the hour" (25:13); the parable of *The Talents*, which consigns the unprofitable servant to outer darkness and to weeping and gnashing of teeth (25:30); that of *The Sheep and the Goats*, which describes the day when the Son of Man comes in his glory, and all the angels with him, and will sit on the throne of his glory to divide the sheep and the goats (25:31 f.). Furthermore, Matthew adds certain details to those of Mark in his picture of the end which is about to come (24:14); he alone mentions the "sign" of the Son of Man in heaven, and the angels coming to the sound of a trumpet (24:30–31). This emphasis in Matthew on the end points to a time when there was a revival of Messianic expectation and excitement (see 24:23 f.). When was this? The time of the rising of Bar Kochba against Rome (about A.D. 135) has been suggested— that is, well into the beginning of the second century. The distress of such a war-torn period would also explain Matthew's emphasis on peace. Recall his words, "All they that take the sword shall perish by the sword" (26:52), and the wartime atmosphere is also reflected in Matthew's insistence that "lawlessness" has multiplied in his day.

All this has led many to think of Matthew as a late Gospel. Some have even placed it in the early second century, perhaps A.D. 125, that is, in the period leading up to Bar Kochba. But such a late date is unnecessary. This must especially be asserted since the discovery of the Dead Sea Scrolls. Early Christians lived in the same world that produced the highly organized institutional life of the Dead Sea Sect. It is not impossible that members of the Dead Sea Sect entered the Church after A.D. 68 when their headquarters at Qumran were attacked. If so, they took with them a tradition of organized "church" life which may have influenced Matthew. But even if this were not the case, there would be many other ways in which to conduct its life. There is no need to place Matthew at a late date because it refers to such ways. Nor must it be forgotten that the interest of Matthew in the organization of the Church must not be exaggerated; it is present, in fact, only in very few passages. Similarly, concern with the end of all things cannot be confined to the time of Bar Kochba in the early second century; it existed long before, as Mark itself shows, and was ever recurring. It is best to recognize that Matthew is later than Mark and probably reflects the discussion which took place between Christianity and Judaism after A.D. 70. Nothing makes it necessary to date it after A.D. 90, and it is best to think of it as emerging around A.D. 85, at a time when the Jewish people were reorganizing themselves after the collapse of their state in A.D. 70.

Just as it has been difficult to fix a date for Matthew, so there has been division about the place of its *origin*. The most likely place suggested is Syria. There Christianity was meeting Judaism and Hellenism, and the "omnibus" character of Matthew, that is, its inclusion of so many different points of view, reflects a situation in which the Gospel had to cope with many influences. In particular, it confronted the challenge of a Judaism that was being forced to reassert and reorganize itself.

Matthaean Christianity and the Rabbinic Judaism which developed at Jamnia after the fall of Jerusalem in A.D. 70 were parallel and interacting movements.

This situation helps us to understand why, by and large, scholars have detected certain emphases in Matthew. We may summarize these as follows:

Matthew as the Gospel of the New Law

Probably it is an American scholar, the late B. W. Bacon of Yale University, who most stimulated this approach to Matthew. He made famous what we may call the Pentateuchal approach to Matthew. Following a tradition which he traced back possibly to the second century, he pointed out that apart from the Prologue (Matt. 1, 2), and the Epilogue (Matt. 26–28), the remainder of the material in the Gospel falls into five "books," each of which is terminated by a formula, which occurs in almost identical forms at 7:28; 11:1; 13:53; 19:1; 26:1. The Gospel thus presents the following structure:

Preamble or Prologue: 1–2: The birth narrative.
Book I: (a) 3:1–4:25: Narrative material.
(b) 5:1–7:27: The Sermon on the Mount.

Formula: 7:28–9: *'And when Jesus finished these sayings,* the crowds were astonished at his teaching, for he taught them as one who had authority, and not as their scribes.'

Book II: (a) 8:1–9:35: Narrative material.
(b) 9:36–10:42: Discourse on mission and martyrdom.

Formula: 11:1: *'And when Jesus had finished instructing his twelve disciples . . .'*

Book III: (a) 11:2–12:50: Narrative and debate material.
(b) 13:1–52: Teaching on the Kingdom of Heaven.

Formula: 13:53: *'And when Jesus had finished these parables . . .'*

Book IV: (a) 13:54–17:21: Narrative and debate material. (b) 17:22–18:35: Discourse on church administration.

Formula: 19:1: 'Now when Jesus had finished these sayings . . .'

Book V: (a) 19:2–22:46: Narrative and debate material. (b) 23:1–25:46: Discourse on eschatology: farewell address.

Formula: 26:1: 'When Jesus finished all these sayings, he said to his disciples . . .'

Epilogue: 26:3–28:20: From the Last Supper to the Resurrection.

With the above five blocks of material, Bacon compared the Pentateuch. "The Torah," he wrote, "consists of five books of commandments of Moses, each body of law introduced by a narrative of considerable length, largely concerned with the 'signs and wonders' by which Jehovah 'with an outstretched hand and a mighty arm' redeemed his people from Egyptian bondage. Matthew is a 'converted rabbi,' a Christian legalist. Each of the 'five books' of his 'syntaxis of the logia' of Jesus begins with an introductory narrative and closes with a stereotyped formula linking its discourse to the next succeeding narrative section." On this view the intention of Matthew is to organize the Gospel of the Church, the New Israel, in the same way as the Law of the Old Israel was arranged, that is, in a fivefold manner. It agrees with this that the Jesus presented by Matthew is very much like Moses. In chapter 5, he ascends the mountain, which is a counterpart to Mount Sinai, and from there delivers his "law."

But there are difficulties about Bacon's approach, only some of which can be mentioned here. The formula which ends each group of materials—"and it came to pass when Jesus had finished these sayings"—may be unimportant. Bacon may have read too much into it.

Again, the division of a document into five sections was frequent in Judaism; for example, there were five books of Psalms, so that the fivefold division of Matthew may be a customary one which has no significance for Matthew's theology. But the most serious difficulty is the obvious one that, on Bacon's view of Matthew, the birth narratives are outside the main scheme of the work and, what is more important, the Passion of Jesus and his Resurrection are reduced to mere addenda. Is it really credible that the Passion and Resurrection should be outside the main body of Matthew's work?

It is unlikely, therefore, that Bacon's view of Matthew as a new Pentateuch should be accepted. But Bacon did emphasize an aspect in Matthew which is valid: Matthew was concerned with presenting the moral teaching of Jesus as the Law of the Messiah, that is, as the true interpretation of the old Law. The words of Jesus fulfill the Law of Moses:

Matthew 5:17–20:

Do not suppose that I have come to abolish the Law and the prophets; I did not come to abolish, but to complete. I tell you this: so long as heaven and earth endure, not a letter, not a stroke, will disappear from the Law until all that must happen has happened. If any man therefore sets aside even the least of the Law's demands, and teaches others to do the same, he will have the lowest place in the kingdom of Heaven, whereas anyone who keeps the Law and teaches others so will stand high in the kingdom of Heaven. I tell you, unless you show yourselves far better men than the Pharisees and the doctors of the law, you can never enter the kingdom of Heaven.

Matthew as the Gospel of the New Israel

One reason why many thought that Matthew was a late Gospel was that it pays so much attention to the Church; it is an ecclesiastical Gospel. Certain striking passages dealing with the Church are peculiar to Matthew. These are:

16:18–19:

> And I say this to you: "You are Peter, the Rock; and on this rock I will build my church, and the forces of death shall never overpower it. I will give you the keys of the kingdom of Heaven; what you forbid on earth shall be forbidden in heaven, and what you allow on earth shall be allowed in heaven."

Some have claimed that this passage reflects differences of opinion in the Early Church as to who was leader—was it Paul or James or Peter? Matthew supports the authority of Peter.

In chapter 18, we have a long discussion of Church discipline; parts of this are peculiar to Matthew. Note especially *18:15–20:*

> If your brother commits a sin, go and take the matter up with him, strictly between yourselves, and if he listens to you, you have won your brother over. If he will not listen, take one or two others with you, so that all facts may be duly established on the evidence of two or three witnesses. If he refuses to listen to them, report the matter to the congregation; and if he will not listen even to the congregation, you must then treat him as you would a pagan or a tax-gatherer.
>
> I tell you this: whatever you forbid on earth shall be forbidden in heaven, and whatever you allow on earth shall be allowed in heaven.
>
> Again I tell you this: if two of you agree on earth about any request you have to make, that request will be granted by my heavenly Father. For where two or three have met together in my name, I am there among them.

And, finally, in the last chapter of the Gospel, words are placed on the lips of the Risen Christ, which are peculiar to Matthew, but full of significance for the life of the Church. They assure the Christian community of the continued living presence of Jesus. Such ecclesiasticism must have developed slowly, a fact which means, as we said above, that Matthew in the view of many cannot be dated too early. Matthew already reveals the process which was soon to lead to the emergence of what is called *Catholicism*.

This aspect of Matthew has been increasingly noticed recently, and its direct relation to the life of the Church within which it emerged has been more and more urged. This is emphasized in several ways. The way in which the liturgy of the Church has influenced Matthew has been made clear before (see chapter 11). This is a document, if not designed for public reading, at least aware of the proprieties of public reading. The communal or "churchly" concern of Matthew has been clarified in another way by those who think of Matthew as the product, not of an individual, but of a school of Christians, who were concerned to explain the significance of Jesus by setting him over against the Old Testament and using quotations from the latter to illuminate his life. This school was anxious to take the words of Jesus and apply them to the life of the Church. With this twofold concern they produced Matthew, which at the same time presents Jesus as the fulfillment of the Old Testament and as the source of a kind of "Book of Orders," a Manual of Discipline for the Church. This shows how, although Matthew is expecting the end of all things, he is also concentrating on the life of the Christian Church here and now in the world. The end is sure to come and may come soon; therefore, "Watch and pray." But meanwhile, preparing for the end, living in readiness for it, the Church must go on; and Matthew, throughout his five great discourses, provides guidance for the Church in its various aspects. He provides a *vade mecum* for a Church awaiting the end. Matthew's Gospel moulds the tradition of the words and works of Jesus to provide guidance for his Church. It is the Gospel of the New Israel.

Matthew as the Gospel of Jesus the Christ

With all of this we need not disagree. And yet to make the life of the Church in itself the center of Matthew's concern is to distort his intention. The glowing center of the Church, as of all things for Matthew, is Jesus himself. The glory of the Church is that it is the community in which he is present, "For where two or three have met together in my name, I am there among them" (18:20). The highest promise is that Jesus will be with his own to the end of the age, and the greatest privilege to worship him to whom "All authority in heaven and on earth has been given" (28:16–20). It is not the Church itself, therefore, that is the centre for Matthew, but Jesus.

For this reason it is the Prologue, so often neglected, that gives the clue to Matthew's concern. In the Prologue, usually referred to as the birth narratives, Matthew sets forth the significance of Jesus under four main motifs—as Messiah, New Moses, Creator, Emmanuel.

If we take seriously these four motifs, we see how Matthew thinks of Jesus, the Lord of the Church. He is the Messiah; he is the one who shows us the demand of God as the New Moses; he is the inaugurator of a new creation; he is the very presence of God-Emmanuel. But of whom is all this asserted? The body of Matthew's Gospel gives the answer. It is asserted of a man born in a manger, who was tempted as we are, who dwelt in Galilee of the Gentiles in contact with the unclean and open to all the broken people of that despised land:

> He went round the whole of Galilee, teaching in the synagogues, preaching the gospel of the Kingdom, and curing whatever illness or infirmity there was among the people. His fame reached the whole of Syria; and sufferers from every kind of illness, racked with pain, possessed by devils, epileptic, or paralysed, were all brought to him, and he cured them. Great crowds also followed him, from Galilee and the Ten Towns, from Jerusalem and Judaea, and from Transjordan. (4:23–25)

It is asserted of one who "took our infirmities and bore our diseases" (8:17); of one of whom it is written: "Foxes have holes, and birds of the air have nests; but the Son of Man has nowhere to lay his head" (8:20). It is asserted of one who, when asked who he was, replied:

> Go and tell John what you hear and see: the blind recover their sight, the lame walk, the lepers are clean, the deaf hear, the dead are raised to life, the poor are hearing the good news— and happy is the man who does not find me a stumbling-block. (11:4-6)

Or again, it is asserted of one whose cry has strangely moved the hearts of all those who have heard it:

> Come to me, all whose work is hard, whose load is heavy; and I will give you relief. Bend your necks to my yoke, and learn from me, for I am gentle and humble-hearted; and your souls will find relief. For my yoke is good to bear, my load is light. (11:28-30)

And the one who thus offers rest to all men is misunderstood and, finally, rejected. The force of Matthew's high view of Jesus is clear. The one to whom, at the end of the Gospel, all authority in heaven and on earth has been given, so that his Good News has broken all national boundaries and is no longer confined to the lost sheep of the house of Israel but destined for all nations, is the one who had nowhere to lay down his head. The humiliated Jesus is Judge, Creator, Messiah, Emmanuel, the Living Presence, who is Lord of the Church.

As compared with Mark, therefore, Matthew is more comprehensive in his presentation of Jesus. He knows the "passionate" Jesus of Mark but has brought other fruits of his ministry into clearer view. It is no accident that for most Christians it is Matthew, not Mark, who is most relevant. The Matthaean Jesus is as gentle as he is majestic, as infinite in succor as in his demand, as dear to Gentile as to Jew. And, above all, the Matthaean Jesus is Emmanuel, which, being interpreted, is "God with us," the creator who redeems.

CHAPTER 19

THE GOSPEL OF LUKE

We now turn to the last of the Synoptics—Luke. It has usually been dated between A.D. 80–85, though some would place it later. Its author is generally taken to have been Luke, the companion of Paul (Col. 4:14; II Tim. 4:11). He was possibly a doctor (Col. 4:14) from Antioch in Syria.[21] Most important of all, the author of Luke is also, in the judgment of many, the author of Acts. The recognition that Luke and Acts belong together is the decisive factor in recent interpretation of Luke. In order to bring forth the full significance of this recent interpretation, let us first recall what older scholars emphasized about Luke.

The old view of Luke

A great emphasis was placed on the attention paid by Luke to social relationships, especially those between the wealthy and the poor. Thus the first Beatitudes as they are given in Matthew and Luke are contrasted.

Matthew 5:3	Luke 6:20
How blest are those who know that they are poor; the kingdom of Heaven is theirs.	Then turning to his disciples he began to speak: "How blest are you who are poor; the kingdom of God is yours."

To the Beatitudes of Matthew, Luke has added, in 6:24–26, a list of woes:

But alas for you who are rich; you have had your time of happiness.

Alas for you who are well-fed now; you shall go hungry.

Alas for you who laugh now; you shall mourn and weep.

Alas for you when all speak well of you; just so did their
fathers treat the false prophets.

Wealth for Luke is the "mammon of unrighteousness"; several
of his parables are taken from the world of money, of borrowing and lending. He emphasizes almsgiving, as in 11:41: "Give
for alms those things which are within," and again, "Sell what
you have and give alms," in 12:33. Luke has an "economic"
nuance, as it has been felt, which is less noticeable in Mark
and Matthew.

Perhaps naturally alongside this, it was noticed that Luke
emphasizes the gracious attitude of Jesus to the outcast and the
sinners. The parables that are peculiar to Luke are especially
full of the mercy of God: that of the Prodigal Son (15:11 ff.);
the parable of the Pharisee and the tax-collector—the tax-collector "standing afar off, would not even lift up his eyes to
heaven, but beat his breast, saying 'God, be merciful to me a
sinner'"; the parable of the Good Samaritan (10:30 ff.). Notice
that Samaritans had no dealings with the Jews and were regarded as beyond the pale by the latter; these Luke includes
in Jesus' mercy. And the word tax-collector must be given its
full force. Tax-collectors in first-century Palestine were what we
should call "quislings" or "foreign agents." These Jesus did
not spurn; instead, he offers to stay at the house of one of
them—Zacchaeus (19:1 ff.). But the place where the wideness
of Jesus' mercy most appears is on the cross.

There were two others with him, criminals who were being
led away to execution; and when they reached the place called
The Skull, they crucified him there, and the criminals with him,
one on his right and the other on his left. Jesus said, *"Father,
forgive them; they do not know what they are doing."* (23:
32–34)

The italicized words are peculiar to Luke, and the same is true of the following passage: the whole of it is only found in Luke.

> One of the criminals who hung there with him taunted him: "Are not you the Messiah? Save yourself, and us." But the other answered sharply, "Have you no fear of God? You are under the same sentence as he. For us it is plain justice; we are paying the price for our misdeeds; but this man has done nothing wrong." And he said, "Jesus, remember me when you come to your throne." He answered, "I tell you this: today you shall be with me in Paradise." (23:39–43)

As in the parables already mentioned and in those of the lost sheep and the lost coin, which occur along with that of the prodigal son in chapter 15, Jesus always comes to seek and save the lost.

It was further frequently noted that Luke pays special attention to women. The Western world, especially perhaps the United States, has increasingly recognized the rights of women. The ancient world, by and large, was not so concerned with these. But in Luke, there is an indefinable sensitivity to the claims of women. He alone gives the story of the widow of Nain (7:11 ff.); of Joanna and Susanna (8:3); Martha and Mary (10:38); of the woman with the spirit of infirmity (13:10 ff.); of the woman with the lost coin (15:8 ff.); of the widow and the unjust judge (18:1 ff.).

And, finally, Luke's Gospel was revered for its concern for all peoples. The infant Jesus is a light to lighten the Gentiles (2:32). All flesh are to see the salvation of God (3:6)—a point which is not noted in the parallel passages in Mark and Matthew. And in the saying from Q in Matthew 8:11, which is also found in Luke 13:29, Luke adds, to Matthew's "east and west," the phrase "and from north and south." And the Risen Lord in Luke claims that penitence and forgiveness should be preached in his name "unto all the nations, beginning from Jerusalem" (24:47). It was impossible to ignore the large sympathy of Luke for the Gentiles, but the full significance of this for the understanding of his Gospel was not realized.

Again, the older scholars pointed out the sense of joy (2:10), of prayerfulness (5:16; 6:12; 11:1), and of the holy spirit which pervades Luke.

All the above data—the sympathy with the poor, the outcast, with women and Gentiles, together with the humane atmosphere pervading the Gospel—persuaded scholars that Luke's is the portrait of the humanitarian Jesus, of the gentle Jesus, exquisite in his sensitivity. It was even breathed that Luke had sentimentalized Jesus, as when he describes the crowds of people and of women bewailing and lamenting him and beating their breasts at his Passion (23:26 ff., 48). The Jesus who walks the pages of Luke is lovable and human, but he lacks the fire of the Jesus of Mark and the austerity of the Jesus of Matthew. In Luke, the "strange" Jesus has been domesticated.

Such an interpretation of Luke was only possible—and only barely so even then—when Luke was separated from Acts. With the recognition that the Gospel of Luke and the Acts of the Apostles are two parts of what is to be understood as one work, another understanding of the Lukan Jesus becomes possible.

The new view of Luke

When we refer to a new view of Luke, we do not imply that the old view of it was false; but it was incomplete. What more recent scholars have done is to set the data, which older scholars rightly emphasized, in a larger framework. In this way, they have given to these data a new significance. Just as the individual pieces of a jigsaw puzzle remain the same in themselves, before and after they are arranged, but only yield their real meaning after they have been fitted together into their proper places within the intended framework, so the data in Luke are only seen in their true perspective when Luke and Acts are fitted together.

Let us begin with the last item mentioned above, the emphasis on the Gentiles, which used to be placed alongside similar emphases (on the poor, on women, on outcasts) as simply a mark of the humanitarianism of Luke. Luke's Gospel begins with the infant Jesus who is proclaimed as a light to lighten the Gentiles, and it ends on the same note, as we pointed out above. But Acts also begins with the giving of the Gospel to the Gentiles on the day of Pentecost and ends on the same note. The story of the descent of the Spirit in Acts 2 probably recalls two episodes in the Old Testament—the story of the Tower of Babel in Genesis 11 and of the giving of the Law on Mt. Sinai. In the former, human pride and fear cause mankind to lose the unity of language which it had once enjoyed; that is, they introduce national division. To the giving of the Law on Mt. Sinai, according to the tradition of Judaism, all the nations of the world had been invited, but only Israel had accepted the yoke of the Law: Luke finds that, in the new order of the Gospel, the Spirit, corresponding to and contrasted with the Law given on Mt. Sinai, is poured forth and received by all nations. The Spirit of God, which had been active in Jesus, is the source of world-wide community. Luke has pressed into the story of the day of Pentecost his understanding of Christianity as involving a world-wide community. The disunity of Babel is annulled in the unity of the Spirit. At the coming of the Spirit, writes Luke:

> They were amazed and in their astonishment exclaimed, "Why, they are all Galileans, are they not, these men who are speaking? How is it then that we hear them, each of us in his own native language? Parthians, Medes, Elamites; inhabitants of Mesopotamia, of Judaea and Cappadocia, of Pontus and Asia, of Phrygia and Pamphylia, of Egypt and the districts of Libya around Cyrene; visitors from Rome, both Jews and proselytes, Cretans and Arabs, we hear them telling in our own tongues the great things God has done." (Acts 2:7–11)

Compare with this Genesis 11:1–9. The promise is now given: "And it shall be that whoever calls upon the name of the Lord shall be saved." The Church born of the Spirit includes all. And at the end of Acts, Luke again returns to the same theme. Paul declares to his own people, the Jews: "Let it be known to you then that this salvation of God has been sent to Gentiles; they will listen."

The purpose of Luke, then, in his references to the Gentiles, is not merely to emphasize the kindness of Jesus to all. In the light of Luke-Acts, for so we must think of the two documents, he was concerned to show how God, through Jesus, has been working to lead to the grand climax of a Gospel in which the division between Jew and Gentile is annulled and a salvation for all made available. The description of the infant Jesus as a light to lighten the Gentiles foreshadows Paul at Rome preaching salvation to all. The mission of the world-wide Gospel is already present in embryo in the ministry of Jesus. The disciples whom Jesus called, first the Twelve and then the Seventy (suggesting the elders appointed by Moses and perhaps the number of the nations of the earth), and whom he taught and to whom he entrusted his Kingdom at the Last Supper, were a preparation for the coming great Gentile Church. The latter is foreshadowed in the little flock around Jesus whose sights are already being turned on those outside Israel. There can be no question that for Luke the greatest fact of the first century was the Church in which the division between Jew and Gentile had been annulled, just as for Archbishop William Temple the greatest fact of the twentieth century was the existence of a world-wide Church.

Bound up with Luke's understanding of the ministry of Jesus as foreshadowing, preparing for, and part of the world-wide mission of the Church, is his emphasis on the Spirit. The Gospel begins with the outpouring of the Spirit, not only on John the Baptist in the birth story, but on Jesus at his baptism. The nature of Jesus' ministry is summed up by Luke as follows:

Then Jesus, armed with the power of the Spirit, returned to Galilee; and reports about him spread through the whole countryside. He taught in their synagogues and all men sang his praises.

So he came to Nazareth, where he had been brought up, and went to synagogue on the Sabbath day as he regularly did. He stood up to read the lesson and was handed the scroll of the prophet Isaiah. He opened the scroll and found the passage which says,

The spirit of the Lord is upon me because he has anointed me;
He has sent me to announce good news to the poor,
To proclaim release for prisoners and recovery of sight for the blind;
To let the broken victims go free,
To proclaim the year of the Lord's favour.

He rolled up the scroll, gave it back to the attendant, and sat down; and all eyes in the synagogue were fixed on him.

He began to speak: "Today," he said, "in your very hearing this text has come true." (4:14–21)

But this same spirit that rested upon Jesus was poured forth later on the Christian community on the day of Pentecost described in Acts 2. Throughout Acts, the Spirit is a source of guidance. The point to note is that the Spirit of Jesus and the Spirit on Jesus carries on the life of the Church. And this Spirit is possessed by Jesus as the Messiah; he is also a New Moses, and, above all, he is the suffering Servant of the Lord. Notice, however, that it is as a light to the Gentiles especially that Jesus is Servant, not so much as the suffering Servant who makes atonements for the sins of the world. Luke expounds the person of Jesus in relation to the whole world.

On the other hand, Luke is very conscious that the separation between the Church and the Jewish people, which the entry of the Gentiles into the Church largely created, was already foreshadowed in the life of Jesus. In the very synagogue where Jesus spoke of his call in the Spirit, the people are scandalized by him and reject him. Throughout the Gospel, Luke gives full weight to the rejection of Jesus by his own people. This is marked especially between the first prediction of the Passion of Jesus (9:22) and the Passion itself; Jesus came to his own but they received him not. But through his rejection and humiliation at the hand of his own people, Jesus is able to become the Saviour of the world. In Acts, Luke insists that the death of Jesus was in the purpose of God. Through his death he was glorified. His glorification is witnessed to by his followers, who proclaimed him as the Servant of the Lord, Messiah, New Moses, and Lord. But above all, he is the light of the Gentiles, that is, of all men. It is no accident that, while Matthew traced the genealogy of Jesus back to Abraham, Luke traced it back to Adam.

• Luke, then, links the ministry of Jesus with the life of the Church. He thinks of Jesus as the inaugurator of a world-wide community in which there is neither bond nor free, male nor female. The expectation of an imminent end of all things does not dominate Luke; he thinks of the Church as a settled community, growing in time; it is not feverish either from persecution or from a fervid expectation of the end. The end will ultimately come, but the life of the Church in history is significant. And the life of Jesus in history is significant; it is not only a sign of the end, but a guide to the spirit that should inform the life of the Church. And so Luke treats Jesus more as a historian would than do any of the Gospel writers. He checked his sources; and the humanitarian figure he describes is not his own creation but a real figure who steps out of those sources. It is precisely this kind of figure, one open to the grief of the ages, who is the Saviour of the World. Luke never allows us to forget that the reality of the world-wide community, the Church, ultimately depends upon the reality of Jesus as the friend of the poor, the sick, the outcast, the women, who cried out for care and attention in the first century. Humanitarianism is endemic to his Gospel. The

Spirit of the Jesus he saw walking in Galilee and Judaea as the Friend of Humanity is also the only spirit that can inform the world-wide community with true life.

The three portraits of Jesus

Our survey of the Synoptics is over. They are far more complex than has often been supposed. They share terms and ideas, but they each look at and describe Jesus in different ways. Mark sees him through the glare of Nero's persecutions and presents him as the suffering leader of and model for Christians undergoing fiery trial in first-century Rome. The Markan Jesus is tempered with the kind of suffering which tried and purified and tempered the Puritans of early America. In this sense, the Markan Jesus is a Puritan Jesus. Matthew, concerned to set forth Jesus as the one who fulfills the hopes of Judaism so as to win the allegiance of Israel, pictures a teacher of righteousness who is in part a New Moses offering a New Law, even as, by his living presence, he challenges the Gentile world. The Matthaean Jesus is informed by the kind of dignity, austerity, and yet "earthy" quality which breathes in the statue of Abraham Lincoln in Washington, D.C., which is the quintessence of suffering sensitivity and strong justice. And when we turn to Luke, both the fiery leader of Mark and the lawgiver of Matthew have become the gentle, warm, "humane," and "human" Saviour of the Gentiles, even as he retains his glory. The Jesus of Luke, one feels, might well have uttered the words written on the Statue of Liberty in New York harbour:

> Give me your tired, your poor,
> your huddled masses yearning to breathe free.
> . . . .
> Send these, the homeless, tempest-tost to me.

But, you will ask, since all the evangelists differ so greatly in their presentation of Jesus, can we see him as he was? Is not Jesus himself lost to us behind the mantles cast around him by

Matthew, Mark, and Luke? This question may, however, be given a different twist. May we not also ask whether, if we only had one Gospel, many aspects of Jesus' ministry would have been lost to us? Do not the three Gospels (omitting John for the moment) supplement each other?

Their three portraits deal with the same person, Jesus. The three deal with him out of the same experience of the presence of the living Jesus; that is, the three write after the death of Jesus and after the emergence of the Church, which was born out of the conviction that Jesus was still a living reality among Christians. They share a common theme and a common experience. They share also, to a large extent, a common body of tradition. Matthew, Mark, and Luke witness to the same glory. Where the difficulty emerges is that they each write out of different situations. And the place on which we stand determines what we see. To approach New York from the sea is to be overpowered by the daring of its skyscrapers; to approach it by road is to be made aware of its outreach into the suburbs, Long Island, New Jersey, and beyond; to fly over New York is to recognize the intricate symmetry of its design. Whichever approach is taken, the city itself, in its singularity, is unmistakable. But each approach brings to the foreground one aspect of the city. Taken in isolation, each of these aspects is not false, but disproportionate. Taken together, they provide a rich understanding of New York in its fullness. So is it with the Gospels. The three Gospels with which we have dealt approach Jesus from beyond the great divide, which is the Resurrection, so that the glow of faith is over all that they write. But they approach him from a particular direction. Each bears witness to the fact of Jesus, but the witness of each needs to be supplemented by that of the others. Through their three pictures, we are confronted with one who is unmistakably the same in all three—the same in his compassion and suffering, in his grace and demand. By living with the three Gospels, we may discover that he comes to be more and more recognizable as the same in all three. It is the testimony of many that despite the differences and even contradictions of the Synoptics, he shines clear. One of the latest translators of the Gospels relates his experience with the Gospels as follows:

No one can read the hundredth part of what has been written about the Gospels since they ceased to be regarded as verbally sacrosanct and feel certain that Jesus acted and spoke on each occasion *exactly* as described. On the other hand no one can reasonably doubt that the Gospels are true—the tradition they embody is firmly based on the reports of eye-witnesses. Such a tradition is of course not only selective but liable to interpolations and distortions, as anyone can prove for himself by passing a story round a circle of friends by word of mouth and then comparing the final version with the first. Yet what has impressed me most in the oral tradition as presented to us in the Gospels is its fidelity to detail. Not that we should be surprised at that. Everything that Jesus had said and done was precious both to those who reported him and to their eager audiences. Every word, tone, look and gesture of the Master was carefully reproduced. In fact, when the first Christians spoke about him, I feel that they must have acted the part, so realistic are the descriptions that have come down to us. And I was happy, on returning to the texts after my excursion into controversial literature, to find that I had received a strong impression of this kind when first translating. I had even felt at some points that the logic of Christ's words could not be brought out unless they were spoken as he spoke them, with the gestures that he made. Also that even the narrative portions cannot always be fully appreciated unless they are read aloud, as the Evangelists intended. For it is becoming increasingly clear that the Gospels were prepared not only to be read in private, but to be read aloud, and to be used in church for liturgical purposes. (See *The Origins of the Gospel According to St. Matthew,* G. D. Kilpatrick, 1946; and *The Primitive Christian Calendar,* P. Carrington, 1952.)

Such is the faith I have acquired in the authenticity of the material which our Gospel-writers undertook, as Luke says, "to arrange in narrative form." But it was by no means a foregone conclusion that the stringing together of a number of short narratives and bits of teaching, however true and graphic they might be, would result in an entity that could be called a book, still less a literary masterpiece. It is true that the writers did not feel it their duty, like a modern biographer, to present a balanced view of a whole life, nor to narrate everything in the order of its occurrence—indeed I do not think they always knew it. But they had other difficulties to contend with. They had to arrange their material in suitable sections for liturgical purposes. They had at the same time to create the impression of rapid and relentless forward movement from the divine beginnings to the predestined end. And they had, like the Greek tragic dramatists, to write for an audience who were conscious of that end before the first words of the first line were spoken. That they succeeded as they did constitutes a miracle which is unique in the history of literature and the annals of religion. We can account for it only by remembering that they were inspired by a unique personality. Just as Jesus lived in the oral tradition that preceded the Gospels, so he inspired and unified the writings that eventually summed it up. One might almost say that Jesus wrote the Gospels.[22]

PART III
Paul

. . . a man of little stature, thin-haired upon the head, crooked in the legs, of good state of body, with eyebrows joining, and nose somewhat hooked, full of grace: for sometimes he appeared like a man, and sometimes he had the face of an angel.

(From *The Acts of Paul*)[23]

For the same God who said, "Out of darkness let light shine," has caused his light to shine within us, to give the light of revelation—the revelation of the glory of God in the face of Jesus Christ.   (II Corinthians 4:5–6)

CHAPTER 20

THE SOURCES

So far we have dealt with those writers in the New Testament who consciously recalled Jesus as he lived. Their pictures of him were governed by their present needs and colored by the glow of their faith. But they did look back to Jesus, and an important part of their purpose was to recall him as he was. To put it in other words, Jesus as he lived was a standard to which they referred. They did interpret him, but they always convey the impression of looking back at him across the years from a distance.

In the next chapters, we shall be dealing with documents, the epistles of Paul, where this is not the case. In these epistles, while the Jesus of Galilee and Judaea is taken for granted and remembered, it is not the story of his life in the past which is the chief point of reference. Not history, not even preached history, is their main concern, but the meaning of Jesus and his relevance for the present life of the Church. The partly historical interest of the Gospels gives way to a theological interest. Our previous discussion has shown that such a statement cannot be pressed, but at least we can say that in Paul the theological interest is more exclusively dominant; that is, we meet in him one who reflects upon what the Synoptics have presented in the story of a life. But the reflection upon the story takes place in the hurly-burly of a life which buffeted with the waves of the Mediterranean, endured the flogging of the Synagogue and wrestled with the "care of the churches." Paul's "theology" is a theology wrought, not in the quiet of a study, but in the maelstrom of a missionary life. The details of that life cannot be given here, but no understanding of Paul's intensity is possible unless the tensions of his life be remembered. He was far more industrious and far more often in prison for the sake of the Gospel than any other Christian. Without discussing his pride at the moment, let us recall his words:

> Are they servants of Christ? I am mad to speak like this, but I can outdo them. More overworked than they, scourged more severely, more often imprisoned, many a time face to face with death. Five times the Jews have given me the thirty-nine strokes; three times I have been beaten with rods; once I was stoned; three times I have been shipwrecked, and for twenty-four hours I was adrift on the open sea. I have been constantly on the road; I have met dangers from rivers, dangers from robbers, dangers from my fellow-countrymen, dangers from foreigners, dangers in towns, dangers in the country, dangers at sea, dangers from false friends. I have toiled and drudged, I have often gone without sleep; hungry and thirsty, I have often gone fasting; and I have suffered from cold and exposure.
>
> Apart from these external things, there is the responsibility that weighs on me every day, my anxious concern for all our congregations. If anyone is weak, do I not share his weakness? If anyone is made to stumble, does my heart not blaze with indignation? (II Cor. 11:23–29)

But suffering alone does not make a person important. We must still ask why the figure of Paul deserves the attention that we shall pay him. And the answer is clear: it is fourfold.

What makes Paul important?

First, Paul is important in the New Testament itself. Out of twenty-seven of its documents, thirteen are ascribed to Paul. His written work on this reckoning constitutes about one-fourth of the whole of the New Testament. Moreover, Paul's espistles are the earliest documents within the New Testament, so that they take us nearest in time to the origins of Christianity.

Secondly, the work of Paul in the early Church is of crucial significance in the early days of Christianity.

> . . . Although he did not labour alone, he more than any other was responsible for the rapid spread of Christianity in the mid-1st cent.; albeit unwittingly he can be claimed to have laid the foundations for later Christian theology; he gave the Gentile churches order in worship and in organisation. He understood the Graeco-Roman world, and was yet rooted in Judaism, so that he was able to plant a Palestinian Gospel in an alien world and yet keep it true to its root; while his imperial awareness kept Christianity from conflict on any large scale with Rome.[24]

As a dominant formative influence in the growth of early Christianity, Paul deserves the closest scrutiny.

Thirdly, the epistles of Paul have been of extraordinary importance in the later history of Christianity. It could be argued that some of the most creative movements in the history of the Church have been born of a rediscovery of Paul. Let me remind you briefly only of three. In the fourth century, a professor of rhetoric sat weeping in a garden and heard a child singing in a neighboring house, "Take up and read! take up and read!" Taking up the scroll which lay at his side, he read (Rom. 13:13b–14), "not in reveling and drunkenness, not in debauchery and licentiousness, not in quarreling and jealousy. But put on the Lord Jesus Christ, and make no provision for the flesh, to gratify its desires." And the man who became St. Augustine goes on to say: "No further would I read, nor had I any need: instantly, at the end of this sentence, a clear light flooded my heart and all the darkness of doubt vanished away."

Later on, in 1515, Martin Luther, a professor of Theology, found that a passage in Paul became to him, as he puts it, "a gateway to heaven."

> For I am not ashamed of the Gospel. It is the saving power of God for everyone who has faith—the Jew first, but the Greek

also—because here is revealed God's way of righting wrong, a way that starts from faith and ends in faith; as Scripture says, "he shall gain life who is justified through faith." (Rom. 1:16–17)

And that passage set the match to the Protestant Reformation. So, too, later still, in 1738, John Wesley's heart was strangely warmed in Aldersgate Street, London, when he heard someone reading Luther's Preface to the Epistle to the Romans, and the evangelical revival of the eighteenth century was launched.

Finally, Paul is important because he can still speak to modern man. In our time, Karl Barth has moved the world by a commentary on Paul's Epistle to the Romans, which became a bombshell on the theologians' playground. Not only within the covers of the New Testament is Paul important, but in the pages of history.

For all these reasons, I invite you to consider him, because who touches him, not only touches a man, but something of the divine fire. But first, we must examine the sources that are available for understanding him.

The sources for understanding Paul

The sources are of three kinds. First, there is the extra canonical literature dealing with Paul, almost all of which is legendary and historically valueless. Secondly, there are the books of Acts which we shall discuss later; and, finally, the Pauline epistles.

Let us begin with the Pauline epistles. In the New Testament as we have it, there are thirteen epistles ascribed to Paul. But many of these have been examined for a long period of time and found to be non-Pauline. A large degree of agreement has been reached over most of the epistles which we should accept as Pauline, and the present position held by most Protestant scholars may be summarized as follows.

It is generally agreed that the Epistle to the Hebrews should not be regarded as written by Paul. The reasons for this are based upon style and content and seem to me to be conclusive.

Most scholars regard the Pastoral Epistles, that is I and II Timothy and Titus, as second-century documents. They may contain fragments of letters written by Paul (II Tim. 4:6–21; Tit. 3:12–14), but in their main structure they are non-Pauline. It would be an exaggeration to say that the non-Pauline authorship of these epistles is universally accepted among Protestant scholars. There are still excellent scholars who hold to their Pauline authorship. But the language of the Pastorals and the temper of their thought seems to point to a later date than Paul.

There has been considerable debate among New Testament scholars concerning the Pauline authorship of Colossians and Ephesians, especially, and also of Philippians. It is over the authorship of Ephesians that there has been most dispute. We need not enter into the various theories propounded. By and large, they do not compel the conclusion that Ephesians is not by Paul. At least, we may claim that it emerges from circles influenced by Paul. Many still feel that it is unlikely that the mind and heart which created Ephesians can have been other than those of Paul himself.

Granting, then, that we have the following undisputed Pauline documents: Galatians, Romans, I and II Corinthians, I and II Thessalonians, Philemon, Philippians, and the possibly Pauline or near-Pauline documents of Colossians and Ephesians, it must be admitted that we have a fair amount of first-hand material from which to study Paul. But we also have other material, namely, the Book of Acts, which purports to tell us a great deal about Paul.

For the particular purposes of our survey, Acts is important for several reasons. *First, we shall be concerned to discover the background against which we are to understand Paul.* To know Paul, we must know the world out of which he came; was it one in which Hellenistic forces predominated or was he a child of

Judaism untouched by Hellenism? To answer these questions accurately would take us a long way toward understanding the Apostle. And the Book of Acts does tell us much about him—his birth, his education at the feet of Gamaliel, and his career. We must, therefore, ask what weight should be given to this document in our study of Paul.

Secondly, we are concerned to understand Paul as a Christian. This means that we must ask how he is related to other Christians. Often in the past it has been asserted that Paul was a kind of solitary Christian who had his own peculiar brand of Christianity; between him and the primitive Church, a great gulf was fixed. By his peculiar conversion, he had entered into the Church in an extraordinary way and was, therefore, cut off from the life of the Church. But, however impressive Paul must have been and however different from other Christians, he must have been in some relation to them. And, since Acts purports to give us a description of the life of the earliest Christian communities, it could be, if reliable, a major source for helping us to understand how Paul stands in relation to these.

And *thirdly,* it must not be overlooked that, in a sense, Paul dominates Acts—at least the second half. What the precise aim of Acts was we need not now enquire, but at least it purports to give the career of Paul of Tarsus as a Christian.

The historical value of Acts

Thus, because of the kind of material that Acts deals with, any student of Paul must ask: What is the value of Acts as a historical source for understanding Paul? On this question scholars have been very divided. Let us begin with radical scholars first. Many have claimed that Acts is a very unreliable document. It is unreliable because of two things. First, it is of a late date. Some regard it as written in the first quarter of the second century. This means that its picture of the primitive Church was dated from the beginning. Secondly, the author of Acts was less concerned with what the earliest days of the Church were like—that is, with history as such—than with what the Church should be like in his own day. It tells us a good deal about what the author of Acts thought the Church should be and what Christian sermons should be in his own day, but little as to what the Church actually was at first and what the first sermons actually were like. Acts, in short, is not history pure and simple, but history with a purpose—the purpose of edifying Christians at the time when it was written. On these two grounds, many have suggested that we should not place too much reliance on the historicity of Acts, so that its value for understanding Paul is minor.

On the other hand, others have dealt with both the date and historical value of Acts more gently. Older scholars, for example, insisted that behind the early chapters of Acts there were very early sources written in Aramaic. One American scholar, Professor C. C. Torrey, argued that the whole of Acts 1–15 is a translation from an early Aramaic source. Few have followed Torrey, but there have been many who have claimed that parts of Acts 1–12 are drawn from early written or oral sources of extreme value. It must be admitted that at the moment, source criticism in Acts, as in the Synoptic Gospels, is not always highly valued, but there are still scholars who insist that the early chapters of Acts do give us reliable knowledge of the primitive Church in its earliest days.

And, even if the early chapters of Acts may be open to question, it has to be recognized that in the second half of Acts, where the author is dealing with Paul, he drew upon what seems to have been his own diary. In this section, therefore, the witness of Acts must be given much attention, although even here scholars have been divided as to the real value of the traces of the diary to which I refer.

What then are the sources which we have for Paul? I shall

assume that the non-canonical sources are largely legendary and historically of little if any value. What shall we say about the Epistles and Acts? Three positions can be taken:

1. We may regard Acts as so unreliable historically that we have to depend entirely, or almost entirely, on the Epistles.

2. We may take the Epistles as primary but take Acts with utmost seriousness as containing reliable information which must be reconciled with the Epistles. This is the position taken by British scholars usually.

3. We may take a mediating position. The Epistles are primary, but while we should not twist their evidence to fit that of Acts, Acts does provide valuable information which deserves to be considered as historically significant. This position is held by J. Munck.

In the following pages, Acts is taken as a serious source for early Christianity and Paul, although primary importance is given to the Epistles.

CHAPTER 21

THE BACKGROUND OF PAUL

I am a part of all that I have met . . .

So speaks the Ulysses of Tennyson. And his words are profoundly true of us all; they are certainly true of Paul. What were the worlds that he met, which were a part of him and of which he was a part? There were three main influences upon Paul. He lived in the world of the Roman Empire, which means that he was open to Hellenistic influences. He was probably a Roman citizen, so that imperial thoughts were no strangers to his breast. And, finally, he was born a Jew and was proud of this, so that Judaism bore him and nourished him. There can be little question that Athens, Rome, and Jerusalem were all tutors of Paul. The question is—to what extent did each of them exert their influence? Admitting that he was open to all the winds that blew from all three directions, which wind, in his case, was strongest? Debate still goes on over this question, and I shall attempt to point out its bare bones.

The Hellenistic background

The first avenue along which critical scholarship approached Paul was that of Hellenism. Paul had written in Greek. Many scholars had been trained in classical Greek and so it was natural for them to look at Paul through Greek eyes. And at the end of the last century and the beginnings of the twentieth, this was a very popular way of interpreting Paul. Certain things seemed obvious. For example, there are four things where it seems clear that Paul thinks as a Greek. He contrasts the flesh and the spirit, as the Greeks did; he increasingly gave up Jewish ideas about the end of the world and adopted the more Greek idea of the immortality of the soul, for example, in II Corinthians 5; his understanding of Christ as Lord points to Greek usage—the Greeks knew gods many and lords many; and, lastly, his teaching about baptism and the Eucharist can only be understood in the light of the Graeco-Roman world, which was familiar with the baptismal and sacramental rites of dying and rising saviours.

Today few scholars would accept any of these positions thus simply. For example, take the dualism of flesh and spirit. I recently examined the notion of the flesh in Plato but found little to substantiate the idea that the Pauline doctrine of the flesh owes anything to classical Greek sources. Many older nineteenth-century scholars had a preconceived notion of what they thought was Hellenistic or classical Greek thought and applied this to Paul without justification or proof. They ignored material which connected Paul with primitive Christianity and with Judaism because they approached the Apostles too exclusively through the classical tradition.

In the twentieth century, the approach to Paul through the Hellenistic world has been continued, however, by what we may call the "History of Religions School." Representatives of this approach claimed that, by the first century, oriental cults and Hellenistic religions had merged to create a longing for salvation and immortality through initiation into mysteries. They claimed that Paul drew upon the language of these mysteries to expound Christianity. Already, before Paul, Christianity had been Hellenized; the process of Hellenization began in Antioch in Syria. There, Christian congregations transferred to Jesus the title *Kyrios,* Lord. And out of this worship of Jesus as Lord, Paul developed his theology. These positions have been criticized on several grounds. It has been pointed out

that there is no evidence for the existence of any cult centering in a "Lord" such as this school refers to. And the terminology which it traced to the Mystery Religions is now seen to be
native to Judaism. Any heavy emphasis on the Hellenism of
Paul must come to terms with the following facts:

a. That Paul regarded himself as unmistakably a Jew (Phil.
3:4b ff.; Rom. 9:3b).

b. To deny this Jewishness demands that we dismiss a great
deal of Acts as unhistorical.

c. To understand Paul as deliberately importing mystery
terminology into the interpretation of the Gospel is psychologically unlikely. This can be safely asserted because of the dis-
gust at immorality so often contained by the Mysteries which
Paul's letters reveal.

There are many other reasons against taking Paul as a Hel-
lenizer of Christianity, but I must pass on.

Hellenistic Judaism

A modified form of the Hellenistic approach to Paul is that
put forward by Jewish scholars. According to these scholars,
Paul was indeed a Jew, but it should never be forgotten that
he was *not* a Palestinian Jew, but rather one born outside
Palestine in Tarsus. Tarsus was a center of philosophy, and
Paul would inevitably have been exposed to the influence of
Greek thought. Moreover, the Judaism which Paul knew in
Tarsus was an inferior kind of Judaism, modified and corrupted
by Hellenistic influences, both philosophic and religious. These
scholars urged very strongly, as we shall see, that, if Paul had
known true Palestinian Judaism—that is, the best "Rabbinic"
Judaism of his time—he would not have been so open to
Christian influences. The only Judaism he knew was an inferior, Hellenized Judaism. I shall deal further with this position later. Here I merely state that it is unsatisfactory. But

Jewish scholars have at least recognized that Paul was a Jew, even though an inferior one, and this brings me to the next avenue along which Paul has been approached.

The Old Testament, Apocalyptic and Rabbinic Judaism

Those who have emphasized that Paul above all was a Jew have, however, emphasized different elements within his background as a Jew.

First, in the nineteenth century, some scholars were content with pointing to the Old Testament as an adequate explanation of the so-called "Jewish-element" in Paul. But between Paul and the Old Testament there stands what we call Judaism. It is not possible to ignore this, and a direct, simple appeal to the Old Testament as an explanation of Paul's Jewishness is inadequate. The Judaism of Paul was not exhausted by the Old Testament.

And the second approach along the lines of Judaism is particularly associated with Albert Schweitzer. He especially emphasized the relationship between Apocalyptic Judaism and Paul, that is, that Judaism which concentrated on the passing of the present order and the coming of a new order. He took the teaching of Judaism about the end of all things seriously, and, in his very great work *The Mysticism of Paul the Apostle* (1931), he argued that Paul shared with the early Church the conviction that through the life, death, and resurrection of Jesus the Messianic Kingdom had drawn near; that the end was at hand and had begun. Those who are in Christ share in the new life of the Messianic Age, in a world-wide redemption that has taken place in him. It is from this point of view that Schweitzer interprets the whole of Paulinism. Essentially, Schweitzer's position has been endorsed by the two most recent significant interpreters of Paul, Schoeps and Munck.

The strength of Schweitzer's position is evident: it explains why Paul was *understood* by the earliest Christians, whose view of the end he shared; and how he was increasingly misunderstood by later Christians, who became more and more Hellenized and unable to appreciate Paul's emphasis on the end of all things. It also does justice to the undoubted fact that Paul's whole thinking was concerned with the end. But it does not do justice to other aspects of Paul's thought. These are only to be accounted for by recognizing that Paul, however steeped in the apocalyptic tradition of Judaism, also had affinities with Pharisaic Judaism or what later became Rabbinic Judaism.

This is the third avenue along which Paul has been approached—the avenue of Pharisaism or Rabbinism. This is the position which I urged in *Paul and Rabbinic Judaism*. My argument for this would be somewhat as follows.

Paul a Jew

Consider the following passages from Paul's Epistle to the Romans, the manifesto of his faith:

> I am speaking the truth as a Christian, and my own conscience, enlightened by the Holy Spirit, assures me it is no lie: in my heart there is great grief and unceasing sorrow. For I could even pray to be outcast from Christ myself for the sake of my brothers, my natural kinsfolk. They are Israelites: they were made God's sons; theirs is the splendour of the divine presence, theirs the covenants, the law, the temple worship, and the promises. Theirs are the patriarchs, and from them, in natural descent, sprang the Messiah. (9:1–4)

At the very least, these words reveal one who was consciously a Jew, proud of his people and of their place in history. Moreover, he ascribes to that same people a role in the future history of mankind which we can hardly exaggerate. So far from thinking that, with the coming of the Messiah, the specific role of his own people was over, submerged in and subordinated to that of the Gentiles, he ascribes to Israel after the flesh—

that is, to Jewry as such—a special place in the purpose of God. He does not precisely define this place, but merely says that the union of the New Israel, that is, the Christian Church, with the Old Israel, that is, the Jewish people as such, would—in his mystifying phrase—be "life from the dead." By this, he at least meant that Judaism was necessary to the deepest or highest life of the New Israel. I shall, in the light of all this, assume therefore that Paul was a Jew.

A Palestinian Jew

To deny this obvious fact, however, has been impossible, even for those in Israel who find Paul alien. Can we go further and define more nearly what kind of Jew was this Paul? Because there are Jews and Jews. Was Paul a true Jew—comparable, let us say, to Hillel or Akiba? Many have denied this, and claimed that Paul, far from being rooted and grounded in Palestinian Judaism, was a typical product of Hellenistic Judaism. The debate recently stirred up by Prime Minister Ben-Gurion on the relative merits of Jews living in Palestine and those outside is probably as old as Judaism itself. Certainly it occupied first-century Judaism. Were the Jews of the Diaspora quite as authentically Jewish as those who lived in Israel? This question has invaded Pauline studies.

Thus some Jewish scholars, Claude Montefiore and Joseph Klausner, in particular, have emphasized the fact that Paul was born outside Palestine and, therefore, could not have been aware of the full wealth of pure Palestinian Judaism. The Judaism in which he was brought up in Tarsus, in Asia Minor, was of necessity inferior to the Palestinian Judaism of such figures as Hillel and Shammai, Johanan b. Zakkai, and other teachers. Had Paul been a Palestinian, he would have encountered the true Judaism of the land of Israel itself. It was because he knew only this second-hand, diluted, and even "corrupted" Judaism that Paul left the religion of his fathers and embraced a new faith. Paulinism is only a possibility on the soil of an inferior Judaism of the Diaspora.

What shall we say to this understanding of Paul? First, we may doubt the claim made that a Jew born in Tarsus of necessity knew only a Judaism inferior to that of Palestine. Living in the Diaspora, as many an exile from his motherland knows, could and often did lead to a more intense devotion to the religion of the motherland. Very often the best native is the native abroad. We can be fairly certain that Paul's home was a bit of Palestine in the Diaspora, where the religion of his fathers in its warmth, purity, and depth was observed. Secondly, the old distinction which scholars have drawn for decades between Palestinian and Diaspora Judaism has now been seen to be false. It should not be forgotten that for three centuries, under the Seleucids, Palestine had been open not only to a Greek occupation but to one that deliberately aimed at the Hellenization of the country. The extent to which Palestinian Judaism was thereby Hellenized has been increasingly recognized. The number of Greek words that have crept into Jewish literary sources; the Greek terms such as *bêma, Sanhedrin,* and others used to describe the institutions and ornaments of Judaism; the extensive evidence drawn upon by Professor Goodenough of Yale, in his monumental works on *Jewish-Symbols in the Graeco-Roman World,* to show how Hellenistic and Jewish images were intermingling in the first century in Palestine as in the Diaspora; and the way in which even Rabbinic methods of exegesis reveal Aristotelean and other Greek influences—all these elements show that the Judaism of Palestine was not a watertight compartment shut off from all Gentile influences but a religion which was inevitably open to Hellenization. Thus, there was no pure Judaism in Palestine to be set over against a less pure Judaism in the Diaspora. Rather, currents poured the Diaspora influences freely into Palestine and made the gulf between the motherland and the Diaspora far less than scholars have often

claimed. Judaism in Palestine itself was surrounded by Hellenistic influences, while—through the Temple Tax, through the
visits of pilgrims to the Holy Land, and through the intercommunication made possible by the ubiquitous synagogue which
already before A.D. 70 had probably become the living centre of
Israel—the Judaism of the Diaspora was continually influenced
by and made similar to that of the mother country.

On the above two counts, even if Paul was a Diaspora Jew,
it does not necessarily follow that he was therefore outside the
main stream of Judaism. But there is a further point to be
considered. Is it quite clear that Paul *was* brought up in the
Diaspora? There is no doubt that he was born in Tarsus in
Cilicia in Asia Minor. What is not so clear is how long he
lived there. Recently, a Dutch scholar, Professor Van Unnik of
Utrecht, has suggested, very plausibly, that, while Paul was
born in Tarsus, he was brought up in Jerusalem. The crucial
passage is the following in Acts 22:3 which reads:

"I am a true-born Jew," he said, "a native of Tarsus in Cilicia.
I was brought up in this city, and as a pupil of Gamaliel I
was thoroughly trained in every point of our ancestral law. I
have always been ardent in God's service, as you all are today."

Notice the terms *born, brought up, trained;* note also their
sequence. There is considerable evidence that these terms, in
this sequence, were traditional: they were used to describe a
man's birth, upbringing, and technical education. Clearly,
though he was born in Tarsus, the significant part of Paul's
life was spent in the Holy City and that at the feet of
Gamaliel. He may, indeed, have left Tarsus when he was a few
weeks or months or years old, at an age before the environment of that city could have deeply influenced him. This
means that those who have emphasized that Paul, from his
earliest days, had been open to the impact of Greek philosophies such as Stoicism, which was especially popular at Tarsus,

to the attraction of Mystery Religions with their insidious corruptions, and to the Hellenistic ethos generally—have all been mistaken. In Paul, we confront not a Diaspora Jew at all but a true son of Palestine acquainted with the best Rabbinic Judaism of his day.

A Pharisaic Jew

And, at this point, we must take seriously the further evidence of the Epistles and of Acts. In Galatians 1:13 f., Paul tells of his former life in Judaism—how he "advanced in Judaism beyond many of [his] own age among [his] people, so extremely zealous was [he] for the traditions of [his] fathers." So, too, in Philippians 3:5 f., he tells us that he was "circumcized on my eighth day, Israelite by race, of the tribe of Benjamin, a Hebrew born and bred in my attitude to the law, a Pharisee; in pious zeal, a persecutor of the church; in legal rectitude, faultless." When we turn to Acts, we find him sitting at the feet of Gamaliel, acquainted with the High Priest (Acts 9:1), able to speak in Hebrew (Acts 21:40), "a Pharisee, a son of Pharisees" (Acts 23:6). Everything, therefore, points to the fact that Paul was not only a Jew but a Pharisaic Jew, probably one of the strictest of his kind. He was no inferior product of the Diaspora but one bred and nourished in Israel. The picture of Paul as a Hellenistic Jew has to be abandoned.

So far, then, we have established that Paul was, first, a Jew and, secondly, a Palestinian, Pharisaic Jew. But the question now faces us whether after he became a Christian he regarded himself as having ceased to be a Jew.

One thing is certain. During the earliest phases of his missionary work, he went first to the Jewish Synagogues. It might be argued that this was merely a matter of organizational convenience, since the Synagogues, widespread throughout the Mediterranean world, provided Paul with a ready-made platform for the preaching of Christianity. But, while this fact doubtless influenced Paul, this was not the chief factor in his insistence on preaching first to the Synagogue. Behind this lay the conviction that salvation was from the Jews and that the Gospel which he preached should first be offered to them. Even in the Fourth Gospel, written at a time when the lines between Judaism and Christianity were beginning to be clearly drawn, it was still believed among Christians that "salvation was from the Jews." (John 4:22, where Jesus says to the woman of Samaria: "You worship what you do not know; we worship what we know, for salvation is from the Jews.")

Not only did Paul, as long as he was permitted to do so, first take his message to the Synagogues (see, for example, Acts 18:1 f.), but there is considerable evidence that he continued to observe the Law. The details of the various pertinent texts cannot be given here, but he explicitly states that to the Jews he became as a Jew (I Cor. 9:20), he may have circumcized Titus (the passage in Galatians 2:1–3 is ambiguous), who was to him probably a kind of pupil or "shm'a." In Acts 21:17–26, there is an illuminating account of how far Paul was prepared to go to conciliate or to win over his compatriots. It deserves quotation in full:

> So we reached Jerusalem, where the brotherhood welcomed us gladly.
>
> Next day Paul paid a visit to James; we were with him, and all the elders attended. He greeted them, and then described in detail all that God had done among the Gentiles through his ministry. When they heard this, they gave praise to God. Then they said to Paul: "You see, brother, how many thousands of converts we have among the Jews, all of them staunch upholders of the Law. Now they have been given certain information about you: it is said that you teach all the Jews in the gentile world to turn their backs on Moses, telling them to give up circumcising their children and following our way of life. What is the position, then? They are sure to hear

that you have arrived. You must therefore do as we tell you. We have four men here who are under a vow; take them with you and go through the ritual of purification with them, paying their expenses, after which they may shave their heads. Then everyone will know that there is nothing in the stories they were told about you, but that you are a practising Jew and keep the Law yourself. As for the gentile converts, we sent them our decision that they must abstain from meat that has been offered to idols, from blood, from anything that has been strangled, and from fornication." So Paul took the four men, and next day, after going through the ritual of purification with them, he went into the temple to give notice of the date when the period of purification would end and the offering be made for each one of them.

Thus the practice of Paul suggests that his concern with his own people persisted after he had become a Christian; that he had not ceased to feel as one with them. We have already quoted passages from Romans which place this beyond doubt. It is significant, *very* significant, that the last scene in which Paul appears in the Book of Acts (and it is the very last scene in the book) reveals Paul in discussion with Jewish elders, expounding to them the meaning of his faith. To the very end, therefore, we may assume that Paul was anxious to remain in dialogue with his own people.

But it is not only in his practice that Paul reveals his essential Jewishness. The same emerges from the basic structure of his thought. To prove this statement would require volumes. Here we merely point to a few areas where this truth emerges with great clarity.[25]

In the following pages, we shall see that in his understanding of man, sin, the Church and, indeed, in all the main concepts that he uses, Paul draws upon the world of the Rabbis. Finally, we must note a broader sense in which Paul's thought is determined by Judaism. The Christian dispensation or event was understood by Paul as an act of redemption. But the word redemption for him, as a Jew, carried with it the rich connotation of the Exodus; to claim that there was "redemption" in Christ was to claim an Exodus through him—that is, an Exodus from the realm of slavery to sin, the old Egypt, to the life of a new Canaan. Christianity for Paul is a specific kind of Judaism with a new Exodus and a new Moses "in Christ." In other words, Pharisaic, Rabbinic Judaism is essential to his understanding.

New light from the Dead Sea Scrolls

Recently, a fourth avenue has opened up to the understanding of Paul. It is not a wholly new avenue. We knew of its existence before, but most scholars had thought that it was insignificant. I shall call it the Essene avenue. It is made far better known to us in the Scrolls from the Dead Sea. At numerous points, such as justification by faith, the flesh and the spirit, these do illumine the world of Paul in a new way. As yet, this avenue has been little explored; but that it is a significant one for Pauline studies, few will deny. Those who travel along it are constantly bringing new light on Paul.

In view of all the above, there can be little question that it is Judaism that furnished the most potent influence that worked on Paul. But here I want to remind you again of what I have constantly insisted upon—that the old division between Hellenism and Judaism, the Hellenic and the Hebraic, is no longer rigidly tenable. We should recognize that Paul was a Jew and a Pharisaic Jew, but also at the same time a Hellenized Jew. And, further, he was also a Romanized Jew. I shall only refer to the Roman element in Paul. It comes out, not only in his pride in his Roman citizenship, but also—if we believe some scholars—in the massiveness of his missionary strategy in which, concentrating his work in the great cities like

Ephesus, Corinth, Rome, he aimed at building a Christian Church on the model of the vast Empire of Rome.

In any case, it is well to recognize that Paul is a highly complex figure. Open to Athens and the Hellenistic world and to Jerusalem—to Apocalyptist, Pharisee, and Essene—he was also a citizen of Rome. It is to such a man that the Gentile Church mostly, if not exclusively, owes its growth.

CHAPTER 22

ON THE ROAD TO DAMASCUS

Paul, then, is the product of several worlds—the Greek, the Roman, and the Jewish. A complex figure, highly sophisticated and highly trained, Paul became a Christian. It is true that Shakespeare once refers with a touch of mild contempt to the extreme simplicity of Christians, but it is no simple figure that we meet in Saul of Tarsus. What made him become a Christian? To answer this question we have to examine the event referred to as his "conversion," but more accurately to his "call." What was its significance? The conversion is described in Acts 9:1–19; 22:4–16; 26:9–18. There is a reference to it in Galatians 1:11–17. We reproduce here Acts 9:1–9 and Galatians 1:11–17:

Acts 9:1–9

Meanwhile Saul was still breathing murderous threats against the disciples of the Lord. He went to the High Priest and applied for letters to the synagogues at Damascus authorizing him to arrest anyone he found, men or women, who followed the new way, and bring them to Jerusalem. While he was still on the road and nearing Damascus, suddenly a light flashed from the sky all around him. He fell to the ground and heard a voice saying, "Saul, Saul, why do you persecute me?" "Tell me,

Galatians 1:11–17

I must make it clear to you, my friends, that the gospel you heard me preach is no human invention. I did not take it over from any man; no man taught it me; I received it through a revelation of Jesus Christ.

You have heard what my manner of life was when I was still a practising Jew: how savagely I persecuted the church of God, and tried to destroy it; and how in the practice of our national religion I was outstripping many of my Jewish contemporaries in my bound-

Acts 9:1–9

Lord," he said, "who you are." The voice answered, "I am Jesus, whom you are persecuting. But get up and go into the city, and you will be told what you have to do." Meanwhile the men who were travelling with him stood speechless; they heard the voice but could see no one. Saul got up from the ground, but when he opened his eyes he could not see; so they led him by the hand and brought him into Damascus. He was blind for three days, and took no food or drink.

Galatians 1:11–17

less devotion to the traditions of my ancestors. But then in his good pleasure God, who had set me apart from birth and called me through his grace, chose to reveal his Son to me and through me, in order that I might proclaim him among the Gentiles. When that happened, without consulting any human being, without going up to Jerusalem to see those who were apostles before me, I went off at once to Arabia, and afterwards returned to Damascus.

This event has been understood from several points of view:

The visionary approach

Some have been content merely to assert without discussion that Saul of Tarsus had a vision of Jesus as the Messiah. This vision, inexplicable and strange, overwhelmed him. He became convinced that Jesus of Nazareth was alive and had appeared in the character of a supernatural Lord, a glorious heavenly being. But however true to the stories of the conversion in Acts this may be, it is not enough for us merely to state that this happened. Must we not seek to understand not only what happened but why? The attempt to answer this question has led to the next approach to Paul's conversion.

The psychological approach: the conversion leads to self-understanding

We must begin by getting rid of certain false notions which the term "conversion" suggests to us. This word today suggests a change from a morally bad life to a morally good life. The word evokes pictures of men sodden by drink suddenly enabled to walk in sobriety; of men accustomed to beating their wives and neglecting their children suddenly becoming kind, good fathers. "Conversion" is a passage from dissipation to morality.

But there is no evidence that Paul was at any time immoral or a profligate who needed moral rehabilitation. He was a morally serious Jew, dedicated to the observance of the Law; a Roman citizen of established social position. Conversion in his case was not a change from debauchery to morality.

But there was a change in Paul's life. What was it? Let us recognize at once that, as a Jew, Paul was always an outsider in the Graeco-Roman world. The gulf of Jewishness always remained between him and his Gentile neighbors. This meant that he was always insecure. What provided a check to this insecurity? It was pride—pride in his people Israel. Over fifty times in his epistles Paul refers to "pride." The classic passage is in Philippians 3:4–5:

> If anyone thinks to base his claims on externals, I could make a stronger case for myself: circumcized on my eighth day, Israelite by race, of the tribe of Benjamin, a Hebrew born and bred; in my attitude to the law, a Pharisee.

This was written thirty years after he had become a Christian, but you can still feel the thrill of being a Jew pulsating through his words.

How could he express his love for and pride in Israel? In one way only: by living as a Jew, that is, keeping the Law rigidly. To obey the Law became the end of his life, and he found his delight in the Law. Or did he? Paul was a perfectionist; he had to excel; not enough for him the ordinary compromises of life. He had to fulfill the Law absolutely to the last degree. This was his nature—to be obedient in all. But he could not be obedient in all. His acts he could control but not his desires; he knew that he could not give up the evil thought, however hard he tried.

Thus Paul—intense, ardent, perfectionist—became a man of

inner conflict or frustration. And it was to get rid of this frustration that he persecuted Christians; to persecute them became the supreme test of his zeal. Zeal—fanatic zeal—often turns to hatred. "Lord, how I love thy Law," says one of the Psalmists, and then: "Do I not hate them, O Lord, which hate thee? I hate them with a perfect hatred."

And, on the road to Damascus, this man of conflict, who had staked everything on the Law, found, on his way to attack Christians, that he could not go on with the butchery. Zeal for the Law had led him to what he could not do—to persecution. He could not be the perfect Pharisee. And so his pride was gone. The Law demanded persecution; and he found himself unable to go on with it. He was not capable of perfection. There was a deadlock. And the outcome was that Paul decided to throw in his lot with the one whom he had persecuted. Pride in the Law gave place to pride in the cross. He accepted his failure and trusted in God to do with him what he would, and he found freedom in this trust.

Paul's conversion meant a new self-understanding. Previously, he had believed that he himself could achieve the good life by keeping the words of the Law. The cross revealed to him that he could not—that all his strivings after righteousness were ineffective. In his conversion, Paul came to recognize this. Paul had thought that he could be blameless; that he could establish his righteousness; that he could even, perhaps, hide behind his own righteousness. He came to see in his conversion that this very belief, this very understanding of himself, was what he had to forego.

From this point of view, then, the conversion was a psychological crisis in self-understanding. But this view faces two difficulties. First, there is little, if any, evidence in the Epistles of Paul to support it. It is generally recognized that the Epistles do not depict a Paul who was frustrated and suffering under the Law. And, secondly, the details in the accounts of Paul's conversion in Acts and Galatians suggest something different. For this, we must turn to the next view of Paul's conversion.

The prophetic approach

This has only recently been propounded by Professor Johannes Munck of Denmark in his work, *Paul and the Salvation of Mankind*. He dismisses all psychological theories of the conversion because there is no evidence for them. Paul was blameless under the Law (Phil. 3:6). Munck rejects any psychological preparation for the conversion in Paul's life, and emphasizes the following points.

First, *the suddenness of the conversion*. All we know about Paul before this event is that he was on his way to Damascus to persecute Christians; that he was already a Jew, well-established in Judaism. He was not prepared for any event such as the conversion; he was, as he puts it, "seized" or "snatched" as if by something or someone from "the blue."

Next, *the accounts in Acts speak of a necessity that was laid upon Paul*. In 26:14, the Risen Lord says to him, "Saul, Saul, why do you persecute me? It hurts you to kick against the goads." This phrase, "to kick against the goads," has often been understood psychologically as referring to the pangs of conscience that Paul had against the Law in his pre-Christian days. But Munck gives it a new interpretation: it means "Why do you kick against the destiny that God has laid upon you?" And what is this destiny? It is the necessity laid upon Paul to preach the Gospel (I Cor. 9:16). "For if I preach the gospel, that gives me no ground for boasting. For necessity is laid upon me. Woe to me if I do not preach the gospel!" Here is the heart of the matter. With this agrees the next point.

All the accounts of the "conversion" are like the accounts of "the call" given to the great prophets in the Old Testament. The "conversion" of Paul is a call like the call of Amos,

Isaiah, Jeremiah, Ezra, and Ezekiel. Compare, just to cite one example, the description of the call of Jeremiah with that given in Galatians 1.

> Now the word of the Lord came to me saying,
> "Before I formed you in the womb I knew you,
> and before you were born I consecrated you;
> I appointed you a prophet to the nations." (Jer. 1:4-5)

The details given in Acts recall similar accounts, for example, in I Enoch 14:8–16:4. Here Enoch's experience is like that of Paul in form. The following items occur: The seeing of a strong light; the vision of the Lord; the falling of the men visited to the ground; the raising up of the prostrated; the call to prophecy.

It is clear that Paul's experience falls in line with that of the great prophetic figures of Israel's past. Through this peculiar revelation of the living Jesus, Paul became convinced that he was called by God to be an apostle to the Gentiles from his mother's womb. He became convinced through this "peculiar" experience that he had a "peculiar" part to play in bringing the whole of the Gentile world to faith in Jesus. He had a "peculiar" place in the Providence of God as God was winding up all things. Paul, in fact, became convinced that it was on the effectiveness of his work as an apostle to the Gentiles that the consummation of all things depended. He was the key-figure in the drama of the end to which Judaism no less than the Christians had looked forward.

This view of Paul's conversion has certain weaknesses. It reads back into the single initial event of the conversion what only became clear to Paul much later; it confuses the oak with the acorn. The conversion was the beginning of Paul's awareness of his own role in history, not its end. And again the emphasis on the totally unprepared suddenness of the conversion makes it difficult to attach a profound meaning to it. An event that is wholly unprepared for, completely cut off from any possible antecedent, could not have had the consequences that the conversion had for Paul. It would be too odd to be significant.

The approach through the Church of the crucified

The last sentence leads on to the last approach to be mentioned. What were the antecedents of the conversion? Can we set it within the framework of Paul's life? When we ask what happened immediately before Paul's conversion, the answer is clear: it was his persecution of the followers of Jesus. When we further ask why he persecuted these, two answers suggest themselves: the nature of the Christian community and the nature of the Messiah that it proclaimed. First, these Christians proclaimed a Messiah who had been crucified. Most Jews, as we saw, had certainly not anticipated a Messiah who should suffer. No Jews, we may be certain, had anticipated a Messiah who should endure the shameful death of crucifixion. Such a death in the light of Deuteronomy placed Jesus under the condemnation of the Law. To Paul's Pharisaic mind, to proclaim Jesus as Messiah was to proclaim that one whom the Law had condemned was upheld by God. This was tantamount to denying the validity of the Law. To a Pharisee, such a proclamation was anathema and had to be opposed.

We do not know whether Paul had seen Jesus in the days of his flesh; he never claims to have done so and, apparently, failed to recognize Jesus when he saw him in the vision on the road to Damascus. But the possibility is not to be ruled out that before his conversion Paul had heard much about Jesus. He had seen the martyrdom of Stephen; he must have heard criticisms of Jesus by the Pharisees. Had he heard words of Jesus such as, "They that are whole need not a physician, but they that are sick: I came not to call the righteous but sinners"? Had words such as these set the demon of doubt wandering forever in his heart? We do not know. But we do know that he must have realized that a challenge to the understanding of the Messiah which he had always cherished was being issued by Christians. They proclaimed a Messiah accursed by the Law. This was a staggering fact. The question of the nature of the Messiah was being forced upon Judaism. And Paul's initial answer was violent.

But along with this question went another. Implicit in the Church's proclamation was the claim that the Messiah whom the Jews had long expected and yearned for had appeared to them; that God had chosen to reveal his final emissary to people who by Jews such as Paul, at least, would be regarded as second-rate and possibly even worse. To Paul, it would have seemed inconceivable that God should have sent his Messiah to such ignorant, unprepared, insignificant people as those who followed Jesus. They were what Paul would have regarded as "people of the land"—boorish, untutored, irreligious. "The people of the land" was a phrase used, not only with the kind of contempt with which I often heard the horrible phrase "poor white trash" used in the South, but with hatred. The disciples were not the kind of people to whom God could have sent his Messiah. The Messiah would certainly appear among those most fitted to receive him, the righteous who kept the commandments zealously. The claim of Christians that they had received the Messiah was an impossible one, an affront to those who had kept the fires of piety and purity and "true religion" alive in Israel. The effrontery of the Church had to be countered; Christians had to be annihilated. And Saul "breathed out" threats and murder against the disciples of the Lord. To wipe out this new movement was to serve the God of Israel. Notice that the affront of the crucified Messiah was one with the affront of the "arrogance" of the Church.

Then on the road to Damascus Paul was confronted with the challenge of the truth. He was overcome by it; he could not go on with his butchery; a new life began for him. The accounts of Paul's conversion in Acts, both in their form and content, strike us as strange and unreal. We find it difficult to believe that such an event ever took place, because in modern society normal men are not expected to have such experiences. To see visions, among us, is a mark of abnormality. But anthropologists have long taught us that what may be normal in one culture may be abnormal in another. Normality varies from culture to culture. Joan of Arc would be very odd in modern America. In the culture in which Paul had been brought up, prophetic persons were expected to have visions. The vision of Paul on the road to Damascus fits in with the visionary experience of many others among his people. So there is no reason at all to doubt the form given to Paul's experience in Acts. Paul had other visions to which he refers. But he does distinguish between his vision at his conversion and all his other visions. His seeing of the Lord on the road to Damascus was different from his seeing him at other times. His other visions were private ones which he did not want to share; his vision of the Lord on the road to Damascus was like that given to other Christians. It was a shared vision. Its reality we need not doubt.

The results of the conversion

What was its result? For convenience, we separate the inseparable. First, Paul became convinced that Jesus of Nazareth was in fact the Messiah—the ultimate, final figure of history. The inconceivable had happened. The final representative of God to Israel and to the world had been crucified. The way of the Law had been subordinated to the way of the Cross. God had in fact raised Jesus. He had, therefore, approved of Jesus. But this meant that Jewish expectations of God's final actions in history had been erroneous. Paul had now to reckon with this new fact that God had chosen a person who was condemned by the Law to establish his purposes and had drawn near through the shame of Jesus. He had to reassess the role of Law and the way of salvation.

Secondly, but indivisible from the above, Paul came to know that the followers of Jesus, after all, had been right. God had visited the "unworthy." He had caught Judaism by surprise. The expectation that God rewarded men on the basis of their worthiness was a mistaken one. He had come not where he was expected to come—to those who had rigidly strained for his coming, but to those who thought themselves unworthy of his presence, to the despised "people of the land."

This made Paul's head swim. And he had to face an even more staggering fact. If God had, indeed, visited these "people of the land," would he not also visit the Gentiles? The answer could not be in doubt. All the conversion accounts connect Paul's vision with a call to the Gentile world. The God who had given his Messiah freely to the despised among the Jews, would also include all in his mercy. The barriers between Jew and Gentile were down. The Gentile world had become the object of God's grace.

Two things, therefore, converge in Paul's conversion. The awareness of the Lord as Jesus—that is, of the ultimate as crucified—and the awareness of the people of God as despised Christians. The recognition of Jesus as Lord is inextricable from the recognition of his followers as the people of God. This is strikingly brought out in the conversion stories themselves. In each, it is emphasized that, in persecuting Christians, Paul was really persecuting Jesus. "Saul, Saul, why persecutest thou me . . ?" . . . "I am Jesus whom thou presecutest." To reject the humiliation of the Church was to reject the Messiah. Later, Paul was to know that to accept the humiliation of the Church was the way to accept the Messiah. But, at this point, let us again merely note the revolutionary change involved in the acceptance of Jesus as Messiah and of "Christians" as the people of God. It was the encounter with the Church, behind which

and in which stood Jesus of Nazareth as Messiah, that turned
Saul of Tarsus into Paul the Apostle.

If this approach be anywhere near the truth, then one important result follows. It has often been asserted that Paul was
sharply divided from other Christians. He has been pictured as
a solitary colossus among a multitude of mediocre Christians
with whom he had very little in common. A great gulf was
fixed, not between him and Jewish Christians only, but between him and all Christians. But, if it was partly, at least,
through the Church itself that Paul was led to his deeper understanding of God, such a view is hardly likely. And, in fact,
in the deepest things, Paul was at one with other Christians.
Paul was converted, not only through the Church, but into
the Church.

That this was so appears when we examine the main items
in Paul's thought. In his treatment of Baptism and the Eucharist
he is not removed from what other Christians believed. Like
other Christians, he drew upon the words of Jesus for moral
guidance. Like other Christians, he used the hymns and the
creedal formulae which were the common property of the
Church. In his understanding of Jesus and of his death, of the
Spirit and of the Church itself, Paul shares with other Christians a common treasury of thought. This is not to reduce Paul
to the intellectual and spiritual level of all other Christians; it
is to recognize that, great as he was, he was not a peculiarity in
the life of the Church but a profundity. He set about expounding the Christian faith, which was his through his conversion,
not from outside the Church but from within it. In short, as he
himself makes clear, the Gospel that he preached was not his
own peculiar property, certainly not what he himself had "in-
vented" for the world, but a tradition, that is, something that
had been handed down to him from those who were in the
Church before him. "I delivered unto you," he tells the
Corinthian Church, "that which also I received." Christianity

for Paul was no merely individual possession but a common tradition. How his genius enabled him to interpret this common tradition which centered in a crucified Messiah, both to his own day and, indirectly, for all time, we shall examine in the following chapters.

CHAPTER 23

MAN AND THE UNIVERSE

Not all people are likely to be drawn to Paul. The world in which he lived and the way in which he thought are so alien to us that he strikes us as "odd." How can this "stranger" mean much to modern men?

Even more disturbing than Paul's strangeness is his intensity. He disturbs. He threatens, much as a poet who rejects all our values stabs us. As the preceding chapters have assumed, the question of the true way of life and of his relation to God was a matter of life and death for Paul. He had a compulsive need to be "right." He was nothing if not enthusiastic. Highly intelligent people ("the cold men apart"), who scorn enthusiasms, are not likely to appreciate him. To the insensitive of this world, as to Agrippa, he will even appear slightly mad. You may recall how in *Tom Jones*, Parson Thwackum, asked about his religion, replies in true bucolic fashion: "When I mention religion, I mean the Christian Religion; and not only the Christian Religion but the Protestant Religion; and not only the Protestant Religion but the Church of England." But such an attitude, in which the problems of life and destiny can be neatly pigeonholed and conveniently settled, was not for Paul. He was of the race of Jacob, a wrestler,

> . . . anxious for the future and in throes
> Of travail for perfection out of reach.[26]

Paul's it was to strive and not to yield, more from distrust of himself than of heaven and earth. To understand his response to Jesus Christ and his Church, we must understand his previous plight; how he regarded heaven and earth and himself; and why he so desperately sought a means of meeting the riddle of the universe.

The universe

Like others of his day, Paul recognized three areas of existence, which are all interrelated: the human—the world of humanity; the subhuman or the material—the world of nature; the superhuman—a world of invisible powers beyond man's control. As thus set forth, these divisions are too neat. The stars and planets, for example, would belong both to the subhuman and superhuman worlds. To the whole of these divisions, taken together, Paul gives the name *The Cosmos,* The World. Very often he regards the whole world—not the world of man only but the totality of the universe—as separated from and opposed to God. Why is this so?

The answer that Paul gives to this question is that the World had fallen under the domination of superhuman powers which were evil. He calls these by the following names:

1. *Angels:* for Paul, these are usually forces of evil. They lie in wait to injure men; they infest men with diseases; they corrupt. They are of significance not only in the lives of individual men. Behind the governments of the nations, manipulating them often, are angels. These are in control to pervert the nations. The term "authorities" is sometimes applied to these.

2. *Principalities and Powers:* these are unseen powers. They are also called "things in heaven," or "the spirits of wickedness in the heavens," or "the world powers of this (evil) age," or "the rulers of this world."

3. *The elements of the world:* the elemental demons of the world (the exact meaning of this phrase is not clear).

4. Supreme among the demons is *Satan:* he is the enemy of God and man. This awareness of a world of demonic forces surrounding human existence was familiar in first-century Judaism. In the Synoptics, the ministry of Jesus is, in part, an attack upon Beelzebub, that is, Satan. But Jesus, like those who wrote the Dead Sea Scrolls, knows of good angels as well as evil ones, whereas Paul refers most often to evil powers.

Coupled with his recognition of unseen powers of evil, Paul also shares another idea with Judaism which again and again breaks out in his writings. Judaism recognized that nature was in the hands of God, but that there were aspects of nature which still evaded his control. The dragon of the deep, subdued by God at creation, had not been wholly conquered. There always remained in nature an element opposed to the Creator. And not only so; as a result of Adam's fall, the universe itself had been affected. In the fall of man, nature fell, so that man found himself in a world in which nature itself is corrupted. For example, the beasts of the field have become ferocious. The wolf cannot lie down with the lamb; nature is "red in tooth and claw."

As if all this were not enough, Paul is also aware of Hellenistic ideas about the world. Two developments profoundly influenced the Graeco-Roman world, astronomy and astrology. In the earliest days of Greece, the universe was regarded as a flat disk arched by the ceiling of the heavens; it was compassable, even small. But in the fourth century B.C., man's ideas of the universe suddenly expanded. Aristarchus of Samos (c. 310–230 B.C.) estimated that the sun was three hundred times as large as the earth and one hundred and eighty earth diameters away. At the same time, the realm of the atmosphere was separated from the realm of the heavens. The heavens were divided into eight spheres; in the first seven, there were wandering stars, in the eighth, fixed stars. The wandering stars were the Moon, Mercury, Venus, the Sun, Mars, Jupiter, Saturn. These astronomical developments led men to think that the universe was immense, and they themselves of little significance. And after death what hazards the soul of man had to face before she could reach heaven!! She had to pass all the long way through the spheres of the wandering stars. The abode of the soul after death was no longer the now almost comfortable, nearby Hades, located under the earth, but an unbelievably distant Heaven. The infinite spaces filled men with awe.

This awe was turned to fear and despair by another development, the growth of astrology. By the first century, fatalistic ideas, starting probably in Babylon, had spread throughout the Graeco-Roman world. According to these, what happened on earth was determined by the shape of the sky, the movements of the planets and the stars. These moved without pity; and, as they moved, so was man's life shaped. An individual's fate was eternally fixed by the position of the planets at his birth; the stars in their courses ruled the world. This belief fell upon the Hellenistic world with the malign force of an epidemic of disease. It was one of the most terrible doctrines that ever oppressed humanity. But we can understand how such fatalism appealed to men, even as it drove them further into despair. It suited an age when the individual counted so little. Those who had known the ruthless advance of armies and the decay of their home states with their old securities and supports knew how puny and helpless were all their efforts to change things. They could well believe that the universe itself was governed by inhuman forces. It was natural to think that the armies of Rome, for example, were merely the earthly counterpart of the armies of a still more cruel Fate ruling the stars and planets. From these there was no escape. In the first century, especially, there was a strong sense that the universe was in bondage to corrupt powers. A "sympathy" ran through all things; the universe was one whole, but it was not stable; change and decay were everywhere. There was a living premonition that the universe, because of the rule of the planets, was soon to undergo inevitable conflagration and destruction. And since even in death the soul confronted hostile planetary and astral powers, there was also in the Hellenistic Age a very marked emphasis on the fear of death. Fate and Death became twin ogres which held mankind in bondage.

But, you will ask, could Paul, as a Jew, believe in the supremacy of the unseen angelic-demonic forces and of Fate and Death as did his Roman and Greek contemporaries? Could a Pharisee, such as Paul, have shared in such views? On the answer to this question depends Paul's answer to the problem which these powers posed to men. There can be no doubt that he took seriously the reality of the unseen angelic powers. But, as a Jew, he also held that their power was ultimately due to man. Particularly was this the case with the angelic powers which stood behind the political, governmental powers of the world. These had been assigned to the various nations by God himself. It was man who, by according to them a reverence which was not their due, had lent to these powers their demonic character. Similarly, the evil in the physical universe was bound up with the fall of man; it was through man's sin that the universe became corrupt. Fundamentally, therefore, the fault for the evil of the angelic powers lies with man.

But what of the belief in Fate? Surely man could not be blamed for having been set in a world governed by the planets! In this connection Paul uses the terms and concepts of the Hellenistic world without himself believing in the reality of their crippling dominance. At no point does he allow that the astrological powers are in control of the universe; it was God himself who had allowed them to be in control. Paul had a full awareness of the plight of men—Jew and Greek—in his day. He felt the force of their fear of unseen forces of evil, of Fate and Death; but whereas many of his Hellenistic contemporaries would claim that the fault was not in themselves but in their stars, in the last resort Paul would have insisted that

> the fault . . . is not in our stars,
> But in ourselves that we are underlings.[27]

Men are now underlings to the forces of evil. But the responsibility for this terrible fact lies with man himself. To put all this in other words: whereas the Graeco-Roman world found the major threat to its existence in Fate and Death, Paul found the major threat in man's sin, from which he believed that the horror of Fate and Death arose. Until man can be delivered from sin, the universe will be in bondage. Consider carefully the following passage from Romans 8:18–23:

> For I reckon that the sufferings we now endure bear no comparison with the splendour, as yet unrevealed, which is in store for us. For the created universe waits with eager expectation for God's sons to be revealed. It was made the victim of frustration, not by its own choice, but because of him who made it so; yet always there was hope, because the universe itself is to be freed from the shackles of mortality and enter upon the liberty and splendour of the children of God. Up to the present, we know, the whole created universe groans in all its parts as if in the pangs of childbirth. Not only so, but even we, to whom the Spirit is given as firstfruits of the harvest to come, are groaning inwardly while we wait for God to make us his sons and set our whole body free.

It follows from what we have just written that Paul would be particularly concerned with man and his place in the universe. In the Hellenistic Age there were many views of man. One especially was prevalent and different from that held by Paul. According to this, there was little distinction between man and God or between the human and the divine. Men could be easily fused with gods. We noted how easily human emperors could become divine beings. To claim to be divine was not regarded

as "odd," as it would be among us, and "divine men" were common. This is somewhat surprising. In the Hellenistic Age men
felt as if they were the flotsam and jetsam of the universe; and
yet this very age could believe in "divine men," that the gulf between man and gods was small. The spirit of the age in its baf-
fling inconsistency in this matter might well find expression in
the words of Hamlet:

> . . . this goodly frame, this earth, seems to me a sterile prom-
> ontory; this most excellent canopy, the air, look you, this brave
> o'erhanging firmament, this majestic roof fretted with golden
> fire, why it appears no other thing to me than a foul and pesti-
> lent congregation of vapours. What a piece of work is man!
> how noble in reason! how infinite in faculty! in form and moving
> how express and admirable! in action how like an angel! in
> apprehension how like a God! The beauty of the world! the
> paragon of animals! And yet, to me, what is this quintessence
> of dust?[28]

God and man

How did Paul confront such an ambiguous view of man?
Unlike his Hellenistic, but like his Jewish, contemporaries, Paul
found a great gulf fixed between God and man. This gulf is
inescapable. Man is creature, not Creator; with qualifications,
he is clay in the hands of the Potter. Any fusion of man and
God is unthinkable. Man is on earth; God is in heaven.

But this does not mean that man is—as Hamlet puts it—
merely "the quintessence of dust." On the contrary, Paul finds
in man what seem, at first sight at least, bridges or points of
contact between the Holy God and man. Thus he refers to the
mind of man. And a Hellenist would ask, "Is not this a divine
element in man? Is not his 'noble reason' a spark of the divine
reason? Is not the mind a higher principle that can guide man?"
Paul does recognize that there is, in the mind of man, a rational
faculty. With this faculty man can recognize and respond to
the law of God, as appears from Romans 7:23–25:

> . . . but I perceive that there is in my bodily members a different law, fighting against the law that my reason approves and making me a prisoner under the law that is in my members, the law of sin. Miserable creature that I am, who is there to rescue me out of this body doomed to death? God alone, through Jesus Christ our Lord! Thanks be to God! In a word then, I myself, subject to God's law as a rational being, am yet, in my unspiritual nature, a slave to the law of sin.

The mind can also plan for action; it can purpose well.

Again, Paul borrowed from his contemporaries the notion of "conscience." Every man born into the world has a capacity to approve the good and to condemn the evil; this capacity expresses itself as a pain following wrongdoing. Paul associates it with a law written on the heart of every man. In Romans 2:15, he writes as follows:

> . . . for they display the effect of the law inscribed on their hearts. Their conscience is called as witness, and their own thoughts argue the case on either side, against them or even for them.

Is not conscience a bridge between God and man? Was not the Greek who claimed that "conscience is a god to us all" right?

However, far more important in Paul's thinking than either the mind or conscience was another way in which man might be open to God, that is, the "spirit." The term "spirit" is used in two main senses in Paul; first, of a normal endowment or characteristic of man as man. The term sometimes denotes the self of a man, as in I Corinthians 16:17–18:

> It is a great pleasure to me that Stephanas, Fortunatus, and Achaicus have arrived, because they have done what you had no chance to do; they have relieved my mind [spirit]—and no doubt yours too. Such men deserve recognition.

But in a very large number of cases "the spirit" refers to "supernatural" influences, as in Galatians 4:6 and Romans 8:14–17:

To prove that you are sons, God has sent into our hearts the Spirit of his Son, crying "Abba! Father!" (Gal. 4:6)

For all who are moved by the Spirit of God are sons of God. The Spirit you have received is not a spirit of slavery leading you back into a life of fear, but a Spirit that makes us sons, enabling us to cry "Abba! Father!" In that cry the Spirit of God joins with our spirit in testifying that we are God's children; and if children, then heirs. We are God's heirs and Christ's fellow-heirs, if we share his sufferings now in order to share his splendour hereafter. (Rom. 8:14-17)

Here the Spirit of God is able to bear witness with our human spirit; there is a way open from the one to the other; the human spirit can be open to divine influences. To modify Tennyson by the change of a capital: "Speak to Him thou for He hears, and Spirit with spirit can meet"[29] —Man has, in his spirit, a point of contact with the Spirit of God.

The body and the flesh

This means that man can be receptive to God or directed toward God. He can live for God because his spirit, which is sometimes like his will, can be open to the prompting of God, to the power of God impinging upon him. To the human personality in this condition—as open to God and directed toward God—Paul applies the term "body." It is difficult for us to use it in this way. To us "body" suggests the physical aspect of man, man as part of physical nature or, less often, the self, as in such phrases as: "He is somebody," by which we mean "some important person or self." These meanings are found in Paul, but his most important use of the term is the one first indicated: it denotes man in an attitude of openness or obedience or co-operation with God. It is as if Paul defines a man, not in terms of any properties, physical or other, but in terms of his direction or his stance or the way in which he is turned. Man as he is directed toward God for Paul is a "body," and this "body" can be raised from the dead; the personality as open to God is "body."

All the above suggests that Paul's view of man is a high one. Is he not possessed of mind, of conscience, of spirit? Can he not be directed as a "body," in his totality, toward God? All this is true. Man can be open to God; but he also can be and, in fact, is closed to God; he is against God. When man is in this condition, that is, living in rebellion against God, Paul uses the term "flesh" to describe him. Such a man is living "according to the flesh." The term "flesh" suggests to us the physical aspect of man. The "sins of the flesh" are those in which physical appetites are indulged. Paul does use "flesh" in this sense. But it also has for him a deeper meaning. "The flesh" suggests man as he is weak, mortal, creaturely, merely human, and, above all, as he is opposed to God or directed away from God.

Again, therefore, Paul uses a term, not to express a physical characteristic, but an attitude or direction. To live after the flesh is to live in opposition to God's claim; it is to follow the devices and desires of our own hearts, to turn to our own way and away from God. On the more obvious level, this often means living sensually, that is, self-indulgence of a physical kind. But it is possible and, indeed, more usual, to live "after the flesh," as Paul understood this phrase, where there is no sexual or physical indulgence at all. Where life is turned in upon itself, in self-concern and self-assertion, away from God, there is life "after the flesh." It may be outwardly most respectable, but inwardly rotten, dry, and parched. Where there is no openness to God, "the flesh" is in control.

Why did Paul choose the term "flesh," which is also used of the physical nature of man, to denote this attitude of hostility to God? Did he think the physical flesh, the appetitive life of man, in itself evil? Did he have the kind of distaste for everything physical that we can sense, let us say, in Aldous Huxley's work? Or, again, was Paul an ascetic, who thought of physical impulses as unworthy and to be shunned, thwarted, and "beaten black and blue"? There is no evidence that this was so. Paul nowhere claims that the flesh itself is evil. To claim this would be to claim that existence itself is evil; and this, as a Jew, Paul could never admit. The world, as God made it, was good. Why, then, does Paul call the misdirected life as a life "after the flesh"? Probably because, although not corrupt in itself, the flesh, the seat of the physical appetites of man, is easily corrupted. This is the point where man is prone or likely to succumb to evil. To describe this, Paul uses a military term. The flesh, he asserts, is the "base of attack" for sin. The flesh, not in itself evil, has become a base of attack within man from which an enemy has conquered him; it is, to change the metaphor, a bridgehead for the invasion of sin.

The flesh, in this sense, is the Achilles' heel of man. Without that heel Achilles is helpless; it is necessary to him; it is beneficial; but, at the same time, it is this heel that makes Achilles vulnerable and, finally, brings him to the dust. So is it with the flesh. It is not evil but weak; it is open to the suggestiveness of sin.

The consequences of this we shall turn to in the next chapter. The present chapter may be summed up in an image. I once lived in an eighteenth-century house in East Anglia. On the edge of the lawn was what looked like the pride of the garden. It was a pear tree. In summer, when it was in full foliage and fruit, it was an unforgettable sight. It was perfectly shaped; its branches had been pruned to form a full half circle; and a myriad of golden pears gleamed appetizingly among the leaves. It was the delight of my eyes. But when I went to pick the pears I discovered to my dismay that every pear was marked by a small black dot and rotten. And, on closer inspection, it turned out that the whole tree—in trunk, branches, and leaves as well as fruit—had a curious disease. The pride of the garden was under the blight. So was man for Paul, and not only man, but the whole garden of the universe.

CHAPTER 24

THE ANCIENT ENEMY

The candid incline to surmise of late
   That the Christian faith may be false, I find;

I still, to suppose it true, for my part,
   See reasons and reasons; this, to begin:
'Tis the faith that launched point-blank her dart
   At the head of a lie—taught Original Sin,
The Corruption of Man's Heart.

           —Robert Browning[30]

President Coolidge, who was not accustomed to wasting words, had once been to a service of worship. On being asked what the minister had preached on, he replied with the mono-syllable: "Sin." On being pressed as to what the preacher had said about it, he merely answered, "He was against it." The words of Coolidge were typically laconic; but in the New England village where he grew up, everybody thought that he knew what was meant. In his generation, the idea of sin had not become unfashionable. But quite recently I heard a distinguished British philosopher urge American students to give up the out-moded concept of sin. To think and talk, and certainly to write, about it, he said, is a form of immature morbidity. The word "sin" is certainly increasingly shunned, and the reason for this is understandable: sin has often been confused with trivial faults and puritan peccadilloes. But that what Paul meant by sin should be ignored and abandoned is another matter.

In the last chapter we noted without explanation that the

universe and man were corrupted because what Paul calls "sin" had secured a base of operation in man. What did Paul mean by "sin"? In a general sense he uses several words for it. By some of these he simply means the willful breaking of the Law, that is, a transgression. To steal a neighbor's good is sin, in the sense of transgression; a law is broken, just as driving past a red light at an intersection is a transgression.

But the term which Paul uses most often for sin is *harmartia*. This has a far wider meaning than simple transgression. The fundamental idea which it contains is that of missing the mark. To sin is to miss one's intended goal; it is to be misdirected. This means for man to miss the glory of God for which he was intended. In the light of our discussion of the term "glory" in chapter 4, this means to fail to share in God's activity and purposes. It is to this fact of misdirection that the word "sin" points; it points to man's estrangement from the God who made him and the purpose that God has for him. Sin, then, is misdirection and estrangement.

But sin is also conceived by Paul as an active force or power which causes this misdirection. He seems to think of sin as a kind of personal reality: it pays wages; it can die and revive; it arouses desire in man. Paul uses language of it that suggests a personal will of evil. We have seen that it attacks man through his flesh. Its power can be seen in its effectiveness. Let us recall the tree in my garden; every pear was rotten, and the whole tree was rotten. So is it with sin.

First, every man is attacked by sin and falls into its power. Note the following passages:

For we have already formulated the charge that Jews and Greeks alike are all under the power of sin. This has scriptural warrant:
"There is no just man, not one;
No one who understands, no one who seeks God.
All have swerved aside, all alike have become debased;

There is no one to show kindness; no, not one.
Their throat is an open grave,
They use their tongues for treachery,
Adders' venom is on their lips,
And their mouth is full of bitter curses.
Their feet hasten to shed blood,
Ruin and misery lie along their paths,
They are strangers to the high-road of peace,
And reverence for God does not enter their thoughts." (Rom. 3:
    9–18)

. . . all, without distinction. For all alike
have sinned, and are deprived of the divine splendour [glory]. (Rom.
    3:22–23)

Every man is in the flesh and like Paul himself finds a law of
sin at work in himself.

> I discover this principle, then: that when I want to do the
> right, only the wrong is within my reach. In my inmost self
> I delight in the law of God, but I perceive that there is in my
> bodily members a different law, fighting against the law that
> my reason approves and making me a prisoner under the law
> that is in my members, the law of sin. Miserable creature that
> I am, who is there to rescue me out of this body doomed to
> death? (Rom. 7:21–24)

But, secondly, the whole man, not only every man, has fallen
under the power of sin. Through the weakness of the flesh,
Paul claims that corruption has, in fact, spread throughout
man's being. The mind, a faculty able to recognize God and his
demand and to direct conduct, has itself become corrupt. It
cannot be regarded as "noble reason." It is not a bit of the
divine in man which remains uncontaminated. It, too, has been
stained by sin. This does not mean that Paul is contemptuous
of man's rational powers. He does not connect reason itself
with pride as did Alexander Pope:

> In pride, in reasoning pride, our error lies.

Reason is a victim of, not a source of, sin. Paul is not anti-intellectual; he fights no war against the "eggheads" of his day, as such. But he does know that "eggheads," like all men, are open to the attack of sin, that is, can be misdirected. Human intellectual pursuits are not exempt from the blight. Clever "devils" are not rare.

So, too, "conscience," so often thought of as the pure and undiluted voice of God, has been contaminated. It, too, can be weak, says Paul; it can mistake morbid scrupulosity for morality and succumb to the pressures around it; it can become hurt and hardened. Both conscience and mind can be so conformed to this evil world that they have to be renewed. This is the implication of Romans 12:1–2 and 9:1–2:

> Therefore, my brothers, I implore you by God's mercy to offer your very selves to him: a living sacrifice, dedicated and fit for his acceptance, the worship offered by mind and heart. Adapt yourselves no longer to the pattern of this present world, but let your minds be remade and your whole nature thus transformed. Then you will be able to discern the will of God, and to know what is good, acceptable, and perfect. (Rom. 12:1–2)

> I am speaking the truth as a Christian, and my own conscience, enlightened by the Holy Spirit, assures me it is no lie: in my heart there is great grief and unceasing sorrow. (Rom. 9:1–2)

Without the renewal to which Paul refers here, mind is a blind guide of the blind. Only as conscience is brought into relation with a power capable of renewing it can it be taken as the voice of God: this is the implication of Romans 9:1–2. Paul does not only appeal to his own conscience, but to that conscience as enlightened by the Holy Spirit.

Such then is Paul's understanding of the human condition. The Universe as a totality, human society as a whole, is misdirected. And every man is throughout corrupted. Not all men individually are equally tainted; there are real differences between men; not all are equally corrupted. But this is not the significant fact. The significant fact is that all have fallen short of God's glory. Like a ship, whose crew and passengers include "saints" and "sinners," the just and the unjust in varying degrees, but which is bound on the wrong course so that all aboard are "doomed" to disaster and that willy-nilly, so is the frail barque of humanity. Its members are varied; but the fact that determines their condition is that they are all misdirected. The unseen powers of evil that hold the powers of this world—governmental and other—in thrall, the stars and planets in their tyrannical sway, and sin, the malignant power that lies behind all other malignancy—these are on the bridge.

But to state that all mankind and the universe itself are misdirected is not illuminating, however true. Does Paul help us to understand further the causes of this corruption and misdirection? There is no rational explanation of it possible. When President John F. Kennedy was killed by an assassin's bullet, many people cried out at "this senseless act." When all the possible explanations for it have been stated, the meaningless waste of dedicated talent and the unjustifiable national and personal tragedy remain. In that act evil appeared as meaningless. We cannot expect Paul to explain sin; it is essentially without "reason." But Paul does suggest its origin. He thinks, in fact, of three sources for it. They are all sources which Judaism itself had previously proposed.

The fall of Adam and its consequences

In Romans 5:12, we read:

> It was through one man that sin entered the world, and through sin death, and thus death pervaded the whole human race, inasmuch as all men have sinned.

And in Romans 5:18–19, we read:

It follows, then, that as the issue of one misdeed was condemnation for all men, so the issue of one just act is acquittal
and life for all men. For as through the disobedience of the
one man the many were made sinners, so through the obedience of the one man the many will be made righteous.

In these passages Paul asserts that there is a connection which he
does not explain clearly between the sin or disobedience of the
first man, Adam, and the sin of all men. But how can the act of
Adam affect all men? Three answers have been given to this
question.

(a) Paul meant to assert that Adam directly caused those who
followed him to sin. He did this because all men who followed
him were of his blood. But his blood was the blood of a sinful
man. He had injected into the bloodstream of all men a kind of
virus or germ which willy-nilly made them sin. But there is no
suggestion of such a biological idea in Paul and we may safely
pass it.

(b) Paul meant to assert that once Adam had sinned, the
world was a different place. Adam had been born into a sinless
world, but all who followed him were born into a world in which
sin was a fact: their environment had been corrupted. And since
our environment affects us, sin became natural to man. This idea
of the environmental results of Adam's sin appealed to those who
have emphasized that man is a creature of his external environment. But there is nothing in Paul to support this interpretation;
it is a twentieth century misinterpretation of his thought.

(c) The most probable view is that Paul is thinking of Adam
as a figure who represents all men. The meaning of the name
"Adam" is "man": he stands for all men, so that what he does
affects all men. This idea is bound up with the way in which
Semitic peoples—Jews and Arabs and others—thought. A man
belonged to his own family: everything he did affected his family. A man belonged to his tribe: everything he did affected his

tribe. A man belonged to a nation: everything he did affected his nation. A man is bound up in a common bundle of life with his own people.

Some years ago I was in West Germany in a part occupied by the American troops. One day an American soldier murdered a German in conditions of horrible cruelty. Immediately this was reported in the German newspapers. People spoke of the terrible standards of all Americans. The murderer, who on examination admitted that he had never heard of President Truman, had given all Americans a bad name: when he fell, all Americans fell: he represented America. In a similar but even more vivid way, Paul thought of Adam as having given a bad name to all mankind. In him we all fell: Adam represented mankind.

One thing it is important to recognize. The Jews of Paul's day held that although all men sinned in Adam, nevertheless every man is responsible for his own sin. Consider the following passages:

. . . In 2 Baruch 54:15–19, we read:

For though Adam first sinned
And brought untimely death upon all,
Yet those who were born from him
Each one of them has prepared for his own soul torment
   to come,
And again each one of them has chosen for himself glories
   to come.
Adam is, therefore, not the cause save only of his own soul
But each of us has been the Adam of his own soul.

In the above the responsibility of each individual is emphasized. In 4 Ezra 3:21–2, however, we read as follows:

For the first Adam, clothing himself with the evil heart, transgressed and was overcome; and likewise also all who were born of him. Thus the infirmity became inveterate; the Law indeed was in the heart of the people, but (in conjunction) with the evil germ; so what was good departed and the evil remained.

Again in 4:30–2:

For a grain of evil seed was sown in the heart of Adam from the beginning, and how much fruit of ungodliness has it produced unto this time, and shall yet produce until the threshing-floor come!

Again in 7:116 f.:

And I answered and said: This is my first and last word; better had it been that the earth had not produced Adam, or else having produced him, (for thee) to have restrained him from sinning. For how does it profit us all that in the present we must live in grief and after death look for punishment? O thou Adam, what hast thou done! For though it was thou that sinned, the fall was not thine alone, but ours also who are thy descendants! For how does it profit us that the eternal age is promised to us, whereas we have done the works that bring death?

Paul leaves us with a question: how do we sin inevitably and yet by our own choice?

Idolatry and its consequences

Consider the following passage from Romans 1:18–24:

For we see divine retribution revealed from heaven and falling upon all the godless wickedness of men. In their wickedness they are stifling the truth. For all that may be known of God by men lies plain before their eyes; indeed God himself has disclosed it to them. His invisible attributes, that is to say his everlasting power and deity, have been visible, ever since the world began to the eye of reason, in the things he has made. There is therefore no possible defence for their conduct; knowing God, they have refused to honour him as God, or to render him thanks. Hence all their thinking has ended in futility, and their misguided minds are plunged in darkness. They boast of their wisdom, but they have made fools of themselves, exchanging the splendour of immortal God for an image shaped like mortal man, even for images like birds, beasts and creeping things.

For this reason God has given them up to the vileness of their own desires, and the consequent degradation of their bodies, because they have bartered away the true God for a false one, and have offered reverence and worship to created things instead of to the Creator, who is blessed for ever; amen.

In this passage it is claimed that sin arose because men turned from the worship of the true God, whom of themselves they could know, to worship the things that he had made. This again is an idea which Paul shared with others in Palestine. A passage in *The Testament of the Twelve Patriarchs* reads:

Sun and moon and stars change not their order; so do ye also change not the law of God in the disorderliness of your doings. The Gentiles went astray, and forsook the Lord, and changed their order, and obeyed stocks and stones, spirits of deceit. But ye shall not be so, my children, recognizing in the firmament, in the earth, and in the sea, and in all created things, the Lord who made all things, that ye become not as Sodom, which changeth the order of nature.[31]

Again, in an old Jewish source there is a story about Abraham. He is claimed to have discovered the existence of God by reasoning back to a First Cause. When he refused to accept idolatry, King Nimrod demanded that he should worship fire. The following argument is then recorded:

Abraham replied to him: "We should rather worship water which extinguishes fire." Nimrod said to him: "Then worship water." Abraham retorted: "If so we should worship the cloud which carries water!" Nimrod said: "Then worship the cloud." Abraham retorted: "If so, we should worship the wind which disperses the cloud!" Nimrod said: "Then worship the wind." Abraham retorted: "Rather should we worship the human being who carries the wind."[32]

In Romans 1:18–24, we might claim that Paul sees in a corruption of religion the root of sin. At that very point where man would be expected to be "safe," that is, his worship, he is most liable to corruption.

The evil impulse and its consequences

In chapters 1 and 5 of Romans, Paul considers the history of sin in the world and mankind at large. In the following passage from Romans 7, he is thinking of sin as it works in the life of the individual:

> I do not even acknowledge my own actions as mine, for what I do is not what I want to do, but what I detest. But if what I do is against my will, it means that I agree with the law and hold it to be admirable. But as things are, it is no longer I who perform the action, but sin that lodges in me. For I know that nothing good lodges in me—in my unspiritual nature, I mean—for though the will to do good is there, the deed is not. The good which I want to do, I fail to do; but what I do is the wrong which is against my will; and if what I do is against my will, clearly it is no longer I who am the agent, but sin that has its lodging in me.
>
> I discover this principle, then: that when I went to do the right, only the wrong is within my reach. In my inmost self I delight in the law of God, but I perceive that there is in my bodily members a different law, fighting against the law that my reason approves and making me a prisoner under the law that is in my members, the law of sin. Miserable creature that I am, who is there to rescue me out of this body doomed to death? God alone, through Jesus Christ our Lord! Thanks be to God! In a word then, I myself, subject to God's law as a rational being, am yet, in my unspiritual nature, a slave to the law of sin. (15–25)

In this and other passages, Paul is probably thinking of what he had learned from his Jewish teachers. Long before Paul, the view had arisen that two impulses are implanted in man, a good and an evil impulse. Jewish thinkers concentrated most on the evil impulse:

> God created Man from the beginning
> And placed him in the hand of his *yetzer* (impulse).
> (Ecc. 15:14)

Some held that the evil impulse was located in the kidneys, others that it was in the heart; some personified it as an evil spirit. There were different opinions on these matters, but the function of the evil impulse was clear: it urged or inclined man to sin, and it was especially connected with sexual sin or lust; it led to unchastity and idolatry.

From the above, we may gather, then, that Paul connects the origin of sin, from one point of view, with the simple fact of human solidarity, that all men are bound together in the common bundle of life, so that one man's sin affects every other man:

> In Adam's sin
> We sinned all.

From another point of view, he connected sin with the corruption of "religion" "worship," and, from still another, with the evil impulse in which Judaism believed.

But it was not with the origins of sin that Paul was concerned, but with its reality. Its results are only too clear. Indirectly, as we saw, Paul traced the whole misdirection of the universe to man's sin. But he directly connected two things with it—wrath and death, both of which it is difficult for us to appreciate in the same way as Paul.

Sin calls forth the anger or wrath of God, as in Romans 1:18:

> For we see divine retribution [wrath] revealed from heaven and falling upon all the godless wickedness of men.

This seems to mean that God is angry at human conduct and acts to punish man. Many have found it difficult to accept such a view. Anger is an irrational emotion in which one loses one's self-control. It is condemned by all moralists; it is a "brief madness." Surely God cannot be guilty of it. Both Hellenistic and modern thinkers have often urged strongly that God cannot be angry.

But if so, what does Paul mean by the wrath of God? Simply, we are told, that the universe is so constructed that, if man sins, he is punished. If a child pushes his finger into the fire, he suffers. This is not because the fire is "angry," but because there are certain laws which govern the physical order. So, too, there are spiritual laws which govern moral order. When a man sins, God is not angry. But the moral laws of the universe are at work and punishment comes automatically. God is never angry, but sin is always punished. Paul, in fact, never asserts that God is angry but that "the wrath" is at work; that is, that there is a process at work by which man reaps what he sows.

Such an explanation is attractive but probably wrong. Paul was a Jew. He had been reared on the Old Testament which everywhere refers to God's wrath—not a capricious, unaccountable, fitful "anger," but an indignant response to the sin of man. The personal God of the Old Testament responded to evil in a personal way. Anger is the other side of God's mercy, an expression not of his unruly passion but of his infinite pathos. "To feel" is not only to show mercy but to react against evil. "It is because [God] cares for man that his anger may be kindled against man." So writes Professor Abraham Heschel, and his other words deserve quotation: "Admittedly, anger is something that comes dangerously close to evil, yet it is wrong to identify it with evil. It may be evil by association, but not in essence. Like fire, it may be a blessing as well as a fatal thing—reprehensible when associated with malice, morally necessary as resistance to malice. Both alternatives are fraught with danger. Its complete suppression, even in the face of outbursts of evil, may amount to surrender and capitulation, while its unrestrained drive may end in disaster. Anger may touch off deadly explosives, while the complete absence of anger stultifies moral sensibility. Patience, a quality of holiness, may be sloth in the soul when associated with the lack of righteous indignation. "For everything there is a season, and a time for every matter under heaven: . . . a time to keep silence, and a time to speak, a time to love, and a time to hate" (Eccles. 3:1, 7, 8).[33] With this Paul would probably agree.

The other direct result of sin is death. This is expressed clearly in Romans 5:12–16:

> Mark what follows. It was through one man that sin entered the world, and through sin death, and thus death pervaded the whole human race, inasmuch as all men have sinned. For sin was already in the world before there was law, though in the absence of law no reckoning is kept of sin. But death held sway from Adam to Moses, even over those who had not sinned as Adam did, by disobeying a direct command—and Adam foreshadows the Man who was to come.
>
> But God's act of grace is out of all proportion to Adam's wrongdoing. For if the wrongdoing of that one man brought death upon so many, its effect is vastly exceeded by the grace of God and the gift that came to so many by the grace of the one man, Jesus Christ. And again, the gift of God is not to be compared in its effect with that one man's sin; for the judicial action, following upon the one offence, issued in a verdict of condemnation, but the act of grace, following upon so many misdeeds, issued in a verdict of acquittal.

Here again we meet a difficult idea. Is not death a natural phenomenon, an inevitable accompaniment of our decaying physical powers?

> The woods decay, the woods decay and fall
> And after many summers dies the swan.

This is natural. Shakespeare expresses this fact in *Hamlet* in lines where the king chides Hamlet for mourning his father too much.

> 'Tis sweet and commendable in your nature, Hamlet,
> To give these mourning duties to your father:
> But, you must know, your father lost a father,
> That father lost, lost his, and the survivor bound
> In filial obligation for some term
> To do obsequious sorrow: but to persevere

In obstinate condolement is a course
Of impious stubbornness; 'tis unmanly grief:
It shows a will most incorrect to heaven,
A heart unfortified, a mind impatient,
An understanding simple and unschool'd:
For what we know must be and is as common
As any the most vulgar thing to sense,
Why should we in our peevish opposition
Take it to heart? Fie! 'tis a fault to heaven,
A fault against the dead, a fault to nature,
To reason most absurd, whose common theme
Is death of fathers, and who still hath cried,
From the first corse till he that died to-day,
"This must be so." . . .[34]

But it is the king, the murderer of his own brother, who so speaks. To Hamlet himself, "a beast that wants discourse of reason" would have mourned his "father" longer. To die is natural; yes, but also to mourn; death does have a sting. And Paul, in a way in which he does not explain, connects this sting with sin. "The sting of death is sin."

For Paul, then, the condition of man is desperate. Not all men individually are equally corrupted by evil; there are real differences between men. But this is not the significant fact. The significant fact is that all have fallen short of God's glory; all are misdirected under the wrath of God and the shadow of Death. It is not only that individual men are misdirected, but that the whole of society is in this plight, that makes Paul cry out: "O wretched man that I am, who shall deliver me from the body of this death?"

To many, such a view of the condition of mankind is morbid, unrealistic, exaggerated, the fruit of a gigantic neurosis. It repels. It does so because so many moderns have a directly opposite view. The following quotations by modern scholars contrast sharply with what Paul claims. The distinguished British scientist, Sir James Jeans, wrote as follows:

We no longer believe that human destiny is a plaything for spirits, good and evil, or for the machinations of the Devil. There is nothing to prevent our making the earth a paradise again—except ourselves. The scientific age has dawned, and we recognize that man himself is the master of his fate, the captain of his soul. He controls the course of his ship, and so, of course, is free to navigate it into fair waters or foul, or even to run it on the rocks.[35]

The President of the Chicago Natural History Museum thinks:

But if we listen to the anthropologists, who can scientifically demonstrate that it is not color of skin, or type of hair or features, or difference of religion, that creates problems between peoples, but factors for which man is responsible and which he can control or change if he will, then we shall at least come within sight of that better world which we now realize we must achieve if we are not finally to perish as victims of our own perversity.[36]

Another anthropologist considers that "man makes himself."

But not all moderns think in this way. One anthropologist has called the idea that man controls civilization "an anthropocentric illusion." Man is fashioned from the day he is born by the society into which he comes. The environment, the culture, moulds him willy-nilly. We do in Rome as the Romans do. There is no escape from the dead hand of culture. The following are the words of an eminent anthropologist:

The culture of the present was determined by the past, and the culture of the future will be but a continuation of the trend of the present. Thus in a very real sense, *culture makes itself*. At least, if one wishes to explain culture scientifically, he must proceed *as if* culture made itself, *as if* man had nothing to do with the determination of its course or content. Man must *be* there, of course, to make the existence of the culture process possible. But the nature and behavior of the process itself is self-determined. It rests upon its own principles; it is governed by its own laws.

. . . . The English language, the Christian religion, our political institutions, our mills, mines, factories, railroads, telephones, armies, navies, race tracks, dance halls, and all the other thousands of things that comprise our civilization are here in existence today. They have weight, mass, and momentum. They cannot be made to disappear by waving a wand, nor can their structure and behavior be altered by an act of will. We must come to terms with them as we find them today. And they will be tomorrow what their trend of development in the past dictates. We can only trot along with them, hoping to keep up.[37]

This is not unlike the realism of Paul, unrelieved by his faith. Or recall the famous essay by Freud, *A Difficulty of Psycho-Analysis*. He refers to three blows that have wounded the self-love of humanity: the *cosmological* one, which revealed to man that he was no longer the center of the physical universe; the *biological* blow, which revealed to him that he does not differ from but originates in the animal race; and, finally, the *psychological* blow, the most wounding of all, which revealed to him that part of the activity of his own mind has been withdrawn from his control and from the command of his will by unconscious processes. Man is not so much a master of his fate as the sport of the universe. But Paul had experienced all these blows; he had reeled under their punch. He knew our modern predicament. But his realism was not unrelieved. How Paul reacted to these blows is part of the relevance of the New Testament to modern man.

CHAPTER 25

HOPE FULFILLED:
A PHILOSOPHY OF HISTORY

To see that mankind is misdirected is one thing; to believe that it can be redirected is another. What makes Paul significant is that he makes the stupendous claim that he has encountered a power to redirect the world. Realism is common; pessimism cheap; but the faith of a Paul is "rarer than radium."

Since he believed that the whole world is misdirected, for Paul any claim to turn it from its fatal course would have to be on a world scale. Paul was naturally concerned with his own destiny as a person, but he recognized that he himself was only part of a total situation; his own problem was bound up with the problem of the whole world; not self-understanding was his concern but the understanding of himself as a member of the people of Israel and of the human race. He did not think of himself merely as an "individual" but as a member of the tribe of Benjamin, a Hebrew of the Hebrews, of the seed of Abraham, a son of Adam. His own redirection depended upon the redirection of the race, just as surely as the destiny of a boy or girl in the slums of Harlem is bound up with the remaking and redirection of New York and of White America.

The hope of Judaism

But the Jews, to whom Paul belonged, had long wrestled with the problem of misdirection in their own life and in the life of the world, and out of this wrestling a daring hope had been born.

This hope may be expressed roughly as follows: Judaism came to regard the world as the creation of the One God, which was intended to reflect the oneness of its Maker, to be a unity. In the beginning, this oneness was a reality; the cosmos as a totality, man included, "obeyed" God. But sin entered upon the scene, and with it disunity of all kinds: this disunity expressed itself as enmity between man and man; in the family, between Cain and Abel; within the nation itself, between rich and poor; then between Jew and Gentile; and particularly and fundamentally, of course, between man and God. However, despite man's fall, Judaism continued to believe that God was still God, and that, therefore, ultimately his will would be done.

How would this take place? It would take place in the future; but there were different ways in which this future was conceived. Some thought that a Messianic figure, a Son of David, powerful like the first David, would arrive and inaugurate his kingdom on this earth. Others despaired of this earth entirely and looked for a supernatural figure, the Son of Man, who should inaugurate a new heaven and a new earth. Probably we are not to think of any one well-defined and generally accepted Messianic expectation, but of a rich variety of expectations much intermingled. However conceived, the end would be like the beginning; just as at the creation God's will gained untrammeled obedience from the created order and from man himself, so at the end there would be a corresponding obedience. The result of this obedience would be the inauguration of unity, i.e., the re-creation of the broken unity between man and man, and between man and God.

But we must grasp how this obedience, which was to characterize the end, was conceived. One thing is certain. The *condition* of God's reign would be the devoted observance of the Law. Only when men were worthy of it would God's reign begin; it waited upon Israel's loyalty; the decisive factor in its coming would be Israel's obedience. The unity of the end of the days would be unity in the Law, and man would bring it to birth by his obedience to the Law.

Another thing was equally certain. The *consequence* of God's reign would be the observance of the Law by all. But what, then, of the Gentiles? Would they obey the Law? Judaism was always divided on this question. There were always "liberals" who thought that at the end all the scattered people of Israel would be regathered into their own land and that all the heathen nations would be converted to the Lord God of Israel. Consider, for example, the following early passage from Isaiah 2:2–4 which remained to haunt the people of Israel always:

> It shall come to pass in the latter days
>   that the mountain of the house of the Lord
> shall be established as the highest of the mountains,
>   and shall be raised above the hills;
> and all the nations shall flow to it,
>   and many peoples shall come, and say:
> "Come, let us go up to the mountain of the Lord,
>   to the house of the God of Jacob;
> that he may teach us his ways
>   and that we may walk in his paths."
> For out of Zion shall go forth the law
>   and the word of the Lord from Jerusalem.
> He shall judge between the nations,
>   and shall decide for many peoples;
> and they shall beat their swords into plowshares,
>   and their spears into pruning hooks;
> nation shall not lift up sword against nation,
>   neither shall they learn war any more.

But there was a different, hostile attitude toward the Gentiles, and by the first century in some quarters this had hardened. The various pagan powers that had oppressed the people of Israel—Assyrians, Babylonians, Greeks, and, in the first century, Romans—had given them ample cause to hate the Gentile world. The Jews then, as in our own time, had seen "the sullen majesty of man" in their midst in its unbelievable cruelty. Some gave up all hope for the conversion of the Gentiles and only expected a decent minimum moral standard—the Noachian commandments —from them; they were only capable of this; some agonized over them in pity; others condemned them lock, stock, and barrel— "they are like ants' spittle!" It was law-abiding Israel that alone could constitute the people of God; the sphere of redemption was Israel and the Law. The only way by which an alien could hope to share in the glorious future "at the end of the days" was by naturalization in the Jewish people. A great liberal Jewish scholar has summed up the matter as follows:

> The particularist doctrine of the Rabbis was that the heathen nations could not be 'saved.' They were doomed to hell. Yet sometimes the heart of the Rabbis smote them for this cruel doctrine, even as the heart of some Christian theologians smote them for a similar teaching. For if the heathen knew no better and had never heard of the one true God how could their doom be justified? . . . Hence the theory of the 'seven prophets' who 'warned' them. But these prophets had ceased long ago. What then? Well, then came the Law which arranged for the reception of proselytes. Ever since, the nations could become Jews if they chose. The proselytes of each generation are a warning to all their contemporaries. The warning is unheeded; therefore the doom of hell is justified.[38]

This was the point at which the hope of Israel was ambiguous. But, notice, it was ambiguous at the very point which touched the majority of mankind, who were "without God and without hope in the world."

Paul was the heir of the hope of Israel to which we have referred—a constant hope, however varied. He knew that the angelic forces of evil were real; the Hellenistic world could assert the inexorable reality of fate and his own experience could testify to the "exceeding wickedness of sin." But Paul remained always assured that history was the scene of God's activity and plastic to his will. "At the end of the days" he would reign. The

Lord would be One and his people One. But the ambiguity about the Gentiles? We can be sure that Paul shared it.

Born in no mean city, a Roman citizen, Paul would early have been brought into contact with Gentile life. Despite its sensuality and idolatry, the varied and colorful life of the Hellenistic world would appeal to him as we know that it attracted other Jews through the post-exilic period. It would have been quite unlike the Paul revealed to us in the Epistles and in Acts to disregard the life and fate of the majority of the people around him. But at the same time, of course, the very fascination of Hellenism would make him more intensely aware of his Jewishness. In any case, Paul, like the author of 4 Ezra, must have been compelled, in his studies as in his personal contacts, to consider "the lesser breeds without the Law" and to wonder at the fate of "the many" who were doomed to destruction. His very extreme devotion to the Law may have been the shadow of an agony he felt for those without the Law; his human sympathies would be in conflict with his creed.

Paul, therefore, as he confronted the misdirection of the world was not without hope. But his hope was fulfilled so unexpectedly, in a way so utterly staggering to him that he was temporarily blinded. It was fulfilled in a manner which at first he would have thought impossible—in Jesus of Nazareth. He encountered the claim that this Jesus, who had fraternized with publicans (quislings) and sinners, people outside the Law, and who had finally died like a common criminal on a cross, under the curse of the Law, was the Messiah, the final figure of "the end of the days." He encountered the claim that this impossible final figure of history had gathered his own Messianic community from among the "people of the land," irreligious boors; that God was fulfilling the hope of Israel, not through the devout keepers of the Law, but through second-rate Jews from Gentile Galilee—Peter, James, John, and their ilk. He encountered the

still more audacious claim, which initiated and confirmed the
other claims, that this accursed Jesus had been raised from the
dead. The resurrection from the dead, the very mark of the end
of the days in Jewish expectation, had begun; the final age of
history was inaugurated. The end was upon the world!

Paul not only encountered this claim; what is still more, he
was led to believe it. And perhaps because he was a trained
Pharisaic scholar, Paul came to see more clearly and feel more
deeply than the earliest disciples the full significance of what
they said about Jesus as the Messiah. With the rapier of one of
the great minds of history, he penetrated to the heart of the matter. The hope of Judaism, he had been taught, could only be
fulfilled among men who had achieved obedience to the Law
and merited God's favor, that is, among "the good." In Jesus,
Paul encountered one who had not waited for worthiness but
had come to the unworthy: "I came not to call the righteous but
sinners." While men were yet willfully and woefully misdirected,
the love of God toward them had become manifest and active
in Jesus. A new factor had entered the field of history: Paul
called it the "grace" of Jesus, God's love in action in him—un-
expected, persistent, unlimited love toward the undeserving. Its
supreme manifestation was in the resurrection—the coming
again of Jesus to his own who had betrayed him and, above all,
his coming to Paul himself, the arch-persecutor. This grace
could and did give to history a new direction.

Henceforth, Paul was committed to Jesus of Nazareth, as the
Messiah, the final figure of history, the object of his ultimate
concern, the one who had redirected history. But such a phrase
—redirected history!—is so easily written! Could it be true? In
what sense was it true? To answer these questions we must now
set forth Paul's understanding of history. This he owes to Judaism, but to Judaism illumined, for him, by the fact of Christ.
How then does he interpret the place of Jesus Christ in history?

The centrality of Christ in history

The first fact is that Jesus is the point of decisive change in history. Judaism, as we saw, had looked forward to a passing of this present, evil Age and the coming of a new Age, when good would triumph. Like those who wrote the Synoptic Gospels, Paul is convinced that the new Age had dawned in the coming of Jesus. Paul sets forth certain antitheses which make this clear. Consider the following examples:

1. *The old and the new man:*

By baptism we were buried with him, and lay dead, in order that, as Christ was raised from the dead in the splendour of the Father, so also we might set our feet upon the new path of life.

For if we have become incorporate with him in a death like his, we shall also be one with him in a resurrection like his. We know that the man we once were has been crucified with Christ, for the destruction of the sinful self, so that we may no longer be the slaves of sin, since a dead man is no longer answerable for his sin. (Rom. 6:4–7)

Stop lying to one another, now that you have discarded the old nature with its deeds and have put on the new nature, which is being constantly renewed in the image of its Creator and brought to know God. (Col. 3:9–10)

2. *Life in the flesh and in the spirit:*

You, my friends, were called to be free men; only do not turn your freedom into licence for your lower nature, but be servants to one another in love. (Gal. 5:13)

I mean this: if you are guided by the Spirit you will not fulfil the desires of your lower nature. That nature sets its desires against the Spirit, while the Spirit fights against it. They are in conflict with one another so that what you will to do you cannot do. But if you are led by the Spirit, you are not under law. (Gal. 5:16–18)

3. *The old and the new creation:*

> When anyone is united to Christ, there is a new world; the old order has gone, and a new order has already begun. (II Cor. 5:17)

Christ has introduced a New Order.

The fullness of time

The new order introduced by Jesus is the fulfillment of what the prophets of the Old Testament had foretold. The coming of Jesus was not a sudden intervention in history but the climax of a long process in which God had been at work in the Old Testament; Jesus came at the "fullness of the time."

> . . . which he promised beforehand through his prophets in the holy scriptures, . . (Rom. 1:1–2)

The image of God

But how is the purpose of God for man to be understood? The following passages make this clear [splendour-glory].

> . . . and in everything, as we know, he co-operates for good with those who love God and are called according to his purpose. For God knew his own before ever they were, and also ordained that they should be shaped to the likeness of his Son, that he might be the eldest among a large family of brothers; and it is these, so fore-ordained, whom he has also called. And those whom he called he has justified, and to those whom he justified he has also given his splendour. (Rom. 8:28–30)
>
> Now the Lord of whom this passage speaks is the Spirit; and where the Spirit of the Lord is, there is liberty. And because for us there is no veil over the face, we all reflect as in a mirror the splendour of the Lord; thus we are transfigured into his likeness, from splendour to splendour; such is the influence of the Lord who is Spirit. (II Cor. 3:17–18)
>
> Stop lying to one another, now that you have discarded the old nature with its deeds and have put on the new nature, which is being constantly renewed in the image of its Creator and brought to know God. (Col. 3:9–10)

PAUL'S CONICAL VIEW OF HISTORY (SIMPLIFIED)

The Universe or Created Order including Man

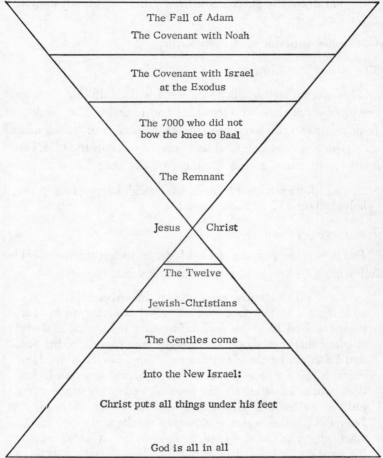

The Fall of Adam

The Covenant with Noah

The Covenant with Israel
at the Exodus

The 7000 who did not
bow the knee to Baal

The Remnant

Jesus   Christ

The Twelve

Jewish-Christians

The Gentiles come

into the New Israel:

Christ puts all things under his feet

God is all in all

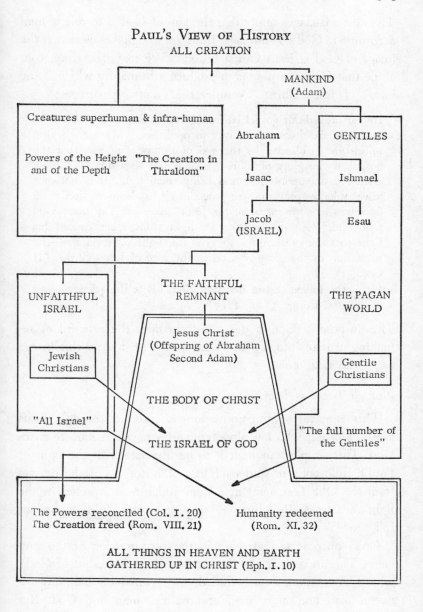

PAUL'S VIEW OF HISTORY
ALL CREATION

MANKIND (Adam)

Creatures superhuman & infra-human

Powers of the Height and of the Depth   "The Creation in Thraldom"

Abraham   GENTILES

Isaac   Ishmael

Jacob (ISRAEL)   Esau

UNFAITHFUL ISRAEL   THE FAITHFUL REMNANT   THE PAGAN WORLD

Jewish Christians

Jesus Christ (Offspring of Abraham Second Adam)

Gentile Christians

THE BODY OF CHRIST

"All Israel"

THE ISRAEL OF GOD

"The full number of the Gentiles"

The Powers reconciled (Col. I. 20)
The Creation freed (Rom. VIII. 21)

Humanity redeemed (Rom. XI. 32)

ALL THINGS IN HEAVEN AND EARTH
GATHERED UP IN CHRIST (Eph. I. 10)

The above passages imply that the aim of God is to renew man according to God's own image. But Paul also makes clear that the image of God is Jesus Christ himself. We may, therefore, conclude that God's purpose is to produce a humanity which is the image of Jesus Christ. Consider the following passages:

> And if indeed our gospel be found veiled, the only people who find it so are those on the way to perdition. Their unbelieving minds are so blinded by the god of this passing age, that the gospel of the glory of Christ, who is the very image of God, cannot dawn upon them and bring them light. It is not ourselves that we proclaim; we proclaim Christ Jesus as Lord, and ourselves as your servants, for Jesus' sake. For the same God who said, "Out of darkness let light shine," has caused his light to shine within us, to give the light of revelation—the revelation of the glory of God in the face of Jesus Christ. (II Cor. 4:3–6)
>
> He is the image of the invisible God; his is the primacy over all created things. (Col. 1:15)

The purpose of God is the transformation, the renewal or remaking of man into the image of Jesus Christ. And this brings us to the next point.

Not all Israel is Israel

This renewal or transformation is possible through Jesus Christ himself, who has already given a new direction to mankind. This simple statement is to be understood in the light of Paul's philosophy or understanding of history. This he derives from the Old Testament and from Judaism interpreted in the light of Christ. Roughly, we may state this "philosophy" as follows:

God's purpose was at work in the very creation of the universe. The universe is not the outcome of chance, but of God's will. The creation, man included, was created for harmony between man and man, man and nature, man and God. But through the sin of Adam, God's purpose was thwarted. God made a new beginning with man, however, in a covenant with Abraham; the promise is given that in him all the nations of the earth would be blessed. Abraham responded to the call of God, and through him there came into being a people of God, a people chosen by an act of God's free will and grace. But God's purpose was not automatically secured through the single act of the choice and response of Abraham. Those who were physically descended from Abraham were not all responsive to God's call as their father Abraham had been, so that not all who were physically connected with Abraham were really his children. Thus of Abraham's two sons only Isaac, who was the child of God's promise, was recognized as a true "son"; Ishmael, the natural son of Abraham by Hagar was rejected. Similarly, Jacob, the son of Isaac, is the object of God's love, but Esau, his brother, of God's hatred. Merely physical membership in Israel is not enough; by itself, physical descent means little. Thus, as Paul puts it, not all Israel is Israel; that is, not all Jews have responded in obedience to God's demand. Indeed, the majority of those physically descended from Abraham have been disobedient and are consequently not considered his true children. In the time of Elijah, there were still seven thousand who did not bow the knee to Baal. A remnant did remain. But this remnant became increasingly smaller; in the day of Isaiah, it was a very small remnant. And, as Paul came to see the history of his people, it became increasingly small, until, as we are told in Galatians 3:16, there is only one person who can be said to be the true descendant of Abraham, and this person is Jesus. In him alone is the promise to Abraham fulfilled. Paul makes use of the difference between a singular and plural noun to make his point:

> Now the promises were pronounced to Abraham and to his "issue." It does not say "issues" in the plural, but in the singular, "and to your issue"; and the "issue" intended is Christ. (Gal. 3:16)

Jesus alone represents the people of God's promise. He is the apex of a triangle—a "triangle" within which progressively the "people of God," the true descendants of Abraham, have become increasingly fewer and from which his "false" descendants have been increasingly excluded. A process of exclusion comes to its culmination in Jesus.

The beginning of the New Israel

The process of exclusion in the history of Israel, which is a record of God's failure to create a people for himself in the world, is the counterpart of that misdirection which Paul discovered in the Gentile world. Both Israelites and non-Israelites were involved in the same fundamental misdirection, although the *symptoms* of this misdirection were not always the same. But in Jesus of Nazareth the misdirection was checked. By the obedience of his life, which issued in death on the cross, the process of exclusion was reversed. Jesus inaugurated a countermovement of inclusion; some among his own people recognized in Jesus the true seed of Abraham and joined in allegiance to him. They constituted a "new" remnant, the beginning of a New Israel. This New Israel was made up of those who had seen and responded to the grace of Jesus, the Christ. They were not only Jews by descent. They soon included Gentiles, and they are destined to include not only all Gentiles but also all Jews who, at present, reject the claims that Jesus is the final figure. In this way, in the emergence of a New Israel, which is to bring all to the recognition of Jesus as the Final One and of God as all-in-all, Paul claims that the whole historic process has been given a new, decisive turn. And not only human history. Jesus has set in motion in history a spirit that will in the end bring all things—human, superhuman (the angels, the principalities and powers) and subhuman—into the blessing of God. The misdirected universe will be redirected and restored to him who made it. And the purpose of all this, as we have seen, is that man may regain the image of God that he had lost through the fall of Adam; and, since Christ *is* the image of God, to be like Christ, to grow into his maturity, is the purpose of God for man. And for the universe? That all powers in heaven and earth, all things, may share in the glory of God. Consider the following passages:

> As in Adam all men die, so in Christ all will be brought to life; but each in his own proper place: Christ the firstfruits, and afterwards, at his coming, those who belong to Christ. Then comes the end, when he delivers up the kingdom to God the Father, after abolishing every kind of domination, authority, and power. For he is destined to reign until God has put all enemies under his feet; and the last enemy to be abolished is death. Scripture says, "He has put all things in subjection under his feet." But in saying "all things," it clearly means to exclude God who subordinates them; and when all things are thus subject to him, then the Son himself will also be made subordinate to God who made all things subject to him, and thus God will be all in all. (I Cor. 15:22–28)
> He is the image of the invisible God; his is the primacy over all created things. In him everything in heaven and on earth was created, not only things visible but also the invisible orders of thrones, sovereignties, authorities, and powers: the whole universe has been created through him and for him. And he exists before everything, and all things are held together in him. He is, moreover, the head of the body, the church. He is its origin, the first to return from the dead, to be in all things alone supreme. For in him the complete being of God, by God's own choice, came to dwell. Through him God chose to reconcile the whole universe to himself, making peace through the shedding of his blood upon the cross—to reconcile all things, whether on earth or in heaven, through him alone. (Col. 1:15–20)

The philosophy which we have outlined may be set forth in the form of the two cones, drawn on page 302. But to make the picture of it complete, so as to include all things, the diagram on page 303 should be consulted.[39]

The daring of Paul's faith

For Paul, then, Christianity is not a hole-and-corner matter, but a sweeping understanding of history which is clear, dynamic and, granting Paul's assumption about Jesus, inspiring. This is partly why Paul has molded so much of history. Henry Ford is reported to have said that "history is bunk." Historians have sometimes failed to trace any pattern in history but merely a succession of events without design or purpose. But the forces that have moved the world in our time have offered "philosophies" or "interpretations" of history. Nazism did so and so does Marxism. To move men, their existence as a whole has to be interpreted, and because Paul does this he has remained a towering figure. To put him in strange company, he is among those, like Marx, who have moved the world by their "philosophy," except that his "philosophy" rests from beginning to end on the reality and power of Jesus of Nazareth.

Modern anthropology can help us to appreciate the magnitude of what Paul asserts about Jesus. As we saw, some anthropologists claim that man is determined by his culture; I am what I am because I was born at a particular time and place; I am bound hand and foot to the social and cultural and political forces that have surrounded me from the very day of my birth. A recent anthropologist, after urging the need to understand culture, goes on to say: "To be sure, understanding culture, will not . . . alter its course or change the 'fate' that it has in store for us, any more than understanding the weather or the tides will change them."[40] This is the kind of fatalism that Paul faced in the Graeco-Roman world. Other anthropologists are less certain. According to these, change can, indeed, take place within a culture in one of two ways—by the impact upon it of other different cultures, or by the emergence within it of a new unpredicted, unpredictable "person," the great man who so surpasses his own people that he can bring about changes. And even so, the great man is always a product of his own culture, however much he transcends it. But from Paul's point of view, since the whole world is misdirected, there can be no new culture to change it; and since man as man is corrupted, no one man can emerge from within human culture to redirect it. And yet it is of the essence of Paul's belief that the world—the totality of human culture—has been given a new direction; the cultural drift toward decay has been stopped; the "satanic mills" of culture and society, the power structures of the world, the accumulated weight of the customs that corrupt the world— all these have been annulled and fate itself despoiled by Jesus Christ. The question, then, is inevitable: who or what was Jesus Christ, the ground of Paul's hope?

CHAPTER 26

THE GREAT PAULINE METAPHORS

Before we discuss what the redirection of the universe by
Jesus Christ meant for Paul in the depths of his own personal
life, we must note the various ways in which he described this
redirection. He used metaphors which came naturally to him,
but which, despite our vague familiarity with them, are strange
to us. Imagine a Jew of the first century, by some strange twist
of time and chance, opening a Science Supplement of *The
New York Times* or a scientific journal of our day. The dia-
grams, pictures, figures would not only be strange to him but
unintelligible, mystifying, and even terrifying. But when we
read the epistles of Paul—a Jew living twenty centuries ago in
Palestine—we look into a mind that is, in some ways, as strange
to us as the twentieth-century scientific mind would be to him.
Images and metaphors which illumined his contemporaries,
now, because of their remote strangeness, confuse and mystify.
The language of Paul is likely to tax not only the imagination
and intelligence but even the patience of a twentieth-century
reader. We cannot expect to be able to understand him easily,
and it is only with such a caution that we turn to the great
metaphors in which the Apostle interpreted his faith.

These metaphors can be conveniently grouped as they are
derived from the following realms:

1. The Exodus   3. The Sacrificial System
2. The Creation   4. The Law

It would be impossible to deal with all the metaphors indicated in detail here: only the most significant ones can be mentioned from each category.

Metaphors derived from the idea of the Exodus

As we saw in earlier chapters, the hope of the future in Judaism was pictured partly in terms derived from the experience of Israel in the Exodus. The final deliverance "at the end of the days" would be like the first deliverance from Egypt; the final redeemer, the Messiah, would be like the first redeemer, Moses. This conception governs much of the interpretation of Jesus in the New Testament; it certainly emerges clearly in Paul. One passage in particular shows how he compares the time of the Exodus with that of the emergence of the Church:

> You should understand, my brothers, that our ancestors were all under the pillar of cloud, and all of them passed through the Red Sea; and so they all received baptism into the fellowship of Moses in cloud and sea. They all ate the same supernatural food, and all drank the same supernatural drink; I mean, they all drank from the supernatural rock that accompanied their travels—and that rock was Christ. And yet, most of them were not accepted by God, for the desert was strewn with their corpses.
>
> These events happened as symbols to warn us not to set our desires on evil things, as they did. Do not be idolaters, like some of them; as Scripture has it, "the people sat down to feast and stood up to play." Let us not commit fornication, as some of them did—and twenty-three thousand died in one day. Let us not put the power of the Lord to the test, as some of them did—and were destroyed by serpents. Do not grumble against God, as some of them did—and were destroyed by the Destroyer.
>
> All these things that happened to them were symbolic, and were recorded for our benefit as a warning. For upon us the fulfilment of the ages has come. (I Cor. 10:1–11)

The marvel of the events of the Exodus had so impressed themselves upon the memory of the Jews that they transferred them to the ideal future, and Paul follows the tradition of his people in seeing in the work of Messiah-Jesus a kind of repetition of the Exodus. For a parallel in American history to the impression made on the Jewish mind by the Exodus, we might refer to the great depression of the thirties. What strikes Europeans coming to America is how profoundly the United States was influenced by that catastrophe. But the terms in which deliverance from it were conceived were the ones natural to an industrial nation. America experienced not a New Exodus but a New Deal—terms derived from business. However, the parallel is a very pale one. When he wanted to inspire his generation of Americans in the sixties, President Kennedy did *not* go back to the Roosevelt terminology of the thirties, whereas Paul returned to the terminology of the Exodus from the first century A.D. to the tenth century B.C.

But it was not only a general parallel which Paul saw between what happened at the Exodus and "in Christ"; he used terms which were especially filled with meaning by the Exodus. These were:

REDEMPTION

The following verses reveal the use of this term in Paul:

. . . and all are justified by God's free grace alone, through his act of liberation in the person of Christ Jesus. (Rom. 3:24)

You are in Christ Jesus by God's act, for God has made him our wisdom; he is our righteousness; in him we are consecrated and set free [liberation-redemption]. (I Cor. 1:30)

The term "redemption" comes from a verb usually translated "to redeem." The verb was used in classical Greek of ransoming a prisoner of war, setting him free from his captivity by the payment of money. But, as used by Paul, the term is best understood in the light of the Old Testament and Judaism.

The root meaning of the Hebrew verb meaning "to redeem" is *"to get back," "to acquire for its rightful owner something or someone lost to another."* Thus a slave who was captured could be "redeemed," that is, brought back to freedom after he had lost it either by the payment of money or by some other means.

The Old Testament applied this notion of "redemption" to God's liberation of Israel from Egypt. Consider, for example, the following (where the verb "to redeem" not the noun "redemption" is used):

> Say therefore to the people of Israel, "I am the Lord, and I will bring you out from under the burdens of the Egyptians, and I will deliver you from their bondage, and I will redeem you with an outstretched arm and with great acts of judgment. (Exod. 6:6)
>
> Thou hast led in thy steadfast love the people whom thou hast redeemed, thou hast guided them by thy strength to thy holy abode. (Exod. 15:13)
>
> Remember thy congregation, which thou has gotten of old, which thou has redeemed to be the tribe of thy heritage! Remember Mount Zion, where thou has dwelt. (Ps. 74:2)
>
> Thou didst with thy arm redeem thy people, the sons of Jacob and Joseph. (Ps. 77:15)

Notice that although the metaphor suggests to us a payment, in fact, as applied to God's activity, there is no such suggestion. In Second-Isaiah especially, the metaphor was used of God's bringing Israel back from exile in Babylon, as in Isaiah 41:14:

> Fear not, you worm of Jacob,
> You men of Israel!
> I will help you, says the Lord;
> Your redeemer is the Holy One of Israel.

There are many places where God is the Redeemer.

Paul, then, in applying the term "redemption" to the work of Jesus Christ had a long tradition behind him. Just as Israel had been redeemed from Egypt, so the Christian community, the New Israel, had been redeemed, "rescued," from bondage in the "Egypt" of sin. True, Paul does not use the term "redemption" frequently, but the idea of a New Exodus pervades his thought.

One thing is particularly to be emphasized. Only in two passages is the redemption about which Paul speaks regarded as a future possibility and not as a present possession. Just as the Synoptic Gospels proclaim that in Jesus a new order had already been inaugurated, so Paul insists that in him a redemption has already taken place. But as we shall see, this does not remove all sense of a future culmination of the redemption which has already begun. Paul asserts both a present and a future redemption.

ADOPTION

In one passage particularly Paul considers Christians as people who have been adopted as his sons by God through the ministry of Jesus. The passage, in Galatians 3:23–4:7 is too long to quote in full: we quote only 4:4–7:

> . . . but when the term was completed, God sent his own Son, born of a woman, born under the law, to purchase freedom for the subjects of the law, in order that we might attain the status of sons.
>
> To prove that you are sons, God has sent into our hearts the Spirit of his Son, crying "Abba! Father!" You are therefore no longer a slave but a son, and if a son, then also by God's own act an heir.

The term "adoption" is also to be understood in the light of the Exodus. The word "adoption" itself does not occur in the Old Testament, but it is clear that at the Exodus the Old Testament considered that Israel became a "son" of God. Thus the passage of the Christian from slavery to sin to "sonship" is a parallel to what happened at the Exodus, where Israel achieved that status. Among the Rabbis whom Paul must have known, the notion that Israel became God's "son" at the Exodus was a commonplace. So it is that this rich, moving metaphor of God's act in making Jew and Greek, male and female, bond and free his "sons" in Christ by adoption evokes the memory of the Exodus. Perhaps we may claim that while the term "redemption" emphasizes the initiative of God in this act, the term "adoption" emphasizes the grace of God in his dealings with man in Jesus Christ: not because of any worthiness in those whom he adopted did God act but out of his mercy. The thought implied is the same as that frequently expressed in Deuteronomy in such verses as the following:

> It was not because you were more in number than any other people that the Lord set his love upon you and chose you, for you were the fewest of all peoples; but it is because the Lord loves you, and is keeping the oath which he swore to your fathers, that the Lord has brought you out with a mighty hand, and redeemed you from the house of bondage, from the hand of Pharaoh king of Egypt. (Deut. 7:7-8)

LIBERTY

Paul does not often use the express term "liberty." But his epistles are full of the sense of barriers long standing being broken down. In Galatians, the term "liberty" does break forth with force in 5:1 and 5:13:

> Christ set us free, to be free men. Stand firm, then, and refuse to be tied to the yoke of slavery again. (Gal. 5:1)

> You, my friends, were called to be free men; only do not turn your freedom into licence for your lower nature, but be servants to one another in love. (Gal. 5:13)

There can be little doubt that when Paul thinks of the Christian life as "free," he is thinking of it as a New Exodus,

parallel to the first when Israelites who were slaves in Egypt
were set free, although in Galatians it is an illustration drawn
from the history of Hagar that he uses.

Metaphors drawn from the idea of Creation

In addition to the Exodus, the act of Creation occupied
Paul as he attempted to interpret the significance of Jesus. In
fact, in Judaism the Creation and the Exodus were often
joined together in thought. Judaism saw in the Exodus the
activity of the Creator himself. It was, therefore, natural for
Paul to connect Jesus not only with a New Exodus but with
a New Creation. Jesus has introduced a new order which can
only adequately be compared with the "new order" introduced
by God's act of creation. The book of Genesis is not far from
Paul's thought as he interprets the Gospel. This emerges in
several ways:

THE NEW CREATION

In certain passages, Paul uses the expression "a new creation."
Consider the following:

> It is not ourselves that we proclaim; we proclaim Christ Jesus
> as Lord, and ourselves as your servants, for Jesus' sake. For
> the same God who said, "Out of darkness let light shine," has
> caused his light to shine within us, to give the light of revela-
> tion—the revelation of the glory of God in the face of Jesus
> Christ. (II Cor. 4:5–6)
> When anyone is united to Christ, there is a new world [cre-
> ation]; the old order has gone, and a new order has already
> begun.
> From first to last this has been the work of God. He has rec-
> onciled us men to himself through Christ, and he has enlisted
> us in this service of reconciliation. What I mean is, that God
> was in Christ reconciling the world to himself, no longer hold-
> ing men's misdeeds against them, and that he has entrusted us
> with the message of reconciliation. We come therefore as Christ's
> ambassadors. It is as if God were appealing to you through

us: in Christ's name, we implore you, be reconciled to God! Christ was innocent of sin, and yet for our sake God made him one with the sinfulness of men, so that in him we might be made one with the goodness of God himself. (II Cor. 5:17–21)

In the former passage, the reference is directly to the emergence of the universe: a new universe has emerged in Jesus Christ. In the latter passage, the idea may be that the "individual" Christian is a new creature. If we take both passages together, the concept emerges that "in Christ" man is a new creature in a new creation. Such is the newness of what Jesus Christ has achieved that only in terms of creation can it be expressed.

PEACE

It agrees with all the above that, in describing the effects of the coming of Jesus Christ, Paul makes use of the story of the Fall, and this not only, as we shall see later, by ascribing to Jesus the title of "The Last Adam." He enters into the very spirit of the story of the Fall. One of the elements in that story was the hatred that emerged—hatred toward God on the part of Adam and hatred toward man—his own brother Abel —on the part of Cain. True, it is not explicitly stated in Genesis that Adam hated God, but he did rebel against him and break his commandment. For Paul, as a result of that first transgression, a principle of rebellion, revolt, and independence from God had entered into human existence. To this condition we may ascribe the description "hatred toward God." Paul came to regard man's relationship to God as one of alienation. Man needs to be reconciled to God, to make peace with him. The following passages make this clear by implication:

For if, when we were God's enemies, we were reconciled to him through the death of his Son, much more, now that we are reconciled, shall we be saved by his life. But that is not all: we also exult in God through our Lord Jesus, through whom we have now been granted reconciliation. (Rom. 5:10–11)

Notice how after these verses Paul refers to Adam; his thoughts are at the first creation.

Colossians 1:20 again is significant; it reads:

> and through him to reconcile to himself all things, whether on earth or in heaven, making peace by the blood of his cross.

Here Paul recognizes that man and nature were at enmity with God but that the death of Jesus has removed this enmity. For Paul, the whole ministry of Jesus was designed to achieve this end: it was a ministry of reconciliation, as in II Corinthians 5:17–21; which we have quoted already. One of the great gifts of Christ was "peace."

In this connection one thing needs to be clearly understood. Paul never asserts that God hates man; it is man who hates God. Just as he avoids claiming that God is angry with man, so Paul avoids ascribing hatred to God. On the contrary, God is concerned with the work of reconciliation. It was God who was "in Christ" reconciling the world to himself. He took the initiative in removing the barrier placed by man against him. The attitude of God toward man always is and has been and will be one of love. This is part of Paul's Gospel. The Gospel does not imply any change in God's attitude toward man but does, where it is appropriated, work a change in man's attitude toward God.

The result of this change is that the Gospel introduces what Paul calls *"peace."* In five passages, Paul refers to God as the God of peace.

> The God of peace be with you all. (Rom. 15:33)
> the God of peace will soon crush Satan beneath your feet. (Rom. 16:20)
>
> And now, my friends, farewell. Mend your ways; take our appeal to heart; agree with one another; live in peace; and the God of love and peace will be with you. (II Cor. 13:11)

The lessons I taught you, the tradition I have passed on, all that you heard me say or saw me do, put into practice; and the God of peace will be with you. (Phil. 4:9)

May God himself, the God of peace, make you holy in every part. (I Thess. 5:23)

As the third item cited makes especially clear, the term "peace" in Paul certainly retains the sense of concord or agreement or pleasant relationships between man and man. But it means more. It again recalls for Paul the scene described in Genesis 1. Primordially, man was at peace in a world at peace. Everything that God had made was good; order and peace had been called out of chaos. But this peace had been disturbed by the fact of sin, which had introduced misdirection, created a world at dispeace or at "poor peace," as a modern poet has put it. We are all too familiar with this fact in a world which "puts its peace in impossible things." But for Paul, as we have reiterated, "in Christ" the condition of misdirection has been reversed. There is peace instead of dispeace. Just as God, at the creation, had called out order and peace from chaos, so in the new creation "in Christ." Man is now in a new situation in which his enmity toward God has been removed; he is at peace because newly directed. Within his life there is still struggle but no frustration; there is still discomfort but no despair, because "in Christ" God is with him. Peace in this sense becomes essentially trust in life itself as lying in the hands of God and directed "in Christ." No one is likely to call Paul a peaceful man. He knew little "peace of mind" in his labors; yet this "stormy petrel," this turbulent man, knew "a peace that passeth understanding" because he was convinced that life was redirected by his Lord.

Metaphors drawn from the realm of sacrifice

A Jew such as Paul, who was aware of the power of sin, must have thought much about the sacrificial system of Judaism, which was regarded as the means ordained by God to remove the taint of sin. In his attempts to interpret the meaning of Jesus Christ, and especially his death, he naturally turned to the language of sacrifice. Some sacrificial terms which he used we can only note. Christ was for him the Passover Lamb slain for Christians or, again, the First-fruits. On one term alone can we enlarge. We do so because of its importance in the history of Christian thought, where it has played a significant role for ill as well as for good.

In Romans 3:21–26, we read as follows:

> But now, quite independently of law, God's justice has been brought to light. The Law and the prophets both bear witness to it: it is God's way of righting wrong, effective through faith in Christ for all who have such faith—all, without distinction. For all alike have sinned, and are deprived of the divine splendour, and all are justified by God's free grace alone, through his act of liberation in the person of Christ Jesus. For God designed him to be *the means of expiating sin* [*hilastêrion*] *by his sacrificial death, effective through faith.* God meant by this to demonstrate his justice, because in his forbearance he had overlooked the sins of the past—to demonstrate his justice now in the present, showing that he is both himself just and justifies any man who puts his faith in Jesus.

Here Paul asserts certain of his central convictions:

1. That now through Jesus Christ a new order, apart from the Law, though witnessed to by the Law and Prophets, has emerged.

2. This new order has been made possible solely by God's grace; because all, without distinction, had sinned.

3. The means whereby the sin of the whole world can be removed is faith in Jesus Christ whom God had set forth as the means for this, that is, to transliterate the Greek word used by Paul, as a *hilastêrion.*

Often the term *hilastêrion* has been translated by the word "propitiation." This was so in the familiar King James Version. This translation stated that Jesus had been set forth by God as a means to pacify God: the implication was that God was angry with men and poured forth his wrath or anger on Jesus and was thereby pacified. We have seen, however, that Paul does not think of God as being hostile to man and, therefore, as one who needed to be pacified. Recently, a new translation of *hilastêrion* has been offered, that of "expiation": roughly, the meaning of the verse concerned would be, then, that God has set forth Jesus as the means whereby the stain of sin may be removed.

But where did Paul find this word? What is its background? Almost certainly, it comes from the sacrificial practices of Judaism, and possibly from the ritual of the Day of Atonement. Once a year the High Priest of the Jewish people, on the Day of Atonement, after elaborate self-purification, entered the Holy of Holies in the Temple at Jerusalem and sprinkled the blood of a sacrificial victim on the *hilastêrion*, the mercy seat, and thereby removed the sin of all the people. Paul declares in Romans 3 that Jesus is the place where this act of removing sin is *really* performed—Jesus, who died publicly, is the effective means of cleansing the stain of sin from mankind.

Metaphors drawn from the realm of Law

Here again, it is only with the chief metaphor drawn from the realm of Law that we can pause. In most books on Pauline theology it is on this—the concept of justification—that the greatest emphasis is laid. Ever since the Reformation, justification by faith has been regarded by most Protestants as supplying the central motif in Paul's thought.

What, then, is to be understood by "justification." The term is only comprehensible in the light of the Old Testament and Judaism. The idea that Paul wants to convey by the term does not fit into the use of it in classical Greek. In the latter, "to justify" someone is to deal with him according to his deserts, that is, to deal with the guilty as guilty; to give a man his due punishment or reward. But this is almost the exact opposite of what Paul means by the verb "to justify" and the noun "justification."

The image which the term "justification" evokes is that of a judge dealing with a criminal. But, notice, *not* a Western judge. In a Western Court of Law, let us say in Britain or America, the judge sits aloof. He hears evidence for and against the accused. He sifts the evidence. As impartially as possible, he comes to a decision on the basis of the Law and precedent. As objectively as he can, he pronounces judgment —to set free or condemn the person on trial. The marks of a good judge are severe aloofness, dispassionate examination of evidence, immovability.

But such was not the case in Ancient Israel. Let us visit a court of law in the time of David or Solomon. The king sits to hear the evidence, yes. But, as soon as he is convinced of the rights and wrongs of the case concerned, he ceases to be an impartial judge in our Western sense. He intervenes now with passion to do right for the accused before him or to punish him. Especially was the king expected to intervene on behalf of the oppressed—to set him free, to take his part, to "justify" him, that is, put him in the right.

"Justification" as Paul understood it

Such is the background of the term "justification." Paul would argue somewhat as follows: God, the eternal judge, has seen the plight of man, bound by sin. In Jesus of Nazareth, he has come to the side of man, the sinner: he has given him a new direction. Like an Eastern king on behalf of his subjects, God has intervened in mercy on man's behalf; that is, he has set him in the right, given him a new status or direction. He has, thereby, proved himself the friend of publicans and sinners. But all this has one startling implication. God does not deal justly with men; he does not give to each according to his deserts. He justifies the ungodly and to do this is to transcend all legal relationships between God and man. In fact, the relationships between man and God—in the light of Jesus—cannot be expressed in terms of law at all. Paul saw in the mercy of the ministry of Jesus and in the grace of God's love in him a pledge of the universal, everlasting mercy of God to all mankind, and not only a pledge but an intervention of God in man's destiny to place him in the right or to correct his misdirection.

We may carry the illustration from the ancient eastern law court still further. When the king, as judge, intervened on behalf of the accused, the accused was passive; of himself he could do nothing. Paul seems to think of man's condition in a similar light. Man himself can do nothing to change his misdirection; the act by which this change is achieved is solely that of God. All is due to God's free favor or grace.

But this raises an acute problem. Does the redirection of man, which is justification, make those who are redirected good? Does moral achievement go along with justification? Do those whom God treats as righteous and redirects become righteous? Or, since justification is a pure act of grace, in which man is passive, is the moral condition of those who are redirected a matter of indifference?

In answer to these questions, which Paul's insistence on grace alone as the ground of justification raises, three positions have been urged. First, there is no moral connotation to be given to justification; it is sheer grace. Secondly, justification, as redirection, implies that those justified are, thereby, made righteous. Thirdly, justification implies ultimately, though not immediately, the moral re-creation of the person justified. The justified, at last, will be made or will become righteous. Into the many arguments for and against each of these positions, we cannot enter here. One thing can be said. The experience of redirection, that is, of being turned from the way of death and fate and sin to the way of life and hope, when appropriated, must always evoke gratitude. The response of the redirected man is one of thankfulness. And since gratitude may be regarded as the most ethical of all the emotions (a man who has known no gratitude is morally dead), justification, which must, when appropriated, issue in gratitude, contains within itself the power of moral renewal.

What Paul meant by "faith"

But what is this appropriation to which reference has been made? It is that act by which not only justification, but all the other benefits of Christ's work—redemption, adoption, liberty, new creation, peace, expiation—are all taken up into a person's own life and made real to him. And this act is referred to by Paul as "faith." Without this appropriation all these metaphors remain dead words without significance, but with it they spring to life. What, then, does Paul mean by "faith"?

The term "faith" has been so frequently misinterpreted that it has to be rescued from many false notions. The most obvious misinterpretation is that which equates it with a kind of irrational credulity. The ability to believe in obviously "impossible" things has been regarded as a mark of "faith." It must be admitted that there is much in the Biblical records, taken out of context, to encourage such crude credulity among modern men. But with credulity of this kind Pauline faith has little to do. Again, a common (and understandable) error has been to interpret faith as "faithfulness" or "fidelity." It is customary among religious people to refer to the "faithful few" who, for example, despite all odds keep open the doors of some dying Church across the years, and to equate their dogged persistence with "faith." Admirable as such doggedness often (though not always) is, it is not "faith." More frequently still, especially among Protestants, it has been a common practice to equate "faith" with assent to some doctrine or creed. For example, belief in the inerrancy of scripture or in the literal truth of the Virgin Birth have often been regarded as criteria of "faith." Such a concern with doctrinal correctness is often understandable in a shifting, religious scene, but it should not dictate our understanding of "faith." And at the opposite extreme, although springing from the same desire to escape from the shifting sand of contemporary life, there are those who have equated faith with a kind of intense, mystical spirituality, attainable only by the few, which ensures a private vision of Christ that sets those who enjoy it apart from all others. As we shall see later, Pauline "faith" has little to do with such private experiences (not to use the word "indulgences").

But what, then, does "faith" mean for Paul? He deals with it most directly in the Epistle to the Romans in 3:21–4:25. There he sets "faith" over against "works." Perhaps we may summarize his thought as follows. Man may approach life and its many demands in the belief that he himself, in his own strength, can meet these demands and fulfill them: he can, in short, work out his own salvation: he can stand four-square to all the winds that blow and by his own achievement conquer. To live in this belief is to court self-righteousness, pride, and, at the last, despair. This is true of all men; it is true particularly of the religious man who, like the Jew, counts on his own obedience to the Law.

On the other hand, man may recognize his own insufficiency to meet the demands of life and particularly the demands set before him in the Law and yet, in the light of the mercy revealed in Jesus Christ, trust life to work in and through him to his good. Faith is trust in life as coming from God, the All-Sufficient, who is also the All-Merciful revealed in Jesus. Faith is self-knowledge and self-abandonment. Professor C. H.

Dodd has summarized the Pauline understanding of faith in Romans in the following unforgettable words: "For Paul, faith is that attitude in which, acknowledging our complete insufficiency for any of the high ends of life, we rely utterly on the sufficiency of God. It is to cease from all assertion of the self, even by way of effort after righteousness, and to make room for the divine initiative."[41] We may well end this chapter, as we ended the previous one, with a question: "Who is the Jesus who inspires such faith?"

CHAPTER 27

THE NEW PERSON AND HIS NEW PEOPLE

The last chapter closed with a question: "Who is this Jesus who had redirected mankind and become for Paul the center of history?" We may begin to answer it by referring to the words of an unknown man which are recorded in an essay by his friend Hazlitt on the theme "On Persons One Would Wish to Have Seen." Hazlitt presents the matter in the following famous passage:

> [After many names had been discussed] "There is only one other person I can ever think of after this," continued H——; but without mentioning a name that once put on a semblance of mortality. "If Shakespeare was to come into the room, we should all rise up to meet him; but if that person was to come into it, we should all fall down and try to kiss the hem of his garment."[42]

Mr. H—— here expresses what is probably the attitude of most people who have heard of Jesus. He compares Jesus with other men and yet, almost instinctively, sets him apart from other men. He recognizes Jesus as a man among men but as one who is also different in quality from all others. In the earliest days of the Church, Christians were so overwhelmed by the figure of Jesus that they found it easier to think of him in terms of God than of man. They seemed to have asked the question: "How could such a person as Jesus have been merely man? He must have been more than man!" But most modern Christians have been like Mr. H——. They find it easier to think of Jesus, first, as a man and have tended to ask the question, which will arise naturally in any present-day twelfth-grade class, "How could even a person such as Jesus be more than man?" The ancient world thought easily in terms of "gods"; the modern world thinks easily only in terms of man.

In Paul these two emphases meet. We saw that for Paul, Jesus had redirected history. But this view of Jesus necessarily implied two things. First, Jesus must have been someone who was not controlled by this world. One who was himself wholly involved in and governed by the misdirection of history could not redirect it. One who redirected history had to stand beyond or outside history to be able to do this. An ancient Greek philosopher once exclaimed:

> Give me but one firm spot on which to stand,
> and I will move the earth.

The leader who can lift the world has to rest outside the world. So for Paul; his understanding of the work of Jesus in history demanded that he should think of Jesus as one coming into human history from outside it or as having his base, as it were, outside it. Paul's very understanding of the significance of Jesus led him, therefore, to think of him in "divine" terms.

But, secondly, to redirect history, Jesus had also to be fully involved in history. The lever to raise the world has to touch the world, that is, be in real contact with it. So, too, to redirect the world, Jesus had to grapple with it, soil his hands with the dirt of mankind and share its blood, toil, sweat, and tears. Jesus, in short, had to know sin. And so Paul recognizes not only a divine aspect in Jesus but a fully human one: Jesus is man among men. A concrete, tangible figure in history, flesh of our flesh and bone of our bone, and yet one who is so outside it that he has power to redirect it; in the world though not of the world—such is the Jesus of Paul. This twofold emphasis we shall examine in turn.

Jesus and God

GOD IN CHRIST

At all points in the activity of Jesus, Paul saw the activity of God himself. Just as the writers of the Synoptic Gospels saw the active will of God revealed in the ministry of Jesus—in the healing of the sick, the forgiveness of sin, the words of grace and authority—so Paul was convinced that in Jesus, God was at work. The following passages are significant:

> It is not ourselves that we proclaim; we proclaim Christ Jesus as Lord, and ourselves as your servants, for Jesus' sake. For the same God who said, "Out of darkness let light shine," has caused his light to shine within us, to give the light of revelation—the revelation of the glory of God in the face of Jesus Christ. (II Cor. 4:5–6)

The God who was at work in the very creation of the universe has now revealed himself in the face of Jesus Christ.

> For we know that if the earthly frame that houses us today should be demolished, we possess a building which God has provided—a house not made by human hands, eternal, and in heaven. In this present body we do indeed groan; we yearn to have our heavenly habitation put on over this one—in the hope that, being thus clothed, we shall not find ourselves naked. We groan indeed, we who are enclosed within this earthly frame; we are oppressed because we do not want to have the old body stripped off. Rather our desire is to have the new body put on over it, so that our mortal part may be absorbed into life immortal. God himself has shaped us for this very end; and as a pledge of it has given us the spirit. (II Cor. 5:1–5)

God was at work in Jesus to deliver the world from its sin. Similarly, the death and resurrection of Jesus are always regarded by Paul as acts of God, as in Romans 1:4, where Jesus is "designated Son of God in power according to the Spirit of holiness by his resurrection from the dead." Compare 5:10; 6:1–11.

In all such passages as the above Jesus is the means through which God has acted; he is the channel of the Divine purpose and activity. "God was in Christ," writes Paul (II Cor. 5:19). Does he go further? Only in one place does he seem to call Jesus by the name "God," that is, in Romans 9:5. But the NEB translates this: "Theirs are the patriarchs, and from them, by natural descent, sprang the Messiah. May God, supreme above all, be blessed for ever! Amen." (See the NEB notes.) As the NEB makes clear, even here it is not certain that Paul ascribes the title "God" to Jesus. But elsewhere he describes Jesus in ways which make it clear that for him Jesus has a peculiar status. The following terms are particularly important.

THE LORD

In Philippians 2:6–11 we read as follows:

> For the divine nature was his from the first; yet he did not think to snatch at equality with God, but made himself nothing, assuming the nature of a slave. Bearing the human likeness, revealed in human shape, he humbled himself, and in obedience accepted even death—death on a cross. Therefore God raised him to the heights and bestowed on him the name above all names, that at the name of Jesus every knee should bow—in heaven, on earth, and in the depths—and every tongue confess, "Jesus Christ is Lord," to the glory of God the Father.

This passage is probably a pre-Pauline Christian hymn which Paul has made his own. Because of his obedience unto death, God has exalted Jesus, so that "every tongue should confess that Jesus Christ is Lord, to the glory of God the Father." Jesus is distinguished from God, the Father, but given the title "Lord." The title emerges again, for example, in Romans 14:8 ff.

> If we live, we live for the Lord; and if we die, we die for the Lord. Whether therefore we live or die, we belong to the Lord. This is why Christ died and came to life again, to establish his lordship over dead and living.

In both the above passages, the event which makes Jesus "Lord" is the Resurrection—when Jesus was known by his followers as living in their midst even though he had undergone death. The title "Lord" is used of Jesus as he was present in the life of the Church, the object of its worship. In this sense, the meaning of the title was like that given to it in Hellenistic religious groups. There were many such who worshipped some "god" or "lord"—Isis, Adonis, and others. At this point, Paul's use of the title "Lord" for Jesus would have meaning for the people of the Roman Empire; it suggested that Jesus was a being to be worshipped. But it would not suggest any uniqueness on his part, because he was one of many lords and gods who were so worshipped.

Does the title have a deeper significance than this for Paul? It probably does. The term "Lord" used by Paul of Jesus is frequently found in the Greek translation of the Old Testament (called the Septuagint). In that book there are two names which are most often used of the Supreme Being—they are the word "God" and the word "Lord." These two terms are not quite interchangeable. The term "God" (Elohim) could be pronounced; but the term translated "Lord," usually written in English as Yahweh, was the one in which God had revealed himself to Moses at Mt. Sinai.

> Then Moses said to God, "If I come to the people of Israel and say to them, 'The God of your fathers has sent me to you,' and they ask me, 'What is his Name?' what shall I say to them?" God said to Moses, "I AM WHO I AM." And he said, "Say this to the people of Israel, 'I AM has sent me to you.'" (Exod. 3:13–14)

This name God had revealed to Israel: he was Yahweh, the God of Israel. As the generations passed by, the exact pronunciation of it became forgotten and it came to be regarded as an "ineffable name"—a name not to be pronounced. Thus when the Old Testament was read, whenever the name *Yahweh* occurred, Jews substituted for it another word *Adonai*, Lord, Master. In the Greek translation of the Old Testament, the word *Yahweh* is translated by "Lord" which is really a translation of *Adonai*, Lord, Master: it refers especially to God as the One revealed to Israel.

When Paul used the title "Lord" of Jesus, it is probable that he was thinking of him as Adonai—the Lord and Master who had in the past revealed himself to Moses but was now present among Christians in Jesus Christ. Jesus is "Lord"—the same Lord who had become the God of Israel, and has now become the Lord of the New Israel, the Church.

Nevertheless, Paul does not especially call Jesus "God." He was a Jew, and the horror of thinking of two Gods was real to his mind. At the same time, he cannot bring himself to deny that in Jesus "the complete being of God" came to dwell. This is the phrase used in the following passage from Colossians 1:15–20:

> He is the image of the invisible God; his is the primacy over all created things. In him everything in heaven and on earth was created, not only things visible but also the invisible orders of thrones, sovereignties, authorities, and powers: the whole universe has been created through him and for him. And he exists before everything, and all things are held together in him. He is, moreover, the head of the body, the church. He is its origin, the first to return from the dead, to be in all things alone supreme. For in him the complete being of God, by God's own choice, came to dwell. Through him God chose to reconcile the whole universe to himself, making peace through the shedding of his blood upon the cross—to reconcile all things, whether on earth or in heaven, through him alone.

Paul is impelled to ascribe to Jesus the highest status or honor possible: he is constrained to call him "God" and only stops at the very verge of this. Instead, he used the term "Lord" and refers to Jesus as "the complete being of God." In this way Paul's intense devotion to Jesus comes to terms with his monotheism as a Jew.

WISDOM

In the passage cited immediately above, the phrase "the complete being of God" is not the only one that is striking. Paul also refers to Jesus as "the image of God." He does not enlarge upon this, but, instead, makes certain explicit statements about Christ. These are:

1. He is the first born of all creation.
2. *In* him were all things created.
3. *Through* him were all things created.
4. *By* him were all things created.

To understand such language we must again take those leaps in time, space, and language to which we have so often referred. How was it possible for Paul to assert that a historical figure, Jesus, was the first born of creation and, indeed, the very agent of the created order? Is not all this fantastic?

There are two ways in which Paul's mind may have worked. According to some, he has applied to Jesus terms and ideas which were familiar among Gnostic groups of his day (see chapter 2) and interprets Jesus as a Gnostic Redeemer. There is no evidence that the figure of a Redeemer existed in Gnosticism in pre-Christian times, so it is unlikely that Paul could have borrowed his understanding of Jesus from that quarter.

It is more likely that, in interpreting Jesus, Paul has used concepts familiar to Judaism. In many passages he calls Jesus "Wisdom," as in the following:

. . . to those who have heard his call, Jews and Greeks alike, he is the power of God and the wisdom of God. (I Cor. 1:24)
for God has made him our wisdom; he is our righteousness; in him we are consecrated and set free. (I Cor. 1:30)

What does it mean to apply the term "Wisdom" to Jesus? The figure of Wisdom is described in the eighth chapter of Proverbs (22-34):

The Lord created me at the beginning of his work,
>   the first of his acts of old.
Ages ago I was set up,
>   at the first, before the beginning of the earth.
When there were no depths I was brought forth,
>   when there were no springs abounding with water.
Before the mountains had been shaped,
>   before the hills, I was brought forth;
before he had made the earth with its fields,
>   or the first of the dust of the world.
When he established the heavens, I was there,
>   when he drew a circle on the face of the deep,
when he made firm the skies above,
>   when he established the fountains of the deep
when he assigned to the sea its limit,
>   so that the waters might not transgress his command,
when he marked out the foundations of the earth,
>   then I was beside him, like a master workman;
and I was daily his delight,
>   rejoicing before him always,
rejoicing in his inhabited world
>   and delighting in the sons of men.

And now, my sons, listen to me:
>   happy are those who keep my ways.
Hear instruction and be wise,
>   and do not neglect it.
Happy is the man who listens to me,
>   watching daily at my gates,
>   waiting beside my doors.

Here Wisdom, which has a kind of semi-personal character, exists before creation, and plays a significant part in the creation itself. Wisdom is both the plan which God followed in building the universe and the architect which he employed. This is the way in which Judaism asserted that the universe is not a haphazard phenomenon, no accident which simply happened, but the outcome of God's purpose, built upon wise plans. Notice, further, that the Wisdom which pre-existed the universe and was employed in its construction, is also the moral guide of men.

> For he who finds me finds life
> and obtains favour from the Lord;
> but he who misses me injures himself;
> all who hate me love death. (Prov. 8:35–36)

In this way, Wisdom in the Old Testament has a role in the creation and structure of the universe and in the moral life of man.

We are now in a position to understand something of what Paul meant when he referred to Christ as the Wisdom of God. It is he who is the pattern on which the universe is founded and constructed; he is the "secret" of the universe. And at the same time, he is the moral guide of men. But there is still a further step. By the time of Paul, the Wisdom described in Proverbs 8 had been equated with the Law, which is the Wisdom of God. So that when Paul called Jesus "Wisdom," he was applying to him a term which Judaism had already applied to the Law. But— to use terms which explain the force of this—the Law was the ultimate authority for Judaism, and obedience to it the ultimate concern for every religious Jew. When, therefore, Paul described Jesus as the Wisdom of God, he proclaimed him to be the ultimate authority over all men; and in obedience to him, men were to find their ultimate concern.

In the above ways, Paul sought to do justice to the significance of Jesus. He was the Lord who had revealed himself to the Church, just as God had revealed himself to the people of Israel as Lord (Yahweh); he was the wisdom of God who had replaced the Law as the ultimate revelation of God and authority over men. In Jesus, God had revealed himself at work; Paul does full justice to this. But Jesus was also "man." Paul had to do justice not only to God in the man Jesus but to the *man* Jesus as the agent of God. In short, Paul had to wrestle with a problem which still, after twenty centuries, baffles Christians: how can this *man* Jesus be the one in whom *God* was at work? To this question Paul gives no answer: he leaves us with a mystery. Part of the reason for this is that his chief concern was not to explain the mystery of who Jesus was but, as we shall see, to expound the significance of what he had done for men. It was the work of Jesus in history and the claim of Jesus upon men that arrested Paul; and only when the central significance of Jesus was challenged, as at Colossae, did he expound the mystery of the Person of Jesus, and even then, he always did justice to the man Jesus. But that he does do full justice to the significance of the man Jesus, as well as to God in Jesus, we shall see.

Jesus, the Man

Attempts have been made, as we saw, to connect the thoughts of Paul about Jesus with the Gnostic Redeemer in whom people in his day trusted for victory over death and fate. But there was at least one point of fundamental significance at which Paul differed from the Gnostics and Mysteries. The Lord in whom he believed was a figure of recent history, who had suffered under Pontius Pilate. The Jesus of Paul was no phantom, mythical God from a remote past but a man among recent men. This fact Paul never ignores.

The view has often been expressed that Paul was not interested in the life-story of Jesus. To him it was the Risen Lord of the Church that mattered, not the carpenter's son from Nazareth who went about doing good. But this position cannot be held. Paul brings out the following details about Jesus:

1. He was born of a woman, that is, he was born a man.
2. He was born under the Law, that is, he was a Jew, of the seed of David.
3. He had certain definable personal characteristics.
4. His words were to be treasured as authoritative.

The fact is that the whole of Paul's understanding of the Gospel demands the historical reality of Jesus of Nazareth as a man; the redirection of mankind accomplished by God could only be achieved by one who had himself grappled with human life, that is, by a man. The question that arises is: What kind of man was he who did this?

The name by which Paul refers most often to Jesus is "Jesus Christ." This double form has often been regarded as a proper name; that is, it is simply the personal name for Jesus, and no emphasis need be placed on the epithet "Christ," which is merely part of the personal designation of Jesus. But this view needs to be questioned. When Paul uttered the name "Jesus Christ," it doubtless recalled to him its Hebrew equivalent: Jesus Messiah or Messiah Jesus. The full Messianic force of the name would be apparent to Paul.

Jesus was the Messiah. This term, in itself, did not evoke any ideas of a divine being. The Messiah of Jewish expectation was to be a human figure, however glorious. But the Messiah was to be the agent of God, the final man. This is the force of the name Jesus Messiah or Jesus Christ for Paul: in Jesus the final, ultimate man had appeared. To call Jesus "Messiah" was the natural way in first-century Judaism of giving him ultimate significance. If Paul had been writing today, we may surmise that he would use our evolutionary terms and claim that in Jesus the evolutionary process had reached its final or highest expression. There is, indeed, one passage in the Epistle to the Romans which has an oddly evolutionary ring:

> For I reckon that the sufferings we now endure bear no comparison with the splendour, as yet unrevealed, which is in store for us. For the created universe waits with eager expectation for God's sons to be revealed. It was made the victim of frustration, not by its own choice, but because of him who made it so; yet always there was hope, because the universe itself is to be freed from the shackles of mortality and enter upon the liberty and splendour of the children of God. Up to the present, we know, the whole created universe groans in all its parts as

if in the pangs of childbirth. Not only so, but even we, to whom the Spirit is given as firstfruits of the harvest to come, are groaning inwardly while we wait for God to make us his sons and set our whole body free [splendour-glory]. (Rom. 8:18–23)

But this hope for the revelation of the "Sons of God" had already been realized in one individual—in Jesus. The groaning of the evolutionary process, as it were, has already issued in the Son, Jesus.

But as the passage just cited makes clear, and as we saw previously, Paul was not given to thinking of men—even of Jesus—in isolation, as mere individuals. The creation was groaning for the revelation of a community—the sons of God. And when Paul thought of Jesus-Messiah it was as of one bound up with a community which he had brought into being with the whole human race. There are two ways in particular in which Paul finds the significance of Jesus, not so much in his individual person, as in his relationship to others.

First, like the writers of the Synoptic Gospels, Paul sees Jesus in and through the Church. Jesus Messiah, as was expected in Judaism, had brought into being a Messianic community, a body of people united in loyalty to him: the Messiah had created his ecclesia. This ecclesia—composed not of the virtuous but of the forgiven—was now the people of God in the world; it was the Israel of God which had taken over the functions of the Old Israel. So close was the relationship between the community created by Jesus and himself, that Paul refers to it as "the body of Christ." Consider the following passage:

For Christ is like a single body with its many limbs and organs, which, many as they are, together make up one body. For indeed we were all brought into one body by baptism, in the one Spirit, whether we are Jews or Greeks, whether slaves or free men, and that one Holy Spirit was poured out for all of us to drink. (I Cor. 12:12–13)

In this passage Jesus seems to be actually identified with the Church (see especially verse 12 where we should expect: "For the Church is like a single body . . . ," but find "For Christ is like a single body . . ."). Jesus is the head of the Church; his life runs through and sustains the Church, as in the following passages:

> He is the head of the body, the Church; he is the beginning, the first born from the dead . . . (Col. 1:18)
> (where Paul is speaking to the Church) But I want you to understand that the head of every man [in the Church as well as outside] is Christ. (I Cor. 11:3)

But it is not only with his own community, the New Israel, that Jesus is related. He is also related to the whole of humanity and has become, in fact, the founder of a new humanity. To grasp the force of this, it is necessary to concentrate on those passages where Paul describes Christ as the last Adam.

> Mark what follows. It was through one man that sin entered the world, and through sin death, and thus death pervaded the whole human race, inasmuch as all men have sinned. For sin was already in the world before there was law, though in the absence of law no reckoning is kept of sin. But death held sway from Adam to Moses, even over those who had not sinned as Adam did, by disobeying a direct command—and Adam foreshadows the Man who was to come. (Rom. 5:12–14)
> It follows, then, that as the issue of one misdeed was condemnation for all men, so the issue of one just act is acquittal and life for all men. For as through the disobedience of the one man the many were made sinners, so through the obedience of the one man the many will be made righteous. (Rom. 5:18–19)
> But the truth is, Christ was raised to life—the firstfruits of the harvest of the dead. For since it was a man who brought death into the world, a man also brought resurrection of the dead. As in Adam all men die, so in Christ all will be brought to life. (I Cor. 15:20–22)
> It is in this sense that Scripture says, "The first man, Adam, became an animate being," whereas the last Adam has become

a life-giving spirit. Observe, the spiritual does not come first; the animal body comes first, and then the spiritual. The first man was made "of the dust of the earth": the second man is from heaven. The man made of dust is the pattern of all men of dust, and the heavenly man is the pattern of all the heavenly. As we have worn the likeness of the man made of dust, so we shall wear the likeness of the heavenly man. (I Cor. 15:45–49)

Jesus is, for Paul, the last Adam, whose obedience cancels out the disobedience of the first Adam and introduces a new humanity, freed from the tyranny of sin and death. As last Adam, Jesus is all men or represents all men as they are obedient to God and "in him" the broken unity of mankind is restored. To understand Paul's thought here, a glance at Jewish teaching about Adam is necessary. In particular, in his development of the idea of the Church as the Body of Christ, Paul is largely influenced by Rabbinic ideas about Adam.

Rabbinic speculation about the creation of the physical body of Adam was very varied and often even grotesque. But it seems that two dominant interests were served by it, the need for emphasizing the unity of all mankind and the duty of love; while, of course, much of the haggadic material on Adam is playful fantasy and not serious theology. First, then, the fact that all men are derived from one ancestor Adam means that in him all men are one. There is a real unity of all men in him; all belong to each and each belongs to all. Thus in *M. Sanhedrin* 4:5 we read: "Therefore but a single man was created in the world to teach that if any man has caused a single soul to perish from Israel, Scripture imputes it to him as though he had caused a whole world to perish, and if any man saves alive a single soul from Israel, Scripture imputes it to him as though he had saved alive a whole world." It was in order to emphasize that in Adam all people were one that such strange stories were circulated as to the formation of Adam's body. According to a

tradition going back to R. Meir (c. A.D. 150), God made
Adam out of dust gathered from all over the earth. "It has been
taught: R. Meir used to say: 'The dust of the first man was
gathered from all parts of the earth,' for it is written, 'Thine eyes
did see mine unformed substance' (Ps. 139:16), and further it is
written, 'The eyes of the Lord run to and fro through the whole
earth' (Zech. 4:10)." (Epstein comments: "This is perhaps another way of teaching the equality of man, all men having been
formed from one and the same common clay.")

Later speculation claimed that his head was formed from the
earth of the Holy Land, the trunk of his body from Babylonian
soil and his various members from the soil of different countries.
"R. Oshaiah said in Rab's name: 'Adam's trunk came from Babylon (38b), his head from Eretz Israel, his limbs from other lands,
and his private parts according to R. Aha from Akra di Agma.'"
Epstein, in the page referred to above, explains that Adam's
head, the most exalted part of his body, comes from Eretz Israel
"the most exalted of all lands, while Akra di Agma was a place
notorious on account of its immorality." Because of this cosmopolitan physical structure of Adam, it followed that a man from
the East and a man from the West were of the same material
formation, and therefore one. In the deepest sense "there was
neither Jew nor Greek." Thus in *Pirke de Rabbi Eliezer* we
read:

> The Holy One, blessed be He, spake to the Torah: "Let us
> make man in our image, after our likeness" (Gen. 1:26). (The
> Torah) spake before Him: Sovereign of all the worlds! The
> man whom Thou wouldst create will be limited in days and
> full of anger; and he will come unto the power of sin. Unless
> Thou wilt be long-suffering with him, it would be well for him
> not to have come into the world. The Holy One, blessed be He,
> rejoined: And is it for nought that I am called "slow to anger"
> and "abounding in love"? He began to collect the dust of the
> first man from the four corners of the world; red, black, white
> and "pale green" (which) refers to the body . . .

Why (did he gather man's dust) from the four corners of the world?

Thus spake the Holy One, blessed be He: If a man should come from the east to the west or from the west to the east, and his time to depart from the world comes, then the earth shall not say, the dust of thy body is not mine, return to the place whence thou was created. But (this circumstance) teaches thee that in every place where a man goes or comes, and his end approaches when he must depart from the world, thence is the dust of his body, and there it returns to the dust, as it is said, "For dust thou art and unto dust thou shalt return." (*ibid.* 3:19)

In addition to all this, of course, Adam was bisexual, so that in him there was neither male nor female. The phrase "This is the book of the generations of Adam" (Gen. 5:1) was interpreted to mean that God revealed to Adam all the generations to come, this really means that all subsequent generations were in him as it were. How naïvely physical was all this speculation is seen from the fact that different individuals were conceived as being derived from or attached to different parts of Adam's body; one might belong to his hair, another to his ear, another to his nose; they literally formed different members of his body. There was speculation also on the meaning of Adam's name; the latter was found to suggest universality or the unity of all mankind in him. We read in 2 Enoch 30:13: "And I appointed him a name from the four component parts, from East, West, South, and from North." A stood for the East (Anatole), D for the West (Dusis), A for North (Arktos), and M for South (Mesembria). The same idea meets us in the Sibylline Oracles where we read: "Yea it is God Himself who fashioned four lettered Adam, the first man fashioned who completes in his name morn and dusk, antarctic and arctic."

Adam, then, stands for the real unity of mankind in virtue of his creation. There is also another factor. The nature of Adam's creation is made the basis of the duty of love, equality, and peace among men. To quote again M. *Sanhedrin* 4:5: "Again but a single man was created for the sake of peace among mankind that none should say to his fellow, My Father was greater than thy Father . . ." Furthermore, R. Simeon b. Azzai (A.D. 120–40) deduced the principle of love from Genesis 5:1, which reads, "This is the book of the generations of Adam . . .":

> Thou shalt love thy neighbour as thyself (Lev. 19:18). R. Akiba said: "That is the greatest principle in the Law." Ben Azzai said: "The sentence 'this is the book of the generations of man' (Gen. 5:1) is even greater than the other."

Genesis 5:1 teaches that all men are the offspring of him who was made in the image of God.

The relevance of all this to an understanding of Paul's doctrine of the Body of Christ is evident. Christians are, according to Paul, united with one another and with Christ; they share with one another and with Christ in one corporeity. This comes out clearly in Paul's treatment of the Last Supper. In I Corinthians 11:29, he writes: "For he that eateth and drinketh unworthily, eateth and drinketh damnation to himself, not discerning the Lord's body." He here refers to those who in their conduct at the Holy Communion forgot their unity with their fellow Christians and with Christ, who failed to recognize that to partake in the Lord's Supper was not merely to participate in Christ but also in their fellow Christians, who are one with Christ. Irregularities at the Table of the Lord, such as prevailed at Corinth, denied the solidarity of all Christians with each other and with their Lord. As Dr. Dodd puts it, "there is a sort of mystical unity of redeemed humanity in Christ," "a new corporate personality is created in Christ." In a quite physical sense, Christians are all one in Christ. This unity Paul calls the Body of Christ. He goes on to develop this concept: the Body is animated by the Spirit—a kind of life-force that manifests itself in different ways, so that there are many members in the One Body, unity in diversity.

The real problem is why Paul should use the term "Body" to

express the unity of the saints with one another and with their Lord. How could a thinker come to produce this conception of the extension of the body of a personal being? How can Paul regard it as so self-evident that he can make use of it without ever explaining it? Paul accepted the traditional Rabbinic doctrine of the unity of mankind in Adam. That doctrine implied that the very constitution of the physical body of Adam and the method of its formation was symbolic of the real oneness of mankind. In that one body of Adam, East and West, North and South were brought together, male and female, as we have seen. The "body" of Adam included all mankind. Was it not natural, then, that Paul, when he thought of the new humanity being incorporated "in Christ," should have conceived of it as the "body" of the Second Adam, where there was neither Jew nor Greek, male nor female, bond nor free. The difference between the body of the first Adam and that of the second Adam was for Paul that, whereas the former was animated by the principle of natural life, was *nephesh,* the latter was animated by the Spirit. Entry upon the Christian life is for the Apostle the putting off of the old man with his deeds and the putting on of the new man. The purpose of God in Christ is "in the dispensation of the fullness of times" "to gather together in one all things in Christ," i.e. the reconstitution of the essential oneness of mankind in Christ as a spiritual community, as it was one in Adam in a physical sense.

We are now in a position to appreciate the rich way in which Paul thought of Jesus. He gave him the highest titles that he knew, save only that of God; but it was only in controversy that he concentrated on the titular status of Jesus. What most concerned Paul was what this Jesus—the Lord, Wisdom—wrought for men in bringing into being not only the New Israel but the New Humanity, a new humanity sustained by his spirit.

CHAPTER 28

THE NEW WAY: IN CHRIST

When I first crossed the Atlantic, the captain of the ship on which I traveled, the S.S. *Britannic*, invited passengers to examine the ship's engines. I have never forgotten the impression of sheer mechanical perfection which those engines made upon me. Their shining pistons moved faultlessly, with effortless efficiency. When I then admired them, I did not imagine that within a few years, despite what seemed a marvel of engineering, the S.S. *Britannic* would have to be scrapped. And yet now, only a decade or so later, this has happened and the proud ship is no more. Atlantic gales and changes in technology have proved too much for her.

In a similar way, it is possible to be impressed by the thought of Paul. Paulinism, as it is called, that is, Paul's system of theology, can be made to appear shining and faultless, its parts fitting each other with an almost mechanical precision like the engines of the S.S. *Britannic*. But if the whole of Paul could be reduced to a neat system of thought, however perfect, both he and his system would have died long ago. The staggering changes in ideas since the first century, and especially in modern times, would long since have consigned Paul and Paulinism to limbo. As a mere system of thought, Paulinism has no more value and no more permanence than other systems. As a system of thought, it deals only with ideas. What does it mean, for example, to claim that Christ has redirected history? Is not history still full of misdirection; is not his claim simply a striking "idea" or "abstraction"? Or, again, what truth can there be in the claim that the Church created by Jesus is to reunite mankind, when the Churches, as we know them, are divided among themselves and are often a divisive force in society? Or, again, what value can there be to such a claim when, for example, a historian can say, with some justification, of the Church in France before the Revolution of 1789 that "no other institution so much deserved to be destroyed"? The cone theory of history offered by Paul is impressive on paper; but has it any life?

It is doubtful whether Paul thought out any system of theology, as such. If he did, it is because he gave it life, that is, changed it from mere theory to fact, that both he and his thought still live. It cannot be sufficiently emphasized that Paul was not only dealing with theological concepts in interpreting Jesus but with living experiences. Life itself as he encountered it was the fabric of his thought, and because of this, Paulinism has not only stood changing climates of thought but also the acids of experience and gale—the tests of life itself. In this chapter, we shall seek to show how the system which we have described above was not simply an abstraction to be reduced to a paper diagram, but a life to be lived: it was animated. But how?

First and foremost, it is to be emphasized again that, for Paul, Jesus Christ was a concrete figure in history. He was not an idea or a mythical figure, but a man of flesh and blood, who had appeared within the bosom of Judaism. He had so showed forth healing, forgiveness, and boundless charity during his life that he had challenged the limits of the existing Judaism with a vision of a wider, freer, deeper Rule of God. And in loyalty to this Rule, he had undergone the shameful agony of crucifixion. He had died. But, after death, he had also renewed his fellowship with his disciples, who had forsaken him in death, and called into being a new Messianic community which was to continue his life.

It was to this living Jesus that Paul ascribed the central place in history. Not to a bare fact of the past, still less to a symbol of some truth, did Paul commit himself, but to a Person who continued to challenge him and sustain him. He described his life as being a life "in Christ"—a life dominated not by a system of thought, however persuasive, but by a living Presence. This life "in Christ" has been interpreted in three main ways.

In terms of mysticism

"Mysticism," a term which is used here in a wide sense to cover all kinds of extraordinary religious experiences, offering peculiar intimacy with and especially absorption in God, has often been ascribed to Paul. Paul was absorbed "in Christ"; he had an intense personal relationship, involving ecstatic, visionary experiences of Jesus. In view of these, he could proclaim with the "mystics" of all the ages:

> I am lost to all the world
> And all the world is lost to me.

Otherworldly contemplation of the Living Jesus—this is what "in Christ" meant for Paul. He belonged to those of the Mystic Way.

That Paul did have strange, "mystical" experiences is clear. Consider the following passage:

> I am obliged to boast. It does no good; but I shall go on to tell of visions and revelations granted by the Lord. I know a Christian man who fourteen years ago (whether in the body or out of it, I do not know—God knows) was caught up as far as the third heaven. And I know that this same man (whether in the body or out of it, I do not know—God knows) was caught up into paradise, and heard words so secret that human lips may not repeat them. (II Cor. 12:1–4)

There are other passages which point to a warm, intimate relationship between Paul and his Lord. "For me," he once wrote, "to live is Christ." But in the very chapter in II Corinthians 12, where Paul recounts his strange, ecstatic experiences, he makes it clear that all such are not important. He does not deny that such experiences occur, but he does not place any high value on them. To be "in Christ" has meant for Paul, and others, "mystical" experiences, but he does not confuse mystical absorption, however fascinating, strange, and satisfying, with the essential meaning of being "in Christ." Those who have such experiences are in no way "superior" to those who do not have them. It is always a temptation to confuse being "in Christ" with having visions, special visitations from God, strange emotional experiences. But for Paul to be "in Christ" did not mean to live in a withdrawn, absorbed, "unworldly" contemplation of and fellowship with Christ, nor an intensely "religious" concentration in the mystical sense. Paul knew the dangers of such an emphasis full well—an irrelevant piety and a false ecstatic irresponsibility in life in the name of religion.

In terms of the imitation of Christ

Another way in which the phrase "in Christ" has been understood concentrates on such a passage as I Corinthians 11:1: "Be imitators of me, as I am of Christ."

Part of the meaning of this verse is that, just as the pupil of a Jewish Rabbi imitated his teacher in word and deed, so Paul, the pupil of Jesus, imitated his teacher. A modern educational psychologist would say that Jesus became the "identifying figure" of Paul, that is, the one with whom he sought to identify himself in every way. There is evidence, to which we shall refer later, that Paul treasured the words of Jesus and appealed to them as guides for conduct. In the Epistle to the Ephesians, which shows the influence of Paul, there is a reference to "learning Christ"; and again, Paul in Colossians thinks of his life as designed to "fill up that which is behind of the afflictions of Christ," which is a kind of imitation of Christ. There is little doubt that Paul regarded himself as a member of the school of Christ in which, in the light of Jesus, he had to unlearn many things—his pride in his own achievements, his religious bigotry

—and to learn many new things. To be "in Christ" was, in part, to learn of Jesus and to imitate him.

But the emphasis of Paul's epistles does not lie on this kind of imitation, althought it is present. In all imitation there is the danger of a mechanical copying, and Paul's emphasis was more on freedom than on imitation, as we shall see. Neither was the aim of Jesus to reproduce little "Jesuses" nor that of Paul to "copy" Jesus.

In terms of dying and rising with Christ

But what then is the main significance of the phrase "in Christ"? It is best understood in the light of its antecedent in the life of Paul. As a Jew, Paul had been "in Israel"; now he was "in Christ." The meaning of being "in Israel" helps us to understand that of being "in Christ."

What did it mean to be a Jew, to be "in Israel"? To answer this question, we turn to the liturgy of the Passover festival when, every year, the pious Jew reminds himself of his membership in the people of Israel and renews his allegiance to it. In this liturgy, the Jew declares that he has relived the experience of his own people. In other words, he has made the history of Israel his own history. The following quotations from the Passover liturgy make this clear.

The youngest competent at the table says:

Wherefore is this night different from all other nights?

The response is given:

We were slaves to the Pharaoh in Egypt, and the Lord our God brought us forth from thence with a strong hand and outstretched arm. If the most holy, blessed be He, had not brought our fathers from Egypt then we, our children and our children's children would have been slaves to the Pharaohs in Egypt. . . .

The significance of the rite for the individual will be clear from the following:

Four times does the Bible refer to the enquiring son. This indicates that the Bible thought of four kinds of enquiring sons —the wise son, the wicked son, the simple son, and the one that is too young to enquire himself. . . .

Which is the wise son's question? "What mean the testimonies and the statutes and the judgements which the Lord our God hath commanded you?" (Deut. 6:30) Thou must answer him by telling him of the laws of the Passover down to the law that no *aficoman* may follow the Paschal lamb. Which is the wicked son's question? "What mean you by this service?" (Exod. 12:26.) When he thus says YOU he *purposely excludes himself and so rejects one of the principles of Judaism.* Therefore mayest thou retort upon him by quoting (Exod. 13:8): "This is done because of that which the Lord did for ME when I came forth from Egypt."

Or again:

In every generation *each one of us* should regard himself as though *he himself* had gone forth from Egypt, as it is said (Exod. 13:8): "And thou shalt show thy son in that day, saying, This is done because of that which the Lord did unto ME when I came forth out of Egypt." Not our ancestors alone did God redeem then, but he did US redeem with them as it is said (Deut. 6:23): "And he brought US out from thence that he might bring US in to give US the land which he sware unto our fathers."

Therefore we are in duty bound to thank, to praise, to glorify, to exalt, to honour, to bless, to extol, and to give reverence to Him who performed for US, as well as for our forefathers, all these wonders. He has brought US forth from bondage to freedom, from sorrow to joy, from mourning to festival, from darkness to bright light, and from slavery to redemption. Now, therefore, let us sing before Him a new song, Hallelujah!

The true Jew, then, is one who has so entered into the history of his people that that history has become his own history, just as the true American is one who has, in his own experience, crossed the Atlantic with the Pilgrim Fathers, wrestled with the wilderness of early America, fought the War of Independence and the Civil War, and sat down at the table with Washington, Jefferson, Lincoln, and Lee. To be "in Israel" meant to recapture and re-enact the experience of the people of Israel, to make its history living, contemporary history.

Let us turn to the phrase "in Christ" and consider such passages as the following:

> For if we have been united with him in a death like his, we shall certainly be united with him in a resurrection like his. (Rom. 6:5)

> But if we died with Christ, we believe that we shall also live with him. (Rom. 6:8)

"In Christ" Paul re-enacted the death and resurrection of Jesus. How deep this concept of dying and rising with Jesus was in his thought appears from his treatment of baptism and the Lord's Supper. Baptism, the rite by which a person generally entered the Church, signified the going into death with Jesus and rising with him, as in the following verse:

> By baptism we were buried with him, and lay dead, in order that, as Christ was raised from the dead in the splendour of the Father, so also we might set our feet upon the new path of life. (Rom. 6:4)

Similarly, by participating in the Lord's Supper, the Christian remembers and recalls into the present the Jesus who died but is alive. The phrase "Do this in remembrance of me" means, in part, "Do this with a view to recalling me into your present life." In the Last Supper, it is not a figure in the past who is remembered only, but a Living Lord who is recalled so that his presence is experienced anew. Both Baptism and the Lord's Supper bring the Jesus of the past into the present.

Paul claims that he has already died and risen with Christ. Because he so strongly believed that he was one with Christ in the new humanity formed by him, as he was one with Adam in the old humanity, he could believe that he already shared in the victory of Christ over evil in the resurrection. Dying and rising with Christ was a sharing in what Christ had already achieved; it was to be one with him; it was to be an extension of his life—his eyes, his ears, his feet to serve in the world. And it was at the same time to be one with all other Christians who were "in Christ." For Paul, there could be no individual Christian but only Christians, bound up with each other because they were bound up with one Lord.

But here we discover a paradox in Paul. Because he had died and risen with Christ, so that the life of Christ was now his life, it might be thought that he had no more to do. Was not all achieved? Was not history redirected "in Christ"? Not so! The decisive event of history had taken place. Jesus had died and risen, but even though Paul shared in these "events," he still had to make the death and resurrection of Christ his own. A demand was still placed upon him. He had died and risen with Christ, but he still had to die and rise. This paradox he expresses in the well-known verses: "Work out your own salvation with fear and trembling. For it is God which worketh in you both to will and to do of his good pleasure" (Phil. 2:12–13). It so happens that I am writing these words in a farmhouse in The Vaud, Switzerland. Mme Bécholet, the farmer's wife, has just quoted to me an old French saying. Speaking of the necessity of Sunday labor on a farm, she said: "Le bon Dieu gouverne le monde, mais il ne trait pas." ("The good God governs the world, but he does not do the milking.") Paul would have agreed. His dying and rising with Christ were already a fact assured because of his solidarity with Christ; but they were also to be achieved.

But how were they to be achieved? Let us begin with "dying with Christ." The death of Jesus had greatly occupied Paul, and he sought to explain it in many ways. But above all, he understood that death as the supreme expression of obedience to God.

> Bearing the human likeness, revealed in human shape, he humbled himself, and in obedience accepted even death—death on a cross. (Phil. 2:8)

Similarly, it is by his act of obedience that Jesus, the last Adam, undoes the disastrous results of the disobedience of the first Adam.

> For as through the disobedience of the one man the many were made sinners, so through the obedience of the one man the many will be made righteous. (Rom. 5:19)

The death of Jesus arose as the inevitable consequence of his obedience to God in a misdirected world. To die with Christ is to share in his obedience and, thereby, to lay oneself open to the death that comes from this. It is to be ready to undergo the consequences of obedience. It is to refuse to be a mere spectator of life or simply to taste it for one's own ends, but to share in that obedience that redirects the world. It is to volunteer to live "in Christ" in obedience to God in a disobedient world, which means to die to one's own interests. It is to be expendable; to give freely because we have received freely.

When we turn to the other side, "the rising with Christ," we encounter what has again constantly occupied Paul's thought. To us in the twentieth century, it is the visions of the Risen Christ as recorded by Paul and the Gospels that occasion question and incredulity. To a first-century Jew it was otherwise. What staggered Paul was not that there had been a resurrection, but that Jesus, the Risen One, had chosen to appear to men who had betrayed him. Paul was not alone in his surprise. Because it is so incredible, the New Testament

emphasizes that Jesus first appeared after the crucifixion to
Peter, who despite his protestations of loyalty had betrayed
Jesus three times before the cock crew twice. Paul emphasizes
the sheer grace of the coming of Jesus to him who had persecuted his followers. The wonder of the resurrection is the
wonder of forgiveness—forgiveness to those who had failed.
This wonder breaks through the following words of Paul's:

> In the end he appeared even to me; though this birth of mine
> was monstrous, for I had persecuted the church of God and am
> therefore inferior to all other apostles—indeed not fit to be called
> an apostle. However, by God's grace I am what I am, nor has his
> grace been given to me in vain; on the contrary, in my labours
> I have outdone them all—not I, indeed, but the grace of God
> working with me. (I Cor. 15:8–10)

To rise with Christ is to share in his forgiveness; it is to live
the life of forgiveness. It is not enough to wrestle with the
evil of the world in obedience, but to wrestle with it so as also
to forgive. (See also chapter 40.)

"Dying and rising with Christ," therefore, is a demand to
live in obedience and forgiveness. But this obedience and forgiveness are rooted "in Christ." I once heard the great math-
ematician and philosopher, Lord Russell, broadcast for the
British Broadcasting Corporation. He described how lonely
man is in this cosmos. As he once wrote (I quote freely),
ultimately, when the universe runs down, "the whole temple
of man's achievement must inevitably be buried in the debris
of a universe in ruins." The cosmos is indifferent to man. But
Lord Russell pleaded for two virtues even in such a cosmos
—kindness and tolerance: these we must cling to in the cold
world. But is not this a kind of whistling in the dark to keep
up one's courage? Paul's call for obedience and forgiveness is
different. He is not whistling in the dark, but appealing to a
fact—the fact of Christ, in gratitude for whom the demand
for obedience and forgiveness wells up in his breast. His dying

and rising with Christ are already assured and yet to be achieved. The difference between Paul and Lord Russell is that the latter looks out on a bleak world, whereas Paul was assured that Jesus' death and resurrection had redirected the cosmos, created a new community which sustained him and poured forth a new spirit in the world, and that his moral endeavor took place, not against the background of an indifferent cosmos, but within the context of the new community and of a new Spirit. To illustrate again from the military sphere, to which Paul himself also turned, we may recall Napoleon's emphasis on the spirit of his armies and the importance of his presence for his troops. Facing overwhelming odds, 50,000 men against 200,000, he is once reported to have claimed: "Mais 50,000 hommes et moi cela fait 150,000!" ("But 50,000 men and I makes 150,000.") The war in which Paul was engaged was the antithesis of that which engaged Napoleon, but the presence of the Spirit created in him also a courage to overcome. Recall Romans 8:35–39:

> Then what can separate us from the love of Christ? Can affliction or hardship? Can persecution, hunger, nakedness, peril, or the sword? "We are being done to death for thy sake all day long," as Scripture says; "we have been treated like sheep for slaughter"—and yet, in spite of all, overwhelming victory is ours through him who loved us. For I am convinced that there is nothing in death or life, in the realm of spirits or superhuman powers, in the world as it is or the world as it shall be, in the forces of the universe, in heights or depths—nothing in all creation that can separate us from the love of God in Christ Jesus our Lord.

CHAPTER 29

THE NEW WAY:
THE SPIRIT AND THE LAW OF CHRIST

We suggested in the last chapter that, because Paul took the fact of Christ with desperate seriousness as a challenge to obedience, his thought was not merely a system but a way of life "in Christ." But he also expressed his understanding of the Christian life in another way. The life "in Christ" is life "in the Spirit." This is not surprising, because Paul thinks of Jesus Christ and of the Spirit as so closely related that, at times, they seem to be identical for him, and the Church "in Christ" or "his body" is naturally the community of "the Spirit."

But the term, "the Spirit," is peculiarly difficult for us to comprehend. There are many reasons for this. The term "spirit" has such a wide range of reference that it is very loose. As we saw, it can be used, for example, of the "spirit" or enthusiasm inspired by a Napoleon, who was in many ways the antithesis of Jesus. In religious contexts, too, the term has so vague a connotation that it is exceedingly difficult to define. Probably no Christian concept has been more debased than that of the Spirit—it has been confused with uncontrolled emotional excesses, irrational and even immoral practices, as in much revivalist religion depicted in modern American novels; and yet perhaps no Christian concept has borne such richness of connotation—it has been the vehicle of the highest religious experience.

Furthermore, the original Biblical conception of the Spirit has been confused, under the influence of non-Biblical ideas with which it has been colored, throughout the history of the Church. The reason for this is simple. Most, if not all, religions have some concept of "spirit," and the specifically Christian concept has been open to "corruption" from many quarters.

Thus it is that, before we can begin to describe the Pauline teaching on "the Spirit," we have to rid ourselves especially of two very common misinterpretations of it. Very often it has been confused with what is vaguely referred to as the "Spirit of the world or universe" (*anima mundi*). This is originally, perhaps, a Stoic concept—that a spirit runs through the whole of the created order. It dwells in the spirit of man also—which is part of the spirit of the cosmos. A spirit indwells the world, and it is of this spirit that Paul speaks. In modern English poetry, this can best be illustrated from Wordsworth. In *Tintern Abbey*, to use the most well-known example, he speaks of:

> A motion and a spirit, that impels
> All thinking things, all objects of all thought,
> And rolls through all things . . .

So are we to understand Paul, it has sometimes been claimed. But this is to misunderstand him. Paul does not often deal with the natural order; but when he does, he traces in it not "the Spirit" but the revelation of God's power, as in Romans 1:19-20:

> For all that may be known of God by men lies plain before their eyes; indeed God himself has disclosed it to them. His invisible attributes, that is to say his everlasting power and deity, have been visible, ever since the world began, to the eye of reason, in the things he has made. There is therefore no possible defence for their conduct.

What Wordsworth calls a "spirit that rolls through all things," Paul would probably find an expression of the Wisdom of God. For him, the Spirit is not an ever-present, indwelling characteristic of the natural order but a power which invades man from beyond nature. Indeed, the whole connection of the Spirit with Nature—which is so congenial to us moderns and which has been encouraged by English poets, such as Milton and Wordsworth, and by a long tradition of hymn writers, medieval and modern—this has no basis in Paul and little basis in the whole of Scripture.

Another misconception has to be removed. The term "spirit" is likely to conjure up in the mind of a modern reader the opening chapters of Charles Dickens' *A Christmas Carol*, where the ghosts of Christmases Past, Present, and To Come appear to Scrooge. Or again, to recall haunted houses. The very name "Spiritualism" has been given to the cult of unseen powers or spirits from another world. This understanding of "spirit" has a long history. In many first-century cults of the Hellenistic world, contact with "spirits" was familiar. But all attempts at connecting Paul's understanding of the Spirit with such cults have failed. It is best, therefore, to discard almost all our preconceived notions of "spirit" when we seek to understand Paul, and certainly to forget all about ghosts, spooks, and "Spiritualism."

Two fundamental facts are to be recognized. Paul was a Jew: his conception of the Spirit is derived from his Jewish inheritance. But Paul became a Christian: his Jewish inheritance came under the influence of Jesus Christ. It is these two facts—Judaism and Jesus Christ—that govern the peculiar Pauline understanding of the Spirit.

To begin with, the term "Spirit" is used in the Old Testament for the physical phenomenon of the "wind," for an attribute of man, and for the invasive power of God in human life. It is with this last that we are mainly concerned. Despite

Genesis 1:1, where the Spirit of God is mentioned in connection with creation, the Spirit is concerned not with nature but with the life of man—with the endowment of judges to lead Israel, and especially with the gift of prophecy. The belief grew up that "at the end of the days," in the Messianic Age, God would intervene in human affairs. He would do this through his Messiah but also through his own Spirit, that is, his own power, his own dynamic presence as "Spirit." The misfortunes and sins of the people of Israel had become so great that the prophets especially claimed that only an invasion of the power of God himself, of his Spirit, could change Israel. This view is expressed with impressive force in the following passages from Ezekiel 37:1–11.

The hand of the Lord was upon me, and he brought me out by the Spirit of the Lord, and set me down in the midst of the valley; it was full of bones. And he led me round among them; and behold, there were very many upon the valley; and lo, they were very dry. And he said to me, "Son of man, can these bones live?" And I answered, "O Lord God, thou knowest." Again he said to me, "Prophesy to these bones, and say to them, O dry bones, hear the word of the Lord. Thus says the Lord God to these bones: Behold, I will cause breath to enter you, and you shall live. And I will lay sinews upon you, and will cause flesh to come upon you, and cover you with skin, and put breath in you, and you shall live; and you shall know that I am the Lord."

So I prophesied as I was commanded; and as I prophesied, there was a noise, and behold, a rattling; and the bones came together, bone to its bone. And as I looked, there were sinews on them, and flesh had come upon them, and skin had covered them; but there was no breath in them. Then he said to me, "Prophesy to the breath, prophesy, son of man, and say to the breath, Thus says the Lord God: Come from the four winds, O breath, and breathe upon these slain, that they may live." So I prophesied as he commanded me, and the breath came into them, and they lived, and stood upon their feet, an exceedingly great host.

Then he said to me, "Son of man, these bones are the whole house of Israel. Behold, they say, 'Our bones are dried up, and our hope is lost; we are clean cut off.'"

The dry bones of Israel's existence could only be made to come alive by the invasion of God's own Spirit.

This concept of the Spirit, then, as the invasive power of God, Paul inherited from Judaism. But he also shared with the early Church the conviction that with the coming of Jesus the "end of the days" had begun, the Messianic Age had dawned. He saw in the life of the Church the marks of God's invasive power: the Spirit or "Power" which was to characterize the end of the days had come. It had come through Jesus. But it required a Paul to see the significance of this for the interpretation of the Spirit. What did Paul do to justify such a claim?

The Spirit before Paul

Let us first ask what most Christians before Paul seem to have understood by "the Spirit." To judge from Acts and from Paul's epistles, the very first days of Christianity were marked by intense enthusiasm. This we should expect. Few great movements of history have been born without cataclysmic, dynamic, intense emotional manifestations. And the birth of the Church was no exception. Professor Amos N. Wilder once suggested to me that the first days of the Church were like the falls of Niagara—accompanied by sound and foam and mists, in which the tremendous force of the water is obscured by its secondary manifestations.

So did the impact of the Spirit of Jesus fall upon the first generation of Christians. They were so overwhelmed that at first they failed to distinguish the sounds and the foam and the mists from the deep underlying forces which Jesus had set loose. Thus, they were impressed by the strange phenomena of speaking with tongues, by the extraordinary healings, enthusiastic emotional expressions. There is no need to doubt the historicity of such phenomena, and his is a dull mind who does not understand how easy it was in the earliest days of the Church to confuse the Spirit with the ecstatic phenomena of religious excitement.

The Spirit in Paul

It was into such a situation that Paul entered. He at once recognized its challenge. He could not deny the phenomena of ecstasy and enthusiasm; nor did he seek to do so. Indeed, he shared in such phenomena. But he brought to their explanation a critical, rabbinic mind which, in its sobriety, distrusted emotion and recognized that enthusiasm alone could not be made a criterion of the Spirit.

Fortunately, in I Corinthians, we find Paul's discussion of the Spirit. He corrects the misunderstandings of the Corinthians. We may summarize his treatment as follows.

1. Fundamental to any interpretation of the Spirit is the recognition that it is the relation of the Spirit to Jesus that matters. Paul urges that all "spiritual" phenomena are to be tested by their relation to Jesus. It is as if he were saying to early Christians: "In the Niagara of events in which you are engulfed, the underlying power is Jesus Christ himself, who is the touchstone by which you measure all other phenomena." This is the force of the words in I Corinthians 12:3.

> For this reason I must impress upon you that no one who says, "A curse on Jesus!" can be speaking under the influence of the Spirit of God. And no one can say, "Jesus is Lord!" except under the influence of the Holy Spirit.

The Spirit or "power" of God *is* the Spirit of Jesus.

2. The Spirit can find expression in a variety of activities. I Corinthians 12:4 reads:

> There are varieties of gifts, but the same Spirit.

These gifts are enumerated by Paul in the following order—wisdom, knowledge, faith, healing, miracle, prophecy, tongues. The significance of the order in which Paul lists these gifts will appear later.

3. Despite this diversity in expression, the Spirit is one and creates unity. Disunity among Christians is a sign of the absence of the Spirit.

> For Christ is like a single body with its many limbs and organs, which, many as they are, together make up one body. For indeed we were all brought into one body by baptism, in the one Spirit, whether we are Jews or Greeks, whether slaves or free men, and that one Holy Spirit was poured out for all of us to drink. (I Cor. 12:12-13)

4. It agrees with this last that the most excellent manifestation of the Spirit is what Paul calls *agapê*, which is usually translated in English by the term "love." This term, *agapê*, is almost a creation of the Gospel to describe the unmerited, overflowing, persistent, creative good will of God toward man and of man toward man "in Christ." The classic description of *agapê* occurs in chapter 13 of I Corinthians:

> Love is patient; love is kind and envies no one. Love is never boastful, nor conceited, nor rude; never selfish, not quick to take offence. Love keeps no score of wrongs; does not gloat over other men's sins, but delights in the truth. There is nothing love cannot face; there is no limit to its faith, its hope, and its endurance. (I Cor. 13:4-7)

The last sentence in the above passage supplies us with another mark of the activity of the Spirit. The Spirit is not only rational in its content, but it strengthens the bonds of the community; it builds up the common life of the Church. Because speaking with tongues does not do this, Paul lists it last in his description of the gifts of the Spirit. More important than any ecstasy are wisdom, knowledge, faith, and, above all, "love," intense, burning, consistent good will toward men.

Paul impresses on the Corinthians that enthusiasm without understanding, ecstasy without knowledge, intensity of experience without love, are all of secondary worth. The true marks of life in the Spirit, Paul expresses in memorable words:

> But the harvest of the Spirit is love, joy, peace, patience, kindness, goodness, fidelity, gentleness, and self-control. (Gal. 5:22–23)

The Spirit, which is Jesus himself living in the community of those who love him, bears "fruit." The suggestion seems to be that life "in the Spirit" is spontaneous or effortless. The Christian has merely "to live out" in his conduct the impulses supplied to him by the Spirit of Jesus. He is to live what he is "in Christ" or "in the Spirit." Paul seems to be saying: "Love Jesus, and do what you like," that is, "Simply follow the moral instructions given by the Spirit: enjoy the liberty from all formal directions or laws and give rein to your impulses, impulses now born of the Spirit of Jesus. Against those impulses and their fruit there is no law." But in other parts of his epistles, Paul seems to suggest that even the life "in Christ" and "in the Spirit" also has its law.

The Law of Christ

To understand this apparent paradox, it is necessary to go back a little. We saw that for Paul the chief expression of the Spirit is *agapê* (love), and that he describes what he means by *agapê* in I Corinthians 13. But we must ask: "From where did Paul derive this description?" There seems only one possible answer to this question. He derived it from Jesus himself. The name Jesus could easily be substituted for the term "love" (*agapê*) in I Corinthians 13 to supply a description of his character. This is simply another way of saying that it is the figure of Jesus—the tradition about him which he had received—that determines Paul's understanding of love and of the Spirit. We have previously noted that he almost equates the Spirit with Jesus.

It follows that when Paul writes of the Spirit, he is thinking always of the Spirit of Jesus; his understanding of the Spirit is always controlled by what he knew of Jesus. But, among other things, he knew of the demand which Jesus had placed upon his disciples. The ministry of Jesus had been one of infinite grace and freedom. But it had also opened up to men new vistas of obedience and placed before them absolute standards such as those we read of in the Sermon on the Mount. Thus it is that the life "in Christ" or the life in "the Spirit" for Paul is also a life under a law—the law of Christ, which is the law of love. Paul explicitly states in one passage that he is the "inlaw" of Christ, that is, bound by Christ's law.

In setting forth in precise terms the moral demand placed on Christians, or, as he would think of it, the Christian *way*, Paul draws on two sources.

First, he draws upon a tradition of the sayings of Jesus which he had inherited from the Church. Sometimes he distinguishes sharply between what Jesus had commanded and his own commandment or opinion. Consider the following passages:

> To the married I give this ruling, which is not mine but the Lord's: a wife must not separate herself from her husband. (I Cor. 7:10)
> On the question of celibacy, I have no instructions from the Lord, but I give my judgement as one who by God's mercy is fit to be trusted. (I Cor. 7:25)

But, in other places Paul, mingles the words of Jesus with his own words, so that the words of Jesus are not clearly distinguishable but present echoes or reminiscences of what Jesus himself had said. For example, in Romans 12:14–21, the thoughts of Jesus are clearly present and Paul has drawn upon them, but loosely.

Call down blessings on your persecutors—blessings, not curses. With the joyful be joyful, and mourn with the mourners. Have equal regard for one another. Do not be haughty, but go about with humble folk. Do not keep thinking how wise you are. Never pay back evil for evil. Let your aims be such as all men count honourable. If possible, so far as it lies with you, live at peace with all men. My dear friends, do not seek revenge, but leave a place for divine retribution; for there is a text which reads, "Justice is mine," says the Lord, "I will repay." But there is another text: "If your enemy is hungry, feed him; if he is thirsty, give him a drink; by doing this you will heap live coals on his head." Do not let evil conquer you, but use good to defeat evil.

Secondly, the Christian way is not only informed by the words of Jesus, which Paul treasured, but also by many ethical traditions, which Paul borrowed from Jewish and Hellenistic sources. The epistles of Paul often end with sections dealing with moral exhortation. These have been examined thoroughly and have revealed a common pattern which is probably derived from Jewish and Hellenistic Codes. The following tables reveal this pattern: the pattern is not identical in all the epistles but it is clearly traceable.

Order in Colossians 3:8–4:12

(1) *Putting off*

3:8. *But now ye also put off all these;* anger, wrath, malice, blasphemy, filthy communication out of your mouth: 9. Lie not one to another, . . .

(2) *The New Creation*

seeing that ye have put off the *old man with his deeds;* 10. And *have put on the new man, which is renewed in knowledge after the*

Order in Ephesians 4:22–6:18

(1) *The New Creation*

4:22. *That ye put off concerning the former conversation the old man,* which is corrupt according to the deceitful lusts; 23. And be renewed in the spirit of your mind; 24. And *that ye put on the new man, which after God* is created in righteousness and true holiness.

(2) *Putting off*

25. *Wherefore putting away lying,* speak every man truth with his neighbour: for we are members one of another. 26. Be ye angry, and

image of him that created him:
11. Where there is neither Greek nor Jew, circumcision nor uncircumcision, Barbarian, Scythian, bond nor free: but Christ is all, and in all. 12. Put on therefore, as the elect of God, holy and beloved, bowels of mercies, kindness, humbleness of mind, meekness, longsuffering; 13. Forbearing one another and forgiving one another, if any man have a quarrel against any: even as Christ forgave you, so also do ye. 14. And above all these things put on charity, which is the bond of perfectness. 15. And let the peace of God rule in your hearts, to the which also ye are called in one body; and be ye thankful.

sin not: let not the sun go down upon your wrath: 27. Neither give place to the devil. 28. Let him that stole steal no more; but rather let him labour, working with his hands the thing which is good, that he may have to give to him that needeth. 29. Let no corrupt communication proceed out of your mouth, but that which is good to the use of edifying, that it may minister grace unto the hearers. 30. And grieve not the holy Spirit of God, whereby ye are sealed unto the day of redemption. 31. Let all bitterness, and wrath, and anger, and clamour, and evil speaking, be put away from you, with all malice; 32. And be ye kind one to another, tenderhearted, forgiving one another, even as God for Christ's sake hath forgiven you.

5:1. Be ye therefore followers of God, as dear children; 2. And walk in love, as Christ also hath loved us, and hath given himself for us an offering and a sacrifice to God for a sweetsmelling savour: 3. But fornication, and all uncleanness or covetousness, let it not be once named among you, as becometh saints; 4. Neither filthiness, nor foolish talking, nor jesting, which are not convenient; but rather giving of thanks. 5. For this ye know, that no whoremonger, nor unclean person, nor covetous man, who is an idolater, hath any inheritance in the kingdom of Christ and of God. 6. Let no man deceive you with vain words: for because of these things cometh the wrath of God upon the children of disobedience. 7. Be ye not therefore partakers with them. 8. For ye were sometimes darkness, but now are ye light in the Lord: walk as children of the light: 9. (For the fruit of the Spirit is in all goodness and righteousness and truth;) 10. Proving what is acceptable unto the Lord. 11. And have no fellowship with the unfruitful works of darkness, but rather reprove them. 12. For it is a shame even to speak of those things which are done of them in secret. 13. But all things that are reproved are made manifest by the light: for whatsoever doth make manifest is light. 14. Wherefore he saith, Awake thou that sleepest, and arise from the dead, and Christ shall give thee light: 15. See then that ye walk circumspectly, not as fools, but as wise. 16. Redeeming the time, because the days are evil. 17. Wherefore be ye not unwise, but understanding what the will of the Lord is.

(3) The Worship of God

16. *Let the word of Christ dwell in you* richly in all wisdom; *teaching and admonishing one another in psalms and hymns and spiritual songs,* singing with grace in your hearts to the Lord. 17. And whatsoever ye do in word or deed, do all in the name of the Lord Jesus, giving thanks to God and the Father by him.

(3) The Worship of God

18. And be not drunk with wine, wherein is excess; but be filled with the Spirit; 19. Speaking to yourselves in psalms and hymns and spiritual songs, singing and making melody in your heart to the Lord; 20. Giving thanks always for all things unto God and the Father in the name of our Lord Jesus Christ;

(4) *Submit yourselves*

18. *Wives, submit yourselves unto* your own husbands, as it is fit in the Lord. 19. *Husbands,* love your wives, and be not bitter against them. 20. *Children,* obey your parents in all things: for this is well pleasing unto the Lord. 21. *Fathers,* provoke not your children to anger, lest they be discouraged. 22. *Servants,* obey in all things your masters according to the flesh; not with eyeservice, as menpleasers; but in singleness of heart, fearing God:

(4) *Submit yourselves*

21. Submitting yourselves one to another in the fear of God: 22. *Wives* submit yourselves unto your own husbands, as unto the Lord. 23. For the husband is the head of the wife, even as Christ is the head of the church: and he is the saviour of the body. 24. Therefore as the church is subject unto Christ, so let the wives be to their own husbands in everything. 25. *Husbands,* love your wives, even as Christ also loved the church, and gave himself for it; 26. That he might sanctify and cleanse it with the washing of water by the word, 27. That he might present it to himself a glorious church, not having spot, or wrinkle, or any such thing; but that it should be holy and without blemish. 28. So ought men to love their wives as their own bodies. He that loveth his wife loveth himself. 29. For no man ever yet hated his own flesh; but nourisheth and cherisheth it, even as the Lord the church: 30. For we are members of his body, of his flesh, and of his bones. 31. For this cause shall a man leave his father and mother, and shall be joined unto his wife, and they two shall be one flesh. 32. This is a great mystery: but I speak concerning Christ and the church. 33. Nevertheless let every one of you in particular so love his wife even as himself; and the wife see that she reverence her husband.

6:1. *Children,* obey your parents in the Lord: for this is right. 2. Honour thy father and mother; which is the first commandment with promise; 3. That it may be well with thee, and thou mayest live long on the earth. 4. And, ye *fathers,* provoke not your children to wrath: but bring them up in the nurture and admonition of the Lord. 5. *Servants,* be obedient to them that are your masters according to the flesh, with fear and trembling, in singleness of your heart, as unto Christ; 6. Not with eyeservice, as menpleasers; but as the servants of Christ, doing the will of God from the heart; 7. With good will doing service, as to the Lord, and not to men: 8. Knowing that whatsoever good thing any man doeth, the same shall he receive of the Lord, whether he be bond or free. 9. And, ye *masters,* do the same things unto them forbearing threatening: knowing that your Master also is in heaven; neither is there respect of persons with him.

(5) *Watch and Pray*

4:2. *Continue in prayer, and watch in the same with thanksgiving;* 3. Withal *praying* also for us, that God would open unto us a door of utterance, to speak the mystery of Christ, for which I am also in bonds: 4. That I may make it manifest, as I ought to speak. 5. Walk in wisdom toward them that are without, redeeming the time. 6. Let your speech be always with

(5) *Stand and Resist*

10. Finally, my brethren, be strong in the Lord, and in the power of his might. 11. Put on the whole armour of God, that ye may be able to stand against the wiles of the devil. 12. For we wrestle not against flesh and blood, but against principalities, against powers, against the rulers of the darkness of this world, against spiritual wickedness in high places. 13. Wherefore

grace, seasoned with salt, that ye may know how ye ought to answer every man. . . . (Personal details follow here.)

take unto you the whole armour of God that ye may be able to withstand in the evil day, and having done all, to stand. 14. Stand therefore, having your loins girt about with truth, and having on the breastplate of righteousness; 15. And your feet shod with the preparation of the gospel of peace; 16. Above all, taking the shield of faith, wherewith ye shall be able to quench all the fiery darts of the wicked. 17. And take the helmet of salvation, and the sword of the Spirit, which is the word of God:

(6) Stand

12. Epaphras, who is one of you, a servant of Christ, saluteth you, always labouring fervently for you in prayers, that ye *may stand perfect* and complete in all the will of God.

(6) Pray and Watch

18. Praying always with all prayer and supplication in the Spirit, and watching thereunto with all perseverance and supplication for all saints. (K.J.V.)

In these two ways—by appeal to the words of Jesus and to the ethical tradition of Judaism and Hellenism—Paul preserved the moral aspect of the Spirit. The Spirit of Jesus could not be divorced from the moral demand of Jesus himself and, in matters upon which Jesus had not touched, from the best tradition of Judaism and Hellenism.

Our treatment of the Christian life is over. It is for Paul a life "in Christ," "in the Spirit," "in the law of Christ," and as such it is a life in the community, the Church, which Jesus had called into being. Paul has remained a living force in history because he "lived" in this way. His theology was merely the intellectual expression of a life he lived—a way of life to which, by its contagion, he drew others.

PART IV

The Fourth Gospel

So the Word became flesh; he came to dwell among us, and
we saw his glory, such glory as befits the Father's only Son,
full of grace and truth.   (John 1:14)

> With this ambiguous earth
> His dealings have been told us. These abide:
> The signal to a maid, the human birth,
> The lesson, and the young Man crucified.

> But not a star of all
> The innumerable host of stars has heard
> How He administered this terrestrial ball.
> Our race have kept their Lord's entrusted Word.

> Of His earth-visiting feet
> None knows the secret, cherished, perilous,
> The terrible, shamefast, frightened, whispered, sweet,
> Heart-shattering secret of His way with us.

> No planet knows that this
> Our wayside planet, carrying land and wave,
> Love and life multiplied, and pain and bliss,
> Bears, as chief treasure, one forsaken grave.

> Nor, in our little day,
> May His devices with the heavens be guessed,
> His pilgrimage to thread the Milky Way,
> Or His bestowals there, be manifest.

But, in the eternities,
Doubtless we shall compare together, hear
A million alien gospels, in what guise
He trod the Pleiades, the Lyre, the Bear.

Oh be prepared, my soul!
To read the inconceivable, to scan
The infinite forms of God those stars unroll
When, in our turn, we show to them a Man.
—Alice Meynell, "Christ in the Universe"[43]

CHAPTER 30

INTRODUCTION: DATE AND AUTHORSHIP

In the previous pages we have crossed the rugged plateau of the Synoptic Gospels, the volcanic uplands of Paul and now—to carry the geographic metaphor further—we approach the serene heights of the Fourth Gospel. Sometimes those who have been at home in the Pauline eruptions have not found the serenity of the Fourth Gospel congenial, and the reverse is also true. Archbishop William Temple wrote: "Bishop Gore once said to me that he paid visits to St. John as to a fascinating foreign country, but he came home to St. Paul. With me the precise opposite is true. St. Paul is the exciting, and also rather bewildering, adventure; with St. John I am at home."[44] Perhaps those who have wrestled with moral failure are more at home with Paul, and those who have wrestled with the meaning of the world with John. In any case, to enter John after the Synoptics and Paul is to enter into fresh fields and pastures new.

But is it quite fitting to study John *after* the Synoptics and Paul? This has been the usual custom. The assumption has been that John is the summit of the New Testament, a summit only to be climbed after the lower heights of the Synoptics and Paul have been scaled. Just as students of Shakespeare are advised to begin with the simpler *Richard II* or *The Merchant of Venice* before they attempt the profundities of *Hamlet, Macbeth,* or *King Lear,* so the simplicities of the Synoptics and the cataclysmic insights of Paul have often been deemed to serve as a proper prelude to the Johannine profundities.

Such an approach to John, as a solitary climax, out-topping all the New Testament, must be challenged. Certainly the Synoptics can no longer be regarded as simple, straightforward documents whose meaning can be easily discerned; they are not merely chronicles of the events of Jesus' ministry but profound interpretations of them. Paul was a creative thinker. To regard the Synoptics and Paul as largely introductory to John is to ignore the depths which they all share. But we may go even further. Much as it is from the mountain top that the contours of the valley, its lights and shadows, become visible in true perspective, so in a real sense it is from the serene heights of the Fourth Gospel that we can best recognize the significance of the Synoptics and Paul. From this point of view, it would be best to approach the Synoptics and Paul after reading John.

A personal reminiscence may make this clear. Professor C. H. Dodd once told me that it was his study of the Fourth Gospel, which emphasizes that in the coming of Jesus Eternal Life is a present reality, that opened his eyes to those passages which reveal the same truth in the Synoptics. The Fourth Gospel provided him with the key to much that was hidden in the Synoptics. This truth was also emphasized by Sir Edwyn Hoskyns and Noel Davey in their work on the Fourth Gospel. Indeed, they claim far more for the Fourth Gospel:

> The test that we must in the end apply to the Fourth Gospel, the test by which the Fourth Gospel stands or falls, is whether the Marcan narrative becomes more intelligible after reading the Fourth Gospel, whether the Pauline Epistles become more transparent, or whether the whole material presented to us in the New Testament is breaking up into unrelated fragments. . . .
>
> A commentary upon the Fourth Gospel can therefore be no more than a preliminary work. It leads on to further study of the Pauline Epistles and the synoptic gospels.[45]

It follows that the Fourth Gospel should constantly be related to the Synoptics and to Paul in the real expectation that what was dark in them is illumined by the light of that Gospel. Just as it is at the end of the road that all the twists and turns of the journey are recognized for what they are, so from the climax of the New Testament, the Fourth Gospel, the tortuous intricacies and riddles of the Synoptics and Paul can appear in a new light, and the end of the road reveals the meaning of what was previously obscure.

One assumption is made in such a view of the Fourth Gospel: it is that that Gospel stands near enough to the Synoptics and Paul to illumine them; that the Fourth Gospel is within the reach of the Synoptics and Paul, as it were; it is not so far removed from them in time as to be unconnected with them. And this raises the first questions with which we must briefly deal— the date and authorship and sources of John.

When was it written?

Discussion of the date of John turns around two types of evidence which seem to be contradictory: the evidence of early manuscripts suggests that the Fourth Gospel is early; the evidence of the Church Fathers who first used it suggests that it is late. Let us look at these in turn.

THE TEXTUAL OR MANUSCRIPT EVIDENCE

There are three papyrus manuscripts or fragments of the Fourth Gospel which belong to the second century A.D. These are:

1. A fragment of the Fourth Gospel coming probably from Egypt, usually dated before A.D. 150. This is the earliest known fragment of the New Testament in existence. It is found in the John Rylands Library in Manchester, England.

2. Fragments of the Fourth Gospel, dated around A.D. 150, were edited by British scholars, and are now found in the British Museum, London. (Some deny that the fragments contain Johannine materials.)

3. A papyrus discovered in 1955, dated around A.D. 200, contains the whole of the Fourth Gospel. It is called the Bodmer Papyrus after the man who acquired it, Martin Bodmer of Geneva.

The above data mean that by A.D. 200 the Fourth Gospel was well known in Egypt; probably it was known among Christians in Upper Egypt in the first half of the second century, possibly by A.D. 125, and was deemed worthy of quotation. For a Gospel to have reached Upper Egypt and achieved such a status by A.D. 150 implies that it was written considerably earlier, probably by the end of the first century, that is, between A.D. 90 and 100.

The textual evidence, therefore, suggests an early date for the Fourth Gospel.

THE EVIDENCE OF THE CHURCH FATHERS

This evidence is in striking contrast to what was suggested by the textual evidence mentioned above, because the first author to quote the Gospel under the name John is Theophilus of Antioch, A.D. 180. All the Church Fathers before this time cannot certainly be proved to have used the Fourth Gospel.

There are reasons which can be suggested for this fact. Possibly it was heretics who first used John. As we shall see, heretics called Gnostics, who emphasized a kind of "gnosis" or "knowledge" as a way to salvation, could find much that was congenial in the Fourth Gospel. Perhaps a Gnostic preference for John gave the Gospel a bad name among the Church Fathers so that they avoided its use. But this remains only a possibility.

We are faced, then, with contradictory evidence. The manuscripts suggest an early date; the use of the Gospel by the Church Fathers a late date. If the Gospel were very early, the neglect of it by the Fathers becomes more and more difficult to understand, so that a very early date is excluded. But a very late date is also excluded by the manuscript evidence; this evidence points to a far earlier date than the quotations in the Fathers would suggest. Probably John should be placed somewhere between A.D. 90 and 100. It is not so far removed in time from the other Gospels and Paul to be irrelevant for their interpretation. On the other hand, recent attempts to push the Fourth Gospel very early into the second half of the first century because of its alleged affinity with the Dead Sea Scrolls must be rejected; such a date makes the silence of the Fathers inexplicable and makes it impossible to account for certain data in the Gospel, for example, the indications that it was written after A.D. 70 when Christians were being deliberately weeded out of the synagogues in chapter 7.

Who was the author?

Just as over its date, so there is division over the authorship of the *Fourth Gospel*. There are two main schools.

1. *The Conservative point of view: the author was the Apostle John*. The claim that the author was the Apostle John (John the Disciple of Jesus) rests on the following grounds:

THE EVIDENCE OF THE FATHERS OF THE CHURCH

Polycarp (A.D. 60–155), Bishop of Smyrna, who had been taught by the Apostles, regarded the Fourth Gospel as written by John the Apostle. This is apparently a strong piece of evidence. Moreover, the Fathers who do attribute the Gospel to John the Apostle were fully aware of the differences between John and the other Gospels and yet persisted in ascribing it to the Apostle.

THE EVIDENCE OF THE GOSPEL ITSELF

There are abundant data in the Gospel itself which point to Apostolic authorship. These may be gathered under five heads:

1. In John 21:24, the author is claimed to be a disciple. "This is the disciple who is bearing witness to these things, and who has written these things; and we know that his testimony is true."

2. The author knew Judaism so well that he must have been a Jew (see 5:10, 7:22 f., 51; 8:17): his language has Semitic undertones.

3. The knowledge of the geography of Palestine which he reveals suggests that the author was a Palestinian Jew.

4. The author seems able to correct the Synoptic account of the ministry of Jesus. For example, many claim that the date of the Last Supper in John is more accurate than that given in the Synoptics. But this implies that the author of John must have been very closely associated with the disciples of Jesus, if not a disciple himself.

5. It is the constant tradition of the Church that the author is to be identified with the Beloved Disciple mentioned in the following passages:

> One of his disciples, whom Jesus loved, was lying close to the breast of Jesus; (13:23)

> When Jesus saw his mother, and the disciple whom he loved standing near, he said to his mother, "Woman, behold your son!" (19:26)

> So she ran, and went to Simon Peter and the other disciple, the one whom Jesus loved, and said to them, "They have taken the Lord out of the tomb, and we do not know where they have laid him." (20:2)

> That disciple whom Jesus loved said to Peter, "It is the Lord!" When Simon Peter heard that it was the Lord, he put on his clothes, for he was stripped for work, and sprang into the sea. (21:7)

> Peter turned and saw following them the disciple whom Jesus loved, who had lain close to his breast at the supper and had said, "Lord, who is it that is going to betray you?" (21:20)

This Beloved Disciple, moreover, was the Apostle John. In view of all this there developed what we call the conservative approach to the Fourth Gospel according to which the author was the Apostle John, the Son of Zebedee. We are, therefore, very directly in touch with Jesus and his disciples in the Fourth Gospel. The long discourses which occur throughout the Gospel preserve both the more intimate teaching which Jesus gave to his disciples and the reflection upon this of the Church within which John lived. John attained a ripe old age at Ephesus and long pondered the meaning of what Jesus had done and taught. Out of his memory and his contemplation the serene Gospel emerged.

2. *The Liberal Point of View: the Gospel cannot be the work of an Apostle.* The conservative position has been severely attacked on several grounds, which may be summarized as follows:

THE INTERNAL EVIDENCE OF THE GOSPEL IS AGAINST APOSTOLIC AUTHORSHIP

1. The order of events and the content of John are so different from those of the Synoptics that both cannot preserve direct apostolic witness. If it be held that Peter's recollections are preserved in Mark, even to a very minor degree, how can we consider that John preserves the memories of another apostle? For example, John places Jesus' cleansing of the Temple early in the ministry; the Synoptics place it late. Is it likely that the Apostle John should have placed the cleansing so differently from the Synoptics?

2. The Fourth Gospel occurs, quite obviously, at the end of a long development of Christian thought; it is only understandable as the culmination of a movement of thought which included Paul, the Synoptics, and Hebrews. And, in addition, it also presupposes the rise of the Gnostic movement, which it both reflects and combats. All this means that John must belong to a period when the Apostles could no longer be alive.

3. Many details to which the conservative scholars point as supporting the apostolic authorship are dubious. Did the author know Judaism as well as the conservative scholars claim? In 18:13, he wrongly thinks of the High Priesthood as annually

elected. The name by which he refers to the Sea of Galilee is "the Sea of Tiberias," but this name was only used in the second century. In fact, the knowledge of Palestine revealed in the Fourth Gospel is such as might be gained by any pilgrim; it does not require that the author be a Palestinian Jew.

4. The reference to the author as a disciple in 21:24 f. occurs in a chapter which is certainly an addition to the Gospel. Chapter 21 may be the work of a disciple but not the whole Gospel.

In view of all these facts, the Liberals urge that John the Apostle was not the author of the Fourth Gospel. And they find their position confirmed by other data.

THE EVIDENCE OF THE CHURCH FATHERS DOES NOT SUPPORT THE APOSTOLIC AUTHORSHIP

In this connection the Liberal school has one strong and two weak arguments. To begin with the two weak ones. They urge, in the first place, that there is a long tradition that John the Apostle died a martyr's death at an early age, so that he could not have written the Fourth Gospel. All that needs to be stated is that this tradition is a very unreliable one, and need not be taken seriously. Similarly, the second difficulty posed by the Liberal School may be met. The question is asked why, if the Gospel was written by John the Apostle, the Church was so slow in accepting it as part of the Canon or its authoritative documents. But, as we saw, the ease with which the Gospel could be made to serve the ends of the heretic Gnostics sufficiently explains this.

It is more difficult to dispute the remaining point made by the Liberal School. The external evidence cited by the conservatives in support of the Apostle's authorship is not convincing. Apart from the vagueness of Irenaeus's reference to Polycarp, it is significant that the latter himself makes no claim to having known the Apostle John and never cites him. Moreover, since John is such a common name, the very person referred to by Irenaeus as John, the disciple, may not have been the Apostle at all.

Thus, on the evidence of the Gospel itself and of the Fathers of the Church, the apostolic authorship has been denied.

The discussion outlined ends in a stalemate. Is there a way out? The suggestion has been made that two persons bearing the name of John have been confused. Papias (A.D. 63–130), Bishop of Hierapolis in Asia Minor, refers to John the Presbyter, who lived in Ephesus at the end of the first century. And some have argued that this John was the author of the Fourth Gospel. He was confused with the Apostle. But this is pure conjecture. There is no way out of the above stalemate; the author we cannot know by name.

But the discussion of authorship has not been fruitless. If the data to which both the conservatives and the liberals appeal are all taken seriously, two things appear to be clear.

First, there is a real connection between the Fourth Gospel and the apostolate: whether through John the Son of Zebedee or Andrew or other apostles (there are indications of this), we cannot say: *the Gospel has a Palestinian root.*

Secondly, the Gospel as it stands points to an extra-Palestinian milieu: it looks to the far horizons of the Higher-paganism of the Graeco-Roman world: *the Gospel has a Hellenistic spread.*

These two factors suggest that while the author of the Fourth Gospel is unlikely to have been an apostle, he did draw upon early sources which contained the apostolic testimony. In the last resort, it is not the name of the author that matters but the value of the tradition upon which he drew and the use he made of it. This leads us to the sources behind the Fourth Gospel.

CHAPTER 31

THE SOURCES
BEHIND THE FOURTH GOSPEL

A young girl, who was wearing what seemed to her father a bizarre hat, on being asked why she wore such a thing, replied: "It's the fashion." There seem to be fashions not only in clothes but in scholarship; at least, there is a tendency for scholars at certain times to concentrate on the same things. In the nineteenth century, it was "fashionable" to emphasize that the Fourth Gospel was a unity; that is, the work throughout of one hand.

The twentieth century introduced a new "fashion." Probably owing to the influence of Old Testament studies, which had revealed various sources behind many of its documents (as had classical scholars behind Homer), New Testament students increasingly asked what materials the author of The Fourth Gospel had used. Perhaps the word "fashion" suggests "caprice"; and in fairness, it must be stated that there were many elements in The Fourth Gospel which seemed to point to different sources. We note, as examples, the following data:

1. John 20:31 reads as follows:

> Those here written have been recorded in order that you may hold the faith that Jesus is the Christ, the Son of God, and that through this faith you may possess eternal life by his name.

This verse seems to be the end of the Gospel, but it is followed by chapter 21, which appears to have been added after the whole Gospel had been written.

2. There are several places where the connection between parts of the Gospel is broken as if different sources had been combined. The following are examples:

. . . but the world must be shown that I love the Father, and do exactly as he commands; so up, let us go forward! (14:31)

After 14:31 we have the phrase: "So up, let us go forward." But 15:1 continues as if this had not been uttered.

At 4:54 Jesus is in Galilee; but in 5:1 he is in Jerusalem. If 7:15–24 be read before 7:1–14 the meaning is clearer.

3. There are certain inconsistencies which might be due to the joining of different sources:

a. 4:1–2

A report now reached the Pharisees: "Jesus is winning and baptizing more disciples than John"; although, in fact, it was only the disciples who were baptizing and not Jesus himself.

b. 2:13–3:21 constitute a problem. Nicodemus visits Jesus early in his ministry, before any hostility had been aroused and when Jesus had only performed one sign, in Cana of Galilee. But Nicodemus speaks of the signs that Jesus had performed; he is already afraid and visits Jesus by night.

4. The sequence of events in the trial of Jesus is confused. It would be improved if 18:24 were placed between 18:13 and 18:14.

To account for these data, two theories have been propounded. First, the dislocations in the Gospel have been claimed to be due to an accidental confusion of pages. The Gospel was written by one author, but somehow its pages came to be mixed up. This could easily have happened. From early copies of the Gospel, in parchment or papyrus, in book (codex) form, pages could fall apart and be wrongly replaced. The fact that the sections alleged to have been displaced are all about the same length suggests that they might be single pages. The following rearrangements, among others, have been proposed:

a. 3:22–30 should come between 2:12 and 2:13. This restores the connection between 3:21 and 3:31. It also improves the itinerary in chapter 2.

b. Chapter 6 should be between chapters 4 and 5 to improve the itinerary.

c. 7:15–24 should be after 5:47. It now interrupts the connection between 7:14 and 7:25; and it continues the argument of chapter 5.

d. 10:19–29 should stand after 9:41 to restore the connection between 10:18 and 10:30. This would also provide a better relation to the miracle of chapter 9.

e. Chapters 15 and 16 should be before 14:31, which is surely the end of the Farewell Discourses.

The difficulty in accepting such proposals is that the new arrangements put forth create their own difficulties; they cause as many problems as they solve.

Secondly, then, the data have suggested that the author has combined different materials and, in joining them, has forgotten or neglected to cover up his seams. It is not necessary to recount all the theories that have been held about John's sources. By and large, the problem of sources has narrowed itself down to two major considerations.

On the one hand, most scholars recognize that there is a remarkable unity over a great deal of the Fourth Gospel. There seem to be basic documents behind John which many have been able to recognize. The Gospel itself has provided evidence that there are different sources behind its narrative and its discourse materials. Accordingly, two sources at least have been postulated to lie behind John—a Book of Signs upon which he drew for his narrative, and a source containing Revelatory Discourses.

The unity of the Fourth Gospel

But not all have accepted such a division. The style of the Fourth Gospel is remarkably uniform throughout; the narratives and the discourses are so closely and naturally intertwined that they seem always to have belonged to each other. As for the inconsistencies and discontinuities or breaks in sequence to which we referred above, these are important only if the author were concerned primarily with giving a chronicle of events. But it is certain that this was not his primary concern. The author of the Gospel would not be troubled by the breaks referred to; like the rabbis, he could move from theme to theme with a grand indifference to the chronological and other niceties which trouble a western historian.

In short, whatever the sources which John used, he has so absorbed them—that is, reflected upon and digested them—that he has made them his own, so that we may treat his final Gospel as a unity. There is an old Welsh saying: "Gather your meal wherever you may, but bake your own loaf." This is precisely what the author of the Fourth Gospel has done. The final product is his own—and it is unmistakably one.

Did John know the Synoptics?

On the other hand, there is one aspect of the question of John's sources which must command attention. The assumption has frequently been made that the Fourth Gospel draws upon the Synoptics. In the following passages, there seems—as has been claimed—to be direct dependence:

The story of the anointing of Jesus at Bethany. (Compare Mark 14:3–9 with John 12:1–8; the language of both passages is very similar.)

The healing of the impotent man at Bethesda in John 5:8 ff. recalls Mark 2:9.

The feeding of the five thousand in John recalls that in Mark.

In addition to passages where the language recalls that of the Synoptics, the sequence of events in the Fourth Gospel often recalls that in the latter. The basic outline of the ministry is the same–the work of the Baptist, a journey from Galilee to Judaea, the crucifixion in Jerusalem and the resurrection. The following crucial events, among others, are the same:

The work of John the Baptist	1:19–36	compare	Mark 1:4–8
The feeding of the five thousand	6:1–13	compare	Mark 6:33–44
The walking on the lake	6:16–21	compare	Mark 6:45–52
Peter's confession	6:68 f.	compare	Mark 8:29
The entry into Jerusalem	12:12–15	compare	Mark 11:1–10
The anointing at Bethany	12:1–8	compare	Mark 14:3–9
The Last Supper	13:1–17:26	compare	Mark 14:17–26
The arrest	18:1–11	compare	Mark 14:43–52

On these and other grounds it has been argued that John used Mark and Luke; his use of Matthew is less clear. In any case, the tradition upon which the Synoptics drew was known—so it is claimed—to John.

But if John were dependent on Mark and Luke, or indeed merely on the tradition lying behind them, certain *omissions* in his work are very difficult to understand. These are:

The actual baptism of Jesus
The temptation in the wilderness
The cure of demoniacs and lepers
The association of Jesus with outcasts and sinners
The transfiguration
The institution of the eucharist
The agony in Gethsemane (in a developed form)
The cry of despair on the cross

Again the *style* of John is so very different from that of the Synoptics that a common reservoir of tradition for both is hard to imagine. This difficulty is intensified when John generally avoids parables in favor of allegories, and introduces long discourses where the Synoptics have none.

Furthermore, in matters of *geography* and *chronology* John differs. In John, the ministry lasts three years; in the Synoptics, about one year. In John, Jerusalem is mentioned often from chapter 2 onward; in the Synoptics, Jesus visits it only in the last week of his ministry.

An independent source

Not surprisingly, therefore, many have not been convinced that John drew upon the Synoptics and even upon the same tradition as lies behind the Synoptics. Rather, John rests upon an independent tradition which offers an avenue to Jesus different from those offered by Matthew, Mark, and Luke. British scholars especially have claimed that an early Palestinian tradition—not preserved in the Synoptics—is found in John. We note two things:

1. The Semitic character of the language of *The Fourth Gospel* points to a Palestinian tradition.

2. Even where it most clearly suggests Hellenism, as in the Prologue, for example, the Gospel also has affinities with Palestinian Judaism.

In the light of this, and many supporting details, the late T. W. Manson claimed that John drew upon a tradition which began in Jerusalem, moved to Syria, and later was carried to Ephesus, where the author of the Fourth Gospel used and illumined it. The relation of this tradition to the Synoptics remains obscure.

Two other British scholars have carried the matter further. Gardner-Smith re-examined the language and style of those passages in John which were claimed to rest on the Synoptics. He concluded that John was not dependent on the latter. In a great work, *Historical Tradition in the Fourth Gospel,* C. H.

Dodd has argued that John draws upon a Southern-Palestinian tradition, cherished by Jewish Christians, possibly at Jerusalem. It was transplanted outside Palestine without being much changed. This tradition is not that which lies behind the Synoptics, although it is like it. Often it clarifies what in the Synoptics is obscure. It is quite distinct, however, and forms the starting point for John's theological interpretation of Christianity.

In summary, to judge by the latest work on the sources of the Fourth Gospel, we have in it an independent and yet early avenue to Jesus. But this is a long and tortuous avenue, which crosses many frontiers—those of the Semitic world of the ancient Near East in Palestine and of the Hellenized world of the Eastern Roman Empire. It is because it provides an avenue of interpretation in terms of these two cultures that the Fourth Gospel offers a new perspective from which to see Jesus. How it makes use of the riches of these two cultures to set forth the glory of Christ, we hope to show in the following pages.

CHAPTER 32

GOSPEL FOR TWO WORLDS: THE JEWISH BACKGROUND

Writings which have a universal appeal are of two kinds. On the one hand, there are those which concentrate on a limited or local theme and penetrate through it to the center of all things: intense devotion to the particular, however commonplace, engenders universality. It was at such universality that Wordsworth aimed—"to choose incidents and situations from common life . . . tracing in them, truly though not ostentatiously, the primary laws of our nature." (Preface to the Second Edition of *Lyrical Ballads*) On the other hand, there are writings which become universal in their appeal because their canvas is so wide that they encompass more than one culture and by their very scope suggest the vast variety and complexity of life. Such, for example, is the appeal of Tolstoy's panoramic *War and Peace*.

The Fourth Gospel belongs to this second group. As the above surveys of the problem of its date and sources suggested, it spans the Semitic and the Graeco-Roman worlds. And it is this that lends it such a strange richness. There is nothing merely local in the Fourth Gospel; everything in it has been touched with the color of two worlds in such a way as to make it relevant to all worlds. We shall see that every concept in it seems to have a double thrust—to evoke and to address two worlds. And because it has striven to interpret the glory of Christ to Jew and Greek, it has done so for all men. This chapter will concentrate on its Jewish coloring.

At no time have the Jewish elements in the Fourth Gospel been unnoticed; but well into the twentieth century, most scholars thought of it as a fundamentally Greek document, designed to present Jesus to the Hellenistic world. By and large, it was students of the classics, like William Temple, who felt most at home in the Johannine world. But there has been a radical change. About 1923 or 1924, a Jewish scholar, Israel Abrahams, startled scholars by claiming that to Jews "the Fourth Gospel is the most Jewish of the four." But even before this, the recognition of the Semitic or Jewish character of the Fourth Gospel had begun, and ever since it has advanced by leaps and bounds. The reasons for this may be gathered up as follows:

1. The style is Semitic

The language and style of the Fourth Gospel point to the Semitic world. A personal experience may clarify this point. I turned to reading the Greek New Testament after being immersed for some time in classical Greek. Most of its documents —the Synoptic Gospels, Acts, and the Epistles—I found to present no difficulty in translation. But, to my amazement, the Greek which seemed the most simple in the whole of the New Testament, that of the Fourth Gospel, was the most difficult to understand. The vocabulary was simple, but there was always some strange twist in the structure of the sentences and especially in the relative clauses which made translation difficult. At first I was baffled. But I soon realized that the difficulties arose because the Greek of the Fourth Gospel was more influenced by Semitic (Aramaic) usage than that of any other New Testament documents.

How are we to account for this? In a volume called *The Aramaic Origin of the Fourth Gospel,* a great British scholar, C. F. Burney, claimed that the Gospel was first written in Aramaic and is, therefore, as we now have it, a translation.[46]

Not many have gone as far as this, but neither can many deny the evidence that the author of the Fourth Gospel thought as a Semite.

2. *The author knew Judaism*

The detailed Rabbinic knowledge revealed in the Gospel suggests that the author was not only aware of Judaism on a superficial level but acquainted with it from within. He refers to a specific commandment from the Law of Moses.

> In the Law Moses has laid down that such women are to be stoned. What do you say about it? (Jn. 8:5)

He is familiar not only with the occurrence of the various festivals of Judaism but with the passages from the Old Testament which were read at them. Some scholars have claimed that the whole Gospel is built around the chief Jewish Festivals and is governed in its thought by the Scriptural passages which were connected with the Festivals. See 2:23 (Passover); 6:4 (Passover); 7:2 (Tabernacles); 10:22 (The Feast of the Dedication); 13:1 (Passover); 5:1 (may refer to Tabernacles); 11:56 (Passover). What is certain is that the author of the Gospel was steeped not only in the Old Testament but in the liturgical tradition of Judaism.

There are several points where only a detailed familiarity with the exegesis of the Rabbis can explain the materials used by the author. One illustration must suffice here. In John 8:56, we read as follows:

> Your father Abraham was overjoyed to see my day; he saw it and was glad.

Whence did John derive this idea that, centuries before, Abraham saw the days of the Messiah? It is not present in the Old Testament. But it does occur in a Rabbinic interpretation of a passage in Genesis. Genesis 24:1 reads as follows:

Now Abraham was old, well advanced in years, and the Lord had blessed Abraham in all things.

The phrase *"advanced in years,"* used by the Revised Standard Version, is really a paraphrase of Hebrew words which mean *"went into the days."* A literal translation of Genesis 24:1 would be: *"Now Abraham was old and went into the days."* The Rabbis interpreted the phrase *"into the days"* to mean: *"Abraham saw before the Lord into all the history of his people up to the Messiah."* John 8:56 shows that the author of the Fourth Gospel was familiar with the Rabbinic interpretation. This, in turn, means that he knew the subtleties of the Rabbis from the inside.

But Judaism did not merely serve as the background for the author's understanding of Jesus; it is the concepts of Judaism that supply him with some of the most striking metaphors and images to set forth the glory of Jesus. Let us consider some of the great affirmations that are placed on the lips of Jesus:

1. (From the discussion between Jesus and the Woman of Samaria.)

"Sir," the woman said, "you have no bucket and this well is deep. How can you give me 'living water'? Are you a greater man than Jacob our ancestor, who gave us the well, and drank from it himself, he and his sons, and his cattle too?" Jesus said, "Everyone who drinks this water will be thirsty again, but whoever drinks the water that I shall give him will never suffer thirst any more. The water that I shall give him will be an inner spring always welling up for eternal life." "Sir," said the woman, "give me that water, and then I shall not be thirsty, nor have to come all this way to draw." (4:11–15)

2. 6:35

Jesus said to them: "I am the bread of life. Whoever comes to me shall never be hungry, and whoever believes in me shall never be thirsty."

3. 8:12

Once again Jesus addressed the people: "I am the light of the world. No follower of mine shall wander in the dark; he shall have the light of life."

Such claims, explicit or implicit, to be "the Living Water," "the Bread of Life," "the Light of the World" are only to be understood over against similar claims that were made by Judaism for the Law, which it regarded as the perfect, unchangeable revelation of God. John claims for Jesus what Judaism had claimed for the Law. The following illustration is drawn from a very large body of materials.

As water is gratis for all, so is the Torah gratis for all. As water is priceless, so is the Torah priceless. As water brings life to the world, so the Torah brings life to the world. As water brings a man out of his uncleanness, so the Torah brings a man from the evil way into the good way. As wine cannot keep good in vessels of gold and silver, but only in cheap earthenware vessels, so the words of the Torah keep good only with him who makes himself lowly. Like wine, words of the Torah rejoice the heart; as wine grows better by keeping, so the words of the Law become better as a man grows older.[47]

In addition to the familiar metaphors to which we have already referred, there is one phrase the force of which can easily be missed in an English translation. In the Old Testament and in Judaism, great importance was attached to the name of God. God had a hidden name which was not to be pronounced. Consider the following passages:

See now that I, even I, am he, and there is no god beside me; I kill and I make alive; I wound and I heal; and there is none that can deliver out of my hand. (Deut. 32:39)

I am the Lord, that is my name; my glory I give to no other, nor my praise to graven images. (Is. 42:8)

Therefore my people shall know my name; therefore in that day they shall know that it is I who speak; here am I. (Is. 52:6)

God's hidden name is *"I am he."* And the Fourth Gospel applies this hidden name to Jesus; the name reserved for the Divine Presence is used to assert that in Jesus that Presence is realized among men. The best example of this Johannine usage is found in John 18:1–7.

> After these words, Jesus went out with his disciples, and crossed the Kedron ravine. There was a garden there, and he and his disciples went into it. The place was known to Judas, his betrayer, because Jesus had often met there with his disciples. So Judas took a detachment of soldiers, and police provided by the chief priests and the Pharisees, equipped with lanterns, torches, and weapons, and made his way to the garden. Jesus, knowing all that was coming upon him, went out to them and asked, "Who is it you want?" "Jesus of Nazareth," they answered. Jesus said, "I am he." And there stood Judas the traitor with them. When he said, "I am he," they drew back and fell to the ground. Again Jesus asked, "Who is it you want?" "Jesus of Nazareth," they answered.

As Jesus reveals who he is by pronouncing the Divine Name his opponents draw back; they are overwhelmed by numinous awe in the presence of the Divine.

To conclude this chapter, two things more may be noticed. Throughout the Gospel the author shows an acquaintance with Jewish Messianic expectations at an intimate level. The origin of the Messiah is to be obscure (7:27); he must perform signs (7:31); he is to come from Bethlehem (7:42); he will abide forever (12:34). Such references to the Messiah point to one who was within Judaism in no superficial manner.

Equally striking as evidence of Jewish motifs is the section which, at first encounter, gives the impression of being thoroughly Hellenistic, the Prologue (regarded either as 1:1–14 or 1:1–18). True the terminology of the Prologue immediately casts around the Gospel a philosophic, Hellenistic aura. But the same terminology can also evoke central concepts in Judaism. In fact, there is hardly a statement in the Prologue which cannot be paralleled in Jewish literature dealing with the Wisdom of God, which in turn was equated with the Torah (the Law). To this we shall return later.

Enough evidence has been presented above—and much more could be given—to make it clear beyond the shadow of a doubt that the author of the Fourth Gospel was familiar with the deepest concepts in Judaism and capable of using them in the interests of his faith. But his was not a "one track mind." Intimately familiar with Judaism it was but not confined by it; it ranged beyond its confines to the wider Graeco-Roman world and the complexities of the Hellenistic Age.

CHAPTER 33

GOSPEL FOR TWO WORLDS:
THE HELLENISTIC BACKGROUND

The Fourth Gospel is the chameleon among the Gospels. However much recognition be given to its Jewishness, its affinities with the Hellenistic world are unmistakable. At one moment it evokes Judaism, the next the religions and philosophies of the Graeco-Roman world. The same images and metaphors which speak with power to Jews also do so to Gentiles. They shift without warning from one nuance to another, now Semitic, now Hellenistic. It is not only that the Gospel, despite its Semitic undertones, is written in Greek, but that its words and concepts are thoroughly at home in the cultured pagan circles of the Graeco-Roman world. The Gospel startles us by its direct use of Semitic ideas, but it is also informed by the sophisticated subtlety of the Hellenistic world.

This is what might be expected in the first century. In New York City at the present time the coexistence of large Christian and Jewish groups has led to all sorts of intermingling between them, so that it has become fashionable to refer to "The Judaeo-Christian Tradition" or to "Judaeo-Christian Ideas or Values." The situation in the first-century Graeco-Roman world was similar. Judaism and Hellenism were not sealed off from each other, each occupying a "watertight" compartment. Rather, they were constantly impinging upon each other. Judaism, even in Palestine, was Hellenized and Hellenism was Judaized (see chapter 3).

Thus the Fourth Gospel, which is in dialogue with Judaism,

is also in dialogue with Hellenism; it uses the terms of Jerusalem and Athens at one and the same time. And before we refer to its use of more or less strictly Hellenistic categories, we must recognize that it confronts also a fusion of Judaism and Hellenism. Thus, for example, one of the most striking terms used by John of Jesus, the term "The Word," was familiar to the Jewish intelligentsia of the Hellenistic world.

The meaning of "The Word"

We can illustrate this from the work of a Jew who lived in Alexandria in the first century. He is known as Philo Judaeus (c. 20 B.C.–c. 50 A.D.), and is, without question, the most important figure among the Hellenistic Jews. Philo used the term "The Word" to denote the mediator between the Supreme God, the ground of all Being, and the world of things. The Word enabled the Supreme God, who himself could not come into contact with corruptible things, to create the universe and yet remain separate from it. In this Word—which to us imperfect men is "a god" (theos) but to be distinguished from the Supreme God, the God (ho theos)—are summed up all the ideas of which phenomena are mere copies. The Word is the Supreme Idea; it is the archetypal light, the law of nature. The use of the term "word" suggests that God had "spoken." The Word, therefore, existed in two forms. It resides in the mind of God, the Supreme Being, as a concept or thought, but it also has an "uttered" or a "manifested" existence when God has given his thought utterance. There can be no question that when the Fourth Gospel refers to The Word, a Hellenistic Jew such as Philo would immediately find his curiosity whetted. For such Jews the question "What is the nature of the Logos?" would be as burning as the question "What is the purpose of the evolutionary process?" to a twelfth grader in a modern high school. (The accompanying diagram gives a summary of Philo's scheme.)

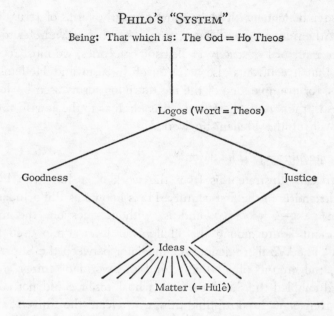

PHILO'S "SYSTEM"

Being: That which is: The God = Ho Theos

Logos (Word = Theos)

Goodness   Justice

Ideas

Matter (= Hulê)

The Logos is at the head of all ideas: it is invisible because
it is not like anything perceptible: it comprehends
in itself the whole intelligible cosmos.
It exists in two forms:
1. As Reason or Mind itself: it is the Rational,
    Sovereign Principle of the human soul.
2. As Speech, the offspring of Reason.

The Hermetica

But the term "The Word" would also be understood in circles not in direct contact with Judaism. Among Hellenistic
seekers after truth, this term and others that John used would
be very familiar. John appealed to the Higher-pagans of his
day, to Greek religious intelligentsia as they are revealed to us,
for example, in documents called *The Hermetica*. Let us glance
briefly at these.

To understand *The Hermetica* it is necessary to glance at
the soil in which they emerged. Throughout the period when

the New Testament writings were being written, there were all sorts of refined, intellectual people in the Graeco-Roman world who were seeking for a religious anchorage. They were beyond the reach of the popular religions; these they treated with contempt. But they were also dissatisfied with the cold emphasis on reason in the traditional philosophical schools. They had often learned at the feet of Plato, who had warmth as well as reasonableness, but they had become tired of the cut-and-dried, arid teaching of other popular philosophers. Where could they be at peace? To meet the needs of such people, there arose a kind of philosophic mixture or amalgam, a synthesis of Platonism and other philosophies. Groups of spiritual intellectuals gathered together. They formed philosophical or religious societies of what they considered the elite or "the spiritual." They sought for God in little enclaves of intellectually superior people, often marked by piety and sensitivity. It was out of such groups or cells of "spiritually cultivated" seekers that *The Hermetica* came. The people who wrote down *The Hermetica* lived after the first century, but there is much in *The Hermetica* which can be traced back to that period. What are the marks of this material? The following are the chief.

1. *The emphasis on tradition or ancient, received truth.* The material in *The Hermetica* was a tradition handed down from a distant past, from mouth to mouth, from group to group. It was thought to have come originally from the God Thrice-Great Hermes who was none other than the God Thoth, the scribe of the Egyptian Gods. From Thoth the priests of Egypt had derived their wisdom. In turn they had handed it down to Pythagoras (540–510 B.C.), and the latter had passed it on further to the great Plato himself. The teaching of *The Hermetica*, therefore, was ancient truth.

Why was there such an emphasis on the antiquity of the teaching? The reason lies in the nature of the first century.

It was a time of the failure of nerve (see chapter 2). Refined, sensitive, disillusioned people felt that the only wisdom worth having was what did not belong to the degenerate present but had come from the distant past. Only a few had the courage to think independently; most preferred to shelter in the shadow of ancient authorities. There is a similar phenomenon in modern society where many find satisfaction in a cult of the medieval or even in the primitive (Gaugin was a symptom of this); and in the Church in this century there have been several backward looking movements, calling for a return to Aquinas or Calvin or Luther. In times of confusion and uncertainty, the traditional appeals strongly.

2. *The emphasis on "knowledge."* The ancient tradition which was cherished in *The Hermetica* emphasized that salvation came by what was called *Gnôsis*, "knowledge." But the term "knowledge" has to be carefully defined. In reaction to the cold reason of the schools, the Hermetists urged the need for a knowledge higher than the merely rational—a superior, direct knowledge of ultimate reality. Such knowledge could not be gained by the exercise of the mind alone, but only from a revelation communicated in ancient tradition. Not the penetration of reason was important but mystical awareness of the truth handed down, culminating in a vision of the Divine.

3. *Immortality and true life.* The knowledge referred to above conveys to the spiritual, who receive it, immortality and true life. It is expressly stated, indeed, that the end of knowledge is deification. Those who possess it become "gods."

4. *The sources of "knowledge."* There were opposing views as to how "knowledge" could be attained. According to some, "knowledge," which is salvation, is conveyed in and through the world.

> Holy art Thou, whose brightness has not darkened
> Holy art Thou, of whom all nature is an image.

More often God himself, as Mind, gives "knowledge." In the seventh book of *The Hermetica* we read:

> For He cannot be known by hearing, nor made known by speech, nor can He be seen with bodily eye, but with mind and heart alone.

And the mind, whence is it? God himself is mind and he gives light and life.

5. *Mind is related to The Word.* The Mind which is God is also related to what is called The Word. We can gather some notion about The Word from the first tractate of *The Hermetica.* The contents of the first book may be summarized as follows.

> The seer, who is in an ecstatic state, is given a vision from the God, Poimandres. He is allowed to see the truth about the nature of things. He sees, in this vision, light stretched out to infinity. After an interval, darkness enters and it becomes what is called a wet nature, violently agitated.
>
> Next a "holy word" comes out of the light. At this, fire leaps up from the wet nature: air follows upon the fire. The fire and the air then take their places in the upper regions. They leave behind a mixture of earth and water which are kept in perpetual motion by the word.
>
> There follows an interpretation of the vision:

> The Light=Mind, Reason, The Primal God
> The Word=The Son of the Primal God

After this explanation the vision continues. In the light, the seer sees a whole universe—the idea or archetypal form of our universe. This idea of the universe has always existed. The Counsel of God saw this idea: the idea was copied and in this way the elements came into being.

In the following part of the vision, the Primal God, Mind, gives birth to a second mind, The Demiurge, who in turn creates seven administrators—the Planets which in their orbit are to embrace the physical universe. At this juncture the Word becomes united with the Demiurge. Together they set the

The "System" of *The Hermetica*
The Primal God
Light stretching to Infinity. This is Mind or Reason

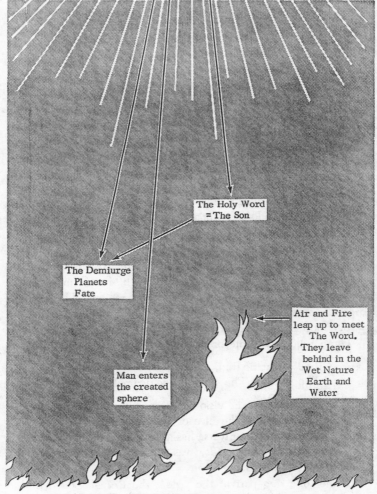

The Holy Word
= The Son

The Demiurge
Planets
Fate

Air and Fire
leap up to meet
The Word.
They leave
behind in the
Wet Nature
Earth and
Water

Man enters
the created
sphere

DARKNESS: A WET NATURE VIOLENTLY AGITATED

planets in motion. The revolution of the planets in turn causes the emergence of irrational living things—birds, animals etc.

But what of the creation of man? This is now described in terms which may reflect the influences of Genesis 1. Mind (=The Primal God), who is life and light, gave birth to Man in his own image. Mind loved Man, and gave him authority over all his creatures. But Man conceived the desire to create for himself. He entered the created sphere: in his descent the astral powers imparted something to him. As a result Man became human. Reaching the framework of the heavens, he saw Nature. Nature fell in love with him and he returned her love. Descending into the irrational sphere, Man became one with Nature. He has now a twofold character: he is both immortal and mortal. He is Lord of creation in virtue of God's gift, but subject to Fate in virtue of his union with Nature. Out of this union mankind is born.

Here, then, is an elaborate myth. Man is immortal but through attachment to matter, which is involved in the exercise of the sexual instinct, he becomes mortal. How is he to escape from this involvement with matter? There is one way only. It is by "knowledge"—knowledge of what he is and whence he came, imparted to him by the tradition. If a man knows that he was created by Mind, who is light and life, he will find salvation. "If, being made of life and light, you learn to know that you are made of them, you will go back into life and light." To know one's origin and destiny, this is the way of salvation.

The process of salvation is described in Tractate 13 of *The Hermetica* in terms of Rebirth in the form of a secret discourse between the Thrice-Great Hermes and his son Tat. A part of it runs as follows:

TAT: I know not, thrice-greatest one, from what womb a man can be born again, nor from what seed.

HERMES: My son, the womb is Wisdom, conceiving in silence; and the seed is the true God.

TAT: And who is it, father, that begets? I am wholly at a loss.

HERMES: The Will of God, my son, is the begetter.

TAT: Tell me this too; who is the ministrant by whom the consummation of the Rebirth is brought to pass?

HERMES: Some man who is a son of God, working in subordination to God's will.

TAT: And what manner of man is he that is brought into being by the Rebirth?

HERMES: He that is born by that birth is another; he is a god, and son of God. He is the All, and is in all; for he has no part in corporeal substance; he partakes of the substance of things intelligible, being wholly composed of Powers of God.[48]

Compare with the above John 3:3 (and other passages):

In truth, in very truth, I tell you, unless a man has been born over again he cannot see the kingdom of God.

It has been necessary to refer at such length to Philo and *The Hermetica* because only when the world of thought which they represent is recognized can the thrust of the Fourth Gospel be appreciated. The terminology of John is the terminology of Hellenistic Judaism and the Higher-paganism. But this is not only attested by the use of the terms "The Word of Jesus," but by other Johannine terms which must be noted.

John's emphasis on "knowledge"

The noun for "knowledge" (*gnôsis*) does not occur in the Fourth Gospel, but the verb "to know," from which it comes, appears more often in it than in any other document in the New Testament. The following passages are noteworthy:

Turning to the Jews who had believed him, Jesus said, "If you dwell within the revelation I have brought, you are indeed my disciples; you shall know the truth, and the truth will set you free." (Jn. 8:31–32)

I am the good shepherd; I know my own sheep and my sheep know me—as the Father knows me and I know the Father—and I lay down my life for the sheep. (Jn. 10:14–15)

Thomas said, "Lord, we do not know where you are going, so how can we know the way?" Jesus replied, "I am the way; I am the truth and I am life; no one comes to the Father except by me." (Jn. 14:5–10)

"If you knew me you would know my Father too. From now on you do know him; you have seen him." Philip said to him, "Lord, show us the Father and we ask no more." Jesus answered, "Have I been all this time with you, Philip, and you still do not know me? Anyone who has seen me has seen the Father. Then how can you say, 'Show us the Father'? Do you not believe that I am in the Father, and the Father in me? I am not myself the source of the words I speak to you: it is the Father who dwells in me doing his own work." (Jn. 14:5–10)

This is eternal life: to know thee who alone art truly God, and Jesus Christ whom thou has sent. (Jn. 17:3)

In such passages "eternal life" or "salvation" is to be attained by "knowledge." In another passage, John 13:3, Jesus possesses the kind of knowledge—of his own origin and destiny—which the Hermetist desired:

During supper, Jesus, well aware that the Father had entrusted everything to him, and that he had come from God and was going back to God, rose from table.

Clearly the emphasis on knowledge in John spoke to a need of his day.

Associated with John's concern with "knowledge" is his striking use of the adjective "true" or "real," as in the following verses:

The real light which enlightens every man was even then coming into the world. (Jn. 1:9)

That is how the saying comes true: "One sows, and another reaps." (Jn. 4:37)

They said, "What sign can you give us to see, so that we may believe you? What is the work you do? Our ancestors had manna to eat in the desert; as Scripture says, 'He gave them bread from heaven to eat.'" Jesus answered, "I tell you this: the truth is, not that Moses gave you the bread from heaven, but that my Father gives you the real bread from heaven. The bread that God gives comes down from heaven and brings life to the world." (Jn. 6:30–33)

Thereupon Jesus cried aloud as he taught in the temple, "No doubt you know me; no doubt you know where I come from. Yet I have not come of my own accord. I was sent by the One who truly is, and him you do not know." (Jn. 7:28)

I pass judgement on no man, but if I do judge, my judgement is valid because it is not I alone who judge, but I and he who sent me. (Jn. 8:16)

This is eternal life: to know thee who alone art truly God, and Jesus Christ whom thou has sent. (Jn. 17:3)

This is vouched for by an eyewitness, whose evidence is to be trusted. He knows that he speaks the truth, so that you too may believe. (Jn. 19:35)

John's emphasis on "truth"

Similarly striking is the frequency with which the noun "the truth" occurs in the Fourth Gospel—in all, twenty-five times. Contrast Matthew, Mark, and Luke where it only occurs 1, 3, and 3 times, respectively. For our purpose, the following examples may serve:

But the hour is coming, and now is, when the true worshipers will worship the Father in spirit and truth, for such the Father seeks to worship him. God is spirit, and those who worship him must worship in spirit and truth. (Jn. 4:23–24)

And you shall know the truth, and the truth will make you free. (Jn. 8:32)

Consecrate them by the truth; thy word is truth. (Jn. 17:17)

Many of the references to "true" and "the truth" are best understood in the light of ideas, ultimately going back to Plato, which were familiar in the Hellenistic Age. As we saw before, Platonism distinguished two orders, that of eternal existences and that of spatial, temporal phenomena. Only what belongs to the former order is real or true. And it was with the true or the real in this sense that the Hermetist, for example, was concerned. Consider the following words from the thirteenth book of *The Hermetica*:

HERMES: I rejoice, my son, that you are like to bring forth fruit. Out of the Truth will spring up in you the immortal brood of virtues; for by the working of mind you have come to know yourself and our Father.[49]

HERMES: The mortal form changes day by day; it is altered by lapse of time, and becomes larger and smaller; for it is an illusion.

TAT: What then is real [true], thrice-greatest one?

HERMES: That which is not sullied by matter, my son, nor limited by boundaries, that which has no colour and no shape, that which is without integument, and is luminous, that which is apprehended by itself alone, that which is changeless and unalterable, that which is good.[50]

A religious inquirer of the kind who would be interested in the speculations of *The Hermetica* would find in the Johannine references to "the true" and "the truth" an echo of what he had already encountered. John would be "speaking his language," as it were.

But the same applies to other terms which litter the pages of *The Hermetica* as those of *The Fourth Gospel*. Even the few quotations extracted above show how the terms "life" and "light" are common to both documents.

Life and light

The word "life" occurs very frequently in John. The aim of Christ is to give life, as in 10:10: "I am come that they might have life and might have it more abundantly." Compare with this sentences from the first tractate of *The Hermetica* (1:24):

"Full well have you taught me all, O Mind," said I, "even as I wished. But tell me furthermore the ascent by which men mount; tell me how I shall enter into Life . . ."

In *The Hermetica,* as we saw, Mind is life and light, and so the Father of all who is Mind consists of life and light. It is over against such concepts that John's references to "coming to the light" (3:20 f.), to the "true light coming into the world" and to Christ as the "light of the world" become telling. John is addressing people to whom such terms were charged with meaning. Ever since Plato had used light as a symbol for God, the term was fully at home in the Hellenistic world.

Enough has now been written to show that along with the coat of Jewish color the Fourth Gospel presents a coat of Hellenistic color in various shades. It uses the religious vocabulary of Jew and Greek; its pages interest them both at one and the same time, as it still interests scholars of the Ancient World. But John would not be flattered by such a statement. It was once said that the most unkind comment that can ever be made on any sermon is: "It was interesting." The same may be said of such a comment on a Gospel. John certainly was not concerned to interest but to challenge. What his challenge was we shall see in the next chapter.

CHAPTER 34

THE CHALLENGE OF THE FOURTH GOSPEL

So far it is the similarities between the Fourth Gospel and the documents of the Graeco-Roman world that have been emphasized. The impression, indeed, may have been given that that Gospel is so much part of its world that, like the chameleon, it takes its whole coloring from its environment. But this is only partly true. In fact, the Fourth Gospel stands out against its own world as an unmistakable challenge in a startling contrast. This double character of the Fourth Gospel, at the same time belonging to and standing against its world, may be illumined by comparison with another castle of my boyhood in Wales—Castell Carreg Cennen. This stands giddily on a steep cliff which falls sheer for five hundred feet. To look at it, on this side, is to see a structure almost suspended in mid-air, its base lost to sight; it erupts without warning, inexplicable and strange, among the soft limestone hills around. But, from the other side, the castle looks quite different. There the ground gradually rises from the river valley till it reaches the outer wall of the castle, which, from this point of view, appears to grow naturally out of the ground, "to belong" to its world after the manner which Frank Lloyd Wright taught us to appreciate. The appearance of the castle depends on the point of view.

So it is with the Fourth Gospel. For one long familiar with the peculiar doctrines and emphases of the Christian Faith, to view that Gospel in the light of the work of Philo of Alexan-

dria, *The Hermetica*, and the philosophic writings of the Hellenistic Age is to be amazed at the similarities between them;
the Fourth Gospel seems to be part and parcel of that Age.
But let us imagine the opposite. Consider a Greek and a Rabbi
at the end of the first century coming across a copy of the
Fourth Gospel. Despite the familiarity of its language, what
would strike them would be the strangeness of the Gospel. It
would erupt forcefully upon them to evoke a shock of incredulity. In fact, both Greek and Jew would be "scandalized" or
"horrified" at what the Fourth Gospel asserted. They would
both be brought up sharply by something inexplicable and
strange which they encountered in John; the Greek by the
scandal of "The Flesh," the Jew by the scandal of "The Now."
Let us consider the latter scandal first.

To the Jews: the scandal of "Salvation Now"

As we have previously seen, one of the strong marks of
Judaism in the first century, as at other periods, was its living
hope for the future. *"At the end of the days,"* a technical
phrase which signified the ideal future when God's will would
be done, the Messiah would appear, there would be a Judgment, a Resurrection, a New Exodus, the return of the Jewish
exiles to Israel, and the manifestation of the true God to the
Gentiles, who would be gathered to Jerusalem to join with
Israel in true worship. All this and much else constituted the
hope of the Jews. But as a hope it remained in the future.

But what did a Jewish reader find in the Fourth Gospel? He
found the staggering claim that what his people had hoped for
"at the end of the days" had already come; that the future of
Jewish expectation had moved into the present. The phrase,
"And now is," rings like a bell in the Fourth Gospel. True, in
one place John refers to a future judgment, but even there its
present reality is also asserted.

In truth, in very truth I tell you, a time is coming, indeed it is already here, when the dead shall hear the voice of the Son of God, and all who hear shall come to life. For as the Father has life-giving power in himself, so has the Son, by the Father's gift.

As Son of Man, he has also been given the right to pass judgement. Do not wonder at this, because the time is coming when all who are in the grave shall hear his voice and move forth. (Jn. 5:25–28)

Throughout the Fourth Gospel the conviction is eloquent that "the ends of the ages" had already come in Jesus of Nazareth. A few illustrations to show this are now presented.

In the very first chapter of the Gospel, the author leaves no doubt that the Messianic hope has been fulfilled. Andrew, the brother of Simon Peter, asserts explicitly in 1:41:

We have found the Messiah (which means Christ).

Philip claims in 1:45:

We have met the man spoken of by Moses in the Law, and by the prophets:

Nathanael is equally emphatic in 1:49:

"Rabbi," said Nathanael, "you are the Son of God; you are king of Israel."

The use of the Hebrew form "Messiah" is doubly significant in such a document as John; it leaves no possibility of misunderstanding Jesus as the fulfillment of the hope of Israel.

But the claim that Jesus was a Messiah, in itself, would not have startled a Jewish reader. After all, many had claimed to be Messiahs, but they had gone with the wind, forgotten as a dream. It was what John asserted about this Messiah that was so startling; this and the nature or character of this alleged Messiah.

Thus John claimed that to encounter this Jesus was to be

judged by him and that this judgment was the last judgment. The last judgment, which Jews awaited in the future, had moved into the present. As John puts it in 3:19:

> Here lies the test: the light has come into the world, but men preferred darkness to light because their deeds were evil. Bad men all hate the light and avoid it, for fear their practices should be shown up.

Even in the passage in 5:25–28 where a future judgment is envisaged, as we saw, its present reality is also indicated. Notice the phrase "is already here" or "and now is": already the voice of judgment is heard.

Along with the idea that the judgment has come, we find that the resurrection of the dead, placed by Judaism in the future, is, for the author of the Fourth Gospel, already taking place in the lives of those who believe in Jesus as the Messiah. In 5:25–28, which has just been cited, John anticipates a future resurrection. But this passage stands alone. More emphasized by John is the conviction that the resurrection has moved from the future into the present for those who believe in Jesus; the resurrection for them has already taken place. Consider John 11:24–26:

> Jesus said, "Your brother will rise again." "I know that he will rise again," said Martha, "at the resurrection on the last day." Jesus said, "I am the resurrection and I am life. If a man has faith in me, even though he die, he shall come to life; and no one who is alive and has faith shall ever die. Do you believe this?"

In this passage Martha gives expression to the traditional Jewish expectation:

> I know that he [Lazarus] will rise again at the resurrection on the last day.

Jesus agrees with Martha that there is a resurrection. But he asserts that he who believes in him shall not know death; he has already experienced resurrection because Jesus himself is, here and now, the resurrection and the life. In Jesus, the resurrection has become present fact.

Other passages deal with the "life of the Age to Come," usually rendered in English as "eternal life." By the first century, Judaism had developed the concept of two ages or worlds: "This Age," characterized by sin, division, and death; and "The Age to Come," when these characteristics would disappear to give place to their opposites. This is how a document from the late first century describes the life of the Age to Come:

> For for you
> is opened Paradise,
> Planted the Tree of Life,
> The future Aeon prepared,
> Plenteousness made ready,
> A city builded,
> A rest appointed,
> Good works established,
> Wisdom preconstituted.
> And death is hidden away
> Hades fled away,
> Corruption forgotten,
> Sorrows passed away
> And in the end the treasures of immortality are
> made manifest. (4 Ezra 8:52-64)

Connected with such expectations were also those Messianic hopes to which we have frequently referred.

Imagine how a Jew familiar with the expectation of The Age to Come would react to the following passages from John's Gospel:

The Jews then disputed among themselves, saying, "How can this man give us his flesh to eat?" So Jesus said to them, "Truly, truly, I say to you, unless you eat the flesh of the Son of man and drink his blood, you have no life in you; he who eats my flesh and drinks my blood has eternal life, and I will raise him up at the last day. For my flesh is food indeed, and my blood is drink indeed. He who eats my flesh and drinks my blood abides in me, and I in him. As the living Father sent me, and I live because of the Father, so he who eats me will live because of me. This is the bread which came down from heaven, not such as the fathers ate and died; he who eats this bread will live for ever." (Jn. 6:52–58)

This passage claims that the ideal conditions of the future, the New Exodus, when the life of The Age to Come, the true manna, would be available, are already present for him who participates in Jesus Christ. As Peter declares in John 6:68, it is he who has "the words of eternal life."

The following verses are also pertinent:

My own sheep listen to my voice; I know them and they follow me. I give them eternal life and they shall never perish; no one shall snatch them from my care. (Jn. 10:27–28)

Notice that in 10:28, the verb is in the present tense. Here and now Jesus gives "the life of the Age to Come." And in a famous verse in 17:3, this life is defined in terms of knowing God and Jesus, whom he has sent, here and now.

After these words Jesus looked up to heaven and said:
"Father, the hour has come. Glorify thy Son, that the Son may glorify thee. For thou hast made him sovereign over all mankind, to give eternal life to all whom thou hast given him. This is eternal life: to know thee who alone art truly God, and Jesus Christ whom thou has sent." (Jn. 17:1–3)

Already in "This Age" Jesus has been given the power to impart the life of "The Age to Come." The future hope has become present possibility through Jesus Christ.

Related to the present reality of the judgment and the resurrection for those who encounter and accept Jesus, are the great affirmations made by Jesus to which we have referred before. In these, again, the present tense of the verb is important. Jesus, here and now, *is* the light of the world and the bread of life and the living water. He brings from the distant horizons of the future the cherished hopes of Judaism and declares them to be fulfilled.

Finally, the Fourth Gospel sets forth the claim that, through the unity of those who believe in Jesus Christ, the world is to know God; and since the Church is already coming into being, the final coming of all nations to the worship of the true God, which Judaism had hoped for, is also in process. The signs of the end of the days are present; the Lord God is to be recognized as One and the people of the world drawn to him through those gathered together by Jesus. This is implied in the following verses from Jesus' prayer in John 17:20–23:

> But it is not for these alone that I pray, but for those also who through their words put their faith in me; may they all be one: as thou, Father, art in me, and I in thee, so also may they be in us, that the world may believe that thou didst send me. The glory which thou gavest me I have given to them, that they may be one, as we are one; I in them and thou in me, may they be perfectly one. Then the world will learn that thou didst send me, that thou didst love them as thou didst me.

Particularly through the cross of Jesus the whole world is to be drawn together, as in John 12:31–33:

> . . . "Now is the hour of judgement for this world; now shall the Prince of this world be driven out. And I shall draw all men to myself, when I am lifted up from the earth." This he said to indicate the kind of death he was to die.

The death of Jesus is both the judgment of the world and the means of its redemption. The drawing together of all men by the magnet of the cross, as it were, is a sign that already the end of the days had begun.

This reference to the presentation of the death of Jesus as a means of the final redemption of mankind brings us back to the theme of this chapter. To most, if not all, Jews such a claim especially could not but be scandalous. It was scandalous enough to point to the figure of Jesus of Nazareth as the Messiah, but to point to a crucified Jesus as such was monstrous. How could the claim be made that such a figure was the judgment, the resurrection, the inaugurator of the New Exodus and of the final unity of mankind? How could the claim be accepted that in him: "Now is the day of salvation"? However much a Jew might have been at home in the vocabulary, style, atmosphere, and concepts of the Fourth Gospel, he would stumble at the claim that all his great expectations for the future were already offered to him by a figure who died on a cross. The response of a Jew to such a claim could not but be one of shock. The force of such a shock might be illustrated by a modern parallel (though in reverse). During World War II, I remember being asked to tea to a friend's home. My friend asked me: "Have you heard the latest news?" On my answering in the negative, he said: "Hitler now thinks he is the Messiah." And I can still recall the shock of incredulity at such a monstrous claim that shook me, just as later at Nuremberg, in Bavaria, I heard that Hitler had applied to himself the great Johannine affirmations: "I am the Bread of Life," "I am the Light of the World." Was such horrendous presumption possible? I have used this illustration, not because the details of the parallel are to be pressed, but to illustrate the kind of incredulity which the Fourth Gospel would inspire in Jewry. Like the disciples mentioned in John 6:66 who, when they realized the significance of Jesus' claims, drew back, so the Jews of the first century would draw back when they encountered the refrain of the "Now" which runs through John's work. Are not the signs of "This Age"—sin, division, death—still with us: how can salvation be "Now"?

To the Greeks: the foolishness of "The Flesh"

A farmer was once going leisurely home from market in a cart drawn by his old mare. Suddenly, as he was going round a corner, an automobile, traveling quickly in the opposite direction, made its appearance and unceremoniously compelled farmer, cart, and mare higgledy-piggledy into the ditch. The farmer, in considerable fury, turned to the driver of the automobile and said: "What do you think I am, to come charging into me like that—an ox or an ass or a bloody-nonsense?" This story was used by a distinguished professor of poetry to describe his first reactions to the poetry of T. S. Eliot. Eliot's poems, when they were first published, seemed to many unintelligible; and the professor asked, as did the old farmer: "What does Eliot think I am—an ox or an ass or . . ." A cultured Greek might well have reacted in a similar fashion to the Fourth Gospel. If the Jew found that Gospel a scandal, the Greek found it foolishness. Why?

We have already noted that in the Fourth Gospel the future had moved into the present. But John not only thought, as a Jew, in temporal terms—of present and future, of "now" and "then," but also as a kind of Platonist, in spatial terms—of two orders of being, the earthly or the lower, and the heavenly or the upper realm, of "here" and "there." And he declared that in Jesus of Nazareth the heavenly realm had penetrated into the earthly: "the things that are above" had entered into "the things that are below": the ideal, true, or genuine world had entered into this world of transitory phenomena. The contrast between these two realms—upper and lower—appears, for example, in the following passages:

> If you disbelieve me when I talk to you about things on earth, how are you to believe if I should talk about the things of heaven?
>
> No one ever went up into heaven except the one who came down from heaven, the Son of Man whose home is in heaven. (Jn. 3:12–13)
>
> He who comes from above is above all others; he who is from the earth belongs to the earth and uses earthly speech. He who

comes from heaven bears witness to what he has seen and heard, yet no one accepts his witness. (Jn. 3:31)

. . . "Our ancestors had manna to eat in the desert; as Scripture says, 'He gave them bread from heaven to eat.'" Jesus answered, "I tell you this: the truth is, not that Moses gave you the bread from heaven, but that my Father gives you the real bread from heaven. The bread that God gives comes down from heaven and brings life to the world." (Jn. 6:31–33)

I have come down from heaven, not to do my own will, but the will of him who sent me. (Jn. 6:38)

At this the Jews began to murmur disapprovingly because he said, "I am the bread which came down from heaven." (Jn. 6:41)

I am that living bread which has come down from heaven: if anyone eats this bread he shall live for ever. Moreover, the bread which I will give is my own flesh; I give it for the life of the world. (Jn. 6:51)

Jesus replied, "My testimony is valid, even though I do bear witness about myself; because I know where I come from, and where I am going. You do not know either where I come from or where I am going." (Jn. 8:14)

Jesus continued, "You belong to this world below, I to the world above." (Jn. 8:23)

As has been stated previously, the contrast indicated in the above verses between "the things above" and "the things below" was familiar in the cultured Graeco-Roman world, because Platonism, in various degrees of purity, had spread everywhere. But this dualism of "the things above" and "the things below" produced a problem. What contact could there be between them? For "the things above" to be in direct touch with "the things below" was considered impossible because this would corrupt "the things above." Consider the following passages from *The Hermetica* (13:6):

TAT: What then is real, thrice-greatest one?
HERMES: That which is not sullied by matter, my son, nor limited by boundaries, that which has no color and no shape,

that which is without integument, and is luminous, that which is apprehended by itself alone, that which is changeless and unalterable, that which is good.

Or again:

HERMES: But if you would be born again, you must cleanse yourself from the irrational torments of matter . . .
. . . Whoever then has by God's mercy attained to this divine birth, abandons bodily sense; he knows himself to be composed of Powers of God, and knowing this, is glad . . .
TAT: Tell me, father, will this body which is composed of divine Powers ever suffer dissolution?
HERMES: . . . The physical body, which is an object of sense, differs widely from that other body, which is of the nature of true Being. The one is dissoluble, the other is indissoluble. The one is mortal, the other is immortal . . .

In view of such a rigid separation between the real ("the things that are above") and the material ("the things that are below"), the need arose for a way of bringing them together indirectly. And out of this need there developed a concern with mediators between them. In Philo of Alexandria, as we saw, The Word fulfilled the function of a mediator. Through The Word, the Supreme God, without himself sharing in the corruption of matter, was able to impress himself upon the material world. But the idea of mediation was also widespread in Stoicism and other "systems." Notice, however, that the mediator or mediators were "concepts" or "ideas"; to give them material substance would be to make them corrupt and, therefore, unable to be in touch with "the things above." The mediators were necessarily incorporeal and to be apprehended by Mind or Knowledge.

It is over against such ideas that the full force of the Fourth Gospel is to be measured. It claims that the Mediator between God and the world, between "the things that are above" and "the things that are below," is a historical personage, Jesus of

Nazareth. To put it in John's own terms: "The Word became flesh." Such a sentence, so familiar to us that it no longer causes comment, would have been shocking to the cultured Graeco-Roman world of the first century. The notion that one in the flesh, and, therefore, corrupt, could mediate "the things that are above" and be the agent of God would have appeared ignorant and incredible. The very idea of The Word was designed to remove the scandal of the flesh. How, then, could The Word be located in the flesh? The mediating Word of Philo was the sum of all ideas: "the things above" could only be comprehended by Mind or Knowledge. But the Fourth Gospel set forth man in the flesh as Mediator and as the medium of revelation. Not an incorporeal Idea to be known by *Gnôsis* (Knowledge), but a figure in history, a man, so the Fourth Gospel asserted, *is* the mediating Word. The Word became flesh in Jesus of Nazareth. But this could not be! It was like claiming that oil and water could mix or that a circle could be square. The statement "The Word became flesh" was, in short, a contradiction in terms. To the cultured Greek and Roman, it was foolishness—a scandal.

The Fourth Gospel, then, chameleon as it is, presented to Jew and Greek a disturbing challenge. The point at which it was scandal to the one and foolishness to the other was ultimately the same—it was the person of Jesus of Nazareth. The cutting edge of the Gospel lay in its claim that in this historical figure The Age to Come had become present, the Real had become actual, The Word had become flesh. It presented to Judaism the scandal of finality, to Hellenism the foolishness of particularity, and the final and the particular figures were one —Jesus.

CHAPTER 35

THE WORD BECAME FLESH

The Fourth Gospel is a labyrinth. But if the conclusion to the last chapter be true, one theme, like Ariadne's thread, runs through it: Jesus of Nazareth is the final fact of history and the expression in time and space of the universal Truth or Reality. This thread can be picked up right at the beginning; the Prologue itself sounds the theme sentence: "So the Word became flesh; he came to dwell among us." The thread can then be followed in the rest of the Gospel. We begin at the beginning with the Prologue.

The Prologue: Jesus as the Word

By the Prologue is meant either 1:1–14 or 1:1–18. The New English Bible renders 1:1–18 as follows:

The Coming of Christ

When all things began, the Word already was. The Word dwelt with God, and what God was, the Word was. The Word, then, was with God at the beginning, and through him all things came to be; no single thing was created without him. All that came to be was alive with his life, and that life was the light of men. The light shines on in the dark, and the darkness has never quenched it.

There appeared a man named John, sent from God; he came as a witness to testify to the light, that all might become believers through him. He was not himself the light; he came to bear witness to the light. The real light which enlightens every man was even then coming into the world.

He was in the world; but the world, though it owed its being to him, did not recognize him. He entered his own realm, and his own would not receive him. But to all who did receive him, *to those who have yielded him their allegiance,* he gave the right to become children of God, *not born of any human stock, or by the fleshly desire of a human father, but the offspring of God himself.* So the Word became flesh; he came to dwell among us, and we saw his glory, such glory as befits the Father's only Son, full of grace and truth.

Here is John's testimony to him: he cried aloud, "This is the man I meant when I said, 'He comes after me, but takes rank before me'; for before I was born, he already was."

Out of his full store we have all received grace upon grace; *for while the Law was given through Moses, grace and truth came through Jesus Christ.* No one has ever seen God; but God's only Son, he who is nearest to the Father's heart, he has made him known.

The original Greek text suggests that the Prologue is like a hymn; in the above we have sought to indicate the hymn and the comments of the author. (The comments are italicized.) Some have claimed that John has taken over a pre-Christian Aramaic hymn and Christianized it by adding certain sections; others that John used a pre-Johannine Gnostic hymn and changed it. We may compare the Prologue, for example, with the following Naassene Gnostic Hymn:

> The world's producing law was Primal Mind,
> And next was First-born's outpoured Chaos;
> And third, the soul received its law of toil:
> Encircl'd, therefore, with an aqueous form,
> With care o'erpowered it succumbs to death.
> Now holding sway, it eyes the light,
> And now it weeps on misery flung;
> Now it mourns, now it thrills with joy;
> Now it wails, now it hears its doom;
> Now it hears its doom, now it dies,
> And now it leaves us, never to return.
> It, hapless straying, treads the maze of ills.

But Jesus said, Father, behold,
A strife of ills across the earth
Wanders from thy breath [of wrath];
But bitter Chaos [man] seeks to shun,
And knows not how to pass it through.
On this account, O Father, send me;
Bearing seals, I shall descend;
Through ages whole I'll sweep,
All mysteries I'll unravel,
And forms of Gods I'll show;
And secrets of the saintly path,
Styled "Gnosis," I'll impart.[51]

In this Gnostic hymn, Jesus saves the world by imparting *Gnôsis*, "Knowledge." The Prologue probably belongs to this genre, whether in Aramaic or Greek, but it sets forth the Christian understanding unmistakably. Jesus does not so much give *gnôsis*, but himself. He does not merely point the way from the Chaos from outside it, but enters into the Chaos and shares in it for the salvation of men: "So the Word became flesh."

The author, then, has either taken an old "hymn" and re-fashioned it or composed his own "hymn." According to some, he had spent many years meditating upon the life of Jesus. After he had written the Gospel, John decided to add a Prologue to explain the significance of what he had already written. The Prologue supplies the clue to the body of the Gospel; the acts and words of Jesus are the very activity of The Word. It is as if John were saying to his cultured pagan readers: "You discuss and speculate endlessly about the meaning of The Word which mediates between God and the world. But you find The Word not by speculation, but by looking at Jesus of Nazareth. No *gnôsis*, however erudite, esoteric, or ancient leads you to The Word. The Word is Jesus. All true *gnôsis* is centered in him." To put the matter in another way, John did not begin with a concept, "The Word," and then proceed to illustrate what "The

Word" meant by referring to the words and works of Jesus, so that the ministry is seen in the light of a concept. On the contrary, for John it is the light of the ministry of Jesus that illumines the concept. The ministry is not secondary to The Word but The Word to the ministry. The term "The Word," as a title for Jesus, only occurs in the Prologue; it does not play a dominant role in the Gospel as a whole.

But it is not necessary to insist that the Prologue was written after the Gospel to agree with all the above. The Word, as a title for Jesus, does not occur in the rest of the Gospel, but the Prologue is full of concepts that frequently appear elsewhere in the Gospel. Compare the following passages:

The Pre-existence of the Logos or Son

When all things began, the Word already was. The Word dwelt with God, and what God was, the Word was. (Jn. 1:1 f.)	. . . and now, Father, glorify me in thine own presence with the glory which I had with thee before the world began. (Jn. 17:5)

Life in the Logos

All that came to be was alive with his life, and that life was the light of men. (Jn. 1:4)	For as the Father has life-giving power in himself, so has the Son, by the Father's gift. (Jn. 5:26)

Life and Light

All that came to be was alive with his life, and that life was light of men. (Jn. 1:4)	Once again Jesus addressed the people: "I am the light of the world. No follower of mine shall wander in the dark; he shall have the light of life." (Jn. 8:12)

Light and Darkness

The light shines on in the dark, and the darkness has never quenched it. (Jn. 1:5)	Here lies the test: the light has come into the world, but men preferred darkness to light because their deeds were evil. (Jn. 3:19)

There are other themes which are common to the Prologue and the Gospel. The very structure of the Prologue—the rejection of The Word by its own (the people of Israel) and its acceptance by the believers (the Church)—foreshadows the whole course of the Gospel. The Prologue is indissoluble from the Gospel, not an addendum. But it is not the philosophical idea of The Word that governs John in the writing of the Gospel. Rather, it is the ministry of Jesus in the flesh that determines the Johannine understanding of The Word. Whether John wrote the Prologue first or last, the heart of the matter is that he sees The Word in the fleshly actuality of Jesus of Nazareth. We shall attempt to understand what this means, confining ourselves in this chapter to "The Word." And in that concept, two currents of thought are conjoined—the Greek and the Hebraic.

The Word: a challenge to the Greek

In Hellenistic circles the term "word" (*logos*) was used for the reason or order which we encounter in our experience. This reason or order can be detected in the following realms:

1. *Nature:* the regularity and constancy of the natural world; for example, the movement of the stars and the round of the seasons. The Word is the scheme or structure of the Universe.

> The General Law, which is Right Reason [Logos] pervading everything is the same as Zeus. (Zeno, *Fragment* 162)

> The whole order of the heavens obeyeth thy [Zeus's] word. (Cleanthes, *Fragment* 537)

2. *Man:* the skill of man in craftmanship. This is implied in the same *Fragment* from Cleanthes.

> But thine is the skill to set even the crooked straight . . . that thy Word should be one in all things: abiding forever.

The term is connected especially with man's intellectual faculty, the mind, in a twofold way. It refers to the reality within the mind, pure thought or, as Byron put it, "voiceless thought," and also to the expression of that reality in speech. The Word includes both "thought" and "word."

One thing must again be emphasized. The Word, the rational principle in Nature and Man, was all-pervading. But in the works of Philo and *The Hermetica,* The Word appears also as a kind of semi-personal figure or entity which mediates between God and the universe. In this way there are anticipations of John in the Hellenistic world.

But in another sense the way had not been prepared for the Fourth Gospel. In Hellenistic circles, The Word had always remained an idea and was necessarily removed from direct contact with matter. At this point John was a scandalous innovator; he asserted the impossible: "The Word became flesh." No cultured Hellenist could easily stomach such a claim.

The full significance of this claim must now be noted. To the Hellenistic mind, then, Reason or Thought or The Word permeated all things. The natural order and the panorama of human life are all informed by The Word.

> Thou hast fitted together all things in one:
> The good with the evil:
> That thy word should be one in all things: abiding forever.[52]
> (Cleanthes, *Fragment,* 537)

To many in the Hellenistic Age, to be united with the universe, to feel at one with Nature, was the goal of desire, because Nature was the expression of The Word. Wordsworth would have appealed greatly to many at that time when he declares that in Nature he felt:

> a sense sublime
> Of something far more deeply interfused,
> Whose dwelling is the light of setting suns,
> And the round ocean and the living air
> And the blue sky, and in the mind of man;
> A motion and a spirit that impels
> All thinking things, all objects of all thought
> And rolls through all things.[53]

Or, again, W. H. Hudson's desire for unspoiled unity with Nature would be understood by the Greek:

Face to face with Nature on the vast hills at eventide, who does not feel himself near to the Unseen?
Out of his heart God shall not pass
His image stampèd is on every grass.[54]

With such experiences of "the splendor in the grass and the glory in the flower," John would doubtless be familiar. Nor does he deny their validity. The Word for him is the agent of creation: "and through him all things came to be; no single thing was created without him." The Word is diffused through the cosmos. The view that "the heavens declare the glory of God and the firmament showeth his handiwork" is consistent with John's thought about The Word.

But The Word is present in the created order only in a secondary and mediated sense. The Word has impressed itself upon Nature but remains at a distance from it. The emphasis in John is elsewhere. We confront The Word not in direct *communion* with Nature, however valuable this may be, but in an *encounter* with a Person, Jesus of Nazareth. "The Word became flesh," that is, directly present in him. The significance of this can best be brought out in terms of John's understanding of The Word as "the light":

All that came to be was alive with his life, and that life was the light of men. The light shines on in the dark, and the darkness has never quenched it.
The real light which enlightens every man was even then coming into the world. (1:9)

The notion that The Word was the Sun, the source of all light, was familiar. The Sun scatters its light everywhere. What John asserts is this: the light diffused throughout the cosmos has been brought to a sharp focus in Jesus. To use a metaphor, Jesus is the lens which draws together the light which illumines the universe to a point of concentration. And that point is one of grace and truth. Not union with Nature or the Infinite is the way to The Word, but response to a historical figure, now living—Jesus. There is room for reverence before Nature because it expresses The Word, but Nature cannot finally lead to The Word. By itself, indeed, communion with Nature or the quest of the Infinite can be even dangerous. In Wordsworth, rooted in the Gospel, communion with Nature passed on to "little acts of kindness and of love" and unstopped the ears to:

> The still, sad music of humanity
> Nor harsh nor grating, though of ample power
> To chasten and subdue.[55]

But communion with Nature, untouched by grace, as in Byron, could be an expression of hate for and withdrawal from mankind, as Childe Harold puts it:

> I live not in myself, but I become
> Portion of that around me; and to me
> High mountains are a feeling, but the hum
> Of human cities torture: I can see
> Nothing to loathe in Nature, save to be
> A link reluctant in a fleshly chain,
> Classed among creatures.[56]

Against all such craving for Nature, the Fourth Gospel sets The Word made flesh in Jesus, who was grace and truth. Against the craving for the Infinite expressed in such a passage as the following from *The Hermetica* (11:20):

Make yourself to grow into immeasurable greatness, leap beyond the body, rise above all time, and become an eternal being, and you will apprehend God. . . .

—against such a craving, John sets the flesh of Jesus as the seat of The Word. In the life of Jesus—hungry, thirsty, tired, marked by conflict, pain, and death—in this life The Word found expression. And all experience of The Word—in Nature and the Supernatural or Infinite—is to be judged in his light.

The personal activity of Jesus is presented to the Hellenistic world as the criterion for understanding The Word.

The Word: a challenge to the Jew

But the Prologue would also challenge a Jew; it would evoke two elements in his faith:

1. *The Wisdom of God.* By the first century, Wisdom had come to be conceived as a semi-personal being, existing before creation, serving as the ground plan on which the universe was built. Indeed, it was not only the plan followed but the instrument used by God in the creation of the universe. At the same time, Wisdom was the moral guardian and guide of mankind. It was a cosmic and redemptive figure.

The Lord created me at the beginning of his work,
  the first of his acts of old.
Ages ago I was set up,
  at the first, before the beginning of the earth. (Prov. 8:22–23)

when he assigned to the sea its limit,
  so that the waters might not transgress his command,
when he marked out the foundations of the earth,
  then I was beside him, like a master workman;
and I was daily his delight,
  rejoicing before him always,
rejoicing in his inhabited world
  and delighting in the sons of men. (Prov. 8:29–31)

For he who finds me finds life
  and obtains favor from the Lord;
but he who misses me injures himself;
  all who hate me love death. (Prov. 8:35–36)

A cultured Jew would see at once that the Prologue was ascribing to Jesus of Nazareth the attributes of Wisdom. And he would be puzzled. How could a historical figure be given such honor?

Part of the difficulty he would experience would be that

Wisdom had also come to be identified with The Law. The Law was perfect, eternal in its validity; it was the ultimate authority in religion in which all wisdom dwelt. A Jew would recognize with a shock that John was setting forth Jesus of Nazareth as the final authority, replacing The Law. This is made explicit in 1:17.

> . . . for while the Law was given through Moses, grace and truth came through Jesus Christ.

In 1:18, the Jewish reader would be reminded of the actual account of Moses on Mount Sinai given in Exodus 33:18 and 20:

> Moses said, "I pray thee, show me thy glory." . . .
> "But," he said, "you shall not see me and live."

Compare with this John 1:18:

> No one has ever seen God; but God's only Son, he who is nearest to the Father's heart, he has made him known.

The relation of Jesus to the Father was qualitatively different from that of Moses.

2. *The Word of God in the Old Testament*. The phrase the Word of God would be familiar to Jewish readers of the Old Testament. It was used of God's communications to his people through figures such as Moses and the prophets. It called for a response in obedience. But time and time again the response was not forthcoming. The Word of God came to his own people but was rejected:

> The ox knows its master
> And the ass his master's crib,
> But Israel does not know,
> My people does not understand. (Is. 1:3)

This history of the rejection of The Word can be read in John's Prologue, 1:11:

> He entered his own realm, and his own would not receive him.

And the following verse suggests the reception of The Word by those who believe in Jesus, 1:12:

> But to all who did receive him, to those who have yielded him their allegiance, he gave the right to become children of God, not born of any human stock, or by the fleshly desire of a human father, but the offspring of God himself.

The Prologue suggests that The Word which had come to Israel in the past, through its leaders and prophets, has now come in a new form—personalized in Jesus. It is in him that the challenge of God has now come. And the challenge is one of grace and truth.

But, finally, the Prologue makes a claim which scandalizes not only Greek and Jew but all men. The Word which became flesh in Jesus Christ was God. The very first verse of The Gospel reads:

> In the beginning was the Word and the Word was with God and the Word was God. (R.S.V.)

The translation of *The New English Bible* is:

> When all things began, the Word already was. The Word dwelt with God and what God was the Word was.

At least the claim is made that The Word is of the same nature as God. We may go further; for John, the words of Jesus are the words of God, his deeds the deeds of God; to see him is to see God. At this point the Prologue passes beyond Hellenistic and Hebraic concepts and asserts the mystery of the incarnation of God in the flesh of Jesus. This claim can only be rejected or received.

> He entered his own realm, and his own would not receive him. But to all who did receive him, to those who have yielded him their allegiance, he gave the right to become children of God, not born of any human stock, or by the fleshly desire of a human father, but the offspring of God himself. (1:12–13)

In the next section we shall examine what it meant that The Word had taken "flesh."

CHAPTER 36

THE FLESH

A previous chapter (33) began with the statement that "The Fourth Gospel is the chameleon among the Gospels." It is "restless"; it suggests one thing, immediately to declare its opposite. Nowhere is this more true than in its treatment of the flesh. In some passages, the flesh has become the very seat of salvation, in others it is of no avail. In this chapter, we shall examine how John regarded the flesh. We shall deal with this in the Prologue, the sacramental "references," and the discourses.

The Prologue

The twofold character of John's attitude to the flesh appears clearly in the Prologue. The climax of the Prologue may be taken to be verse 14:

> And the Word became flesh and dwelt among us, full of grace and truth; we have beheld his glory, glory as of the only Son from the Father. (R.S.V.)

The Word has taken up its tent in the flesh of Jesus; his flesh has become the vehicle of the very principle that creates and governs the world. The life of Jesus in the flesh has become the place of revelation, the expression of the glory of God; it is indeed:

> God's presence and his very self.

Such a claim constituted a revolution for the Hellenistic mind. Was not the flesh the sphere of corruption; was it not the prison of the essential self; was not escape from it, by however costly a redemption, the purpose of existence? And the Fourth Gospel declared that The Word had become flesh. The end of knowledge and the agent of redemption had become one with the source of ignorance and "damnation." The flesh had become the sphere of the union of God and man and had thus become sacramental—the "material" had become the vehicle of the "spiritual." In the light of this, it is impossible to exaggerate the significance that "the flesh" has for John. Paul sometimes had a slight uneasiness about asserting that Jesus had become flesh; he came, he says once, "in the likeness of sinful flesh." John does not hesitate; he plunges into the deep of the Christian revolution: "The Word became flesh."

And yet in the very verses that precede verse 14, another attitude to the flesh is expressed. In verses 12 and 13 we read:

> But to all who did receive him, to those who have yielded him their allegiance, he gave the right to become children of God, not born of any human stock, or by the fleshly desire of a human father, but the offspring of God himself.

A contrast is drawn between those born of the will of the flesh and of the will of God. The former are inferior to the latter. The implication is that those who were merely Israelites after the flesh, that is, by physical descent, had failed to accept Jesus. Physical or fleshly advantages, in themselves, are of no significance.

This point of view is expressed with great force in other passages. In John 3:1–8, we read:

> There was one of the Pharisees named Nicodemus, a member of the Jewish Council, who came to Jesus by night. "Rabbi," he said, "we know that you are a teacher sent by God; no one could perform these signs of yours unless God were with him." Jesus answered, "In truth, in very truth I tell you, unless a man has been born over again he cannot see the kingdom of God." "But how is it possible," said Nicodemus, "for a man

to be born when he is old? Can he enter his mother's womb a second time and be born?" Jesus answered, "In truth I tell you, no one can enter the kingdom of God without being born from water and spirit. Flesh can give birth only to flesh; it is spirit that gives birth to spirit. You ought not to be astonished, then, when I tell you that you must be born over again. The wind blows where it wills; you hear the sound of it, but you do not know where it comes from, or where it is going. So with everyone who is born from spirit."

A sharp contrast is drawn between what is born of the flesh and of the Spirit. Essentially this is the same contrast as that drawn in 1:12–13. But notice with the Spirit is connected also "water"—a physical element. John cannot wholly get away from the flesh even here; he connects the physical water with the Spirit itself.

Consider further the discussion of the bread of life in the sixth chapter. On the one hand, we read in John 6:63 the well-known words:

> The spirit alone gives life; the flesh is of no avail; the words which I have spoken to you are both spirit and life.

The words italicized are very strong. But along with them there is an insistence on the significance of the "flesh." In 6:51, we read:

> I am that living bread which has come down from heaven: if anyone eats this bread he shall live for ever. Moreover, the bread which I will give is my own flesh; I give it for the life of the world.

The bread of life is identified with the "flesh" of Jesus. The hearers of these words are represented as finding them difficult. In 6:52–59, the theme is further expounded; it is again emphatically asserted that the "flesh" of Jesus is the living bread of the world. To eat it is essential. The Greek word used for eating here, "to crunch," is especially colorful; it makes unmistakably clear that physical eating is meant. The whole section is as follows:

> This led to a fierce dispute among the Jews. "How can this man give us his flesh to eat?" they said. Jesus replied, "In truth, in very truth I tell you, unless you eat the flesh of the Son of Man and drink his blood you can have no life in you. Whoever eats my flesh and drinks my blood possesses eternal life, and I will raise him up on the last day. My flesh is real food; my blood is real drink. Whoever eats my flesh and drinks my blood dwells continually in me and I dwell in him. As the living Father sent me, and I live because of the Father, so he who eats me shall live because of me. This is the bread which came down from heaven; and it is not like the bread which our fathers ate: they are dead, but whoever eats this bread shall live for ever."

The sacramental references

In the two passages cited from John 3 and 6, the reference is most probably to the sacraments. To be "born of water" refers to the sacrament of Baptism; to "eat the flesh" of the Son of Man, to the sacrament of the Lord's Supper. Notice that in Baptism and in the Lord's Supper, things of "flesh"—water and bread—have a sacramental significance, that is, they are outward, visible signs of spiritual grace.

But John also reveals an uneasiness about the sacraments. There is no account of the Lord's Supper in the Fourth Gospel. In John 13, the breaking of the bread and the drinking of the cup are replaced by the washing of the disciples' feet by Jesus. What reason was there for this? What could justify the omission of the breaking of the bread and the drinking of the cup? The fact is that John seems to regard the washing of the disciples' feet as of equal significance with the Lord's Supper. Were there Christians who were overemphasizing the Lord's Supper? Then, as always, it was easy to use symbols and to avoid what they signified; to substitute sacraments for that to which they pointed. Is John insisting that the Spirit inculcated by Jesus Christ at the Last Supper, that of foot washing, is more important than the rite of breaking bread? The "flesh" itself, the Lord's Supper itself, is nothing; the Spirit of self-giving is everything. His disciples could know their Lord as much in his stooping to wash Peter's feet as in his breaking of the bread.

And yet, even in this same passage of the washing of the feet, the value of the sacrament of Baptism *as such* is hinted at. This is probably the meaning of the following passage:

> When it was Simon Peter's turn, Peter said to him, "You, Lord, washing my feet?" Jesus replied, "You do not understand now what I am doing, but one day you will." Peter said, "I will never let you wash my feet." "If I do not wash you," Jesus replied, "you are not in fellowship with me." (Jn. 13:6–8)

There is here, probably, a cryptic reference to the need for Baptism. When Jesus seeks to wash his feet, Peter refused to let him do so. The Messiah washing feet! This was inconceivable. Towels do not comport with Messiahs. But Peter has to allow himself to be washed; he has to discover that Jesus has to do for him what he cannot do for himself. He has to undergo Baptism.

All in all, the Fourth Gospel sets forth the "flesh" of the sacraments in two lights. Of themselves they profit nothing, and yet they are not to be ignored. Mechanically observed they are useless; and yet the bread must be eaten and the water of Baptism must be used for cleansing. Rightly understood, the "flesh" of the sacraments is the bearer of life, even though the flesh availeth nothing.

The discourses

But this "sacramental" evaluation of the flesh in John is not confined to the Prologue and to passages dealing with the sacraments only. It runs through the whole of the Fourth Gospel. One aspect of this shall be noted here. In many of the discourses in the Gospel, a recurring order is traceable in the material. First, there is a narrative involving something physical, for example, water or bread. Then the physical element becomes a point of departure for a "spiritual" truth suggested or signified by it. The "flesh" becomes a vehicle for the truth. The following passages illustrate this:

Jesus answered, "In truth, in very truth I tell you, unless a man has been born over again he cannot see the kingdom of God." "But how is it possible," said Nicodemus, "for a man to be born when he is old? Can he enter his mother's womb a second time and be born?" Jesus answered, "In truth I tell you, no one can enter the kingdom of God without being born from water and spirit. Flesh can give birth only to flesh; it is spirit that gives birth to spirit. You ought not to be astonished, then, when I tell you that you must be born over again. The wind blows where it wills; you hear the sound of it, but you do not know where it comes from, or where it is going. So with everyone who is born from spirit." (Jn. 3:3–8)

Here the transition is from the fact of physical birth to spiritual rebirth, and from wind as a physical phenomenon to the Spirit. Things seen suggest unseen things.

Meanwhile a Samaritan woman came to draw water. Jesus said to her, "Give me a drink." The Samaritan woman said, "What! You, a Jew, ask a drink of me, a Samaritan woman?" (Jews and Samaritans, it should be noted, do not use vessels in common.) Jesus answered her, "If only you knew what God gives, and who it is that is asking you for a drink, you would have asked him and he would have given you living water." "Sir," the woman said, "you have no bucket and this well is deep. How can you give me 'living water'? Are you a greater man than Jacob our ancestor, who gave us the well, and drank from it himself, he and his sons, and his cattle too?" Jesus said, "Everyone who drinks this water will be thirsty again, but whoever drinks the water that I shall give him will never suffer thirst any more. The water that I shall give him will be an inner spring always welling up for eternal life." "Sir," said the woman, "give me that water, and then I shall not be thirsty, nor have to come all this way to draw." (Jn. 4:7–15)

The need for physical water leads on to a discussion of the other water which wells up into eternal life.

> Meanwhile the disciples were urging him, "Rabbi, have something to eat." But he said, "I have food to eat of which you know nothing." At this the disciples said to one another, "Can someone have brought him food?" But Jesus said, "It is meat and drink for me to do the will of him who sent me until I have finished his work.
>
> "Do you not say, 'Four months more and then comes harvest'? But look, I tell you, look round on the fields; they are already white, ripe for harvest. The reaper is drawing his pay and gathering a crop for eternal life, so that sower and reaper may rejoice together."

This passage supplies a twofold example of that with which we are concerned; ordinary food suggests another "food"—the doing of God's will; the physical harvest points to a spiritual harvest. Compare the passage in 6:25–28: reflection on the physical bread which perishes leads on to a discussion of the bread of life, the eating of which brings eternal life.

The above examples are only a few out of many others that could be given. The Fourth Gospel was early called the "spiritual Gospel." If by this be meant that it is not concerned with the physical or material world, nothing could be more erroneous. In fact, the precise opposite is true. John believes in a sacramental process, that is, the process of reaching the truth by the frank acceptance of the actual conditions of life and making these a "gate to heaven." Physical phenomena are, for John, means whereby the Infinite God and spiritual realities are made imaginable and a present challenge. Through such phenomena, when they are "sacramental," man's will, mind, affection come into touch with eternal truth and power. There is, for John, a real correspondence between the physical and the spiritual. He could have expressed himself "in Christ" in the words of Francis Thompson:

O world invisible, we view thee,
O world intangible, we touch thee,
O world unknowable, we know thee,
Inapprehensible, we clutch thee.[57]

To conclude this section, let us recall the question with which we started: What is John's intention in declaring that The Word became flesh? The answer we may express as follows. He thereby asserts that the historical figure, Jesus of Nazareth, was a real man—a tangible figure, no mere phantom or insubstantial ghost. Against every understanding of Jesus as a spiritual or ethereal being, he roundly declares his "fleshiness." He is bone of our bone; flesh of our flesh. His human existence has become the sphere for the revelation of God's presence. In him, as man, the invisible became visible; the incomprehensible, comprehensible. And this is in line with what John implies about all physical realities. Aspects of the fleshly, physical world are, in their measure, suggestive or indicative of the non-physical realities. The physical life is a reflection of the eternal life; there is a real correspondence between them both.

But, so far, it is the actual physical existence of Jesus that we have understood by "the flesh." Does John give a wider connotation to this? In the next chapter, we shall show that not only the physical actuality of Jesus, but the whole of his activity is the seat of The Word. What he *did,* as well as what he *was,* constituted a "sign" or "signs" of spiritual reality. His whole history had the character of a "sign." That The Word became flesh meant not only that it became present in the physical actuality of Jesus but in his history.

CHAPTER 37

THE SIGNS: JESUS AND THE WORLD

Recently, there appeared on the front page of *The New York Times* a photograph of Pope Paul VI, giving away his papal tiara as a sign of the concern of the Pontiff and of the Roman Catholic Church for the poor. This act is reminiscent of the signs which frequently occur in the Fourth Gospel.

At the end of the previous chapter, the claim was made that, for John, everything Jesus did pointed, beyond itself, to a truth about Jesus and his significance. The acts of Jesus were "signs," (*sêmeia*). To understand the meaning of the term "sign" is now essential.

The meaning of signs in the Old Testament

In the Old Testament, two kinds of events are distinguishable, although they are not always sharply differentiated. There are events which are *merely* strange or odd; these are usually referred to as wonders (*môphêthôth*). The action of a man jumping from the top of the Empire State Building in New York City to the street below and then walking away unhurt would constitute a "wonder." Such an act would be odd, but not significant. Consider, however, the following passage from Exodus 4:1-9.

> Then Moses answered, "But behold, they will not believe me or listen to my voice, for they will say, 'The Lord did not appear to you.'" The Lord said to him, "What is that in your hand?" He said, "A rod." And he said, "Cast it on the ground."

So he cast it on the ground, and it became a serpent; and Moses fled from it. But the Lord said to Moses, "Put out your hand, and take it by the tail"—so he put out his hand and caught it, and it became a rod in his hand—"that they may believe that the Lord, the God of their fathers, the God of Abraham, the God of Isaac, and the God of Jacob, has appeared to you." Again, the Lord said to him, "Put your hand into your bosom." And he put his hand into his bosom; and when he took it out, behold, his hand was leprous, as white as snow. Then God said, "Put your hand back into your bosom." So he put his hand back into his bosom; and when he took it out, behold, it was restored like the rest of his flesh. "If they will not believe you," God said, "or heed the first sign, they may believe the latter sign. If they will not believe even these two signs or heed your voice, you shall take some water from the Nile and pour it upon the dry ground; and the water which you shall take from the Nile will become blood upon the dry ground."

In this passage, the turning of a rod into a serpent is an odd event; but it is not only called a wonder, but a sign (ôth), because it points beyond itself to the power of Moses' God. The same applies to the other events recorded; they, too, are wonders but also signs.

But an event, which is not in itself odd, can be a sign. The prophets sometimes performed acts which, in themselves, were ordinary, but which are designed to point to a truth. The accounts of such signs are too long to be quoted in full. Examples can be found in Isaiah 20:1 ff.; Jeremiah 27:1 ff.; Ezekiel 4:1ff. In the second passage referred to, the prophet Jeremiah walked about Jerusalem carrying a yoke about his neck to indicate the coming of foreign domination. The act of carrying the yoke was both a sign of domination and something more. This something more can again be illustrated by the gesture of Pope Paul VI. In dedicating his tiara to the poor, the Pope was making a sign—pointing to the concern of the Church. But his action was not merely a sign in this sense. In some measure it was also effective; it helped to bring about more care for the poor. Not only would the actual price of the tiara be given to the poor, but many would undoubtedly be spurred to greater charity by this act. The Pope's sign helped to bring about what it signified. This analogy is not to be pressed, but it is not irrelevant, because in the Old Testament a sign is regarded as something more than a mere symbol; it actually helps to bring about what it signifies.

Signs in the Fourth Gospel

The transition from signs in the Old Testament to signs in the New, and especially in *The Fourth Gospel,* is easy. In the latter, the acts of Jesus are treated as signs, and understood as were the signs which the Old Testament prophets performed. John takes the first half of his Gospel, that is, chapters 2 to 12 to present the signs of Jesus. Many scholars are convinced that he drew upon a special source, a Book of Signs, for these chapters.

Traditionally, seven signs have been recognized:

1. The miracle at Cana of Galilee, 2:1–12.
2. The healing of the nobleman's son, 4:47–54.
3. The healing of the sick man at the pool of Bethesda, 5:1–16.
4. The feeding of the five thousand, 6:1–14.
5. The walking on the water, 6:15–21.
6. The healing of the man blind from birth at Siloam, 9:1–17.
7. The raising of Lazarus from the dead, 11:1–44.

As they stand in John, these signs have been combined with other narratives which may be derived from the same source. Often the evangelist takes episodes or signs which he needs and then makes these a point of departure for dialogues or discourses in which he sets forth the truth of the Gospel. But he follows no fixed pattern. The long allegory of The Good Shepherd in chapter 10 stands alone, attached to no episode or sign; the discourse material in chapter 3, discussing rebirth, is much longer than the narrative, which is very brief. On the other hand, the sign at Cana of Galilee (2:1–12) stands alone without a corresponding discourse and ends merely with an editorial comment. After the cleansing of the Temple (2:13–16) there is only a short dialogue. But the most striking arrangement is that in which John makes the sign or episode the occasion for a long dialogue or discourse. The following examples occur:

1. *Episode* (3:23–26): John the Baptist, at Aenon near to Salim, is questioned about Jesus.
   Discourse (3:27–36): Jesus must increase and John decrease.
2. *Episode* (4:1–8): The woman of Samaria and Jesus at the well.
   Dialogue (4:9–38): On the water of life (v.v. 9–15)
   On worship (v.v. 20–26)
   On mission (v.v. 35–38)
3. *Episode* (5:1–16): The healing of the impotent man at the pool of Bethesda.
   Discourse (5:17–47): On the authority of Jesus.
4. *Episode* (6:1–31): The feeding of the five thousand.
   Discourse-dialogue (6:32–65): On the bread of life.
5. *Episode* (7:1–16): The appearance of Jesus at the Feast of Tabernacles.
   Discourse (7:16–52: 8:12–59): On Messiahship: Christ the Light of the world.
6. *Episode* (9:1–7): The healing of the blind man at the pool of Siloam.
   Dialogue (9:8–41): On judgment.

7. *Episode and Dialogue intermingled* (11:1–53): The raising of Lazarus and the discussion of the resurrection of the dead.

8. *Episode* (12:20–23): The Greeks inquire after Jesus.
Discourse (12:23–36): The Passion.

As the Gospel now stands, episodes and dialogues or discourses have been combined to form seven major divisions, and the whole of chapters 2–12 can be regarded as a Book of Signs, in which John sets forth the meaning of Jesus Christ in terms of his acts. Some have found a development in ideas from one sign to the other; others have claimed that the whole truth of the Gospel is brought out in each sign. To enter into this debate is not possible here. What must be insisted upon is that each part of the Fourth Gospel belongs to the other; the Gospel is to be understood as a whole. No attempt will be made in these pages to trace a logical development from one section to another in John, at all points, but each section does gain in depth if set over against the whole of the Gospel. The following are the divisions of chapters 2–12 suggested by Professor C. H. Dodd in his great work, *The Interpretation of the Fourth Gospel*.[58]

Signs that Jesus brings a New Order: 2:1–4:42

I. THE WEDDING AT CANA: WATER IS TURNED INTO WINE

The section begins with a wedding at Cana in Galilee. The wine fails, but water is turned into wine at the word of Jesus. The purpose of John is not to relate a marvel, but to set forth a sign of the fact that, with the coming of Jesus, the religion of the Law, symbolized by water (see especially 2:6: "Now six stone jars were standing there, for the Jewish rites of purification each holding twenty or thirty gallons") was transformed into the religion of the Gospel, symbolized by the wine (for the use of wine as a symbol for the new order of the Gospel, see also Matt. 9:17; Mk. 2:22; Lk. 5:37), which is better than any wine previously available. Later on, in chapter 15, Jesus declares: "I am the true vine"—the giver of the true wine.

2. THE CLEANSING OF THE TEMPLE: A NEW TEMPLE IS TO ARISE

The theme of "newness" is carried further in the story of the cleansing of the Temple in 2:13–22. The meaning of the cleansing is given in 2:18 f.:

> The Jews challenged Jesus: "What sign," they asked, "can you show as authority for your action [cleansing the temple]?" "Destroy this temple," Jesus replied, "and in three days I will raise it again."

The Jews, naturally, take these words to refer to the actual Temple in Jerusalem. But John, as so often, is playing with words to set forth his message. In 2:21, the explanation is given that the "temple" referred to by Jesus is "his body." The raising of the temple points, therefore, to the resurrection of Jesus.

But the term "body" (especially at Ephesus) was familiar as a term for "the Church." When Jesus spoke of the raising up of the temple, his body, he was suggesting also the coming into being of the Church, through his resurrection. Like the story of the wedding at Cana, the cleansing of the Temple is a sign that in the coming of Jesus a new order has begun; Judaism has given place to the Gospel; the Old Israel to the New Israel, the Church; the old order of purification to a new.

3. JESUS AND NICODEMUS: NEW BIRTH

Two further sections are devoted to the illumination of this theme of newness in terms of a new birth and new worship. In chapter 3, Nicodemus, a leading Jew, recognizes that Jesus is from God but is puzzled by him. (This last may be the reason why he comes to Jesus by night; his attachment to Jesus is uncertain.) Jesus informs him that the new order, here called the kingdom of God, can only be appreciated by those born anew or from above. But Jesus' statement is misunderstood. Nicodemus asks:

> "But how is it possible," said Nicodemus, "for a man to be born when he is old? Can he enter his mother's womb a second time and be born?"

Then the explanation is given as follows:

> Jesus answered, "In truth I tell you, no one can enter the kingdom of God without being born from water and spirit. Flesh can give birth only to flesh; it is spirit that gives birth to spirit. You ought not to be astonished, then, when I tell you that you must be born over again. The wind blows where it wills; you hear the sound of it, but you do not know where it comes from, or where it is going. So with everyone who is born from spirit." (Jn. 3:5–8)

The force of the explanation is that entry into the kingdom of God, or the new order, is only possible by the invasive, dynamic energy of God himself, the Spirit, which cannot be humanly controlled at all. Human effort alone will not avail to gain entrance into the kingdom, but a radical activity of God, symbolized by the water of baptism (this is probably the force of the phrase "from water and spirit"). To recognize in the ministry of Jesus the presence of the kingdom of God is not easy for mundane men; it is only made possible by God himself.

All this puzzles Nicodemus still further. Jesus then goes on to explain that this truth is only accessible to himself, the Son of Man, who, out of God's love for the world, came down from above and, therefore, can reveal the things above, that is, the nature of God's reality or of his kingdom. Jesus, as the light, enters the dark world to offer eternal life to those who believe in him. In this he is the Saviour.

But he is also judge. The object of Jesus' coming into the world was to reveal the truth and to draw men to himself. But, because he came as the light, he judged. As light, by its very nature, reveals darkness, so the coming of Jesus reveals the depth of human darkness in a new way. Many a television artist has learned, to his cost, that the light which pours upon him when he faces the cameras is relentless in its honesty, merciless in its truth; every feature of the face—light and dark— is exposed to view. The cameras are candid. So, too, the light of Jesus is merciless, even though its purpose is mercy. In his light, men saw their own evil with a new clarity. For some, the intensity of this light was too much; they turned away from it to the gentler, more comfortable darkness to which they were accustomed. The light pained their eyes. Like Byron's prisoner of Chillon, who was so long in the dungeon that at last he almost lost the desire to be free, men preferred darkness to the light; they would

> . . . . . have done with this new day,
> Which now is painful to these eyes.[59]

In thus turning away from the light of Jesus, men passed judgment, and even condemnation, on themselves. The supreme test of existence was the encounter with Jesus. To turn away from him was to be judged and condemned, not by Jesus, but by themselves. The following verses give the heart of the matter:

> God loved the world so much that he gave his only Son, that everyone who has faith in him may not die but have eternal life. It was not to judge the world that God sent his Son into the world, but that through him the world might be saved.
>
> The man who puts his faith in him does not come under judgement; but the unbeliever has already been judged in that he has not given his allegiance to God's only Son. Here lies the test: the light has come into the world, but men preferred darkness to light because their deeds were evil. Bad men all hate the light and avoid it, for fear their practices should be shown up. The honest man comes to the light so that it may be clearly seen that God is in all he does. (Jn. 3:16–21)

The closing verses in the above quotation are important. Not anything in human nature or existence, as such, is evil; not life in the flesh, as such. The enemy of man is not any state or condition in which he may find himself, not "in his stars"—as Shakespeare might put it—but in his perverse will, which disobeys and rejects the good when it is revealed. It is this that brings condemnation and death:

> This is death and the sole death
> When a man's loss
> Comes to him from his gain;
> From knowledge ignorance,
> And lack of love
> From love made manifest.[60]

4. JESUS AND THE WOMAN OF SAMARIA: A NEW WORSHIP

In the chapter in John which follows chapter 3, the emphasis on the newness of the order brought by Jesus is continued still further. Consider the following dialogue between Jesus and the Samaritan woman:

"Sir," she replied, "I can see that you are a prophet. Our fathers worshipped on this mountain, but you Jews say that the temple where God should be worshipped is in Jerusalem." "Believe me," said Jesus, "the time is coming when you will worship the Father neither on this mountain, nor in Jerusalem. You Samaritans worship without knowing what you worship, while we worship what we know. It is from the Jews that salvation comes. But the time approaches, indeed it is already here, when those who are real worshippers will worship the Father in spirit and in truth. Such are the worshippers whom the Father wants. God is spirit, and those who worship him must worship in spirit and in truth." The woman answered, "I know that Messiah" (that is Christ) "is coming. When he comes he will tell us everything." Jesus said, "I am he, I who am speaking to you now." (Jn. 4:19–26)

Jesus himself has replaced both Gerizim and Jerusalem, the supreme holy places of Samaritans and Jews respectively, as the place of worship; he himself has become the "place" where God and man meet in spirit and in truth. This new order of worship in and through him is already a present fact. "But the time approaches, indeed it is already here." The phrase "it is already here" is emphatic.

In the first section, 2:1–4:42, we note, then, three ways in which Jesus has introduced a new order. He has replaced the cultic center of Judaism, the Old Temple; he has brought into the very present what Judaism expected at the end of the days: the ultimate judgment takes place here and now in the confrontation of men with Jesus. And, lastly, he has transcended the practice of Samaritan religion and that of Judaism. In Jesus:

> The old order changeth giving place to new
> And God fulfills himself in many ways.

Cultic and Apocalyptic Judaism, and Samaritan and Jewish forms of worship are all transcended in Christ. The whole section closes with the confirmation of Christ as the Saviour of the World by many Samaritans.

Signs that Jesus gives life: 4:64–5:1–47

I. THE HEALING OF THE NOBLEMAN'S SON AND OF THE SICK MAN AT THE POOL OF BETHESDA

Two signs occur in this section, but only one discourse. The story in 4:46–54 is described in 4:54 as the second sign. A nobleman's son who was at the brink of death is given a new lease on life by the word of Jesus. Jesus' word has life-giving power:

> "Return home; your son will live." The man believed what Jesus said and started for home. (Jn. 4:50)

This theme is then carried over into the second story—that of the man who had been sick for forty-two years at the pool of Bethesda (5:1 ff.). For forty-two years he had waited to be cast, at the opportune moment, into the healing waters of the pool, but he had waited in vain. At the word of Jesus, however, he was healed. The sick man had been outside the reach of healing until Jesus came. The two healings in this section, then, illustrate the power of the word of Jesus to give new life.

2. DISCOURSE

The discourse material, which follows both signs, at first sight is not closely connected with them; but at certain points it does revert explicitly to the theme of the signs. Thus, in 5:21 and again in 5:26 the life-giving power of the Son is that of the Father:

> As the Father raises the dead and gives them life, so the Son gives life to men, as he determines. For as the Father has life-giving power in himself, so has the Son, by the Father's gift. (Jn. 5:21, 26)

And again, in 5:39-40, Jesus is the fountain of life:

> You study the scriptures diligently, supposing that in having them you have eternal life; yet, although their testimony points to me, you refuse to come to me for that life.

The intricacies of the whole discourse material in 5:17-47 cannot be traced here. Its main thrust is that the Father, out of love for his Son, has given his own power of giving life to Jesus. The power of God is present in Jesus.

A sign that Jesus is the bread of life: 6:1-58

THE FEEDING OF THE FIVE THOUSAND

The sixth chapter records the feeding of five thousand people who were following Jesus. Jesus provides physical bread for the hungry multitudes. The meaning of this sign is then expounded in three parts:

(1) 6:26-34. The food of Eternal Life is understood in terms of the manna given to the people of Israel in the wilderness. The claim is made that it is not through Moses but in Jesus that God gives eternal life—the true bread.

Jesus answered, "I tell you this: the truth is, not that Moses gave you the bread from heaven, but that my Father gives you the real bread from heaven. The bread that God gives comes down from heaven and brings life to the world." (Jn. 6:32–33)

(2) 6:34–51. Christ is and gives the bread of life.

I am the bread of life. Your forefathers ate the manna in the desert and they are dead. I am speaking of the bread that comes down from heaven, which a man may eat, and never die. (Jn. 6:48–51)

(3) 6:52–59. Jesus gives the bread of life in the Eucharist and through his indwelling in the life of the Christian.

Jesus replied, "In truth, in very truth I tell you, unless you eat the flesh of the Son of Man and drink his blood you can have no life in you. Whoever eats my flesh and drinks my blood possesses eternal life, and I will raise him up on the last day. My flesh is real food; my blood is real drink. Whoever eats my flesh and drinks my blood dwells continually in me and I dwell in him." (Jn. 6:53–56)

A sign that Jesus is the light of the world: Conflict with the Jews: 7:1–8:59

JESUS AT THE FEAST OF TABERNACLES

The best commentary on this section are the words:

I came not to send peace but a sword.

There is here no act of Jesus which can be called a sign; instead, the appearance of Jesus in the Temple at Jerusalem, on the Feast of Tabernacles, gives rise to six dialogues which reveal both commitment to and hatred of him. The very presence of Jesus stirs controversy, and in itself is a sign that a time of conflict has begun. Jesus' very appearance inspired loyalty and murderous opposition. Why?

The only action which lies behind this section, as we stated, is the visit of Jesus to Jerusalem to attend the Feast of Tabernacles. But in Judaism, this feast was associated with the Day of Judgment, the Day of the Lord, when God would establish his universal kingdom.

> Then every one that survives of all the nations that have come against Jerusalem shall go up year after year to worship the King, the Lord of hosts, and to keep the feast of booths [that is, The Feast of Tabernacles]. (Zech. 14:16)

THE RITUAL OF THE FEAST: WATER AND LIGHT: THE UNUTTERABLE NAME

Associated with this Feast were certain rituals. First, water from the pool of Siloam was poured over the altar in the Temple at Jerusalem in order that the rains for the coming year might be blessed, rain being the means to life. Secondly, gigantic candelabra were brightly lit in the Temple so that they would illumine every court in Jerusalem. These two aspects of the Feast probably lie behind words which Jesus uttered:

> On the last and greatest day of the festival Jesus stood and cried aloud, "If anyone is thirsty let him come to me; whoever believes in me, let him drink." As Scripture says, "Streams of living water shall flow out from within him." (7:37–38)

Later Jesus uttered the words:

> I am the light of the world. No follower of mine shall wander in the dark; he shall have the light of life. (8:12)

Water and light—terms used of the Law, the ultimate revelation in Judaism—are found in Jesus. He is the living water of revelation, the light of revelation to the whole world. Even more, in 8:21–30 Jesus is given the very name of God, *"I am He"*—the term used for the hidden name of God in Judaism and associated with the Feast of Tabernacles.

> That is why I told you that you would die in your sins. If you do not believe *that I am what I am,* you will die in your sins.

CRITICISMS OF JESUS

This section, therefore, brings together claims that the Johannine Christ makes. But these claims are set over against and partly called forth by criticisms made of him. John has here gathered the Jewish objections to the Messianic claims of Jesus. These are:

1. Jesus was an ignorant man (7:14-24).

How is it that this man has learning, when he has never studied? (7:16-17)

The answer is that Jesus' teaching is that of God.

Jesus replied, "The teaching that I give is not my own; it is the teaching of him who sent me. Whoever has the will to do the will of God shall know whether my teaching comes from him or is merely my own." (Jn. 7:16-17)

This answer raises the question of the relation of Jesus' teaching to that of Moses. The claim is made that Jesus' conduct on the Sabbath does not differ fundamentally from that of his opponents; but the theme is not developed (7:19-24).

2. Jewish tradition claimed that when the Messiah came the place of his origin would be unknown. But the origin of Jesus of Nazareth was known, so that he could not be the Messiah. The answer given to this was that the Jews only thought that they knew Jesus' origin; in fact, he was from God.

Thereupon Jesus cried aloud as he taught in the temple, "No doubt you know me; no doubt you know where I come from. Yet I have not come of my own accord. I was sent by the One who truly is, and him you do not know. I know him because I come from him and he it is who sent me." (Jn. 7:28-29)

3. Witness borne by a person to himself was not valid. Self-praise is no recommendation. In 8:12-19, it is objected that Jesus bears witness to himself. But Jesus asserts that God is his witness.

I pass judgement on no man, but if I do judge, my judgement is valid because it is not I alone who judge, but I and
he who sent me. In your own law it is written that the testimony of two witnesses is valid. Here am I, a witness in my
own cause, and my other witness is the Father who sent me.
(Jn. 8:16–18)

The above accusations and their rebuttal take place between
Jesus and the people, but in the background are the chief priests
and the Pharisees, who sent the Temple police to arrest Jesus.
As he more and more divides the people, the opposition to Jesus
mounts. Aware of the situation, Jesus speaks of his death, "of the
lifting up [that is, crucifixion] of the Son of Man" (8:28) and
of the Jews' intent to kill him. This leads to the amazing claim of
Jesus in 8:58:

Truly, truly, I say to you, before Abraham was, I am.

And the last words of the section are:

They picked up stones to throw at him, but Jesus was not
to be seen; and he left the temple. (8:59)

JESUS AND THE WORLD

The whole section 7:1–8:59 may, therefore, be taken as a
commentary on the verse in the Prologue 1:11: "He came to his
own realm and his own would not receive him." The light and
life (8:12) and the very presence of God (*I am he*) has appeared to Israel and to the world (7:4, 36; 8:12) only to be rejected. The presence of Jesus in itself is a sign of the Divine
Presence, and it is accompanied by three things:

First, *the judgment of this world*. Jesus exposes the wickedness of the world's ways (7:7). He does this, not because he
judges men (7:16), but because men in rejecting him judge
themselves. Jesus judges although he is no judge.

Secondly, *the sifting of this world*. In the presence of Jesus,
men are compelled to take sides, to be for him or against him.
Even before he goes to the Feast, men are divided by him:

> . . . and there was much whispering about him in the crowds.
> "He is a good man," said some. "No," said others, "he is leading
> the people astray." However, no one talked about him openly,
> for fear of the Jews. (7:12–13)

This division runs through the dialogues. Those who accept and
those who reject Jesus join opposite camps. Jesus is a two-edged
sword cleaving the hearts of men and, thereby, sifting them.
Neutrality in his presence is impossible.

Thirdly, *the opposition of the world*. In this section, the death
of Jesus, which in previous chapters had only been hinted at,
becomes inescapable; he will be "lifted up" on the cross. The
confrontation of Jesus and the world can have only one end.
From this section onward, it is the death of Jesus that more and
more comes to the fore.

A sign that Jesus brings judgment: 9:1–10:21, 10:22–39

A connection between the different parts of this section is not
obvious, but it does exist. The stream of thought probably runs
as follows.

THE MAN BORN BLIND

In 9:1–41, a man born blind is given his sight by Jesus. This
healing of the blind man is a sign of the fact that Jesus is the light
of the world (9:5). But John is primarily concerned here, not
with Jesus as the light, but as the judge of those who encounter
his light.

THE PHARISEES AND JESUS

Jesus had healed the blind man on a Sabbath day. But, ask
the Pharisees, would a man from God so desecrate the Sabbath?
The blind man's condition was not urgent; he had been blind
from birth; another day would make little difference to him;
would not a man of God have waited to heal him on a week-
day? In this way the Pharisees call good evil and evil good; they

refuse to rejoice generously in the healing activity of Jesus. They consider him a commonplace fellow of unknown origin. Confronted with his mercy, they cavil at him. Despite all protests, they condemn both him and the one whom he has healed. The healed man is expelled from the synagogue. Both Jesus and he have been judged and found wanting.

But this is not the last word. At the end, the tables are turned:

> Jesus heard that they had expelled him. When he found him he asked, "Have you faith in the Son of Man?" The man answered, "Tell me who he is, sir, that I should put my faith in him." "You have seen him," said Jesus; "indeed, it is he who is speaking to you." "Lord, I believe," he said, and bowed before him.
>
> Jesus said, "It is for judgement that I have come into this world—to give sight to the sightless and to make blind those who see." Some Pharisees in his company asked, "Do you mean that we are blind?" "If you were blind," said Jesus, "you would not be guilty, but because you say 'We see,' your guilt remains." (9:35–41)

In fact, it is not Jesus and the healed man who have been judged and found wanting, but their judges, the Pharisees. The blind have gained sight; those supposed to see have become blind. True judgment has not been exercised by, but upon, the Pharisees. The leaders of Judaism have been found wanting.

THE GOOD SHEPHERD

The full force of this judgment against the Pharisees must be noted. John was writing at a time when the Christian Church was increasingly being estranged from the Synagogue. After the fall of Jerusalem in A.D. 70, the Pharisaic leaders of Judaism had gathered at a place called Jamnia in order to reorganize the life of the Jewish people. They became convinced that Christianity was a menace to Judaism and so, somewhere around A.D. 80–85, the Pharisaic leaders inserted in the chief prayer of the Synagogue a prayer called *The Birkath ha-Minim* (Blessing—a euphemism for curse—on Heretics) which was designed to exclude Christians from the Synagogue. The Pharisees were putting out of Israel those who had accepted Jesus. The leaders of Israel were rejecting the Messiah and his followers, who had been blind but had been given their sight by Jesus.

It is over against this background that the next section, chapter 10, the allegory of The Good Shepherd, is to be understood. Its imagery is drawn from Ezekiel 34, where Israel is represented as God's flock, and her rulers as false shepherds who prey upon the flock. For this reason, the rulers are cast out and God himself cares for his flock and saves them. Over his flock he will set one shepherd, the Messiah. This imagery is applied by John, in chapter 10, to the Israel of his own day. The Pharisaic leaders have been like thieves and robbers; they have expelled from the flock of Israel a man enlightened by Christ; Christians are cast out of Israel. But Jesus himself is the Good Shepherd set over Israel by God. This Good Shepherd lays his life down for the sheep; Jesus chose to die. But his death is a means of bringing life to his flock, which is no longer confined to the fold of Israel, but draws upon all the world. In 10:16, we read:

> But there are other sheep of mine, not belonging to this fold, whom I must bring in; and they too will listen to my voice. There will be one flock, one shepherd.

Such a claim for Jesus—that he is the Messiah, the shepherd of Israel—inevitably raises conflict. The conflict is given expression in 10:22–39 where it is declared that Jesus is Messiah, but in a far deeper sense than Judaism had anticipated; he is the Son of God (10:36), one with the Father (10:30). No greater claim could be made for him.

A sign that Jesus is the Resurrection and the Life: 11:1–53

Up to this point all the signs presented, except one, where the sign is embedded in the midst of the narrative in chapters

7 and 8, have stood out clearly as independent stories followed by interpretative discourses. But in this section, the sign is inseparably interwoven with dialogue. The dialogue comments on the narrative, and the narrative interpenetrates the dialogue.

1. THE RAISING OF LAZARUS FROM THE DEAD

The story, which serves as a sign, is that Lazarus, a friend of Jesus, is ill at his home at Bethany in Judaea. But, on the ground that his friend's sickness is designed to reveal his own glory as the Son of God, Jesus delays going immediately to his help. It is only after two days, by which time Lazarus is already dead and thus beyond human help, that Jesus returns to Judaea. But notice that he does so at the risk of death at the hands of the Jews. And four days after the entombment, that is, when it is quite certain that Lazarus is really dead and not merely asleep, Jesus raises him from the dead.

2. WHAT IT SIGNIFIES

Such is the narrative which can be reconstructed. The sheer inhumanity of Jesus' conduct in refusing to go immediately to the help of Lazarus alone makes it clear that the mere recital of such a story is not the evangelist's intention. As he relates it, each step of the story becomes the occasion for discussion; the story is for the thought.

On Jesus' arrival, Martha, the sister of Lazarus, converses with him.

> Martha said to Jesus, "If you had been here, sir, my brother would not have died. Even now I know that whatever you ask of God, God will grant you." Jesus said, "Your brother will rise again." "I know that he will rise again," said Martha, "at the resurrection on the last day." Jesus said, "I am the resurrection and I am life. If a man has faith in me, even though he die, he shall come to life; and no one who is alive and has faith shall ever die. Do you believe this?" "Lord, I do," she answered; "I now believe that you are the Messiah, the Son of God who was to come into the world." (Jn. 11:21–27)

Jesus assures Martha that her brother will rise again. She understands him to refer to a physical resurrection of the body expected at the last day. But, as so often in John, a physical phenomenon suggests a spiritual reality. Jesus now claims that what was expected in the future—resurrection at the last day—is already present in him; he has the life-giving power which Judaism associated with the end of all things.

I *am* the resurrection and I *am* the life. (11:25; N.E.B., our italics)

The future powers of Jewish expectation are already at work in Jesus. At the same time, in 11:25–26, we also read:

Jesus said, "I am the resurrection and I am life. If a man has faith in me, even though he die, he shall come to life; and no one who is alive and has faith shall ever die."

To believe in Jesus, here and now, is to pass beyond death into true life which is present in him. Whether life is thought of as a present reality or as a future endowment given in a resurrection at the end of all things or at the Day of the Lord, it is Jesus who possesses it. It is as if John were saying: whether you consider life at its best here and now or life as it will be in an ideal "world to come" to be established in the future, the standard of measurement for it is Jesus Christ; his is the ultimate life, present and to come. True life "now" and "then" means the life of Jesus Christ, who is the giver of life and the conqueror of death.

3. THE SHADOW OF THE CROSS

John asserts this last because, in going up to Judaea, Jesus faced death at the hands of the Jews. But, as his readers know, although Jesus did die, he was alive in their midst; he had conquered death. He had conquered death by dying. Life came through his death. This truth that Jesus could only raise Lazarus by facing the perils of Judaea, that is, through dying to himself, explains why before the story of Lazarus in 11:5–8, and after it in 11:45–57, John has placed references to the threat to his life. The life-giving power of Jesus is connected with his self-sacrifice even unto death.

Signs that Jesus brings life through death: 11:55–12:36

1. THE ANOINTING OF JESUS AT BETHANY BY MARY

Two stories occur in this section, the anointing of Jesus by Mary at Bethany in 12:2–8, and the triumphal entry of Jesus into Jerusalem (12:12–15). The former is interpreted as pointing forward to the burial of Jesus. Jesus refuses to agree that the act of Mary in anointing him with very costly perfume was wasteful. To Judas, the treasurer of the company of the disciples, who had objected that the money would have been better given to the poor, he says:

> Leave her alone. Let her keep it till the day when she prepares for my burial; for you have the poor among you always, but you will not always have me. (12:7)

The act of Mary is a sign that Jesus is to be buried.

2. THE TRIUMPHAL ENTRY OF JESUS TO JERUSALEM ON AN ASS

The other story, the triumphal entry, describing Jesus entering Jerusalem riding on an ass, ends with the words of the Pharisees in 12:19:

> The Pharisees then said to one another, "You see that you can do nothing, the world has gone after him."

This event, then, is a sign that the Lordship of Jesus would be universally recognized. But before the final verse is given, John has made it clear that the one riding on an ass is followed by the crowds because he had raised Lazarus from the dead. It is as conqueror of death, through his readiness to risk his life, that Jesus is to be universally acknowledged.

3. LIFE THROUGH DEATH

It is this thought, that Jesus' power comes through his death, which conquers death, that governs the rest of this section. First, as a seed of grain dies to reproduce itself, so it is the death of Jesus that creates or gathers together a world-wide community.

> Among those who went up to worship at the festival were some Greeks. They came to Philip, who was from Bethsaida in Galilee, and said to him, "Sir, we should like to see Jesus." So Philip went and told Andrew, and the two of them went to tell Jesus. Then Jesus replied: "The hour has come for the Son of Man to be glorified. In truth, in very truth I tell you, a grain of wheat remains a solitary grain unless it falls into the ground and dies; but if it dies, it bears a rich harvest. The man who loves himself is lost, but he who hates himself in this world will be kept safe for eternal life. If anyone serves me, he must follow me; where I am, my servant will be. Whoever serves me will be honoured by my Father."

The Greeks can only see Jesus because he died. And in the following section, which in part corresponds to the scene at Gethsemane in the Synoptics, it is made clear that the lifting up of Jesus on the cross—that is, the hour of his shame—is the hour of his glory; the cross is his crown. And through the death on the cross—his lifting up, as John, using a play on words, calls it—a power is at work which will eventually draw all things to God in reconciliation. At last, the real meaning of Christ's glory, or glorification—terms which have haunted the Gospel right up to this point—is made clear; it is not what men mean by glory—power, worldly success, fame; but the exact opposite—self-giving to the bitter end of the cross. The hour of his death is the hour of Christ. And this hour, in which Jesus' glory appears, is the hour of the judgment of this world.

> Now is the hour of judgement for this world. (12:31)

Judaism had placed the judgment of the world in the future. Its accompaniments were clear—the victory of Israel over its enemies; the condemnation of the Gentiles:

> They all were looking for a King
> To slay their foes and lift them high.

But the judgment, John declares, begins at the death of Jesus, which, viewed from one side is the work of sinful men, but viewed from another is God's act of glorification. The ultimate "lifting up" is that of self-sacrifice. "The mark of the true glory," writes C. H. Dodd, "is precisely renunciation of personal security."[61]

Review of the signs: the death of Jesus the real sign

The life of Jesus, as John has presented it in chapters 2–12, consists, then, of a series of signs that he is the true life and light of men, their judge and their Saviour, the true expression of the glory of God. The presentation of the signs culminates in the death of Jesus as his glorification. To bring forth the significance of the culmination of the signs of Jesus in his death, it is necessary to ask what the relation is between the death and the signs.

Is the death to be understood as a sign like the signs that precede it? For example, is there any essential difference between the act of feeding the multitudes, as a sign that Jesus is the bread of life, and the act of dying on the cross? There is. The signs are pointers to what Jesus is. They refer beyond themselves to a truth about Jesus. What they signify exists in a reality outside them. The turning of water into wine illustrates the truth that with Jesus the old order of Judaism has passed into the new order of the Gospel. But the same truth could be illustrated in another way. The sign is not essential to the truth to which it points, but only illustrative. But the death of Jesus is not simply an illustration or a sign; it is an actual death. It illustrates the love of Christ, yes. But it also *is* the love of Christ in action; it is what it illustrates. In no other way than by actually dying—not illustrating death—could the love of Christ be finally demonstrated as *real*. Let us return to the Pope's tiara. The giving of the tiara to the poor as a sign is understandable. But—with all due reverence—it must be asserted that this "sign" does not carry the conviction of the self-imposed, actual, poverty of St. Francis of Assisi, in which sign and deed were one. So is it with the signs of Jesus as compared with his death. The signs point to the intent and potentiality of Jesus to be the bread of life and the light of the world, to the truth that he is these. But in the cross, the intent of Jesus has become deed; the reality signified in the signs is there made actual. The death of Jesus *is* that to which it points. It not only indicates the principle of self-giving; it is not only a symbol of self-sacrifice: it *is* self-giving. Consider the life of a home. The mother wears a golden ring as a sign of her marriage and of her status as mother in her home. But the ring in itself avails nothing. What draws a family to a mother is a life of self-giving, in which the meaning of the ring is lived out and a mother *is* what her ring signifies her to be. Where sign and life are one, the mother has potency to draw her children to herself. So is it with the death of Jesus; it *is* what the signs had pointed to. As such, as *actual self-giving,* the death of Jesus possesses a reality that the signs do not possess. In it, the idea has become deed; the sign is *really* lived; and so "if I be lifted up, I will draw all men unto myself." Life and power come through the *actual* self-giving. Talk, it is said, is cheap; claims to Messiahship of all kinds are cheap; signs are cheap. But death is not cheap. And, because it costs, it is in the death that the glory is finally revealed. The cross—not as a symbol or an idea—but as an actual act of self-giving is, for John, the point where God's glory is actually seen. Not the sign, not the intent, but the deed is the manifestation of the glory. Drinkwater was right: men have need of the deed.

We know the paths our feet
   should press,
Across our hearts are written
   Thy decrees
Yet now, O Lord, be merciful to
   bless
With more than these.

Knowledge we ask not—knowledge
   Thou hast lent,
But, Lord, the will,—there lies
   our bitter need,
Give us to build above
   the deep intent
The deed, the deed.[62]

Or recall the yearning expressed by Byron for a world where there is no hypocrisy, no separation between word and act. His experience has taught him that "words are not things," or as John would put it, that not all "signs" are real or effective. These are his poignant lines at the end of the third Canto of *Childe Harold's Pilgrimage* (cxiv):

I have not loved the World, nor the World me—
But let us part fair foes, I do believe,
Though I have found them not, that there may be
Words which are things—hopes which will not deceive,
And Virtues which are merciful, nor weave
Snares for the failing: I would also deem
O'er others' grief that some sincerely grieve;
That two, or one, are almost what they seem—
That goodness is no name, and happiness no dream.

For John, in Jesus of Nazareth, the Word is "a thing": Jesus not only gave signs of his intent; he actually died and so became the Lord of Glory. The instinct of Goethe was right when, in seeking to translate the first verse of the Gospel, ". . . In the beginning was the Word," he came to render it by: "In the beginning was the Act." The Word is Jesus as "act," and nowhere is he more "act" than in his death. The symbolism of the cross is bound up with the actuality of the cross; without the actuality the symbolism is trifling.

The Book of Signs is now complete. It is followed by a brief epilogue which sums up its main motifs in 12:37–50. And after this, John turns to a new, though of course intimately related, portion of his work. He has first made it clear that in all his acts Jesus has shown to the world the glory of God.

CHAPTER 38

FAREWELL DISCOURSES:
JESUS AND THE CHURCH

Up to the twelfth chapter, John has portrayed Jesus as a public figure. The signs described have been public signs, like the Feeding of the Five Thousand; the dialogues and discourses have been between Jesus and enquirers, opponents, and the masses. Jesus has been set forth as the life and light, the Saviour and judge of the world. But the response to him has not been universal or enthusiastic. At times, it is true, he was accepted by the multitudes who at one point wanted to crown him King, but not many finally accepted him. He came to his own people and, by and large, they received him not. The signs of Jesus only evoked rejection and the threat of death.

But a few had accepted Jesus; they saw his glory and believed. And from chapters 13 to 17, it is with these and their relationship to Jesus that John is concerned. The point of transition is chapter 13, which presents a highly dramatic picture of Christ stooping to wash the disciples' feet. The one unfaithful member among them departs to betray his Lord, and, after he is gone, the "faithful" are alone with Jesus. In chapters 14, 15, 16, 17, dialogues, monologues and, finally, a prayer unfold the relation of these faithful—the Church—to their Lord and to their God. The glory of Christ in the Church is revealed. The public figure gives place to the private figure of the Church.

Their setting

Chapter 13 gives the setting for all the material in chapters 14, 15, 16, 17. The discourses are uttered as Jesus and his disciples are at the Last Supper, which, according to John, took place before the Passover. But there can be little doubt that, although the Last Supper was not, for John, the Passover meal, it partook of the nature of a new Passover in his thought. Passover ideas were bound up with it.

And there is one aspect of the ritual of the Passover which helps to explain the discourses in John. At the Passover meal it was customary for the head of the household to explain the meaning of the rite in its relation to the Exodus from Egypt. Great delight was taken in expounding that event; discussions about the Exodus and related themes went on often far into the night. The Passover was a festival of the memory and the reenactment of the Exodus and its marks were loving reflection upon, dialogue about, and exposition of that event.

When early Christians commemorated the death of Jesus in the Eucharist, or what we call the communion service, there is every reason to believe that they regarded it as an act parallel to the Jewish Passover festival; it was a new Passover. And probably they continued the practice of expounding the meaning of the new Exodus during the Eucharist; they discoursed about their Lord and their new life in him. This is the setting of the discourses in John. They are probably the meditations which formulated in his mind and, finally, were put into writing, as year by year, especially at the Eucharist, he remembered his Lord's death and reflected upon it.

Who, then, uttered them?

John has placed his discourses on the lips of Jesus. But if they are John's own meditations, how can they be attributed in this way to Jesus? Let us consider the following points:

First, in the Synoptic Gospels, there is much material which is presented as the private communication of Jesus to his disciples, and most of this occurs toward the end of the Gospels, that is, the Passion. For example, Mark 13, containing extended teaching about the end of the world, immediately precedes the Passion. John's presentation of Jesus as giving private instruction agrees with that given of him in the Synoptics.

Secondly, the themes of John 14–16 recur in the Synoptics. Thus, John 14 deals with the same theme as Mark 13; John 14–16 are not unrelated to the tradition as given in the other Gospels.

Thirdly, the consequences of the above two considerations must be drawn. While the material in John 14–17, in its present form, is the meditation of John, it *may* not be unconnected with private teaching that Jesus himself gave. The point of departure for the discourses is Jesus himself.

But, fourthly, whatever their point of departure, their relationship to Jesus, as John understood it, has to be carefully noted. Let us ask how John thinks of Jesus at this point. In chapters 2–12, Jesus constantly looks forward to his "hour," that is, the hour when he should be put to death. This "hour" was to be the final revelation of God's glory in him. From chapter 13 on, John asserts that this hour has arrived.

It was before the Passover festival. Jesus knew that his hour had come and he must leave this world and go to the Father. He had always loved his own who were in the world, and now he was to show the full extent of his love. (Jn. 13:1)

When he had gone out Jesus said, "Now the Son of Man is glorified, and in him God is glorified." (Jn. 13:31)

After these words Jesus looked up to heaven and said: "Father, the hour has come. Glorify thy Son, that the Son may glorify thee." (Jn. 17:1)

What had long been expected—the hour—has now happened. But clearly, the crucifixion of Jesus is still in the future! Yes: but John, in chapters 14, 15, 16, 17, puts his discourses *before* the event which they presuppose, whereas in 2–12 he had usually placed the sign before the discourse. For John, the Jesus who acts and speaks in 14–17 has passed out of this world and already has received the full seal of God's authority. Here we listen to the Jesus who has already become the Lord of the Church in whom John lives and moves and has his being. What we read in 13–17 are the promptings of this living Lord, the fruit of his living Spirit mediated through John. Throughout, this living Spirit is rooted in Jesus of Nazareth who walked in Galilee and Judaea. Chapters 13–17 are not the free composition of John but the fruit of his communion with the living Christ who, as Jesus, had lived, spoken, and died "in the flesh." Throughout, there is the memory of Jesus; throughout, history is in control. But there *is* also interpretation.

To make this point clear, consider the following words from John 14: 25–26:

> I have told you all this while I am still here with you; but your Advocate, the Holy Spirit whom the Father will send in my name, will teach you everything, and will call to mind all that I have told you.

These verses illumine chapters 13–17. What was remembered of Jesus has been illumined and revealed in ever growing fullness by the Spirit. *In this sense,* we may be more in touch in these chapters with Jesus himself than if we simply had his own words. The dormant meaning of his words has been awakened for us by the Spirit informing the great author of the Fourth Gospel.

Perhaps an illustration from English history can help us to understand this. In 1215, King John of England was compelled to sign an agreement with the barons, the merchants, and the

Church in England. By this, he undertook to obey certain specific rules, some of which only applied to the King himself. The agreement was *in fact* simple, concrete and, in itself, on the surface, not revolutionary. To this agreement, however, historians have often attributed the whole later development of British liberties. It is referred to as Magna Charta, the Great Charter. But how is it possible to regard this ancient agreement as the mother of British liberties? Many of the liberties now enjoyed by the British were not envisaged by it. Yes, but in that agreement, the seeds of future developments did lie. In time, its terms were to be so interpreted, its principles so appropriated, and, above all, the spirit that informed it so pursued, as to produce the fruit of British democracy. The Magna Charta as bare fact is not the ground of British liberties; but as appropriated through the centuries, it has become this. No illustration can be logically pressed. But in some such way are the discourses of John in 13–17 related to Jesus of Nazareth. They are not, and yet they are, his words; they are his words illumined under the guidance of the Spirit. That Spirit was, for John, the living presence of Jesus himself.

Their themes

(1) THE FOOT-WASHING (CHAPTER 13)

We are all familiar with the painting of the Last Supper by Leonardo da Vinci. The ages have looked upon it and have loved it. But there is one modern painting which for me ranks with it, and sometimes even impresses me more. It is one by Ford Madox Brown, which you can see in the Tate Gallery in London. The artist has painted Jesus kneeling before a surly, half-ashamed Peter to wash his feet. This painting of the stooping Christ will in time, I think, stamp itself upon the imagination of the world.

It is to that scene that John takes us as he turns to present the Christ of the Church. Oddly enough, despite his strong sacramental interests, the author of the Fourth Gospel does not give us any account of the institution of the Eucharist; he makes no reference to the drinking of the cup or the breaking of the bread at the Last Supper. Instead, he gives us the story, that the Lord Jesus, the night on which he was betrayed, knowing that the Father had given all things into his hands and that he was come from God and went to God, rose from supper and took a towel and girded himself. It has been claimed that every story in the Gospels contains the whole Gospel. This is almost certainly true of this story; and John regards the foot-washing as of a parallel importance to the institution of the Eucharist itself. It leads us to the heart of the Gospel. What does it mean?

In order to make clear what the Last Supper means, John first draws a contrast between the mind of Christ and the act of Christ. Jesus here faces death. Other men have done so. Some have faced death burdened by the weight of a bad conscience; some have found in it a leap into the dark, an adventure into the unknown; some have faced it with Stoic or Agnostic resignation or with cynicism, as the last futile flicker of the human candle. We are all aware that we came into this world from darkness, we live in this world in a kind of twilight, and we depart from it again into darkness. Now John omits the story of Gethsemane, but he retains its substance. "Now is my soul troubled" (12:27). But, even though Jesus knew the agony of Gethsemane, he knew whence he came and whither he went; he is in no ultimate uncertainty. Jesus, knowing that the Father had given all things into his hands and that he was come from God and went to God, knew his origin and his destiny.

John tells us that he knew that his "hour" was come that he should depart out of this world unto the Father. The word "hour" rings here like a bell; it is a haunting word that John plays upon. This was apparently the hour of his opponents—

of vacillating Pilate, the politician; of the cunning ecclesiastic, Caiaphas; of the mob; of Judas. They were all putting aside the pale Galilean once and for all. But it was not their hour, though they knew it not. John tells us of Judas, "He then having received the sop, went immediately out: and it was night."

But Christ was, at this point of darkness, the child of the Day. He knew whence he came and whither he went.

That was his mind: what was his act?

Jesus, well aware that the Father had entrusted everything to him, and that he had come from God and was going back to God, rose from table, laid aside his garments, and taking a towel, tied it round him. Then he poured water into a basin.

Secure of himself in God, rooted and grounded in him, he performed the act of a slave. Knowing the mystery of life and death, he is led to the most menial duty reserved for slaves. Not even a pupil was allowed to wash feet; the pupil could do most things for his teacher, but not this. To wash feet was fit only for slaves.

Because, so we might understand John, Jesus was divine, he took a towel. There is a view of Jesus, which is found in the New Testament itself, which claims that he became divine, or was adopted Son, because he did certain things. His divinity was a reward for his obedience. But this is not John's view. Because Jesus was from God and went to God, he did this act. Washing the disciples' feet is not one of the causes of his divinity, but its result. This, John tells us, is how the Logos in the flesh *acted*; this is its expression—the washing of the disciples' feet. Thus his story becomes not only an act of *prophetic symbolism* but of *divine symbolism*.

What does this mean further for John? First, quite simply that the disciple is called to give himself in this way, as did his Lord. "If I, then, your Lord and Master have washed your feet, ye also ought to wash one another's feet." This act becomes the type of Christian action.

And for the believer who, with the Fourth Gospel, really believes that the Word in Jesus became flesh, and that Jesus took a towel, then all service of humanity, of human flesh, becomes sanctified; the most menial task becomes a possible vehicle of the divine. To believe that the Word was made flesh and that Jesus took a towel, is to be plunged immediately into the life of all flesh. Jesus, the Word, became flesh—not white or black or brown flesh—but *human* flesh and took a towel. This means that wherever human flesh of any kind is exploited, Christians are called upon to fight. Thus the story of the towel becomes a ground for the Christian moral imperative. To believe that Jesus took a towel, is to deliver all human service from the deadly poison of triviality and to raise it to a divine status.

This is why Paul, you will recall, when he asked the Corinthian Church to be generous in their gifts to the poor of the Church at Jerusalem, did not preach a sermon on the duty of giving but merely said: "For you know how generous our Lord Jesus Christ has been: he was rich, yet for your sake he became poor, so that through his poverty you might become rich" (II Cor. 8:9). This act of Christ in Paul as in John becomes the ground of our act.

What does this commitment mean? It means, in the end, the readiness to be baptized with the baptism of Christ in death. Jesus enacts what he expects—their baptism of fire. This is the demand laid upon the believers. But the magnitude of this demand leads to the next point which John brings out.

There is one thing perhaps harder than taking the towel. When Jesus came to Peter to wash his feet, Peter refused to allow him to do so. Why? Probably there are two reasons. His refusal was a mixture of misunderstanding and pride. He had his own conception of the Messiah and, in his view, towels and Messiahs did not comport. The action of Jesus affronted his sense of what was Messianically proper; it outraged his conception of the Messianic dignity. He disliked and rejected this act just as he had rejected the prediction of the suffering of the Messiah.

But there is something more. "If I do not wash you, you are not in fellowship with me." Jesus here claims to do something for Peter that Peter could not do for himself. The act of the foot-washing is ambiguous. It suggests, as we saw, the demand that Peter and the disciples be ready to die with Christ. But it also suggests the opposite; the recognition by Christ that they could not die with him, but would need his cleansing and forgiving baptism; that they—even Peter—would need to rely upon Jesus' act to maintain them; that they would all need his grace, not only Judas, but even Peter.

> Simon Peter said to him, "Lord, where are you going?" Jesus replied, "Where I am going you cannot follow me now, but one day you will." Peter said, "Lord, why cannot I follow you now? I will lay down my life for you." Jesus answered, "Will you indeed lay down your life for me? I tell you in very truth, before the cock crows you will have denied me three times." (Jn. 13:36–38)

(2) THE DEATH AND RETURN OF CHRIST (CHAPTER 14)

Chapter 14—whose real beginning is in 13:31—deals with the death and resurrection of Jesus. Jesus is now facing imminent death; he is in fact "dying." This event provokes no question. His death was an event which every Christian understood in its actuality; it was *there*, a fact of history; he was crucified under Pontius Pilate. And on his death Jesus went to his Father. This occasioned no difficulty also. But what did his return signify? The early Church generally understood by his return—his coming on the clouds of heaven to gather his own from the four corners of the earth so that they might be with him "in heaven" or in a supra-terrestrial world. The return signified roughly what a Seventh Day Adventist might claim to be the end of history, accompanied by the terrors of a day of judgment and resurrection.

But John understands the return of Jesus very differently. While he retains the belief in a future Day of the Lord, his emphasis is elsewhere. What does the return of Jesus mean? These are his words:

> "I will not leave you bereft; I am coming back to you. In a little while the world will see me no longer, but you will see me; because I live, you too will live; then you will know that I am in my Father, and you in me and I in you. The man who has received my commands and obeys them—he it is who loves me; and he who loves me will be loved by my Father; and I will love him and disclose myself to him."
>
> Judas asked him—the other Judas, not Iscariot—"Lord, what can have happened, that you mean to disclose yourself to us alone and not to the world?" Jesus replied, "Anyone who loves me will heed what I say; then my Father will love him, and we will come to him and make our dwelling with him; but he who does not love me does not heed what I say. And the word you hear is not mine; it is the word of the Father who sent me." (Jn. 14:18–24)

Jesus returns to those who, while still on earth, love him and keep his commandments. He comes to dwell with them in his Spirit.

> If you love me you will obey my commands; and I will ask the Father, and he will give you another to be your Advocate, who will be with you for ever. (Jn. 14:15–16)

> I have told you all this while I am still here with you; but your Advocate, the Holy Spirit whom the Father will send in my name, will teach you everything, and will call to mind all that I have told you. (Jn. 14:25–26)

The experience of the presence of the Spirit of Jesus in their own lives—this is the return of Jesus. The coming of the Spirit *is* the Second Advent. And the condition of this coming is made clear. Jesus had given a new commandment of love. But he had not only given a new commandment, he had lived out what this meant; he had given an example—in his death. The kind of self-giving revealed in his life is the condition of his return and indwelling. It is the love revealed among his own which both recalls him to them and convinces the world that they belong to him.

> I give you a new commandment: love one another; as I have loved you, so you are to love one another. If there is this love among you, then all will know that you are my disciples. (Jn. 13:34, 35)

John retains a future hope, but there can be little question that the future about which he is concerned is not that when Jesus would return with the clouds to the sound of a trumpet, the rending of rocks, and the turning of the moon to blood, when history would end with "a bang," as T. S. Eliot puts it. No! He is more concerned with the return of Jesus as life-giving, enlightening Spirit to those who love and serve him, with the abiding presence of the Spirit as the Comforter. Elsewhere he seems to warn that the end of the world is not to be the concern of the followers of Jesus; rather, are they to live here and now in love, and thus know untroubled hearts in the midst of their tribulation.

(3) THE RELATION BETWEEN JESUS AND HIS FOLLOWERS (CHAPTERS 15, 16)

Since John turns the thoughts of his readers away from the future to their present life in love, it is not surprising that, in chapters 15 and 16, he is concerned about the relationship between his followers and Jesus, between the Church and her Lord, who is present in the Spirit in their midst.

That relationship is presented in terms derived from the Old

Testament. There the figure of a vine is used to represent Israel (see chapter 15). The following moving words from Psalm 80:8–19 which recapitulate the history of Israel illustrate this.

> Thou didst bring a vine out of Egypt; thou didst drive out the nations and plant it. Thou didst clear the ground for it; it took deep root and filled the land. The mountains were covered with its shade, the mighty cedars with its branches; it sent out its branches to the sea and its shoots to the River. Why then hast thou broken down its walls, so that all who pass along the way pluck its fruit? The boar from the forest ravages it, and all that move in the field feed on it. Turn again, O God of hosts! Look down from heaven, and see; have regard for this vine, the stock which thy right hand planted. They have burned it with fire, they have cut it down; may they perish at the rebuke of thy countenance! But let thy hand be upon the man of thy right hand, the son of man whom thou hast made strong for thyself! Then we will never turn back from thee; give us life, and we will call on thy name! Restore us, O Lord God of hosts! let thy face shine, that we may be saved! (R.S.V.)

John takes up this image in 15:1.

> I am the real vine, and my Father is the gardener. Every barren branch of mine he cuts away; and every fruiting branch he cleans, to make it more fruitful still. (Jn. 15:1)

Jesus is the true vine; that is, he himself is the true Israel or the people of God. Such a statement can only be understood in the light of what is called the idea of "corporate personality" in the Old Testament and Judaism. The whole of life was regarded as one bundle. Each was bound to each. What one did affected all others. Thus, when a single member of a tribe sinned, all sinned; each was in all and all in each. One member could *represent* or *be* the whole tribe. It is such ideas that inform the notion of Jesus as the true vine; he *is* the true Israel.

As the true Israel, Jesus stands in two relationships. He is intimately related to God. Israel belongs to God. God is the gar-

dener who planted the garden or vineyard of Israel, who prunes
it and makes it "true." God's care for Israel is emphasized in the
following well-known passage from Isaiah 5:1–2, 7.

> Let me sing a song for my beloved, a love song concerning
> his vineyard: My beloved had a vineyard on a very fertile
> hill. He digged it and cleared it of stones, and planted it with
> choice vines; he built a watchtower in the midst of it, and
> hewed out a wine vat in it; and he looked for it to yield grapes,
> but it yielded wild grapes . . . For the vineyard of the Lord
> of hosts is the house of Israel, and the men of Judah are his
> pleasant planting; and he looked for justice, but behold, blood-
> shed; for righteousness, but behold, a cry!

As Israel, Jesus himself stands under the fashioning purposes
of God to which he is obedient; he reproduces God's love in
his own life.

But Jesus, as Israel, is also intimately connected with those
who are tied to him in faith. He is so much part of those who
believe in him that his life flows into their lives. He dwells in
them and they in him. As the vine's life flows through its
branches, so does Jesus dwell in Christians and they in him. By
abiding in Christ, those who believe bring forth the fruit
which the true vine produces. But when that fruit is not forthcoming, God exercises his pruning. And the fruit demanded
is *agapê*, love. The supreme rule is "to love one another." The
Church is to be the community of love, abiding in Christ.

But such a community is, of necessity, hated by the world. A
community of love such as John envisages evokes the scorn and
hate, not the envy and respect, of the world. Lucian, a pagan
writer, had encountered such a community and his words in
response are famous: "See how these Christians love one another." But these words were spoken not in admiration but in
contempt; they are a sneer. In the political sphere, reformers
are often disliked even when they are recognized to be right.
Robert Owen was politely called "one of those interminable

bores who are the salt of the earth"; so in the history of the Church. When a true community of love emerges, it is usually hated by the world. But, though rejected by men, the believers are not alone. There comes to them the Paraclete. This term means "one called to one's defense, an Advocate." For John, the Paraclete is the Spirit of Jesus who returns to his disciples in their need. The Paraclete defends them. At the same time, it judges the world. The work of Jesus in the flesh, in saving and judging, is carried on after his death by the Spirit. The Spirit is Jesus, freed from the limitations of time and space and sense. And since Jesus is the Spirit, the character of the Spirit, so to speak, is governed by the character of Jesus. The Spirit is rooted in the Jesus of history and recalls what he had said. The Spirit guides into the future in the light of Jesus. The two passages 14:25–27 and 16:12–15 make this clear.

(4) INTERCESSION FOR THE CHURCH: CHAPTER 17

In the previous chapters 15 and 16, John has dealt with the present life of the Church as a community of love and of its future life under the guidance of the Spirit. He now gathers his whole aspiration for the Church in the great prayer in chapter 17. Here—in a prayer set in the last hour—Jesus thinks of the Christian community as it existed at the beginning and as it would be in the future.

> But it is not for these alone that I pray, but for those also who through their words put their faith in me; may they all be one: as thou, Father, art in me, and I in thee, so also may they be in us, that the world may believe that thou didst send me. (Jn. 17:20–21)

The prayer is that Christ may dwell in the hearts of Christians as God dwells in Christ. Believers are to be "in Christ" as he is in God. They have been sent into the world as Christ was sent by God. The unity of Christ with the Father is to be reflected in the unity of Christians with Christ and with God.

Christians are to be one as Christ and God are one. The love of God revealed in Christ is to be revealed in the life of his followers; this life of the love of God is eternal life. Because eternal life is the life of love revealed by Christ, it is also possible to assert: "And this is eternal life that they know thee, the only true God, and Jesus Christ whom thou has sent" (17:3). Eternal life is measured by Jesus' life, and especially by his greatest hour—that of the cross. John, therefore, now turns to the Passion of Jesus.

CHAPTER 39

THE PASSION

In chapters 2–12, we saw that John constantly placed the signs before the dialogues and discourses which expounded them; the order is established of Sign-Discourse. But after chapter 12, the cart seems to be put before the horse, and the order emerges of Discourse-Sign. Chapters 14–17 expound the meaning of the Passion *before* the account of the Passion is given. This is very strange. What reasons can there be for this?

It is possible that John is merely governed by literary convention. Mark, Matthew, and Luke all end with the Passion narrative and, possibly, this custom was so strong that John bowed to it and so placed the Farewell Discourses before the Sign which they illumined. Yet it is unlikely that literary convention or the tradition of Gospel writing alone should have so dictated John's presentation.

A theological reason may be proposed. Is John anxious to attach his own understanding of the Passion to the Jesus of history, that is, to the man Jesus who walked in Galilee and Jerusalem? Does he place the Farewell Discourses *before* the Passion narrative because he wants to insist that what he writes in those discourses is not merely his private meditation, spun solely from his own thought, but the mind of Jesus himself? The only way in which John could claim the authority of Jesus for his interpretation of Jesus' death was to root it in Jesus as its point of departure at least. So, although he allows the reader to know that it is the Risen Christ, through his Spirit, who speaks in chapters 14–17, he places the Farewell Discourses so that they are contained within the framework of the earthly ministry of Jesus. In this way he presents the profound interpretation of the cross contained in these chapters as due to the interaction of Jesus and his own meditation in the Spirit.

But, perhaps, no such reasoning is necessary. The Passion narrative and the Resurrection come last in John because they are the climax of his thought, as they are the climax of the ministry of Jesus. The death of Jesus was the hour of glorification, when all the signs of his life were sealed by death, the ultimately real sign. It was the natural culmination of John's work. The meaning of the cross and resurrection set forth *spiritually* in chapters 14–17 has validity only because Jesus did *actually* die and rise again. Not the *meaning* of the Passion and Resurrection is primary, but the *fact* which lies behind it and, alone, justifies it. John—wrongly described as "the Spiritual Gospel"—must give the final place to the brute fact of the cross and the awkward fact of the resurrection. In short, in chapters 2–12, the order Sign-Discourses preserves the priority of history; but in chapters 14–21, it is the order Discourses-Sign that does so. The order in both sections is, therefore, in agreement with John's insistence that the Word became flesh. The flesh of Jesus has the first and last word. The emphasis on the death, which emerges at the end of the Gospel and dictates John's order, runs through all his work.

References to the death of Jesus outside the Passion narrative

There have been attempts to claim that John does not emphasize the death of Jesus. For example, Paul refers to it far more intensely and frequently than John. But this view is not to be followed. From the very beginning of the Gospel, the thought of Jesus' death is present. "He came to his own and his own received him not." These words from the Prologue summarize what was true throughout the life of Jesus for John. The Passion casts its shadow back right to the earliest days of the ministry. There are, in fact, three kinds of passages in the body of the Gospel which deal with the death of Jesus.

There are passages which speak of Jesus being lifted up from the earth:

> No one ever went up into heaven except the one who came down from heaven, the Son of Man whose home is in heaven. This Son of Man must be lifted up as the serpent was lifted up by Moses in the wilderness, so that everyone who has faith in him may in him possess eternal life. (Jn. 3:13–15)

In typical Jewish fashion John uses the image of the serpent in Numbers 21:8–9 to explain the work of Christ on the cross.

> And the Lord said to Moses, "Make a fiery serpent and set it on a pole; and every one who is bitten, when he sees it, shall live."

The serpent is used by John as a symbol of salvation. There can be no doubt that the word "lifted up" refers to the cross. Just as the smitten Israelites in the wilderness found health and life by looking at the uplifted serpent, so the cross would be the means of healing and life. Note that the shame of the cross *is* the exaltation of Christ. There is here a conscious play on the words "lifted up." If we were to translate the underlying Greek word by the English word "elevated," John's point would be clearer. To be elevated in modern English is to succeed in Church and State; a Bishop is elevated to his see; a monarch, to his throne. But Christ, John asserts, was "elevated" when he was crucified; his throne is a cross, and his cross a throne. The same term occurs in 8:27–28:

They did not understand that he was speaking to them about the Father. So Jesus said to them, "When you have lifted up the Son of Man you will know that I am what I am. I do nothing on my own authority, but in all that I say, I have been taught by my Father."

Here the suggestion is that it is in or through the death of Jesus that Jesus is to be known for what he really is—the Divine Presence. The Son of Man can only be fully known "on the cross."

"Now is the hour of judgement for this world; now shall the Prince of this world be driven out. And I shall draw all men to myself, when I am lifted up from the earth." This he said to indicate the kind of death he was to die.

The people answered, "Our Law teaches us that the Messiah continues for ever. What do you mean by saying that the Son of Man must be lifted up? What Son of Man is this?" Jesus answered them: "The light is among you still, but not for long. Go on your way while you have the light, so that darkness may not overtake you. He who journeys in the dark does not know where he is going." (Jn. 12:31–35)

Here the "lifting up" on the cross is presented as the means whereby Christ is to draw all men unto himself and according to one reading, all things. The cross is the ground of the Church and of its universal character. Through the weakness of the cross, the "violence of the love of God," as Bishop Westcott expressed it, was to work to unite people with Christ.

Next there are passages where Christ is said to give his flesh or life for others.

"I am that living bread which has come down from heaven: if anyone eats this bread he shall live for ever. Moreover, the bread which I will give is my own flesh; I give it for the life of the world."

This led to a fierce dispute among the Jews. "How can this man give us his flesh to eat?" they said. Jesus replied, "In truth, in very truth I tell you, unless you eat the flesh of the Son of Man and drink his blood you can have no life in you. Whoever eats my flesh and drinks my blood possesses eternal life, and I will raise him up on the last day. My flesh is real food; my blood is real drink. Whoever eats my flesh and drinks my blood dwells continually in me and I dwell in him." (Jn. 6:51–56)

Here through the giving of his life, that is, through the cross, Jesus will be the means of life. The thought here is probably sacramental. The life that Christ gives to men is mediated through the Eucharist.

I am the good shepherd; the good shepherd lays down his life for the sheep. The hireling, when he sees the wolf coming, abandons the sheep and runs away, because he is no shepherd and the sheep are not his. Then the wolf harries the flock and scatters the sheep. The man runs away because he is a hireling and cares nothing for the sheep.

I am the good shepherd; I know my own sheep and my sheep know me—as the Father knows me and I know the Father—and I lay down my life for the sheep. (Jn. 10:11–15)

The Good Shepherd dies for his sheep. Some have seen in the phrase "lays down his life" a reference to Jesus as a sacrificial victim, but this is to read too much into it. In John 13:37, Peter uses it:

Lord, why cannot I follow you now? I
will lay down my life for you.

The phrase simply refers to dying for another. In 10:15, Jesus is to die for his followers. There is emphasis on the death as the culmination of a whole life given for the sheep in all sorts of service.

Then Jesus replied: "The hour has come for the Son of Man to be glorified. In truth, in very truth I tell you, a grain of wheat remains a solitary grain unless it falls into the ground and dies; but if it dies, it bears a rich harvest. The man who loves himself is lost, but he who hates himself in this world will be kept safe for eternal life. If anyone serves me, he must follow me; where I am, my servant will be. Whoever serves me will be honoured by my Father." (Jn. 12:23–26)

Here again the same principle of self-giving is stated. The context makes it clear that there is a direct glance at the death of Jesus. Only through death can the life of Jesus become effective. John is not merely referring to a general law of self-realization through self-abnegation but thinking specifically of the hour of Christ's glorification in death.

But one of them, Caiaphas, who was High Priest that year, said, "You know nothing whatever; you do not use your judgment; it is more to your interest that one man should die for the people, than that the whole nation should be destroyed." He did not say this of his own accord, but as the High Priest in office that year, he was prophesying that Jesus would die for the nation—die not for the nation alone but to gather together the scattered children of God. So from that day on they plotted his death. (Jn. 11:49–53)

The High Priest, Caiaphas, becomes here for John the unconscious instrument of the Spirit of prophecy and foretells the death of Jesus.

Finally, there is one passage where there is possibly an implication that the death of Jesus is a sacrifice. This is John 1:29:

The next day he saw Jesus coming towards him. "Look," he said, "there is the Lamb of God; it is he who takes away the sin of the world."

These words of John the Baptist stress that Jesus is a lamb given by God. The significance of the term "lamb" has been variously interpreted. Two interpretations give to it a strictly sacrifical reference. Some take the lamb to stand for the paschal lamb. Others refer it to the lamb mentioned in Isaiah 53:7:

> He was oppressed and he was afflicted,
>   yet he opened not his mouth;
> like a lamb that is led to the slaughter,
>   and like a sheep that before its shearers is
>   dumb,
>   so he opened not his mouth.

If either of these interpretations be correct, John thinks of Jesus as a sacrifical victim. But such an approach to the death of Jesus is not marked in the Fourth Gospel.

What emerges from all the above passages is clear. The cross is the work of God (3:16), but it is also the expression of Jesus' own obedience. The death of Jesus is a divine necessity and his free act (3:14; 12:24). The emphasis falls on the cross as the only means for drawing men together; it is the ground of the Church. In the Discourses, it is the way through which the Spirit becomes available to the Church.

One thing is clear: The death of Jesus greatly occupied John. It is true that the Prologue places the emphasis on the coming of Jesus into the world, the assumption of flesh by the Word, as the heart of the Gospel. To use theological language, the main concern of the Gospel is with the incarnation of the Word, the descent into the lower order of a being from another order. But this does not exclude a concern with the cross. This emerges not only from the Passion narrative to which we now turn but from all the passages cited above. The Passion narrative is not only an inevitable, traditional part of a Gospel, which John includes as such. It is rather the inevitable fulfillment of a foreshadowing of the death of Jesus throughout the Gospel.

The characteristics of the Johannine Passion narrative

In many ways the Johannine account of the Passion recalls the Synoptics. Like the Markan account of the Passion, the Johannine is marked by sobriety or matter-of-factness. Although the Johannine materials are more moving than the

Markan, they are not sentimental or emotional. They contain no supernatural interventions by angels or other beings, no attempt to heighten the pain of Jesus or to produce divine alleviations for it. Like the Synoptics, John also finds in the Passion the fulfillment of "Scripture." He introduces quotations from the Old Testament not found in the Synoptics (see 19:34; 36). Other aspects of the Johannine narrative have parallels in the Synoptics; for example, the emphasis on the kingship of Jesus, which Mark had already made clear, is also found in John, but carried further.

This leads us to what is peculiarly emphasized by John. Let us begin with the last point, John's treatment of the kingship of Christ, which is far more prominent than that of the Synoptics.

1. *Christ the Judge: Jesus before Pilate*. Pilate begins by referring to Jesus as the King of the Jews in irony, but is led finally to see that here, indeed, is "a man" and the King of the Jews. The progression of Pilate's thought is as follows:

Pilate then went back into his headquarters and summoned Jesus. "Are you the king of the Jews?" he asked. (Jn. 18:33)

Dialogue

"You are a king, then?" said Pilate. (Jn. 18:37)

Dialogue

Pilate said, "What is truth?" (Jn. 18:38)

"I find no case against him." (Jn. 18:38; 19:4, 6)

"Behold the Man!" (Possibly a cryptic: Behold the Son of Man.) (Jn. 19:5)

Dialogue

From that moment Pilate tried hard to release him. (Jn. 19:12)

Dialogue

"Here is your king." (Jn. 19:14)

And Pilate wrote an inscription to be fastened to the cross; it read, "Jesus of Nazareth, King of the Jews." This inscription was read by many Jews, because the place where Jesus was crucified was not far from the city, and the inscription was in Hebrew, Latin, and Greek. Then the Jewish chief priests said to Pilate, "You should not write 'King of the Jews'; write, 'He claimed to be king of the Jews.'" Pilate replied, "What I have written, I have written." (Jn. 19:19-22)

We see that in the course of the trial the judge is judged; the judged becomes the judge. The theme of judgment runs throughout the ministry; the claim is often made that Jesus, as the light, judges. In the scene before Pilate, this actually takes place. Jesus turns the tables of the court. Pilate, the representative of the world, is confronted with one who discomfits him. The judgment of this world is enacted. The purpose of the scene is to set forth Christ as the judge of the world. Pilate's last act is to write the title of "King" over the crucified. Thou hast conquered, O pale Galilean! And some have even seen in Pilate's famous words, "Behold the man," a confession that the Roman at last recognizes Jesus as "The Son of Man."

2. *Christ's initiative: in his death.* Before Pilate, Jesus, then, is master of the situation. This mastery, if we may so express it, reveals itself in another way. Throughout, John emphasizes the authority and freedom with which Jesus acts. He does not wait upon events; he goes to meet them. For example, he chooses to be arrested. Consider 18:1-9:

After these words, Jesus went out with his disciples, and crossed the Kedron ravine. There was a garden there, and he and his disciples went into it. The place was known to Judas, his betrayer, because Jesus had often met there with his disciples. So Judas took a detachment of soldiers, and police provided by the chief priests and the Pharisees, equipped with lanterns, torches, and weapons, and made his way to the garden. Jesus, knowing all that was coming upon him, went out to them and asked, "Who is it you want?" "Jesus of Nazareth," they answered. Jesus said, "I am he." And there stood Judas the traitor with them. When he said, "I am he," they drew back and fell to the ground. Again Jesus asked, "Who is it you want?" "Jesus of Nazareth," they answered. Then Jesus said, "I have told you that I am he. If I am the man you want, let these others go." (This was to make good his words, "I have not lost one of those whom thou gavest me.")

Here is one with a mission to fulfill which claims his initiative. The words in 18:8–9 are significant:

". . . If I am the man you want, let these others go." (This was to make good his words, "I have not lost one of those whom thou gavest me.")
(Compare 17:12.)

The Good Shepherd cares for his sheep; he preserves his own by dying for them. Notice again how what has been looked forward to or suggested in previous chapters is historically fulfilled by the act of Jesus in his actual death. The task of keeping his followers intact, that is, of creating the new community, Jesus deliberately sets before him. In devotion to this task he, finally, goes to his cross.

3. *The form of Christ's death: the cross.* In the last sentence of the preceding paragraph we used the words: *"goes to his cross."* We wrote this phrase rather than the more natural "goes to his death" quite deliberately, because John laid stress on the fact that it was high on a cross that Jesus died. But this was not because crucifixion "is the most terrible and cruel death which man has ever devised for taking vengeance on his fellow man" (so the Jewish scholar, Joseph Klausner, *Jesus of Nazareth,* pp. 349 ff.), but because its form was for John a symbol. This is not surprising, because in Judaism great attention was paid to the way in which a man died. A Jewish Rabbi of the time of Jesus who was being led to die, when told by Rabbi Gamaliel that he should not weep because ". . . by two more steps thou shalt be in the bosom of righteous men . . . ," replied: "Do I weep because we are to be slain? No, but because we are to be slain in

the same way as murderers, and as the desecrators of the Sabbath were. . . ." It was natural for all early Christians to be puzzled *by the way in which Jesus died*.

Paul saw in the crucifixion, as the form of Jesus' death, a mark of the curse (see chapter 22). What John saw in it is revealed in 12:32:

> And I shall draw all men to myself, when I am lifted up from the earth.

We have previously seen how John in this passage plays with the word "lifted up." The shameful death *is* the elevation of Jesus. Two things meet in the cross. It is the point in history where the Son of Man, who came from above, stooped most; here he descended to the lowest parts of the earth—to the isolation and degradation of crucifixion. But it is also the point in history at which the Son of Man is raised up from the earth to return to his Father. For John, the crucifixion *is* the glorification of Christ; the lifting up on the cross is his going to the Father, his Ascension. The redemptive act of ascent through descent is achieved in the cross. At the cross, Jesus finished his work of giving himself for his followers and for the whole world. This is emphasized in the following:

> After that, Jesus, aware that all had now come to its appointed end, said in fulfilment of Scripture, "I thirst." A jar stood there full of sour wine; so they soaked a sponge with the wine, fixed it on a javelin, and held it up to his lips. Having received the wine, he said, "It is accomplished!" He bowed his head and gave up his spirit. (Jn. 19:28–30)

Jesus had endured unto the end; the new order had been born. The drawing of all men and all things together into one unity had been finally initiated. The cross was the end of the beginning of the Church. The act to which previous passages had pointed forward as the condition for the coming of the Spirit and the creation of the unified community of love had taken place. It was an act in which Jesus consecrated himself to death.

Two symbolic events

The cross, then, is the end of the beginning of the Church. To emphasize this, John relates two events. One, he placed immediately *before* the passage claiming "It is accomplished," the other, immediately *after* it.

The event before "It is accomplished" occurs in 19:25–27:

> That is what the soldiers did. But meanwhile near the cross where Jesus hung stood his mother, with her sister, Mary wife of Clopas, and Mary of Magdala. Jesus saw his mother, with the disciple whom he loved standing beside her. He said to her, "Mother, there is your son"; and to the disciple, "There is your mother"; and from that moment the disciple took her into his home.

This section does not simply indicate the care of Jesus for his mother. John throughout his Gospel has drawn the lines between Judaism and Christianity more sharply than the Synoptics.

> For while the Law was given through Moses, grace and truth came through Jesus Christ. (1:17)

The newness of the Gospel is emphasized (see chapter 37). He gathers the matter up in this passage. The hour will come when Judaism, represented by Mary, was to be taken over into the household of the Church, represented by the beloved disciple. The event at which this finally takes place is the death of Jesus when, as Mark had symbolically put it, the veil of the Temple of Jerusalem was rent.

The events placed after the words "It is accomplished" have been uttered are the following from John 19:31–37:

> Because it was the eve of Passover, the Jews were anxious that the bodies should not remain on the cross for the coming Sabbath, since that Sabbath was a day of great solemnity; so they requested Pilate to have the legs broken and the bodies taken down. The soldiers accordingly came to the first of his fellow-

victims and to the second, and broke their legs; but when they came to Jesus, they found that he was already dead, so they did not break his legs. But one of the soldiers stabbed his side with a lance, and at once there was a flow of blood and water. This is vouched for by an eyewitness, whose evidence is to be trusted. He knows that he speaks the truth, so that you too may believe; for this happened in fulfilment of the text of Scripture: "No bone of his shall be broken." And another text says, "They shall look on him whom they pierced."

There is no reason to doubt that these facts happened. They need not be inventions in order to be symbols. That Jesus' legs were not broken on the cross was probably because he had died soon and did not need to have them broken to hasten his death. But John saw in this a fulfillment of Scripture. Psalm 34:19–20 reads:

> Many are the afflictions of the righteous;
>   but the Lord delivers him out of them all.
> He keeps all his bones:
>   not one of them is broken.

Again, it is possible that John is thinking of the Passover sacrifice. Exodus 12:46 and Numbers 9:12 legislate:

> . . . you shall not break a bone of it . . .

That his bones were not broken, John takes to be a sign that Jesus is the true Passover. Similarly, the lance thrust fulfills prophecy. Zechariah 12:10 reads:

> And I will pour out on the house of David and the inhabitants of Jerusalem a spirit of compassion and supplication, so that, when they look on him whom they have pierced, they shall mourn for him, as one mourns for an only child, and weep bitterly over him, as one weeps over a first-born.

The effusion of blood and water from the side of Jesus—physiologically recognized by medical experts as possible—may have signified two things for John. It was proof that Jesus had really died on the cross. Emphasis on this was necessary because there were many in John's day who denied it and claimed that Jesus had only seemed to die. But more important, the water and blood coming out of the side of the crucified indicate that the means by which eternal life is mediated have their source in Jesus' death. They point respectively to the two sacraments of baptism and the Eucharist. Through the cross these ways to life are available. The cleansing and nourishment of the Christian community, as well as its existence, depend upon the death of Jesus. But its existence is also tied up with what John sometimes seems to treat as inseparable and at other times as separable from the death, that is, the resurrection of Jesus from the dead, to which we next turn.

CHAPTER 40

THE RETURN OF JESUS:
THE RESURRECTION

The death of Jesus is readily understandable as a "real" or actual event in history. But the raising of Jesus (or of any man) from the dead causes difficulty to a modern mind. People die constantly, but they do not return from the dead. Today, the notion of resurrection suggests primitive ideas of spirits leaving the world of the dead to revisit the scenes of their earthly abodes. The notion is an alien and improbable one. In the first century, however, in Judaism and other religions, this was not so. A return from the dead was not only conceivable but, under certain conditions, expected. Here we are again called upon to take a very long leap from the twentieth to the first century. We can be sure that, unlike ourselves, John would not feel any difficulty in believing that a person could and had returned from the dead.

Why John records the resurrection appearances of Jesus

But in the light of what we wrote in the previous chapter, we may well ask: "What need has John for any resurrection story?" The conclusion could easily be drawn that, for him, all was finished on the cross. The cross is the final sign that gathers up into itself all the preceding signs. Has not John made it clear that, in the cross, Jesus was lifted up to be with the Father; that this lifting up includes the "resurrection" and "ascension" to God? And, since this is so, does John need any resurrection appearances? Are they not redundant to his purpose, since he understands the death of Jesus as his glory?

All these questions are reasonable. And yet John does tell us stories about the appearances of Jesus after his death. Why? Because the question of fact becomes again important for him.

We saw that the difference between a sign such as the turning of water into wine and the sign of the cross of Jesus was that the cross was *in fact* the thing it signified; it was an effective sign, whereas the other signs only pointed to or symbolized what they signified. The death of Jesus was a "real," actual death. It occurred not only as a sign, but as a historically significant event which had consequences of grave import.

Now John has made it clear that the death of Jesus *was* the hour of glory; for him, no greater glory is conceivable than the self-giving of Jesus on the cross. In principle, the cross is the end; with it all is finished. And nothing in the resurrection stories in John adds to the glory of Christ. Glory has already shone round about Jesus *supremely* on the cross.

But notice: as a fact in history, the cross, standing by itself, was a failure; a crucified figure could not, merely as a historical fact, be a glorified figure. "I thirst," says the dying Jesus; the disciples all fled. John had need to make clear at what point the cross, which, in principle, was the supreme glory, but in history, had been a shattering defeat, became recognized as the fullness of glory by the disciples. He had to show how the disciples came to see the cross in a new light; he had to present what led them to recognize the glory of the crucified. It is to this end that he records the appearances of the Risen Christ. He records them, not to enhance the majesty of Christ, as Matthew does, for example, in chapter 28:16–20, but to preserve the fact that, as a matter of history, Jesus had overcome death and renewed his fellowship with his own discredited followers; that, at a particular point in time, the disciples "saw" his glory. The stories of the resurrection are necessary to the story of the cross to explain how what was historically a disaster became also, historically, a victory, and how what was a triumph "theologically" became also a triumph experientially. For this reason, John records the resurrection stories. As the Gospel now stands, two chapters are devoted to them. But most scholars have little doubt that chapter 21 is an appendix where stories which are like those in the Synoptics appear. It is in chapter 20 that John reaches the climax of his Gospel.

The meaning of the resurrection

We have said that the historicity, that is, the actual happening, of the resurrection was necessary, for John, to explain the life of the Christian community to which he had devoted chapters 14–17. There the essential meaning of the resurrection (which, to judge from many passages, also seems to be, for John, the Second Coming) is the renewal of the relationship, between Jesus and his disciples, that had been broken by his death. Consider the following passage:

> "I will not leave you bereft; I am coming back to you. In a little while the world will see me no longer, but you will see me; because I live, you too will live; then you will know that I am in my Father, and you in me and I in you. The man who has received my commands and obeys them—he it is who loves me; and he who loves me will be loved by my Father; and I will love him and disclose myself to him."
>
> Judas asked him—the other Judas, not Iscariot—"Lord, what can have happened, that you mean to disclose yourself to us alone and not to the world?" Jesus replied, "Anyone who loves me will heed what I say; then my Father will love him, and we will come to him and make our dwelling with him." (Jn. 14:18–23)

The meaning of the resurrection is the coming of Jesus to his own from beyond "the bourne of time and space," and his indwelling in his followers whom he re-creates by his forgiveness. The cross is the end of the brief beginning of the community of believers whom Jesus had gathered during his earthly ministry; the resurrection is the beginning of its long new life. In chapter 20, John is concerned with how this new beginning happened, that is, how the disciples re-emerged after the cross to be a dynamic community. How John understands the coming of Jesus to his own can be gleaned from the chapter referred to, where the following emphases are clear.

First, this so-called spiritual Evangelist leaves no doubt that, in some quasi-physical manner, Jesus left the tomb in which he had been laid, and appeared to Mary Magdalene; to the disciples behind closed doors; and to Thomas and the disciples.

Secondly, he makes it clear that to see the empty tomb, in itself, was not enough. Peter saw it without understanding it, whereas the beloved disciple "saw" and "believed." At first, "doubting Thomas" refuses to believe without proof positive.

> One of the Twelve, Thomas, that is "the Twin," was not with the rest when Jesus came. So the disciples told him, "We have seen the Lord." He said, "Unless I see the mark of the nails on his hands, unless I put my finger into the place where the nails were, and my hand into his side, I will not believe it."
> A week later his disciples were again in the room, and Thomas was with them. Although the doors were locked, Jesus came and stood among them, saying, "Peace be with you!" (Jn. 20: 24–26)

"Believing" which rests on or demands "seeing" is less praiseworthy than that which needs no "sight." The more excellent way is that of the later Thomas. He, finally, recognizes that tangible proof of the risen body is not essential, and makes the confession: "My Lord and My God." He acknowledges that the august claim made for Jesus in the Prologue—that he was God—is justified. The Gospel has come full circle.

And yet the climax of chapter 20 is not Thomas' confession, but the saying in 20:29:

> Blessed are those who have not seen and yet believe. (R.S.V.)
>
> or
>
> Happy are they who never saw me and yet have found faith. (N.E.B.)

But how do those who have not seen come to believe? The answer is that they believe on the witness of the disciples who did see. And the disciples are given a marked place in John. This leads us to the next emphasis.

Thirdly, for John, everything, in the last resort, rests on the witness of those who "were there." And the essence of the resurrection is that Jesus did, as a matter of history, forgive the failure of his followers and, in his mercy, return to them to renew communion with them. The scholar who, more than any other, has illumined the meaning of the Fourth Gospel in our time has expressed the matter thus: "The divine charity in which Christ died and in which he returned from the dead to forgive and re-establish his inconstant followers is itself the creative power that transformed the whole situation and turned defeat into victory" (C. H. Dodd, *Three Sermons*, p. 31). Just as it was *agapê*, that is, overflowing, persistent love, that led Jesus to the death of the cross, so it was *agapê* that brought him back from the dead. The resurrection—the return of Jesus to his own—was above all an act of forgiveness. It is no accident that John makes Jesus first appear to Mary Magdalene—whose sins were well known—just as the other Gospels make him first appear to Peter, who had denied him three times. Seldom has this truth been more beautifully and perceptively expressed than in the following poem by Amos N. Wilder. Notice that he, too, finds the heart of the resurrection in "a charity [*agapê*] coeval with the suns."

The Third Day

That immovable stone tossed aside,
The collapsed linens,
The blinding angel and the chalky guards:
All today like an old woodcut.

The earthquake on the third day,
The awakened sleeper,
The ubiquitous stranger, gardener, fisherman:
Faded frescoes from a buried world.

Retell, renew the event
In these planetary years,
For we were there and He is here:
It is always the third day.

Our world-prison is split;
An elder charity
Breaks through these modern fates.
Publish it by Telestar,
Diffuse it by mundovision.

He passes through the shattered concrete slabs,
The vaporized vanadium vaults,
The twisted barbed-wire trestles.

A charity coeval with the suns
Dispels the deep obsessions of the age,
And opens heart-room in our sterile dream—
A new space within space to celebrate
With mobiles and new choreographies,
A new time within time to set to music.[63]

The disciples, then, are a forgiven community. And they are addressed as follows:

Jesus repeated, "Peace be with you!" and then said, "As the Father sent me, so I send you." (20:21)

They are called upon to continue the ministry of Jesus in the world; they are commissioned by Christ. But there follow the words:

He then breathed on them, saying, "Receive the Holy Spirit!" (20:22)

The disciples are given the Spirit, and they are to continue the work of forgiveness that Christ had performed during his ministry. The forgiven community has the power to forgive and also to refuse forgiveness. But what does the Spirit mean? The expression *"breathed on them"* recalls Genesis 2:7 when God created man:

. . . then the Lord God formed man of dust from the ground, and *breathed into his nostrils the breath of life;* and man became a living being.
(Notice our italics)

The suggestion is that a new humanity is being born of the Spirit of Christ. A new creation is in process. The Church, the community of the Spirit, is born. This is the meaning of the resurrection, as John has already explained in the Farewell Discourses. The resurrection is the reality of the Living Christ, in the Church, through his Spirit. So it is that the Spirit plays as great a role in the Johannine understanding of the Church as in the Pauline, and demands a chapter to itself.

CHAPTER 41

THE SPIRIT AND THE COMMANDMENT

In our treatment of Paul, we pointed out how exceedingly difficult it is to define precisely the meaning of the term "spirit" in his epistles (See chapter 29). The same is also true of the term in the Fourth Gospel. But, in the latter, there are so many references to the Spirit in the Farewell Discourses that it is easier to present a clearer picture of the peculiarly Johannine conception of the Spirit than of the Pauline. In this respect, we note, the Fourth Gospel differs markedly from the Synoptics, where there is little emphasis on the Spirit, whereas John reveals a developed doctrine of it.

The Spirit outside the Farewell Discourses

Sometimes, in the past, scholars have drawn a distinction between the understanding of the Spirit in the Farewell Discourses and that found in the other parts of the Gospel. It has been claimed that outside the Farewell Discourses John often uses the term "spirit" to denote the "real" over against the "unreal," the ideal unseen over against the phenomenal and visible. The following passages are quoted in support of this view.

> Jesus answered, "In truth, in very truth, I tell you, unless a man has been born over again he cannot see the kingdom of God." "But how is it possible," said Nicodemus, "for a man to be born when he is old? Can he enter his mother's womb a second time and be born?" Jesus answered, "In truth I tell you,

no one can enter the kingdom of God without being born from water and spirit. Flesh can give birth only to flesh; it is spirit that gives birth to spirit. You ought not to be astonished, then, when I tell you that you must be born over again. The wind blows where it wills; you hear the sound of it, but you do not know where it comes from, or where it is going. So with every-one who is born from spirit. Nicodemus replied, "How is this possible?" (Jn. 3:3–9)

But the time approaches, indeed, it is already here, when those who are real worshippers will worship the Father in spirit and in truth. Such are the worshippers whom the Father wants. God is spirit, and those who worship him must worship in spirit and in truth. (Jn. 4:23–24)

The spirit alone gives life; the flesh is of no avail; the words which I have spoken to you are both spirit and life. (Jn. 6:63)

Many of John's Hellenistic readers would certainly under-stand all these passages in the light of the familiar Platonic con-trast between the ideal and the actual, the real and the unreal. But John is not to be so simply understood. The passages are part of the Gospel as a whole and are to be understood in its light. The Spirit is the Spirit of God made familiar in the Old Testa-ment and now present in Jesus. Already, before the Passion, the creative, dynamic Spirit of God is available in Jesus. In him a new order of existence is present; through him men can experi-ence a new begetting; in him men can find the new place for true worship; it is his words that produce life. And all this is so be-cause in Jesus of Nazareth the Spirit abides; the Spirit which he received at baptism abides or remains with him.

John testified further: "I saw the Spirit coming down from heaven like a dove and resting upon him. I did not know him, but he who sent me to baptize in water had told me, 'When you see the Spirit coming down upon someone and resting upon him you will know that this is he who is to baptize in Holy Spirit.'" (Jn. 1:32–33)

There is no need to draw a sharp distinction between what John declares about the Spirit in the Farewell Discourses and in the above passages. But he does draw out new emphases in chapters 14–17; and these constitute the heart of his doctrine of the Spirit.

The Spirit in the Farewell Discourses

When we turn to chapters 14–17, perhaps what immediately strikes us most is the intensely *personal* way in which John speaks of the Spirit. He refers to the Spirit as the Paraclete, Counselor (RSV), or Advocate (NEB); the Spirit takes an active interest in the guidance and defense of the followers of Jesus. And in many passages the Spirit seems to be none other than Jesus himself returned to his people; the Spirit is the Invisible Christ.

> If you love me you will obey my commands; and I will ask the Father, and he will give you another to be your Advocate, who will be with you for ever—the Spirit of truth. The world cannot receive him, because the world neither sees nor knows him; but you know him, because he dwells with you and is in you. I will not leave you bereft; I am coming back to you. In a little while the world will see me no longer, but you will see me; because I live, you too will live. (Jn. 14:15–19)

Notice how John thinks either of the Advocate being with his own for ever or of Jesus being so. The Spirit is the mode or form of Jesus' own presence. Even in 20:22, where the Spirit has been claimed to suggest something external to Jesus which can be imparted to others, this is so, because it is Jesus who imparts the Spirit, and it is his Spirit that he does impart.

We may, then, assume that, for John, the Spirit is another way of speaking of Jesus himself; it is the method of his own presence. This is why the Spirit is so hard to define; it is as hard to do so as to define a person. But, if we cannot precisely *define* the Spirit, the Farewell Discourses especially enable us to state certain things which are clear.

When the Spirit comes

It is made clear that the Spirit comes only after the lifting up of Jesus on the cross. Consider:

> On the last and greatest day of the festival Jesus stood and cried aloud, "If anyone is thirsty let him come to me; whoever believes in me, let him drink." As Scripture says, "Streams of living water shall flow out from within him." He was speaking of the Spirit which believers in him would receive later; for the Spirit had not yet been given, because Jesus had not yet been glorified. (Jn. 7:37–39)

> Nevertheless I tell you the truth: it is for your good that I am leaving you. If I do not go, your Advocate will not come, whereas if I go, I will send him to you. (Jn. 16:7)

The Spirit would take the place of Christ after he was gone; it was to be his presence in the midst of the disciples. Only after his death and resurrection could Jesus say: "Receive the Holy Spirit" (20:22). Does this contradict what we wrote above, that the Spirit was present in the ministry of Jesus before the Passion? No! Because before then the Spirit was geographically bound to the physical presence of Jesus, as it were. Death alone could sever this "geographic" bond, so that, in some way, it became possible to speak of the Spirit apart from Jesus.

Can we fathom how such an emphasis arose in John? Probably there are two reasons for it. First, historically, it was after the cross that the Church did experience the impetus of the power of the Gospel. The Johannine emphasis, in short, is another version of the emphasis on the Day of Pentecost in Acts 2. Secondly, John thought of Christ as pre-existing all things, throned from eternity. For a time he had become "flesh," but only to resume his glory in the heavens after this. This means that Christ's fuller activity had to come after the cross when, freed from the limitations of physical existence, he could resume his untrammelled activity. The Spirit is Jesus set free from the flesh.

Where the Spirit comes

But the Spirit, for John, although now free from the physical presence of Jesus, is still associated especially with the followers of Jesus, the Christian community. The Spirit is now in the world (as Jesus had been), but the world does not receive the Spirit for the same reasons that it did not receive Jesus. It is in the Christian fellowship that the Spirit is found. In this sense John is highly "ecclesiastical"; and for this reason the Farewell Discourses are the most rich treatment of the Church in the New Testament.

> If you love me you will obey my commands; and I will ask the Father, and he will give you another to be your Advocate, who will be with you for ever—the Spirit of truth. The world cannot receive him, because the world neither sees nor knows him; but you know him, because he dwells with you and is in you. (Jn. 14:15–17)

The only passage which implies perhaps that the Spirit will exercise an influence on the world is in 16:8–11:

> When he comes, he will confute the world, and show where wrong and right and judgement lie. He will convict them of wrong, by their refusal to believe in me; he will convince them that right is on my side, by showing that I go to the Father when I pass from your sight; and he will convince them of divine judgement, by showing that the Prince of this world stands condemned.

But even here the Spirit is not at work *directly* in the world. The meaning seems to be that through the Spirit the claim of Christ will be vindicated, so that the world will realize its sin in not believing in him, will acknowledge his righteousness, will know itself judged when he overcomes the powers of sin and darkness. That is, *indirectly* the Spirit in the Church will have repercussions on the world. In this sense, there is an activity of the Spirit on the world, although it is only experienced as the Spirit in the

Church. *Directly*, the Spirit is restricted in its activity to the Church; but *indirectly*, it has universal significance. The Church is, then, the sphere of the Spirit.

Does not this imply a narrow, almost fanatic, view of the Spirit? Does not the Spirit express itself in spheres outside the Church—in the life of man and his history in general, and in creation? Here we have to recognize the confusion that the use of the term "Spirit" has undergone. As we previously wrote, the term "Spirit" has often been used of the "life" that inspires and informs the natural world. But generally, in the Bible, as in Paul and as also in John, the activity of God in history and in creation is expressed in terms of the Word of God, not of his Spirit. The influences that men have called "Spiritual" in nature and in history, John would refer to the Word. The intensely personal, warm presence of the Spirit he confines to the community brought to birth by Jesus. Poets like Milton, musicians like Bach, scientists like Einstein—these are inspired by the activity of God's Wisdom, as Paul would hold, or by The Word, as John would hold. But for John, as for Paul, it is to those who have known Christ as Saviour that the Spirit comes, not to the wise and prudent, but to those who have known him.

What the Spirit does

We may conveniently describe what the Spirit does in terms of the past, the present, and the future.

First, the Spirit is the Spirit of Jesus, a figure who belongs to the past. This is the cardinal fact about the Spirit. The Spirit is not a power free in itself; it is always informed or determined by the historical figure of Jesus. John understands the Spirit in terms of Jesus. And one of the main functions of the Spirit is to bring back Jesus to the Church; that is, to remind the Church of its roots in Jesus of Nazareth; he is the touchstone of all things for the Church. Consider John 14:25–26:

I have told you all this while I am still here with you; but your
Advocate, the Holy Spirit whom the Father will send in my
name, will teach you everything, and will call to mind all that
I have told you.

In the light of these verses, we might claim that the Spirit acts as
the memory of the Church or rather as a spur to its memory.
It delves into the past, back to Jesus himself and brings back to
the Church his words.

Is this function of the Spirit an important one? To answer
this question, let us consider the role of memory in the life of the
Church. The claim will here be made that the very life of the
Christian Church depends upon its memory.

Let us begin by considering the role of memory in individual
lives. "The child is father of the man." A trivial incident in a
man's childhood can affect the whole course of a man's life. It is
said of one of the recent Prime Ministers of England that his
whole career as a statesman was colored, even vitiated, by the
circumstances of his early years, which he could not forget. Not
for nothing do we speak of the formative years of childhood and
adolescence; it is then that the substance of our most vivid memories is formed, and they are powerful. The memory of blessings
ennobles; the memory of injury and sin blights. In any case, no
man can be himself without the capacity to remember—without
the memory of his own identity, his own name, and of his con-
nections with his environment, his own world. To use psychological terms: memory is the principle of personal identity.

But this is not only true of individuals; it is also true of peoples. What is it, for example, that makes a nation? Some have
claimed that speaking a common tongue binds people together in
one nation. But the Swiss have hardly shared a common tongue;
they speak German and French and a dialect. Others have urged
that occupying the same country over a long period creates national awareness. But the Jews have continued as a nation without a common land for centuries. Perhaps Matthew Arnold's

definition of a nation still comes nearest to the truth. "A nation is a community of memories." It is the common awareness of a common past that most creates a nation. What makes the British one people is "1066 and all that"; that is, the memory of countless common experiences throughout the centuries. No nation can persist without this memory. That is why, in its conscious search for national unity, the United States has constantly to recall its great heroes—the Pilgrim Fathers, the Founding Fathers, Lincoln, and others. It is the memory of these that primarily, perhaps, provides the ties that bind.

And the same is true in a profound way of the Christian community. It, too, has to live by its memory. In the Last Supper, the rites are performed "to recall me," that is, to bring Jesus back into the present from the past. Only as it remembers Jesus can the Church live. And so John emphasizes that one of the functions of the Spirit is to remind the Church of Jesus. In short, the Spirit, the Living Presence, is also rooted in the historical figure of Jesus of Nazareth. Through the Spirit, the creative source of the Church in the past—the fact of Jesus—is vividly preserved and experienced in the present; past and present meet in the Spirit.

Secondly, when we consider what the Spirit does more specifically in terms of the present, we are faced with the term "paraclete" which is used as a synonym for it, references to which we have already cited. The term is best translated "Advocate" or "Counsellor." The immediate connotation of the term is that the Spirit comes to the side of Christians as they confront the trials and temptations of their life in the world. As in other passages in the Synoptics, the confrontation of Christians and the world demands boldness, outspoken, unpremeditated courage. It is the Spirit of Jesus, alive in their midst, that enables Christians to meet and exhibit this courage; they are not like orphans in the world, fatherless and helpless; they are blessed with an Advocate.

And, thirdly, the Spirit is not only an agent of conservation, which keeps the Church rooted to its true past in Jesus, and not only a source of courage in present trials; it is also the power that enables the Church to learn, to adapt itself to new truth, to venture into the future. In the passage already cited above, the Spirit is to unfold to the disciples the inner meaning of the words of Jesus, that is, to deepen their insight. It will declare what Jesus during his lifetime could not reveal to his followers because they could not bear it. Jesus had recognized the limitations of his followers; the Spirit can take advantage of their ever greater readiness to learn. For this reason the Spirit is the Spirit of truth (14:17; 15:26). All the above is clear from the following passage:

> There is still much that I could say to you, but the burden would be too great for you now. However, when he comes who is the Spirit of truth, he will guide you into all the truth; for he will not speak on his own authority, but will tell only what he hears; and he will make known to you the things that are coming. He will glorify me, for everything that he makes known to you he will draw from what is mine. All that the Father has is mine, and that is why I said, "Everything that he makes known to you he will draw from what is mine." (Jn. 16:12–15)

The disciples can claim no finality for the truth they have at any point because the Spirit can always reveal more truth to them. The future is open; although the Spirit is memory, it is also teacher. There is truth yet to appear to the Church through the Spirit.

So far, then, the Spirit is the principle of memory, of courage, and of illumination. There is one other aspect of the Spirit— which is, at first sight, more surprising. To this we now turn.

The Spirit and the New Commandment

We have insisted that, for John, the Spirit throughout is the Spirit of Jesus; it is the mode of his presence. It is this that accounts for a surprising fact. Usually, it is customary to think of people who are moved by the Spirit as being free from all law. To follow the impulse of the Spirit is to live spontaneously without thought of what ought or ought not to be. The life in the Spirit is a life above and apart from all law and constraint. On such a view, the Spirit in the Church should have nothing to do with any law or commandment; Christians are beyond law in the freedom of the Spirit.

But this is not what we find in the Fourth Gospel. There the community of the Spirit is also under law—the law of the new commandment of love. There can be little question that Jesus during his earthly ministry had made love central in his teaching.

> Then one of the lawyers, who had been listening to these discussions and had noted how well he answered, came forward and asked him, "Which commandment is first of all?" Jesus answered, "The first is, 'Hear, O Israel: the Lord your God is the only Lord; love the Lord your God with all your heart, with all your soul, with all your mind, and with all your strength.' The second is this: 'Love your neighbour as yourself.' There is no other commandment greater than these." The lawyer said to him, "Well said, Master. You are right in saying that God is one and beside him there is no other. And to love him with all your heart, all your understanding, and all your strength, and to love your neighbour as yourself—that is far more than any burnt offerings or sacrifices." When Jesus saw how sensibly he answered, he said to him, "You are not far from the kingdom of God."
>
> After that nobody ventured to put any more questions to him. (Mk. 12:28–34)

> Hearing that he had silenced the Sadducees, the Pharisees met together; and one of their number tested him with this question: "Master, which is the greatest commandment in the Law?" He answered, "'Love the Lord your God with all your heart, with all your soul, with all your mind.' That is the greatest commandment. It comes first. The second is like it: 'Love

your neighbour as yourself.' Everything in the Law and the
prophets hangs on these two commandments." (Matt. 22:34–
40)

On one occasion a lawyer came forward to put this test question
to him: "Master, what must I do to inherit eternal life?" Jesus
said, "What is written in the Law? What is your reading of it?"
He replied, "Love the Lord your God with all your heart, with
all your soul, with all your strength, and with all your mind;
and your neighbour as yourself." "That is the right answer," said
Jesus; "do that and you will live." (Lk. 10:25 ff.)

I may here quote what I have written elsewhere. "It is customary
to state that Jesus enlarged the understanding of the demand of
love in three ways: (1) by inseparably conjoining the love of
God and man; (2) by reducing *the whole* of the demand of God
to the twofold commandment of love of God and of neighbor, he
gave to these two commandments an unmistakable priority; (3)
by extending the term neighbor to include everybody, he univer-
salized the demand of love. All this is true; but more important is it to recognize that Jesus revealed the nature of love itself. . . . I think here of the revelation of the nature of *agapê*
vouchsafed to us in the pure, unlimited self-giving which is ex-
emplified by Jesus. "Thou shalt love thy neighbor as thyself"—
where the norm is the life and word of Jesus himself—is the commandment of the Messiah."[64] It is also the commandment of the
Spirit. The community of the Spirit is born of the love (*agapê*)
of Christ, as we saw; it is to reflect the same *agapê* in its own
life. The love of God for Christ and of Christ for his own is to
be reciprocated by the community. There is no escape from this
commandment because the Spirit is Jesus and recalls his words.
Where there is no *agapê* the Spirit is not present. Consider the
following passages:

"I will not leave you bereft; I am coming back to you. In a
little while the world will see me no longer, but you will see
me; because I live, you too will live; then you will know that

I am in my Father, and you in me and I in you. The man who has received my commands and obeys them—he it is who loves me; and he who loves me will be loved by my Father; and I will love him and disclose myself to him."

Judas asked him—the other Judas, not Iscariot—"Lord, what can have happened, that you mean to disclose yourself to us alone and not to the world?" Jesus replied, "Anyone who loves me will heed what I say; then my Father will love him, and we will come to him and make our dwelling with him; but he who does not love me does not heed what I say. And the word you hear is not mine; it is the word of the Father who sent me." (Jn. 14:18–24)

As the Father has loved me, so I have loved you. Dwell in my love. If you heed my commands, you will dwell in my love, as I have heeded my Father's commands and dwell in his love. (Jn. 15:9–10)

We close our treatment of John as we did that of Paul—by affirming that the Spirit coexists with Law, the Law of Love. What does "love" mean here?

In his now-famous posthumous work *Markings*[65], the late Dag Hammarskjöld reveals how he came to an understanding of "love." For him, "love" meant a life of active social service, self-surrender, which, with single mindedness, met every demand of the neighbor. It meant an overflowing strength in true self-oblivion, unhesitant and unreserved acceptance of whatever life brought. And Hammarskjöld himself implies that the source of such "love" or "*agapê*" is for him the Spirit of Christ. His understanding of *agapê* occurs in a kind of confession of faith. We find here a definition of *agapê*, in terms of the "noughting" of the self—W. H. Auden's phrase—with which John could easily concur. Always the norm for understanding love is the self-oblivion of Jesus, the Good Shepherd, who laid down his life for the sheep, and through whose death the sheep are preserved as a flock. In his foreword to *Markings*, Auden[66] implies that Hammarskjöld did not always show an adequate awareness of the "flock" of Christians, the Church. At first sight Auden's criticism seems valid. But it is highly significant, perhaps, that, in fact, Hammarskjöld, in the confession of faith to which we have already referred, regards himself as "a member of the community of the Spirit"—a phrase with a very Johannine ring. He, too, knew that only in the communion of saints, where the Spirit is shared, can love remain. It is not from any overflowing of man's own strength—as Hammarskjöld might well be taken to imply— that he can exercise love, but only as he is moved by the Spirit in a community of the Spirit. By its very nature, love neither grows nor remains in isolation or solitariness but always in community. Nowhere is this truth given more adequate expression than in the Farewell Discourses of the Fourth Gospel.

CHAPTER 42

CONCLUSION

Our journey through the Fourth Gospel is over. To what position has it brought us? Let us recapitulate.

The author moved in two worlds which were constantly intermingling—those of Hellenism and Judaism. In one thing they were alike. They were both restless worlds moved by deep and disturbing religious and other quests. The Hellenistic world was depressed, even sometimes haunted, by the fear of death and the grip of fate. It was in search of an escape from a life subject to corruption and decay to true, eternal life, in which death should have no dominion, nor "the years condemn." Many thought that by means of knowledge, that is, truth and light on man's origin and destiny, they might escape from this world into one uncontaminated by sin and the stain of matter, and gain such eternal life. Often a profound pessimism moved over the Hellenistic mind, because it had not found spiritual security.

In the Jewish world, also, there was disturbed anxiety. Many Jews, too, and primitive Christians among them, sought an alleviation of their lot in this world. But usually they put their hope, not in another world, but in an ideal future in this world. They were comforted by the expectation that a day of reckoning and redemption would come when the Lord God would assert his one rule; when he would dwell with his people; when all should know him, all have his commandment in the heart; when sin would be forgiven and God's glory be revealed.

Both these worlds John knew: that which sought escape from

things below by knowledge of things above, and that which pinned its hope to the future. He spoke to both.

To the Hellenistic enquirer he proclaims that the true light, the true life, the true knowledge are not to be found in esoteric doctrines about the origins and destiny of man, but in an encounter with Jesus Christ in which all these are found. But he goes further. Eternal life does consist of light and knowledge, and these are present in Jesus Christ, but it consists also of something greater—the love (*agapê*) which is revealed in Jesus Christ, which is a reproduction or extension of the love of God himself. Eternal life is the life revealed and realized in the love of Christ for his own. Its essence is *agapê*—boundless, unfailing good will, such as God revealed in sending Jesus into the world, and such as Jesus revealed in dying for his own. To share in such *agapê* is eternal life. "This is eternal life: to know thee who alone art truly God, and Jesus Christ whom thou hast sent" (Jn. 17:3). The knowledge that saves and gives eternal life is not to be confused with intellectual knowledge, mystical speculation or esoteric, secret tradition, such as some of the intelligentsia of the Graeco-Roman world cherished. No! It is knowledge which is commitment, surrender, obedience to God and to Christ. Knowledge of Christ in this sense, that is, obedience to the prompting of his love—this is the eternal life which the Graeco-Roman world and all other worlds need.

Similarly, John meets the hopes of Judaism and of primitive Christianity in a startling claim. He asserts that all that Judaism and many primitive Christians had transferred to the future, as only a matter of hope, was already present in the fact of Christ and in the community created by him. Confrontation with Jesus here and now is the judgment: in the life of the community called into being by Christ—*there* Christ dwells with his people, *there* the new commandment is known, *there* the Spirit of God is present. In this community the love (*agapê*) of Christ is creating a new people who reproduce his love (*agapê*) for them in their mutual relationships. To share in this *agapê* is to realize all hopes. This *agapê* is all we know and all we need to know—so might John have written, although he recognizes the need for illumination also.

Both to the Hellenistic world and to the Jewish and primitive Christian world, then, John, finally, offers the one challenge—the challenge to participate in the *agapê* of this new community as the means to eternal life. To this challenge he gradually leads us in his Gospel. In the first part, he presents Jesus as the Word, the Logos, a term which, as we saw, would appeal to the Graeco-Roman intelligentsia. He sets Jesus forth as the light of men, as the bread of life: life and light were concepts that would also appeal to the same intelligentsia. But, in the second section, after chapter 12, there is a change of emphasis. It is the love of Christ in his death, a love rooted in the love of God, that is now to the fore. The philosophically attractive terms—Logos, Light, Life—give place to the more profound concept, Love. The Fourth Gospel is an appeal to all men to share in *agapê,* because, as Professor C. H. Dodd has written: "It is in the exercise of *agapê* that man knows God and shares His life, that God and man are made one, and that the creature returns to the Creator through the eternal Word through which all things were made."[67]

Yet this is not the last word. How is the challenge of this *agapê* brought home to men? It is brought home first and foremost through the witness of believers to the life, death, and resurrection of Jesus of Nazareth. The Fourth Gospel is the witness or testimony of a believer which appeals to men to share in *agapê* by pointing them to this figure. Its primary challenge is to belief in him. And in these last sentences of this book, we come to one of the significant usages of the Fourth Gospel. It uses the term "to believe" in many ways, but its distinctive mark is the use of the phrase "to believe in" or "to believe into." As applied to the Christian's attitude to Jesus, "to believe" denotes not simple credence, not the acceptance of any proposition about him, but commitment to him, the yielding of allegiance to him. It is this commitment that John seeks to inspire in all his readers. For him, to believe in Christ is so to have seen Jesus as to be committed to him. It is possible, as we emphasized, to "see" him —to know all about his life, death and resurrection—and yet not "believe." But where "seeing" him leads on to "believing" in him, there is the true vision which is the knowledge of God; it is to see the glory of God in the face of Jesus Christ. This, then, is believing in Jesus Christ; it is to recognize his elevation in his humiliation, a crown in his cross, the glory of God in the flesh of his life. So to believe is to be led on to abide in Christ as a branch on a vine and to find, in this indwelling, eternal life in the community of those who also believe, so that commitment to Christ demands commitment to those who believe in him, that is, to the new Israel, the Church, and through the Church to the world, because the object of God's activity of *agapê* in Christ and his people is the salvation of the world. The heart of the matter is commitment to Christ. But this commitment is always a response —a response to his prior commitment to his own and to the world. As the author of I John put it: "We love because he loved us first" (4:19).

We can now, finally, understand why at the conclusion of his Gospel in 20:30, John writes:

> There were indeed many other signs that Jesus performed in the presence of his disciples, which are not recorded in this book. Those here written have been recorded in order that you may hold the faith that Jesus is the Christ, the Son of God, and that through this faith you may possess eternal life by his name.

Like the Synoptics and Paul, and all the New Testament writers, the Fourth Gospel points us to one figure, Jesus, as the revelation of the glory of God.

NOTES

1. *Journal of Roman Studies*, Vol. II, Pt. ii, p. 233.

2. *Stoics and Sceptics* (New York and London: Oxford University Press, 1913), p. 92.

3. For a fuller treatment, see my article "The Jewish State in the Hellenistic World" in *Peake's Commentary on the Bible*, ed. by M. Black and H. H. Rowley (New York and London: Thomas Nelson & Sons, 1962), pp. 686–92.

4. W. D. Davies, *Christian Origins of Judaism* (Philadelphia: Westminster Press, 1962), pp. 5–6.

5. Bruno Bauer, *Christus und die Cäsaren* (also in an English translation), Berlin, 1877.

6. A. Drews, *Die Christusmythe* (2 vols., 1909–11); *Die Bestreitung der Geschichtlichkeit Jesu* (1926).

7. E. V. Rieu, *The Four Gospels: A New Translation from the Greek* (Baltimore and London: Penguin Books, 1953), p. xxxiii.

8. A. Resch, *Agrapha, Texte und Untersuchungen*, N.F., xv, 2nd ed., 1906.

9. See J. Jeremias, *The Unknown Sayings of Jesus* (New York: The Macmillan Company, 1957), for the whole subject.

10. See Justin, *Apology*, II, X, XI.

11. Eusebius, *Ecclesiastical History*, III, p. 39.

12. E. V. Rieu, *op. cit.*, p. xix.

13. *The Journal of Religion*, Vol. VI, 1926, pp. 347 ff.

14. John Milton, *Paradise Lost*, from *Milton's Poetical Works* (London: Oxford University Press, 1935), pp. 223 f. Book II, lines 930 ff.

15. *Glauben und Verstehen*, 2nd ed., 1954, Vol. I, p. 208: translation by Stephen Neill, *The Interpretation of the New Testament* (Oxford University Press, 1964), p. 271.

16. Virgil, *Eclogue*, iv:4.

17. Cited by A. T. Davies in *Crwydro Sir Gâr* (Llandybie, 1955), p. 108.

18. See J. Jeremias, *The Central Message of the New Testament* (New York, Scribner, 1965), pp. 9–27.

19. Alfred Lord Tennyson, "Gareth and Lynette," *Idylls of the King and The King's Henchman* (New York: Noble and Noble, 1957), lines 261–70.

20. H. G. Wells, *The Outline of History* (London: George Newnes, Ltd., n.d.), Vol. I, p. 362.

21. *Ecclesiastical History*, III, p. iii, 6.

22. E. V. Rieu, *op. cit.*, pp. xix f.

23. *The Acts of Paul* in *The Apocryphal New Testament*, ed. by M. R. James (London: Oxford University Press, 1926), p. 273.

24. *Peake's Commentary on the Bible, op. cit.*, 767g, p. 878.

25. For a fuller treatment, see W. D. Davies, *Paul and Rabbinic Judaism* (London: 1948; forthcoming Torch Paperback, Harper & Row, New York).

26. T. Sturge Moore, "Jacob" in *Longer Modern Verses*, ed. by E. A. Parker (London: Oxford University Press, 1926), p. 60, lines 312 f.

27. William Shakespeare, *Julius Caesar*, Act II, sc. 1, lines 133 f.

28. William Shakespeare, *Hamlet*, Act II, sc. 2, lines 297 ff.

29. Alfred, Lord Tennyson, *The Higher Pantheism*, VI.

30. Robert Browning, "Gold Hair."

31. *Paul and Rabbinic Judaism, op. cit.*, p. 28.

32. *Ibid.*, p. 29.

33. A. Heschel, *The Prophets*, (The Jewish Publication Society of America, Philadelphia, 1955, pp. 279 ff.).

34. William Shakespeare, *Hamlet*, Act I, sc. 2, lines 87 ff.

35. Cited in *Readings in Anthropology*, ed. by Morton H. Fried. Vol. II: *Cultural Anthropology* (New York: Thomas Y. Crowell Company, 1959), p. 549.

36. *Ibid. Man makes himself* is the title of a book by a well-known scholar.

37. *Ibid.*, p. 555.

38. *A Rabbinic Anthology*, ed. by C. G. Montefiore and H. Loewe (New York and London: The Macmillan Company, 1938), p. 187.

39. From C. H. Dodd, *The Epistle to the Romans* (New York: Harper & Row, 1932), p. 187.

40. *Readings in Anthropology, op. cit.*, p. 566.

41. C. H. Dodd, *op. cit.*, p. 41.

42. *A Century of English Essays* (London: Everyman's Library, 1913), p. 271.

43. Alice Meynell, "Christ in the Universe", in *An Anthology of Modern Verse*, ed. by A. Methuen (London: Methuen and Company, Ltd., 1921), pp. 156–57.

44. *Readings in St. John's Gospel* (New York and London: The Macmillan Company, 1945).

45. Edwyn Clement Hoskyns, *The Fourth Gospel,* ed. by Francis Noel Davey (London: Faber & Faber, Ltd., 1939), Vol. I, pp. 125 f.

46. Published by the Oxford University Press, 1922.

47. *A Rabbinic Anthology, op. cit.,* p. 164.

48. *The Hermetica,* ed. by Walter Scott (Oxford, England: The Clarendon Press, 1924–36), Vol. I, Bk. XIII:2, pp. 239–41.

49. *Ibid.,* Bk. XIII:22A, p. 255.

50. *Ibid.,* Bk. XIII:5–6, pp. 241–43.

51. From *The Refutation of All Heresies* by Hippolytus, tr. by J. H. Macmahon, in The Ante-Nicene Christian Library (Edinburgh: T. & T. Clark, 1868), Vol. I of the writings of Hippolytus, p. 153. On this see J. Jeremias, *op. cit.,* pp. 71 ff.

52. For the above *Fragments,* see C. K. Barrett, *The New Testament Background* (New York: Harper & Row, 1961), pp. 62 f.

53. William Wordsworth, "Tintern Abbey."

54. John Galsworthy in his preface to W. H. Hudson, *Green Mansions* (New York: Alfred A. Knopf Incorporated, 1944), p. viii.

55. "Tintern Abbey."

56. Lord Byron, *The Poetical Works of Lord Byron,* Vol. ii (Boston, 1905), pp. 187 ff. "Childe Harold's Pilgrimage," Canto iii, stanza 72.

57. Francis Thompson, "In No Strange Land" in *An Anthology of Modern Verse, op. cit.,* p. 218.

58. Published in New York and London by the Cambridge University Press, 1953.

59. Lord Byron, *op. cit.,* "The Prisoner of Chillon," lines 15–16.

60. Robert Browning, *Poems of Robert Browning* (Boston, 1896, pp. 406 ff.), "A Death in the Desert," lines 482 ff.

61. C. H. Dodd, *op. cit.,* p. 380.

62. John Drinkwater, "A Prayer" from *Collected Poems,* Vol. I (London: Sidgwick & Jackson, Ltd., 1923).

63. Published in *The Christian Century,* Vol. 82, No. 15, p. 458, April 14, 1965.

64. *The Setting of the Sermon on the Mount,* p. 431.

65. New York: Alfred A. Knopf, 1964, p. viii.

66. *Ibid.,* pp. xxi–xxii.

67. C. H. Dodd, *op. cit.,* p. 399.

BIBLIOGRAPHY

I. Texts:

Revised Standard Version of the Bible, (New York: Nelson, 1957)
The New English Bible, (New York and London: Oxford-Cambridge University Press, 1961)
A Synopsis of the Gospels, by H. F. D. Sparks (Philadelphia: Fortress Press, 1964)

II. Certain books of a semi-popular nature recommended for guidance over the whole field:

Fuller, Reginald H., *The New Testament in Current Study,* (New York: Scribner, 1962)
Hunter, Archibald M., *Interpreting the New Testament,* (Philadelphia: Westminster Press, 1951)
Hunter, Archibald M., *Introducing New Testament Theology,* (London: SCM Press, 1957)
Hunter, Archibald M., *Introducing the New Testament,* (Philadelphia: Westminster Press, 1957)
Hunter, Archibald M., *The Work and Words of Jesus,* (Philadelphia: Westminster Press, 1950)
Jeremias, Joachim, *The Central Message of the New Testament,* (New York, Scribner, 1965)
Kee, Howard C. and Young, Franklin W., *Understanding the New Testament,* (Englewood Cliffs, N.J.: Prentice-Hall, 1960), revised edition, 1965
Price, James L., *Interpreting the New Testament,* (New York: Holt, Rinehart and Winston, 1961)
Wright, G. Ernest and Fuller, Reginald, *The Book of the Acts of God,* (Garden City: Doubleday, 1957)

III. Suggested for further reading on:

A. The Background in General

Black, M. and Rowley, H. H., eds., *Peake's Commentary on the Bible,* (New York: Nelson, 1962)

Cross, Frank M., *The Ancient Library of Qumran and Modern Biblical Studies,* (Garden City, New York: Anchor Books, 1961)

Davies, W. D., *Christian Origins of Judaism,* (Philadelphia: Westminster Press, 1962)

Davies, W. D., *Introduction to Pharisaism,* (Brecon: Memorial College, 1953)

Davies, W. D., *Paul and Rabbinic Judaism,* (London: SPCK, 1948)

Foerster, Werner, *From the Exile to Christ,* (Philadelphia: Fortress Press, 1964)

Gaster, Theodor H., *The Dead Sea Scriptures,* (Garden City, New York: Doubleday, 1956)

Grant, Robert M., *Gnosticism and Early Christianity,* (New York: Columbia University Press, 1959)

McNeile, Alan H., *Introduction to the New Testament,* (Oxford: Clarendon Press, 1953)

Murray, Gilbert, *The Five Stages of Greek Religion,* (Garden City, New York: Doubleday, 1951)

Pfeiffer, Robert H., *History of New Testament Times,* (New York: Harper, 1949)

B. The Old Testament in its Relation to the New

Dodd, Charles H., *According to the Scriptures,* (New York: Scribner, 1953)

Lindars, Barnabas, *New Testament Apologetic,* (Philadelphia: Westminster Press, 1961)

Rowley, Harold H., *The Unity of the Bible,* (London: Carey Kingsgate Press, 1953)

Tasker, Randolph V. G., *The Old Testament in the New Testament,* (London: SCM Press, 1946)

C. The Unity of the New Testament and its Variety

Davies W. D., and Daube, D., eds., *The Background of the New Testament and its Eschatology,* "The Eschatology of Luke-Acts" by Cadbury, H. J., (Cambridge: University Press, 1956)

Dodd, Charles H., *The Apostolic Preaching and its Developments,* (New York: Harper, 1960)

Moule, Charles F. D., *The Birth of the New Testament,* (London: A. & C. Black, 1962)

D. The Synoptic Gospels

Baillie, Donald M., *God Was In Christ,* (New York: Scribner, 1955)

Bornkamm, Günther, *Jesus of Nazareth,* (New York: Harper, 1961)

Bultmann, Rudolf, *Jesus and the Word,* (New York: Scribner, 1958)

Bultmann, Rudolf, *Theology of the New Testament* (New York: Scribner, 1951–55) 2 volumes

Cadoux, C. J., *The Life of Jesus,* (Middlesex: Penguin, 1948)

Carrington, Philip, *The Primitive Christian Calendar,* (Cambridge: University Press, 1952)

Conzelmann, Hans, *The Theology of St. Luke,* (London: Faber & Faber, 1960)

Cullmann, Oscar, *Christ and Time,* (Philadelphia: Westminster Press, 1950)

Cullmann, Oscar, *The Christology of the New Testament,* (Philadelphia: Westminster Press, 1959)

Davies, W. D., *Christian Origins of Judaism,* (Philadelphia: Westminster Press, 1962)

Davies, W. D., *The Setting of the Sermon on the Mount,* (New York: Cambridge University Press, 1964)

Dibelius, Martin, *From Tradition to Gospel,* (London: Ivor Nicholson and Watson, 1934)

Dodd, Charles H., *According to the Scriptures,* (New York: Scribner, 1953)

Dodd, Charles H., *The Apostolic Preaching and its Developments,* (New York: Harper, 1960)

Dodd, Charles H., *History and the Gospel,* (New York: Scribner, 1938)

Dodd, Charles H., *The Parables of the Kingdom,* (New York: Scribner, 1961)

Duncan, George S., *Jesus, Son of Man,* (New York: Macmillan, 1949)

Fuller, Reginald H., *The Mission and Achievement of Jesus,* (Chicago: A. R. Allenson, 1954)

Gerhardsson, Birger, *Memory and Manuscript,* (Uppsala, 1961)

Glasson, Thomas F., *The Second Advent,* (London: Epworth Press, 1947)

Goguel, Maurice, *Jesus and the Origins of Christianity,* (New York: Harper, 1960) 2 volumes

Grant, Frederick C., *The Gospels: Their Origin and Growth,* (New York: Harper, 1957)

Grant, Frederick C., *An Introduction to New Testament Thought,* (New York: Abingdon-Cokesbury Press, 1950)

Hanson, Richard P. C., *Tradition in the Early Church,* (Philadelphia: Westminster Press, 1963)

Harnack, Adolf von, *What is Christianity?,* (New York: Harper, 1957)

Hoskyns, Sir Edwyn C. and Davey, Francis N., *The Riddle of the New Testament,* (London: Faber & Faber, 1957)

Jeremias, Joachim, *The Parables of Jesus,* (London: SCM Press, 1954)

Knox, John, *Jesus: Lord and Christ,* (New York: Harper, 1958)

Kümmel, W. G., *Promise and Fulfillment*, (Illinois: Allenson, 1957)

Manson, Thomas W., *The Teaching of Jesus*, (Cambridge: University Press, 1959)

Otto, Rudolf, *The Kingdom of God and the Son of Man*, (Boston: Starr King Press, 1957)

Richardson, Alan, *The Miracle-Stories of the Gospels*, (New York: Harper, 1942)

Riesenfeld, Harald, *The Gospel Tradition and its Beginnings*, (London: A. R. Mowbray, 1961)

Robinson, James M., *A New Quest of the Historical Jesus*, (London: SCM Press, 1959)

Robinson, James M., *The Problem of History in Mark*, (London: SCM Press, 1957)

Robinson, J. A. T., *Jesus and His Coming*, (London: SCM Press, 1957)

Rowley, Harold H., *The Unity of the Bible*, (Philadelphia: Westminster Press, 1953)

Schweitzer, Albert, *The Quest of the Historical Jesus*, (London: A. & C. Black, 1954)

Scobie, Charles H. H., *John the Baptist*, (Philadelphia: Fortress Press, 1964)

Stendahl, Krister, *The School of St. Matthew and Its Use of the Old Testament*, (Uppsala: C. W. K. Gleerup, Lund, 1954)

Streeter, Burnett H., *The Four Gospels*, (London: Macmillan, 1953)

Tasker, R. V. G., *The Old Testament in the New Testament*, (London: SCM Press, 1946)

Taylor, Vincent, *The Formation of the Gospel Tradition*, (London: Macmillan, 1953)

Throckmorton, Burton H., ed., *Gospel Parallels*, (New York: Nelson, 1957)

Wilder, Amos Niven, *Eschatology and Ethics in the Teaching of Jesus*, (New York: Harper, 1950)

E. Paul and Pauline Theology

Brandon, Samuel G. F., *The Fall of Jerusalem and the Christian Church*, (London: SPCK, 1951)

Bruce, F. F., *The Acts of the Apostles*, (London: Tyndale Press, 1951). Only the Introduction and Commentary

Bultmann, Rudolf, *Theology of the New Testament*, (New York: Scribner, 1951–55) Vol. I

Carré, Henry B., *Paul's Doctrine of Redemption*, (New York: Macmillan, 1914)

Cerfaux, Lucien, *Christ in the Theology of St. Paul*, (New York: Herder and Herder, 1959)

Davies, W. D., *Paul and Rabbinic Judaism*, (London: SPCK, 1948)

Deissman, Gustav A., *St. Paul*, (New York: Hodder and Stoughton, 1912)

Dibelius, Martin, *Paul*, (Philadelphia: Westminster Press, 1960)

Dodd, Charles H., *The Bible and the Greeks*, (London: Hodder and Stoughton, 1954)

Hunter, Archibald M., *Paul and His Predecessors*, (London: SCM Press, 1961)

Kennedy, Harry A. A., *The Theology of the Epistles*, (New York: Scribner, 1920)

Klausner, Joseph, *From Jesus to Paul*, (New York: Macmillan, 1945)

Knox, John, *Chapters in the Life of Paul*, (New York: Abingdon-Cokesbury Press, 1950)

Knox, Wilfred L., *The Acts of the Apostles*, (Cambridge: University Press, 1948)

Knox, Wilfred L., *St. Paul and the Church of Jerusalem*, (Cambridge: University Press, 1925)

Knox, Wilfred L., *St. Paul and the Church of the Gentiles*, (Cambridge: University Press, 1939)

Longenecker, Richard N., *Paul, Apostle of Liberty*, (New York: Harper, 1964)

Montefiore, Claude G., *Judaism and St. Paul*, (London: M. Goshen, 1914)

Munck, Johannes, *Paul and the Salvation of Mankind*, (Richmond: John Knox Press, 1959)

Nock, Arthur D., *St. Paul*, (New York: Harper, 1938)

Porter, Frank C., *The Mind of Christ in Paul*, (New York: Scribner, 1932)

Prat, Ferdinand, *The Theology of St. Paul*, (London and Dublin: Burns, Oates and Washbourn, 1945) Vols. I & II

Ramsay, Sir William Mitchell, *St. Paul the Traveller and the Roman Citizen*, (New York: G. P. Putnam, 1896)

Rawlinson, A. E. J., *Essays on the Trinity and Incarnation*, (New York: Longmans, Green, 1928)

Rawlinson, A. E. J., *The New Testament Doctrine of the Christ*, (New York: Longmans, Green, 1926)

Richardson, Alan, *A Theological Word Book on the Bible*, (London: SCM Press, 1950)

Robinson, J. A. T., *The Body*, (London: SCM Press, 1952)

Rowley, Harold H., *The Biblical Doctrine of Election*, (London: Lutterworth Press, 1953)

Schoeps, Hans Joachim, *Paul*, (London: Lutterworth Press, 1961)

Schweitzer, Albert, *The Mysticism of Paul the Apostle,* (New York: H. Holt, 1931)

Schweitzer, Albert, *Paul and His Interpreters,* (London: A. & C. Black, 1912)

Scott, Charles A. A., *Christianity According to St. Paul,* (Cambridge: University Press, 1932)

Stacey, Walter D., *The Pauline View of Man,* (New York: St. Martin's Press, 1956)

Stendahl, Krister, ed., *The Scrolls and the New Testament,* (New York: Harper, 1957)

Weiss, Johannes, *The History of Primitive Christianity,* (New York: Wilson-Erickson, 1937) Vol. I

Whiteley, D. E. H., *The Theology of St. Paul,* (Philadelphia: Fortress Press, 1964)

Wood, H. G., "The Conversion of Paul," *New Testament Studies,* (Cambridge: University Press, 1955–56)

F. The Fourth Gospel

Bacon, Benjamin W., *The Fourth Gospel in Research and Debate,* (New York: Moffat, Yard, 1910)

Barrett, Charles K., *The Gospel According to St. John,* (London: SPCK, 1960)

Bevan, Edwyn R., *Symbolism and Belief,* (Boston: Beacon Press, 1957)

Bultmann, Rudolf, *Theology of the New Testament,* (New York: Scribner, 1951–55) 2 volumes

Carpenter, Joseph E., *The Johannine Writings,* (New York: Houghton Mifflin, 1927)

Clark, Neville, *An Approach to the Theology of the Sacraments,* (London: SCM Press, 1956)

Coates, J. R., ed., *Bible Key Words,* "Gnosis" by R. Bultmann, (New York: Harper, 1958) Vol. I

Cullmann, Oscar, *The Christology of the New Testament,* (Philadelphia: Westminster Press, 1959)

Cullmann, Oscar, *Early Christian Worship,* (London: SCM Press, 1953)

Dodd, Charles H., *The Interpretation of the Fourth Gospel,* (Cambridge: University Press, 1953)

Dodd, Charles H., *Historical Tradition in the Fourth Gospel,* (New York: Cambridge University Press, 1963)

Drummond, James, *An Inquiry into the Character and Authorship of the Fourth Gospel,* (New York: Scribner, 1904)

Drummond, James, *Philo Judaeus,* (London: Edinburgh, Williams and Norgate, 1888) 2 volumes

Flemington, W. F., *The New Testament Doctrine of Baptism,* (London: SPCK, 1948)

Gardner-Smith, Percival, *St. John and the Synoptic Gospels,* (Cambridge: University Press, 1938)

Grant, Frederick C., *The Gospels: Their Origin and Growth,* (New York: Harper, 1957)

Guilding, Aileen, *The Fourth Gospel and Jewish Worship,* (Oxford: Clarendon Press, 1960)

Higgins, Angus J. B., *The Lord's Supper in the New Testament,* (London: SCM Press, 1954)

Higgins, Angus J. B., *New Testament Essays,* (Manchester: Manchester University Press, 1959)

Howard, W. F., *Christianity According to St. John,* (Philadelphia: Westminster Press, 1946)

Howard, W. F., *The Fourth Gospel in Recent Criticism and Interpretation,* (London: Epworth Press, 1955)

Jackson, Henry L., *The Problem of the Fourth Gospel,* (Cambridge: University Press, 1918)

Johnston, George, *The Doctrine of the Church in the New Testament,* (Cambridge: University Press, 1943)

Lampe, Geoffrey, W. H., *The Seal of the Spirit,* (New York: Longmans, Green, 1951)

Lee, Edwin K., *The Religious Thought of St. John,* (London: SPCK, 1950)

Moore, George F., *Judaism in the First Centuries of the Christian Era,* (Cambridge: Harvard University Press, 1927) Vol. I

Rawlinson, Alfred E. J., *The New Testament Doctrine of the Christ,* (New York: Longmans, Green, 1926)

Richardson, Alan, *Introduction to the Theology of the New Testament,* (London: SCM Press, 1958)

Schweizer, Eduard R., *Church Order in the New Testament,* (London: SCM Press, 1961)

Scott, Ernest F., *The Fourth Gospel, its Purposes and Theology,* (Edinburgh: T. & T. Clark, 1951)

Scott, W., *The Hermetica,* (Oxford, 1924–36) 4 volumes

Smith, Dwight Moody, *The Composition and Order of the Fourth Gospel* (New Haven: Yale University Press, 1965)

Smith, Taylor C., *Jesus in the Gospel of John,* (Nashville: Broadman Press, 1959)

Strachan, Robert H., *The Fourth Gospel, its Significance and Environment,* (London: SCM Press, 1941)

Streeter, Burnett H., *The Four Gospels,* (London: Macmillan, 1953)

Taylor, Vincent, *Jesus and His Sacrifice,* (London: Macmillan, 1937)

Taylor, Vincent, *The Person of Christ in New Testament Teaching,* (New York: St. Martin's Press, 1958)

Westcott, Brooke F., *The Gospel According to St. John,* (Grand Rapids: Erdmans, 1954)

Wolfson, Harry A., *Philo,* (Cambridge: Harvard University Press, 1947) 2 volumes

G. Commentaries

Barrett, Charles K., *The Gospel According to St. John,* (London: SPCK, 1960)

Barth, Karl, *The Epistle to the Romans,* (New York: Oxford University Press, 1953)

Hoskyns, Sir Edwyn C., and Davey, F. N., *The Fourth Gospel,* (London: Faber & Faber, 1939)

Taylor, Vincent, *The Gospel According to St. Mark,* (New York: St. Martin's Press, 1959)

Westcott, Brooke F., *The Gospel According to St. John,* (Grand Rapids: Erdmans, 1954)

Harper's New Testament Commentaries, ed. Chadwick, H., (New York: Harper)

The Interpreter's Bible, (New York: Abingdon-Cokesbury Press, 1951–57)

Moffatt New Testament Commentaries, (New York: Harper, 1928–50)

INDEX OF SCRIPTURE REFERENCES